Aborted Women

Silent No More

Aborted Women
Silent No More

DAVID C. REARDON

Foreword by Nancyjo Mann
Founder of WEBA

Loyola University Press
Chicago

Loyola University Press
3441 North Ashland Avenue
Chicago, Illinois 60657

Library of Congress Cataloging in Publication Data
Reardon, David C.

  Aborted women.

  Bibliography: p. 365
  1. Abortion—United States. 2. Abortion—United
States—Psychological aspects. I. Title.
HQ767.5.U5R38 1987   363.4'6   87-17074
ISBN 0-8294-0578-X
ISBN 0-8294-0579-8 (pbk.)

Book design and production by C. L. Tornatore

To Mary and her children of tears

It is literally impossible to count the people who made this work possible, much less to name them all. Yet trusting that they know who they are, I gratefully acknowledge the help of the hundreds of women who so graciously participated in my survey—often at the expense of reopening painful memories. The importance of their contribution to our better understanding of the abortion experience cannot be over-estimated.

A special thank you is also extended to those women who submitted written and oral descriptions of their personal abortion stories for use in this book. Even those accounts which were not reprinted here because of space limitations were valuable contributions to my own understanding of women and abortion. All of them touched my heart.

I am also deeply indebted to Nancyjo Mann and Lori Nerad for the aid and support they gave me in my research efforts.

Lastly, because my gratitude goes beyond words, I wish to extend my love and thanks to my wife and partner, Kim Ryan-Reardon, for her constant encouragement, compassionate care, and excellent editing. Without her none of this would have been possible.

David C. Reardon

C O N T E N T S

F O R E W O R D

Nancyjo Mann
Founder of WEBA

*"And when Pandora lifted the lid of the gift she had coveted for so long,
out flew plagues and sorrows for all humankind."*

— PANDORA'S BOX

In 1973, the United States Supreme Court legalized abortion on demand throughout the nation. Many hailed it as a great step forward for women. Others called it a terrible crime against unborn children. Since that time, the nation has been torn by the political debate and civil strife between these two groups. Both sides speak of high ideals. Those who defend abortion speak of "freedom of choice." Those who denounce it emphasize the "right to life."

Between these polarized groups lies a third group, a group largely ignored in this battle of ideals and rhetoric. This third group is made up of the women who have actually had abortions. These women do not speak of abortion in terms of political or ideological philosophies. They do not cherish abortion as a utopian freedom, nor do they condemn it as the ultimate vice. They have no patience with such abstract mind-games, because to them, abortion is very real.

These women have confronted the harsh circumstances which demand abortion, and they have struggled with its painful decisions. They have experienced abortion in all its realities, in its relief and in its shame. Theirs is a voice that needs to be heard—indeed, has a right to be heard. For above all others, theirs is the voice of experience.

ix

This book is based on the experiences of women who have had abortions. The hundreds of women who have joined together here to share their stories and insights have done so in order to separate the realities of abortion from the myths and the slogans. They come from all parts of the country, from all walks of life. Some are rich, others poor. Some aborted for reasons of health; some because they could not afford a child. A few aborted because their pregnancies were the result of rape; others because the child they carried might have been deformed. Others aborted purely for the sake of convenience.

But despite their many differences, all these women feel that they were deceived and manipulated. Together, they are determined to save other women from the same fate. For these women, abortion is not some great "privilege" which has been granted to their gender. Instead, they see abortion as a tool by which women have been *abandoned and exploited*.

Contrary to the popular slogan "freedom of choice," women who have experienced it know that abortion is seldom, if ever, a "free choice." Instead, legalized abortion has become a tool for the manipulation and exploitation of women. As will be seen, many of these women were forced to abort by boyfriends and husbands who begged and threatened them to "do the sensible thing." Some were forced to abort by insistent parents. Others were intimidated into abortion by physicians who were afraid of malpractice suits, or by social workers seeking to reduce the welfare rolls. Still others felt forced to abort because of the social prejudice against unwed mothers, or because of a social insistence that they handle their problems alone. But whatever the pressures they faced, all of these women felt backed into a corner and saw abortion as the only way out. They were made to feel trapped and isolated. For nearly all women, abortion is experienced not as an act of "choice," but as an act of despair—their *only* choice.

The price women pay for being abandoned and exploited by the "privilege" of abortion is extremely high. Women who have abortions quickly learn that it is not nearly as "safe and easy" as pro-abortionists* would have us believe. Instead, *abortion is dangerous to both the physical*

---

*Those who defend the right to abortion can be separated into two groups. One group actively encourages abortions and can properly be labeled *pro-abortion*. This group includes population control advocates, social engineers who seek to use abortion to weed out the "unfit," and those who make money by providing abortions (ie., abortionists, abortion clinic staffs, and "family planning" agencies which are funded to make abortion referrals.) Pro-abortionists seek to advance their "causes" by encouraging abortion among selected classes of women.

The second group, those who are *pro-choice*, see nothing to be gained by encouraging abortion, *and mental health of women.* In fact, as we will see, half of all aborted women experience some immediate or long-term physical complications, and almost all suffer from emotional or psychological aftershocks.

Finally, instead of being a giant step forward for women's rights, *legal abortion is the most destructive manifestation of discrimination against women today.* The abortion mentality is sexism incarnate. This sexism is apparent in four ways.

First, with abortions easily and legally available, as well as socially acceptable, it is easier than ever for men to sexually exploit women. When their promises of love end in pregnancy, these uncommitted and selfish men are free to manipulate women into abortions so as to free themselves of unwanted commitments. They whine and pout about "doing the sensible thing," or resort to threats, "If you don't have an abortion, I'll leave you." In either case the end result is the same: the women face the risks and guilts of abortion alone. And if a women resists such coercion, her exploiter can simply deny all personal and financial responsibility for *his* "unwanted" child, saying, "You're stuck with it now, baby. After all, you could have had an abortion." Thus the abortion "choice" is just one more arena in which men condition their love and respect on the basis of women's obedience to their desires.

Second, beyond subjecting women to manipulation and threats of abandonment, the abortion mentality attacks the unique value of female sexuality. This is a result of the pro-abortion rhetoric (generally promulgated by population control zealots) which portrays abortion not as an *alternative* to childbirth, but as *preferable* to childbirth. This attempt to de-sex women, to separate them from their reproductive potential, has eroded the natural pride which women enjoy in being able to conceive and bear children—a creative wonder which no man can duplicate. Instead of praising this unique potential of women, the abortion mentality belittles it, or at best, dismisses it as commonplace. No other public policy has ever attempted to undermine a creative capacity of one half of its population.

Third, women are being abandoned by a society which has no

but perceive it as an abstract right which should not be restricted. On the other hand, pro-choice advocates make no attempt to discourage abortions either.

The vast majority of those who support legal abortion are of the pro-choice viewpoint; but because pro-abortionists seek to advance some personal "cause" through abortion advocacy, they are much more politically active and outspoken than the milder pro-choicers. Pro-abortionists, therefore, have clearly dominated the abortion movement and, as we will see, are responsible for much of the manipulation and exploitation of women today.

Throughout this book, the terms pro-choice and pro-abortion will be used to distinguish between the above two groups.

xi

patience for a problem unique to women—an unplanned pregnancy. Rather than receiving the love and support needed to cope with this challenge, women are offered the easy way out, the "quick-fix," the cover-up—abortion. They are seen as second-rate citizens with second-rate problems, and so they are handed a makeshift solution. They themselves are "socially aborted." Abortion is a superficial and potentially dangerous answer to the problems of a pregnant woman. Abortion is the "cheap love" which society offers as a substitute for costly care and honest commitment. Though offered superficial support in making their abortion decisions, women must always face the consequences alone. Abortion, unlike childbirth, is always a lonely process.

Lastly, while feminists have won women the right to both family and career, the abortion mentality tells women that one must be sacrificed for the other. Women are made to feel that they must "plan" children around their careers, because "unplanned" children will ruin their lives. Thus, abortion is defended with the argument that women are restricted by the limits of their careers, their education, or their finances. Faced with these limits, the sexist abortion mentality says, women are not "strong" enough to survive an unplanned pregnancy, much less to raise an "unwanted" child or endure giving it up for adoption. Instead of helping women to be strong, independent, and capable of handling their lives in spite of the social prejudices against "problem" pregnancies, the expediency of abortion encourages women to be weak, dependent, and incapable of dealing with unexpected challenges. This mentality tells women that they must depend on the technology of abortion to solve their problems for them. Just as in the traditional, male-dominated social order, the abortion mentality dictates to women what they *cannot* do, what they *cannot* handle.

In the simplest of terms, abortion has been sold to women under false premises. We have been lied to, manipulated, and exploited. For too long we have remained silent, too ashamed to speak out, too ashamed to admit our errors. Now this has changed. Those who have experienced abortion firsthand are no longer willing to be silent.

My name is Nancyjo Mann. I am one of the sixteen million women who has had an abortion since 1973. I've seen this from all angles; from the pro-choice side, the pro-life side, and most importantly, from the side of a woman who has experienced abortion. I exercised my "right to choose," and I became a victim of this Pandora's box. It was a pretty, tempting treasure. It promised to solve all my problems and restore full control over my life. But instead, this "right," this "gift," was filled with sufferings and regret which I could never have anticipated or imagined. What follows here is my story. It is not a unique one. Millions of others have been seduced by the same false promises. Mine is but one example of the abortion reality.

Abortion is the result of pressures on a woman's life. The pressures leading up to my abortion began in high school where, like many careless, impatient, and short-sighted teens, my boyfriend and I were sexually active. In my junior year, I became pregnant.

My mother was terribly upset. "Oh, what are the neighbors going to say?" she worried. "You'll shame the family. You've got to have an abortion."

This was in 1970. We lived in Iowa where abortion was still illegal, except when necessary to save a woman's life. This fact, however, did not deter my insistent mother, since abortions were easily available under the "progressive" laws of New York and California. My mother only wanted what she thought was best for me, but I *didn't* want an abortion. I wanted to get married. Fortunately, my father stood by me and my mother learned to accept my decision. This was the first time that abortion was ever in my thoughts.

Being a wife, raising a daughter, and finishing school is rough, especially for a seventeen-year-old. No one goes out of their way to make it easier, either. Instead, it seemed like everyone figured I wanted to face all those pressures alone. After all, I could have had an abortion and saved everyone the hassle.

But I survived. I graduated. And I was happy. Two years later I had my second child, a son. Not long after that, my husband left me. The responsibilities of being a father and a husband had become more than he was willing to handle. The joys of our young married life were no longer worth the pressures of adjustment. He wanted out, and so he left.

No sooner were we divorced that I fell right back into trouble. I was still on the Pill, and so when I began dating a new guy, I figured there was nothing to worry about. After all, I was being "responsible." But despite the wonders of modern contraception, I became pregnant with my third child. Four months later we were married.

Though there was a superficial happiness in this second marriage, it didn't last more than ten weeks. On October 30, 1974, he walked out the front door. My strong, "dependable" husband just couldn't handle the prospect of being responsible for another child. It was too much for him.

I was absolutely stunned by the suddenness of his departure. I was left five and a half months pregnant, with my two young children and no source of income. I didn't know what to do. Finally, I took the kids and drove over to my parents' house. My mother and one of my brothers were there. I was at a loss. "What am I going to do? He left!" I said. They talked to me for awhile and finally my mother said, "Nancy, you're never going to amount to a hill of beans. What man is ever going to want you with three children, let alone the two you already have? With all those kids, you'll probably end up on welfare for the rest of your life. You're never going to be anybody. It's obvious that you'll just have to have an abortion."

If I wasn't upset and depressed enough already, this type of "practical" advice made me feel even worse. I felt totally helpless. I was a failure. . . . How could I resist when everyone was just trying to "do the best thing" for me? They were sincerely trying to help me and they were the only source of support I had. Upset, depressed, tired, desperate, I took the path of least resistance. I adopted the attitudes of those around me. I accepted their decisions as my own. I simply floated along with "what had to be done." Besides, I thought, maybe if I get rid of this "problem pregnancy," my husband will come back to me.

My mother made all the arrangements. She called my ob/gyn, and he said he wouldn't do an abortion, much less a second trimester. He told her that the only one in town that would do it was Dr. Paulino Fong, a prominent doctor in that area. Without losing a moment of time for reflection or doubts, my mother and I went over to see him. When he learned that I was seeking an abortion, he immediately had me brought into an examination room.

After a quick examination, my abortionist told me that I would have to have the abortion done within the next twenty-four hours or I would be outside the limit of the law. Of course this wasn't true, but I didn't know that then. Abortions are legal throughout all three trimesters, right up to the day before birth, and I was still well within the second trimester. He just used this little lie to pressure me into making a quick decision.

But that was only the first lie he told me. The second lie came during my "counseling session," when I asked, "What are you going to do to me if I have this abortion?" All he did was look at my stomach and say, "I'm going to take a little fluid out, put a little fluid in; you'll have severe cramps and expel the fetus." "Is that all?" I asked. "That's it." "OK," I said. It was only later, after the abortion had begun, that I was to learn that what he described as "cramps" was actually the labor process. These "severe cramps" were not just going to make my pregnancy magically disappear. Instead, I was going to go through all the motions of normal childbirth—water breaking, labor pains, etc. The only difference was that the baby I would deliver would be dead.

After telling me I had to have the abortion within the next twenty-four hours, Dr. Fong scheduled me for a saline abortion in the hospital that same afternoon. Ironically, a little while after my abortion a nurse who worked at the hospital told me that Fong always scheduled his abortions for the same day that the patient contacted him. At one time he had admitted patients to the hospital the night before the surgery so that they could be observed and their food intake limited. But when some of his patients had changed their minds during the night, sometimes after questioning nurses about what actually would happen, he began to insist on doing the abortions immediately. Too many patients, and profits, were slipping out the front door.

The third lie in my "counseling" was a lie of omission. He never told me any of the risks involved. Only later did I find out that if he had hit a vein, the saline solution could have made me violently ill or caused any number of other complications, including death. He told me none of this. Instead he made it sound like a simple and relatively painless procedure.

I was so naive. I trusted him. After all, he was a doctor. A respected and educated man. And like everyone else, I had always heard that legal abortion was "safe and easy." It wasn't until he had me on the table that I began to question these illusions. It wasn't until he pulled out an enormous syringe that I became

scared. The needle alone was four inches long. Suddenly I realized that this was not going to be as easy as he had implied.

The first thing he did was withdraw 60 cc's of amniotic fluid.
At that point I started to feel afraid for my baby. I could feel her
thrashing about, scared by this intrusion. I wanted to scream out—
"Please, stop. Don't do this to me!" But I just couldn't get it out. I
was petrified with fear.

After the fluid was withdrawn, he injected 200 cc's of the
saline solution—half a pint of concentrated salt solution. From
then on, it was terrible. My baby began thrashing about—it was
like a regular boxing match in there. She was in pain. The saline
was burning her skin, her eyes, her throat. It was choking her,
making her sick. She was in agony, trying to escape. She was
scared and confused at how her wonderful little home had suddenly been turned into a death trap.

For some reason it had never entered my mind that with an
abortion she would have to die. I had never wanted my baby to
die; I only wanted to get rid of my "problem." But it was too late
to turn back now. There was no way to save her. So instead I
talked to her. I tried to comfort her. I tried to ease her pain. I told
her I didn't want to do this to her, but it was too late to stop it. I
didn't want her to die. I begged her not to die. I told her I was
sorry, to forgive me, that I was wrong, that I didn't want to kill her.

For two hours I could feel her struggling inside me. But then,
as suddenly as it began, she stopped. Even today, I remember her
very last kick on my left side. She had no strength left. She gave
up and died. Despite my grief and guilt, I was relieved that her
pain was finally over. But I was never the same again. The abortion killed not only my daughter; it killed a part of me.

Before that needle had entered my abdomen, I had liked
myself. Though I may have had my share of problems, I had seen
myself as basically a good person. I wasn't into any wild scenes. I
was a good housewife and a loving mother. I was happy to be me.
But when that needle entered my womb, when it pulled out the
nurturing fluid of motherhood and replaced it with that venom of
death, when the child I had abandoned suddenly began its struggle within me, I hated myself. It was that fast. Every bit of self-
esteem, every value I held dear, every hope of which I had ever
dreamed—all were stripped away by the poison of that one vain
act. Every memory of joy was now tainted by the stench of death.

That moment of desperation which had led me to this "healer's table" had now positioned itself as ruler of my life. I had abandoned myself to despair, and despair was my future. There was no way to stop it. There was no way to put everything back the way it had been. I no longer had any control, any choice. I was powerless. I was weak. I was a murderer.

A little while after my baby stopped moving they gave me an intravenous injection to help stimulate labor. I was in hard labor for twelve hours, all through the night. When finally I delivered, the nurses didn't make it to my room in time. I delivered my daughter myself at 5:30 the next morning, October 31st. After I delivered her, I held her in my hands. I looked her over from top to bottom. She had a head of hair, and her eyes were opening. I looked at her little tiny feet and hands. Her fingers and toes even had little fingernails and swirls of fingerprints. Everything was perfect. She was not a "fetus." She was not a "product of conception." She was a tiny human being. The pathology report listed her as more than seven inches from head to rump. With her legs extended, she was over a foot long. She weighed a pound and a half, more than many of the premature babies being saved in incubators in every hospital in the country. But these vital statistics did not mention her most striking trait: She was my daughter. Twisted with agony. Silent and still. Dead.

It seemed like I held her for ten minutes or more, but it was probably only thirty seconds—because as soon as the nurses came rushing in, they grabbed her from my hands and threw her—literally threw her—into a bedpan and carried her away.

To add insult to injury, after my daughter was taken away, they brought another woman into the room to finish the last hour of her labor. But this woman wasn't having an abortion. No, she had a beautiful, healthy baby boy. No words can describe how rough that was on me.

I was released from the hospital eight hours after the delivery. The official report filled out by my abortionist stated that the procedure had been completed with "no complications." Three days later I went back into what felt like labor again, and I passed a piece of placenta about the size of my hand. It had been an incomplete abortion, a fact which had been missed by the pathology lab which had reported the placenta had been delivered "intact."

Soon afterwards I began to withdraw from those who loved me, especially from my family since they had supported and encouraged me to have the abortion. There was a part of me that didn't want to be loved, especially by those who had known me before. I was filled with guilt and sorrow. I felt empty, and I lived under a constant feeling of dread. Newborn infants caught my eye and filled me with longing, but I was afraid to touch them. Whenever a friend would offer to let me hold her baby, I would always refuse. I was too afraid of my own destructiveness. I was terrified that I might somehow hurt another child.

Three weeks after my abortion, I chose to be sterilized by tubal ligation. I couldn't cope with the idea that I could ever possibly kill again. It was too devastating. Too mind boggling. My body which had the potential of creating life was now too easily a host of death.

I became preoccupied with thoughts of death. I fantasized about how I would die. My baby had struggled for two hours. I've tried to imagine myself dying a similar kind of death. If a pillow was put over my face to suffocate me, I would struggle for a bit, but in less than four minutes I would pass out. But she had suffered for *two hours*. Would I be so tormented?

Four months after my abortion, the bleeding and infection were still persistent. Too ashamed to go to my own ob/gyn, I returned to Dr. Fong and he performed a D&C to clean out the uterus. He cut off my cervix and left the packing inside of me. Three weeks later I was grossly rotted out inside. Seven months later, at 22 years of age, I was forced to undergo a total hysterectomy—all because of that "safe and easy," legal abortion.

By this time, I didn't care if I lived or died anymore. I was going through a radical personality change and was becoming increasingly self-destructive. Though I had been shy as a teenager, now I forced myself to become bold and aggressive. If I could only become tough and callous, I reasoned, I would be protected from the hurt. So I began to hang around the tough crowd, imitating their ways, taking on their attitudes. What attracted me to them was their destructiveness—their contempt for the world. Soon I was carrying guns and knives, and biking around with motorcycle gangs and worse. The people I ran with were out to destroy, steal, and maim, and that is what I wanted to do to both others and *myself.*

FOREWORD

The desire to destroy is a double-edged weapon. It is both a sword of wrath and a ritual suicide knife of *har-a-kiri*. I hated the world only as much as I hated myself. By becoming destructive I was able to release my growing hatred towards this world that had abandoned me, abused me and exploited me. At the same time, by running outside of the law, by attacking others, I opened myself up to attack. I signaled the world that I was ready to be punished and even killed. It didn't matter. Anger, defiance, self-punishment and self-destructiveness—all were one, and they were me.

I tried to immerse myself in destruction. I wanted to prove to myself that destroying others didn't hurt. After all, once you've killed, you should be able to do anything. By doing every conceivable wrong, I hoped to strip myself of my conscience. I hoped to destroy all the values I had ever held. If only I could prove to myself that everything was meaningless, including the innocent daughter I had killed through abortion, then perhaps I could have the peace of total meaninglessness.

The natural center of this destructive, escapist world in which I lived, of course, was drugs. I began to fire up on heroin, cocaine—anything and everything I could find. I took acid every day for a year and a half. I smoked an ounce of pot every day. Drugs were my refuge, my comfort, my slow fuse to self-obliteration. Whenever I was stoned, I didn't have to think. If I couldn't think, I couldn't feel; and if I couldn't feel, that was almost as good as being dead. It was a lot better than facing myself.

To earn my living during this time, I became a country pop singer for a small band that played the bars. But singing didn't provide enough to cover my drug expenses, so I began dealing drugs across the state line. Whenever that wasn't enough, I would join a few friends and burgle houses. The extra cash from our "discount sales" helped to tide me over.

On top of all of this, I swiftly became promiscuous. Sleeping around was a way to degrade myself, while at the same time feeding on the false comforts of a sexual embrace. Through these quick and desperate intimacies, I secretly hoped I would someday find the love I so desperately needed, but all I found was sex. Soon this turned into prostituting myself to any man who could supply me with the drugs I needed. The promise of forgetfulness was worth any price.

I lived a life like this for four and a half years. It was a hell that can't be described. During this time, I was constantly pushing my abortion out of my mind. I never talked about it. I never dared to let myself even think about it. But it was never far away. In fact, a boyfriend of mine at that time later told me that almost every time I was stoned (which was every day) I would confess to him in a daze: "I had an abortion. You know, I had an abortion." No more than that. I would just keep telling him I had had an abortion and he just kept telling me, "That's alright. It's in the past. Just forget about it." But I never remembered telling anyone, especially him. To me it was the deepest, darkest secret. It was only when all my conscious barriers were dropped that it came tumbling out.

The subconscious rumblings of my abortion revealed themselves in other ways, too. For example, after my abortion I became deathly afraid of the night. I would *never* go to sleep when it was dark. The night was the time during which I had labored for death. Only at five in the morning, when the new dawn was breaking, the time when my labor had ended and my daughter had been released, did I finally settle down and prepare myself for sleep. Never knowing why, my nights had become a time for escape, a time for restless fear.

Four years after my abortion, my self-destructive attitudes turned into an open desire for death. Suicide beckoned me, and I had no place to turn.

My suicidal desires climaxed on one bitter night in January of 1978. After putting the children to bed, I sat dazed and despondent. What reason did I have to live? My two children were the only people I loved and valued. But did I really even deserve them? I wasn't worthy of their love. And the only love I was capable of giving to them was shriveled and distant. I took more than I gave. They would be better off with someone else. If anything, love for my children was a reason to die, not live. There were no reasons to live. Life was only pain and loneliness.

I was so low. There was no place lower to go. No place to hide. There were no more scraps of comfort to be found in the beds of strangers or the lines of coke. There was nothing. I was nothing.

I cried and I cried. My longing for death had become so overwhelming that I was scared that I was really going to do it.

There was no reason *not* to die. Suddenly, I jumped up and ran into the bathroom and flushed my bottle of sleeping pills down the toilet.

Everything in me wanted to die, but I was scared of death. What was on the other side? Where would I go? I felt like I *needed* to die, but I was afraid to.

This long, dark night was filled with the bitter tears and taste of salt.—Wanting to die. Afraid to die.—My only escape was filled with unknown terrors.

In that brief sort of faith born of desperation, I cried out: "God, you've got to give me a reason to live." But even as the words left my lips, I was certain that it could not be. Even if there was a God, He could never love me after all that I had done. All my life I had ignored Him and mocked Him. Why should He come to my aid? My life was worth nothing.

I finally found sleep that night in the weakness brought by tears. Early the next morning, as if in answer to my faithless plea, hope came to me in the form of a phone call. It was Mark, a friend who seemed to have a knack for always popping into my life when I was in trouble. At first I was mad at him for calling so early in the morning, but it was worth it. His news was great. "Nancy," he said, "I'm down here in Kansas City and there is a studio here that wants to record you!"

"Baby, I've got it made," I yelled. "Kansas, here I come."

The recording date was set for April 28th. For four months I lived on that promise of fame. I practiced eight hours a day and took drugs all night.

Months later, after my recording date in Kansas turned out to be fictitious and my friend Mark dropped out of sight, never to be heard from again, I decided to take my career into my own hands. Leaving my children with my mother, I headed off to Golfport, Illinois. There I hoped I would find the big break which would get me a recording opportunity in Nashville.

Those were my plans, but they were scattered like straw when I was involved in a nearly fatal motorcycle accident. The front wheel simply popped off the bike and I went skidding down the highway at full speed. Instead of Nasvhille, I found myself in the hospital with second and third degree burns covering approximately fifty percent of my body. In some areas, asphalt and gravel were imbedded up to three inches in my flesh. The pain was unbelievable. My vain dreams of glory were gone. I was back into the state of desperation from which I had first called out to God.

I was at the bottom of the barrel. This time, I was certain that I was going to die. I had nothing to lose and everything to gain; so I prayed, "God, please be with me. I need you." And again, He answered my prayer. After having resisted for so long, I allowed Him to become my Lord and Savior. The void in my heart that I had been trying to fill with everything else was finally filled with faith in God. From that moment on, I knew I wasn't going to die.

About nine months after leaving the hospital, I finally started to face the abortion I had tried so hard to bury. It was a very, very painful process. The wounds of abortion run deep, especially when they have been pushed down for so long. I nearly went through an emotional breakdown. I had to relive it all, to sort it all out. But this time the Lord was with me offering support and forgiveness. Step by step we went. But He was patient. It took three years, but finally I was able to forgive myself. That's the hardest part. God's forgiveness is ready and waiting. It's forgiving yourself that's hard.

By 1981, I had not only found peace with my abortion experience but felt drawn to help other women to overcome their pain and hurt. I knew that if I had hurt so much, surely there must be at least one other woman who felt the same. In early 1982 I founded Women Exploited By Abortion (WEBA) to minister to the needs of aborted women, to help them heal their pains. It immediately began to grow on its own. A newspaper article was written, then another and another, followed by radio and television appearances. Women from around the country began contacting me. As it turned out, there was a pent-up demand for a place of refuge, a place where women could share their abortion experiences, share their pain, share their strengths, and rebuild their lives.

With the founding of WEBA, the aftermath of abortion was no longer to be ignored. Women were no longer to be abandoned to silently suffer alone. It was time for this "evil necessity" to be purged in the open light. It was time for people to learn that abortion does not solve problems; instead, it changes them, warps them, and creates new problems. It was time for society to learn that abortion was no favor which women had the "right" to enjoy.

xxii

FOREWORD

It was a trap. A curse. A cheap substitute for love and support. A tool for the manipulation and exploitation of the women society has abandoned.

We are its victims, the aborted women of an unwanting society.

Since its founding in 1982, WEBA has been growing at an exponential rate. As of this date in 1986, there are over one hundred chapters of WEBA scattered around every state in the country. Since the chapters are operated at regional and local levels, there are no accurate figures for the total WEBA membership; but there is no doubt that it is already in the tens of thousands. At the request of women in other countries plagued by abortion, WEBA has opened chapters in Germany, Ireland, Spain, Italy, Japan, Australia, New Zealand, and Africa.

WEBA is the only national organization made up solely of women who have had abortions. As such, it is the only group associated with the abortion issue that speaks with the voice of experience.

The two main functions of WEBA are simply stated:

1) WEBA serves as a refuge and a source of spiritual and emotional healing for women who have had abortions. Offering group support, WEBA members share their experiences and their insights in order to promote the healing of the emotional and psychological scars of the abortion experience. WEBA members learn to turn the pain and loss of abortion into personal growth and compassion for others.

2) WEBA volunteers who have fully reconciled themselves to their abortions speak publicly of their experiences in an attempt to educate the general public, and young women in particular, about the physical, emotional, and psychological side effects of abortion. These speakers make frequent appearances on college campuses, in high schools, and before other organized youth groups. Speakers are also frequently guests on radio and television talk shows.

This book is a reflection of these two WEBA functions. Throughout this volume the reader will share the experiences, the pains, the reconciliations, and the maturing growth of women who have had abortions. For the readers who have themselves undergone abortions, this material will serve to guide and encourage them in coping with their own feelings. To other readers, these case studies will provide a greater understanding of the problems and needs of aborted women and insight into the dilemmas and pressures involved in unplanned pregnancies.

In addition, this book is intended to educate readers about the risks of abortion. Whether one is for or against legal abortion, there can be no doubt that there is an urgent need to better educate women about abortion *before* they are in a position where they may need to consider one. Unfortunately, for a variety of reasons which we will investigate, accurate information about the risks and consequences of abortion is routinely denied to women seeking abortions.

Here are some of the little known facts which we will examine:

■ Abortion providers have undertaken a major effort to cover up the morbidity and mortality rates of legal abortion. This deception has been easily achieved, with the cooperation of the courts, since there is no legal requirement to report abortion-related complications or even to record deaths resulting from abortion as such.

■ The minimum rate of immediate physical complications following legal abortions, based on *reported* figures, is fully ten percent.

■ Long-term complications, usually afflicting the reproductive system, occur in 20 to 50 percent of all aborted women. The risk of reproductive damage is highest for teenagers and for women who abort their first pregnancy.

■ Each year, over 100,000 women suffer the loss of a *wanted* baby to miscarriage, to premature birth, or to other labor complications which result from latent abortion morbidity.

■ Psychiatric and emotional complications following abortion have also been downplayed or ignored by abortion defenders. Pro-abortion studies have arbitrarily ignored psychological complications which do not require hospitalization as being "insignificant."

■ No less than 90 percent of aborted women experience moderate to severe emotional and psychiatric stress following an abortion.

Up to 10 percent require psychiatric hospitalization or other professional treatment. One to two percent (15,000 to 30,000 women per year) suffer such severe trauma as to render them unable to work. In addition, aborted women face a suicide risk nine times greater than that of non-aborted women.

■ Women who abort in the "hard" cases—for rape, incest, when pregnant with a handicapped child, or for reasons of physical or mental health—are much more likely to suffer from severe emotional and psychiatric stress after their abortion than are those who abort purely for reasons of convenience.

■ Post-abortion stress increases the probability that a woman will later become involved in a pattern of child battery.

■ Compared to the rate of illegal abortions prior to 1973, legalization of abortion has resulted in a 10 to 15 fold increase in the number of women aborted each year. Although legal abortions are 3 to 5 times safer than illegal abortions, the much faster rise in *total* abortions performed has offset this advantage. This means that while legalization has reduced the *percentage* of complications and deaths resulting from abortion, the *total number* of complications and deaths resulting from legal abortion is much higher.

Clearly, abortion is not as "safe and easy" as its defenders imply. But women seeking abortions are never given the full truth. The above facts and more can be learned at almost any local library, but they will not be learned at the local abortion clinic. In short, the abortion industry in this country is urging women to exercise their "right to choose" without first ensuring their *right to know*. This is manipulation, plain and simple.

In every one of the thousands of cases documented by WEBA, a full explanation of the possible risks and complications was not given by the abortion provider. Even when direct questions were asked, answers about risks are understated, construed, or avoided. Rather than discuss risks, alternatives, or fetal development, abortion counseling is generally devoted to discussing birth control techniques. Rather than receiving information about the abortion, women are given a sales pitch on birth control and sterilization options—all available at an extra charge, of course.

What is crucial to recognize is that, as a doctor, the abortionist currently enjoys the privilege of telling the patient only what he thinks she should know. Indeed, *abortion is the only medical procedure where the physician and his staff have a "constitutional right" to withhold information about the risks and possible aftereffects of the procedure.* This longstanding practice of limiting information available to abortion patients was made a "constitutional right" in the Supreme Court's 1983 *Akron v. Akron Center for Reproductive Health* decision and later upheld in *Thornburg v. ACOG.*

At best, abortion clinics avoid telling women the truth in order to minimize the natural feelings of fear, doubt, and guilt associated with abortion. They may want to create a comfortable, "safe and easy" view of abortion to minimize stress and, hopefully, accelerate recovery. At worst, they avoid explanation for fear of losing a paying customer. As we will show in the course of this book, the latter motive is extremely prevalent.

In sum, women are told lies; abortionists are taking advantage of their ignorance and vulnerability. They are being patronizingly "guided" to choose abortion for the convenience and profit of others. This type of deceit only serves to aggravate the psychological and emotional aftereffects of abortion. When some physical complication develops, or when unexpected feelings of loss and guilt develop, or when a popular magazine article on the marvels of modern medicine shows the picture of a fetus which is seen to be a baby rather than a "blob of cells," the aborted woman is caught unprepared. She feels betrayed, manipulated, and deceived. Or when she learns that abortion was not her "only choice," that there were alternatives and support groups available of which she had not been informed, she is quite right to complain, "Why didn't anyone tell me of this before?"

This book is part of our continuing effort to provide that warning, to provide that education. Women have a *right to know.* Who is better qualified to teach them than those of us who have learned by our experiences?

We have allowed ourselves to be silenced by our shame for too long. We will be silent no more.

A Survey of Women Who Aborted

Since the mid-1960s, abortion has been a major national issue, the subject of state and Congressional investigations, thousands of articles, and hundreds of books. But most of this attention has been focused on the ideological aspects of abortion: "freedom of choice" versus the "right to life." While those on both sides of the issue have published reams of material investigating whether or not the aborted fetus is a "person," comparatively little has been done to identify and understand the *women* who have abortions—until now.

Who are the women who abort? This is a question which should be answered with more than government statistics of age, race, and marital status. Instead, women who abort must be understood as *people*, a group of women faced with a common problem, seeking a common solution. To understand their needs and to empathize with their lives, we must understand their feelings, their dreams, their joys, and their sorrows. We need to know *who* these women are, *why* they choose abortion, and perhaps most importantly, *how* abortion changes their lives. Knowing the answer to these questions, other women who are faced with unplanned pregnancies will be better prepared to decide when abortion is their best choice, and when it is their worst.

There are two possible approaches to understanding the who, how, and why's of the abortion experience. The first method is a *subjective* approach which looks at the personal stories and reflections of

1

aborted women. The second method is an *objective* approach based on surveys and statistical analyses. Each approach has its own particular strengths and weaknesses. The subjective approach is more detailed and more intimate, but its personal nature makes it more difficult to reach general conclusions. If left to stand alone, one could never be sure whether a particular woman's subjective experiences are typical of aborted women, or whether her experience is a rare exception. Objective data, on the other hand, is better suited for drawing general conclusions: but it is so impersonal that it is good *only* for drawing generalities.

While subjective testimonies and objective surveys each have their weaknesses, when used together they can give us a complete view of the abortion experience. The objective data serves as the foundation, or skeleton, for identifying "typical" patterns, while the subjective testimony adds personal details and "fleshes out" the skeleton, providing it with depth and perspective.

To provide a complete picture of the abortion experience, therefore, this book includes both objective data and subjective testimonies.

Limitations of the Survey

Up to this time, there has been very little quantifiable information about women's experiences before, during, and after their abortions. Many studies have been done, but most have been severely limited in scope, concentrating on the demographic characteristics of aborting women, or only on their immediate, short-term reactions.

Detailed studies of the abortion experience are often blocked by practical and political difficulties. First, many pro-choice groups, such as the National Organization for Women (NOW), have long opposed any survey of aborted women. To these pro-choice advocates, it is not necessary to know *why* women abort or *how* abortion affects their lives, it is only important that their *choice* to abort is respected. Investigations into *why* women abort, they argue, are a violation of the aborted woman's right to privacy.[1] While NOW's position is intended to prevent probing into the private and pain-filled memories of aborted women, the lack of such information has prevented other women from being warned about the potential physical and psychological risks they face if they, too, choose abortion.

A second major obstacle to surveying aborted women is that access to these women is generally controlled by abortion providers. While a few abortion clinics have performed minor surveys of their clients, these surveys are generally superficial and are always limited to only the patients' short-term reactions to their experiences. Most abortion providers have little or no motivation to perform a five- or ten-year post-abortion follow-up study; yet they are the only ones with the names and addresses necessary to perform this research. On the other hand, even if there were a desire on the part of clinics to participate in such a study, there are legal obstacles which would probably prevent them from contacting previous patients for such purposes, since such an outreach effort might violate the former clients' rights of privacy.

Furthermore, even if abortion clinics were willing and able to cooperate in a long-range follow-up survey, the sample obtained would still be distorted by many factors. First, it is known that many women give false names and addresses to abortion clinics in order to protect their anonymity. Second, many women would have moved or married (and thus changed their names) during the course of the five to ten years between the abortion and the survey. Third, many of those who could be reached might refuse to "stir up" their abortion memories in order to answer a survey. Any and all of these factors might bias the results of the survey, since the few who would respond might not be fully representative of aborters in general.

The third limiting factor which has plagued all previous surveys is one of geographical constraints. Over 1.5 million elective abortions are performed each year in the United States. From one-fourth to one-third of all pregnancies are terminated by abortion. The abortion rate, however, is not uniform across the nation. Regional attitudes towards abortion play a major influence on the attractiveness of the abortion option. In more rural states, such as Missouri and Wyoming, less than one-tenth of all pregnancies are aborted. But in such major metropolitan areas as New York City and Washington, D. C., abortions outnumber live births.

The differences in abortion rates around the country seem to be directly related to regional values and social "sophistication." In most rural areas, attitudes toward abortion are generally negative, while urban areas tend to reflect more laissez-faire attitudes. In some large urban areas, however, lax standards are beginning to be replaced by a "social obligation to have an abortion if the conditions for carrying a baby to term are not perfect."[2]

Because all previous studies of aborted women have been performed out of a single clinic or abortion hospital, the results of all prior studies are limited by these regional attitudes and biases. With the

3

creation of WEBA, however, a national, independent, long-range fol-low-up study of aborted women finally became possible. For the first time an identifiable group of aborted women was finally obtainable, without the need to rely on the cooperation (or face the interference) of an abortion clinic. Thus, in order to perform a long-range evaluation of the abortion experience, a survey was prepared and distributed through WEBA chapters in 42 states to 252 previously aborted women. (The complete results of the survey are reproduced in the Appendix.

Comparing Statistics

Before evaluating the survey responses dealing with the abortion expe-rience, however, it is necessary to see whether or not WEBA members are typical of a random sample of aborting women. This can be done by comparing the demographic characteristics of the WEBA women sur-veyed with the national abortion statistics which describe the "typical" aborter.

Age

National Statistics: The majority of all aborters, 55 percent, are between the ages of 20 and 29. Approximately 16 percent of aborting women are 30 years of age or over. The remaining 30 percent of abortions are performed on teenagers, with most teenage aborters in the range of 17 to 19 years of age. Less than one percent of all abortions are performed on girls under the age of 15.[3]

WEBA Sample: At the time of their abortions, 3 percent of the WEBA members sampled were fifteen years old or under, 42 percent were between 15 and 19 years old, 47 percent were between 20 and 29 years old, and 8 percent were 30 years old or more. The youngest aborter in the sample was 12 years old, the oldest aborter was 40. The average age at the time of their abortions was 21.2 years old.

This sample suggests that WEBA members are a relatively close match to the national pattern discussed above, though WEBA's mem-bership tends slightly towards younger aborters. This small variation from national averages might be an insignificant "blip" caused by the sampling process, or it may indicate that younger aborters are more likely to suffer traumatic abortion experiences and therefore be more likely to be attracted to contact an organization like WEBA. Since the evidence to be presented later shows that young women are more likely to be vulnerable to manipulation and exploitation by their boy-friends or parents, we are inclined to believe the latter hypothesis.

Marital Status

National Statistics: Approximately 80 percent of all aborters are reported as being unmarried. Most studies agree that the fear of single parenthood is a primary factor, if not the leading one, in the choice for most abortions.[4]

WEBA Sample: At the time of their abortions, 67 percent of the WEBA members surveyed were single and not engaged, 9 percent were single but engaged to be married, 6 percent were divorced or separated, and 18 percent were married. Again, WEBA members are a close match to the typical pattern of aborters described by national statistics.

Family Size

National Statistics: Approximately 58 percent of aborting women had no children at the time of their abortions. Of the rest, 19 percent already had one child, 14 percent had two, and the remaining 10 percent had three or more children.[5]

In terms of family planning, abortion is seldom used to avoid "excess" children. In fact, national statistics indicate that the more children a woman has, the less likely she is to abort a later child. Instead, most aborting women desire to have children at a later date, under more controlled circumstances. By aborting their first pregnancies, these women seek to delay their wanted children until some time when they have better marital and/or financial security.

WEBA Sample: Of the women surveyed, 73 percent were childless at the time of their abortion, 14 percent had one child, 9 percent had two children, and 5 percent had three or more children. In terms of family planning, only 7 percent indicated that concern over limiting their family size was an important factor in their abortion decisions.

Race

National Statistics: More than two-thirds of all abortions are done on white women. But the remaining one-third which are performed on non-white women is a comparatively high figure, since non-whites constitute only about 13 percent of the total American population. When measured on a per capita basis, non-white women are subjected to twice as many abortions as white women.[6]

This disproportionate concentration of abortions among non-whites stands in stark contrast to the situation prior to 1973, when the rate of abortion (both legal and illegal) among whites was twice as high as that found among non-whites. Before it was elevated to the status of a social right, or even a "social duty," abortion was primarily a middle- and upper-class vice associated with "saving face" or "status climbing." Racial minorities, and the poor in particular, were (and are) generally more accepting of unplanned pregnancies, and are more likely to be opposed to abortion on ethical grounds than is the population as a whole.[7] As we will see, however, minorities today are facing increased social and financial pressures to abort against their wills.[8] The rapid rise of abortion among non-whites, therefore, should be taken as evidence that the pressures which compel non-white women to abort are increasing, not that it has become a more "desirable" alternative among minorities.

WEBA Sample: Of the WEBA members surveyed, 87 percent were white and 13 percent were non-white. This percentage of non-whites is very close to the national percentage of non-whites in the population as a whole, but is only half of what should be expected in a perfect sample of "typical" aborters.

There are two possible explanations for this variance. First, the sampling technique used for this survey was geared towards maximizing input from a wide variety of geographical areas. This sampling method may not have included a proportionate representation of major population centers where there are high concentrations of non-whites. Second, the WEBA network is only four years old and may not have yet reached all segments of the aborting community in proportion to their need. Its public speakers, the majority of whom are white, may be concentrating on reaching out to predominately white groups with whom they are already familiar and have easy access.

Repeat Abortions

National Statistics: Approximately 33 percent of all abortions are performed for repeat aborters. About 70 percent of repeat aborters have had one previous abortion, 16 percent have had two previous abortions, and the remainder have had three or more previous abortions. The number of women resorting to repeat abortions is increasing at a rate of about 3 percent yearly.[9]

WEBA Sample: Of the WEBA members sampled, 24 percent have had more than one abortion. This rate is approximately equivalent to the average national rate of repeat aborters in 1977, which is consistent with the fact that most of the WEBA women surveyed aborted from eight to twelve years ago.

When compared to the national demographic characteristics of the "typical" aborting women, WEBA members roughly fit into the same "typical" pattern. In other words, the WEBA women sampled in our survey are a fair, but not perfect, representation of aborting women in general. Therefore, in their answers to objective questions such as "What circumstances led to your abortions?" or "How long did it take you to make your decision?," the answers of the WEBA members sample are representative of aborting women in general.

When it comes to more subjective questions, however, such as "Are you satisfied with your abortion choice today?," it is uncertain how accurately the answers of WEBA members reflect those of aborting women in general. It cannot be forgotten that WEBA members are women who today regret their abortions, and this regret is clearly reflected in many of their answers. On the other hand, many WEBA members were once very much satisfied with their abortion decisions. If any one point is made clear by this survey and the interviews which follow, it is the fact that *dissatisfaction and regrets over abortion grow with time.*

In general, then, WEBA members represent a matured, reflective point of view of their abortion experiences. The average time between having their abortions and answering this survey is 10.0 years. While most short-term studies, performed only a few months after the abortion, reveal a seesawing ambivalence, a reluctant satisfaction with their choice, this study reflects the long-term view of aborted women. With the privilege of hindsight, the thoughts and feelings of the WEBA women surveyed are endowed with years of self-examination, learning, and change.

In short, because of the nature of the organization, the WEBA members who answered this survey generally represent a more settled and mature view of their abortion experiences—a view which is primarily negative. How deeply this bias influences their answers to a specific question depends on the nature of the question. How accurately their answers reflect the long-term reactions of the general population of aborting women must be judged on whether or not WEBA women represent the attitudes of aborting women in general.

We maintain that WEBA is representative of the aborting population as a whole. This point will be further substantiated in Chapter Two, where we will see that most pro-choice studies have found the same doubts, the same complaints, and the same negative experiences among most aborting women. For now, it is sufficient for the reader to remember that as with all surveys, the following results are approximations based on a selected sample of persons. The results are more valuable for drawing general conclusions than specific ones.

Circumstances Leading to the Abortion

Age and Marital Status

As indicated earlier, 83 percent of the WEBA members surveyed were single, engaged, or separated when they discovered they were pregnant. Their average age at the time of their abortions was 21.2 years; the oldest was 40 and the youngest was 12. Nearly half were under the age of 20.

Use of Birth Control

More than three-quarters of all those surveyed were not using any form of birth control at the time of conception. Lack of contraceptive protection, however, was *not* due to lack of knowledge or lack of access to birth control devices. Over 70 percent of these women were highly informed about birth control alternatives, and an additional 15 percent considered themselves to be moderately well informed. Only 15 percent claimed that they had had little or no knowledge of contraceptive practices. As we will see, these findings are consistent with other studies which have shown that most aborters tend to be highly informed about contraceptives but failed to use them at the time they became pregnant.

A significant number of abortions, however, do occur because of contraceptive failure. In this sample of aborting women, 23 percent were using a form of birth control at the time of conception. The method which failed most often for these aborters was the birth control pill. Forty-four percent of those using contraceptives were on the pill, 22 percent were using a spermicide, 16 percent were using a diaphragm, 9 percent had an IUD in place, and 9 percent were using condoms. In addition, one woman became pregnant even though she had had a tubal ligation, and another became pregnant despite her mate's vasectomy.

After relying on the promises of these "responsible" birth control methods, many of these women felt betrayed by the technology they had trusted to keep them from becoming pregnant in the first place. In general, they felt that the pregnancy was not their fault but rather the fault of a contraceptive failure which they were now "forced" to correct through abortion.

Factors Influencing the Abortion Decision

Situational Factors

The aborted women who were surveyed were given a list of common reasons for aborting and asked to indicate to what degree each of these factors influenced their final decision. The following table summarizes the results from the most frequently cited reason to the least:

Was your decision made for reasons of:	
social acceptance	57%
short-term needs?	37%
financial limits?	28%
long-term needs?	24%
career goals?	18%
mental health?	17%
family size?	7%
physical health?	7%

In addition to these reasons, 41 percent reported "other" reasons that played a primary role in their abortion decisions. The "other" reason most often listed was the result of some interpersonal problems, such as "pressure from boyfriend," or "fear of telling parents." (The

9

influence of other people in the abortion decision was dealt with more thoroughly in a later part of the survey; see the section "Interpersonal Influences.") Several women described the "other" major reasons in their abortion decision in terms of their own immaturity, claiming that the decision was motivated by "selfishness," "embarrassment," "ignorance," "shame," "fright," "aloneness," or because it was the "easy way out." One woman noted that the major reason for choosing abortion was because "I didn't know I had options," while another stated that there was "no other place to go." Three women reported that the major reason for their abortions was the fact they were pregnant by men other than their husbands.

A surprising finding in the "other" category was that approximately 8 percent of the WEBA women surveyed aborted for the "hard" reasons. Half of these "hard case" aborters felt "forced" to abort because their pregnancies were the result of rape, and the other half aborted because of the possibility that the child they carried might be handicapped. This number of "hard case" aborters is from 5 to 20 times greater than that found among the general population of aborting women. The explanation for such a high concentration of "hard case" aborters in this sample lies in the fact that abortion in these "hard cases" is generally more traumatic than in "common case" abortions. "Hard case" aborters, therefore, are more likely to need and be attracted to a support group like WEBA.

Altogether, fully 64 percent of the aborted women surveyed described themselves as "forced" into abortion because of their particular circumstances at that time. Most of these women also indicated that during the time between discovering they were pregnant and having the abortion there was such a high level of emotional trauma that they were unable to thoughtfully and cautiously consider their alternatives. Abortion was simply the most obvious and fastest way to escape from their dilemmas. Over 84 percent state that they would have kept their babies "under better circumstances."

Personal Influences

Presented with a list of persons who may have played a role in their abortion decision, the women were asked to indicate to what degree each of these persons influenced their final decisions. The following table summarizes the results in the order from the most frequently cited interpersonal influence to the least:

Were you encouraged to have an abortion by:	
husband or boyfriend?	51%
abortion counselor?	35%
friends?	24%
parents?	23%
doctor?	23%
social worker	14%
other family members?	14%

Other persons reported to have played a major role in the abortion decisions were "school authorities" and "boyfriend's parents." A few women made other notes at this point such as: "Would have been kicked out if not aborted," "Forced by mother; father opposed," "No other option given," "Lack of support from society," and "Planned Parenthood counselor said under my situation abortion was my best choice."

The opinions and pressures of others plays a major role in the final decision of most aborting women. Asked "Would your choice have been different if any or all of the above had encouraged you differently?," more than 83 percent indicated that they definitely would have chosen *against* abortion.

For the majority of those surveyed, these "significant others" played more than advisory roles in determining the women's final decisions. *Nearly 55 percent of the respondents felt they had been very much "forced" to abort by others.* Another 10 percent felt moderate pressure from others to "do the sensible thing," and only 33 percent felt free to make their own decisions.

In another series of questions, approximately 73 percent indicated they did not feel in control of their own lives when making their abortion decisions. Sixty-one percent said that their lives at that time were very much "controlled by others," and another 12 percent indicated their lives were moderately "controlled by others."

Attitudes Toward Pregnancy

The fact that all of these women chose abortion does not mean that they were all equally opposed to pregnancy and parenthood. Instead, many actually desired to keep the baby but felt that abortion was their

11

"only" alternative, given the pressures of their situations and the demands of those around them.

A majority of those surveyed, 53 percent, described themselves as having felt very "good or excited" about being pregnant. Another 6 percent were moderately pleased, and 31 percent were not at all pleased when they first learned of their pregnancy. In general, it might be concluded, an unplanned pregnancy conjures up mixed emotions. While pleasure is experienced from feeling the creative power of fertility and from imagining the beauties and joys of a newborn child, this pleasure is muted by the distressful realization that responsibility for the child will force changes in future plans and expectations.

The pleasurable side of being pregnant was significant for most of these women. Over 85 percent hoped to bear children at some time in their lives. The problem was that this unplanned pregnancy occurred at an undesirable time. Despite this problem, however, 50 percent of those surveyed gave much consideration to carrying the pregnancy to term, 15 percent gave moderate consideration to childbirth, and 12 percent gave it small consideration. Only 19 percent gave no thought to childbirth, apparently certain of their abortion choice from the first moment they found out they were pregnant.

Most aborters tend to equate childbirth with parenthood. Only 14 percent gave much thought to the option of placing the child up for adoption. For many the possibility of adoption was surrounded by ignorance and myths. For most, there seemed to be only two alternatives: raising the child themselves or having an abortion. Fear of raising the child themselves was also compounded by a general ignorance of the support groups and financial aid programs which might have been available.

Despite the hardships they faced, 59 percent gave strong consideration to keeping the baby, and another 13 percent gave it moderate consideration. Most of the women in this category very much *wanted* to keep the baby but felt "forced" to abort by the demands of those around them.

Perhaps the most revealing discovery was that over 84 percent said they would have been very willing to keep the child "under better circumstances." Less than 2 percent indicated they would not have kept the child under any circumstances. This finding suggests that positive programs to improve the circumstances of women faced with unplanned pregnancies would have a major impact on the abortion rate in America. Most women do not desire abortion and would do almost anything to avoid it, but they need support and help to improve their circumstances and to make parenting (and/or adoption) a reasonable alternative.

Prior Attitudes Toward Abortion

Many studies have shown that before becoming pregnant themselves, most aborted women have "definite moral opinions but little factual knowledge about abortion." These studies have found that until placed in a situation where they themselves are "forced" into an abortion, the majority of aborting women disapprove of it. Compelled by their circumstances, most aborting women feel "forced" to compromise their moral values or compelled to rationalize themselves as being "exceptions" to the rule.[10]

This survey found the same trend, and even the same approximate percentages, as recorded by other researchers. Asked "What were your feelings about abortion prior to becoming pregnant?," 21 percent of the WEBA women responded "unsure." Besides the passage of time which might make it difficult to recall one's earlier attitudes, this high percentage of "unsure" responses suggests that many of these young women simply had never given abortion much thought before they became pregnant. They had no clear opinion to guide them once pregnancy did occur.

Looking at those with a definite opinion, 41 percent indicated a very negative attitude toward abortion, compared to 15 percent who had a very positive view of abortion. The remaining 43 percent were somewhere in between the extremes, indicating limited approval of abortion under "special" circumstances.

Given their doubts about the morality of abortion, most aborting women are strongly influenced by the legal status of the abortion option. Asked "Did the knowledge that abortion was legal influence your opinion about the morality of choosing abortion?," 70 percent said that the law had played a major role in their moral perception of abortion, 6 percent stated that it played a moderate role, and 13 percent said it played little or no role. Taken in context with the above information, this suggests that while most aborting women have a negative moral view of abortion before their own abortions, they find comfort (and grounds for rationalization) in the socio-legal view of abortion. Some, perhaps, even doubt their own moral values, thinking, "If it's legal, it must be all right. I just have to get over my own stupid hang-ups."

Making the Abortion Decision

The period before a woman's abortion is a time of personal crisis. For the vast majority of aborters, external pressures and internal needs demand a quick resolution to the crisis situation. Of the aborted women surveyed, 81 percent felt extremely rushed to make the abortion decision.

For most, the amount of time taken to make the decision was amazingly short. Fifty-one percent decided to abort in less than four days after learning they were pregnant. Several noted that the decision was made within hours. Twenty-four percent took a week to make their decisions, 12 percent took two to three weeks, 6 percent waited four to six weeks before deciding, and 7 percent waited seven weeks or more before deciding to abort. It should be noted that many of these late decisions were not due to indecisiveness so much as changing circumstances. For example, a few women learned only several weeks after becoming pregnant with a wanted pregnancy that there was a risk that the child they carried might be handicapped, and so, usually after the urging of a physician, chose abortion.

Asked "Do you feel you had all of the necessary information to make the decision [to abort]?," 93 percent insisted that they had little or none of the necessary information. Only 3 percent believed they had most or all of the pertinent information. This, however, is one of the questions which is strongly affected by the fact that all of the women surveyed are members of WEBA. It is probable that at the time of their abortions, many or even most of these women felt they had all the information necessary—though many may have felt ignorant of what would be done or about what risks they would face. But looking back on their abortions from an average of ten years later, most of these women acquired information and experiences that were not available to them at that time. What might have seemed like an informed choice then is later seen as ignorant, foolish, and hasty.

Similarly, over 82 percent of the WEBA women stated that their abortion decision was not at all "thought out." Only 9 percent felt it was moderately well thought out, and only 8 percent believed that their decision had been "well thought out" under the circumstances.

Degree of Certainty about the Decision

Given the crisis situations in which they were forced to make their decisions, most of the women were *not* content with their decisions

14

even at the time of their abortions. Approximately 56 percent of those surveyed said they had been extremely dissatisfied with their "only" option, 13 percent were moderately satisfied with their choice to abort, and only 24 percent were happy with their decision and secure in their choice.

For most, then, the decision to abort was filled with ambivalence. Any slight change in circumstances or encouragement from significant persons in their lives (especially husbands and boyfriends) could have brought about a reversal of their choice. In fact, even by the time they committed themselves to go to the clinic, only 39 percent felt very firm in their decision to abort. In contrast, 41 percent felt very uncertain about their decision, and the remainder were somewhere in between. Because of this uncertainty, 44 percent said they were still very actively looking for another option up to the final moments before their abortions.

The low degree of commitment to securing an abortion was also evident in answers to questions relating to illegal abortion. Asked whether or not they would have sought an illegal abortion if a legal abortion had not been available, 75 percent said they definitely would not have sought an illegal abortion, 4 percent said there was a moderate chance they would have sought an illegal abortion, 6 percent stated it was very likely they would have sought an illegal abortion, and 16 percent were unsure.[11] Asked whether or not they would have considered self-induced abortion as a desperate last resort, 89 percent totally rejected that alternative, and only 5 percent said self-abortion would have been strongly considered.

What is clear from all these responses is that the vast majority of aborting women are extremely uncertain about and uncommitted to their abortion decisions. Abortion is a "marginal good" at best. Any minor barrier to securing an abortion, or any perception that there are physical risks to the abortion, or any reasonable hope that her circumstances might be improved so as to make childbearing a reasonable possibility might alter the final decision away from abortion and towards accepting the pregnancy, childbirth, and parenting.

Abortion Counseling and Clinic Services

At most abortion clinics it is assumed that once a woman enters and begins to inquire about abortion, her decision to abort has already been firmly made. Abortion counselors believe it is their role to reassure the woman and ease her through the abortion, not to provide her with information or help her review her decision. The weaknesses of this approach are readily apparent in the survey responses of aborted women.

Rather than being certain of their abortion decisions, 40 to 50 percent of the women surveyed were wavering in their choice and were actually hoping for another option when they first went to speak with the counselor. But instead, 91 percent reported that their abortion counselors offered little or no help in exploring their decision and options. Only 4 percent of the women gave their abortion counselors high grades for being informative and helpful. Overall, 66 percent believed that their abortion counselors were strongly biased toward selling them an abortion as the "best solution." Only 9 percent felt that their counselors had been relatively free of a pro-abortion bias, with another 23 percent saying they were uncertain whether any bias existed.

Adequacy of Information

Even pro-choice surveys agree that most aborting women have little or no prior knowledge about what is technically involved in an abortion, what its risks are, or how developed the fetus is that they are thinking to abort.[12] Over 90 percent of the women surveyed felt that they did not have enough information to make an informed abortion choice. In almost all cases this ignorance was not corrected during abortion counseling.

Having been through their abortions and having learned more about abortion since that time, the WEBA women are almost unanimous in their complaint that abortion clinics did not provide them with enough information to make an informed choice. Even basic information about how the abortion would be performed was generally weak, with 76 percent complaining that they were not given an accurate description of the procedure during their pre-abortion counseling session. While at least "watered-down" descriptions of the abortion procedure are almost always given, many of the women complained that there was no mention of the physical pain involved. Only 16 percent felt that the counseling session had adequately informed them about the technical aspects of the abortion procedure.

In the vast majority of counseling sessions, discussion of the health risks of abortion was also absent. Over 80 percent reported that little or no discussion of risks had taken place, and only 8 percent believed their counselors had adequately discussed the surgical risks of the procedure.

But the worst marks for counseling occurred for failure to provide information about the fetus's stage of development, information which many believed would have been a crucial factor in their final decisions. Over 90 percent of the women stated that the biological nature of the fetus had not been discussed during their counseling session. Only 2 percent said that fetal development had been thoroughly or even moderately discussed.

Some abortion counselors maintain that discussion of the abortion procedure and fetal development are not necessary because women have enough information before coming to the clinic, presumably from high school biology courses. This belief is not supported by the evidence, however. Asked whether or not they had felt "well informed about the procedure and fetus through other sources before seeking an abortion," 90 percent claimed they had little or no prior knowledge, and 5 percent stated they had had only moderate prior knowledge. Only 4 percent claimed to have been well informed about abortion and fetal development through prior knowledge.

While the need for information in all three major areas is not being met, the evidence shows that most clinics do not even want to ensure informed consent. Fully 80 percent of the women surveyed felt their counselors had not encouraged—or had even attempted to discourage—questions about the abortion. Only 5 to 13 percent believed that their counselors were open and willing to answer their questions. When questions were asked, only 8 percent felt that their questions were thoroughly answered, 8 percent believed they received moderately complete answers, and 52 to 71 percent felt that their questions were trivialized or avoided.

In sum, nearly 80 percent of the women surveyed believed that they had been denied pertinent information or had been actively misinformed by their counselors prior to their abortions. Asked what were the most important facts they felt misinformed about, nearly 50 percent complained they had not been told about fetal development. The second most common complaint, mentioned by approximately one-fourth of those surveyed, was that they had not been adequately warned about the physical risks of the procedure. Many also complained that they had not been warned about the pain or about the nature of the procedure in general. The third most common complaint was that there had been no warning about the "psychological after-effects," or the "emotional pain," which would follow their abortion. Finally, several women felt that their counseling had been totally inadequate, stating that "nothing was discussed" or that they had been misinformed about "everything." One women charged that her counselor had led her to believe that she had "no other choice." Another felt lied to by her doctor when he told her that "saline abortion [is] easier than childbirth." And yet another felt that the entire counseling system was a sham of "prejudice and conspiracy against [the] weak and poor," designed to seduce the poor into aborting their children so as to save the rich from the costs of welfare support.

Asked the general question of whether they were "satisfied with the abortion services you received," 18 percent registered high to very high satisfaction, 18 percent were moderately well satisfied, 52 percent were very dissatisfied, and 10 percent were "unsure."

Services at Planned Parenthood Clinics

Some might question whether the poor counseling and abortion services WEBA women received is not, in fact, atypical. It is at least a possibility that WEBA women were the victims of poorly run clinics, and thus were more likely to feel misinformed and exploited. Defenders of abortion might insist that most clinics are in fact better than these.

In Chapter Eight we will examine what most typical abortion clinics are like. But for now, it is useful to compare the possibly "atypical" clinics described above with the nationally respected clinics operated by the Planned Parenthood Federation of America.

Planned Parenthood is the self-proclaimed leader in providing quality family planning and abortion services. Even clinics not affiliated with Planned Parenthood generally agree that Planned Parenthood clinics are the closest thing to the abortion industry's standard. Thus, in order to compare the general results on abortion clinic performance described above with this standard, we separately evaluated those WEBA surveys in which abortion counseling and/or the abortion procedure were performed at a Planned Parenthood clinic.

Of the 252 women surveyed, 21 percent received their counseling and/or their abortions at a Planned Parenthood facility. Sixty percent stated that their Planned Parenthood counselor had very strongly encouraged them to choose abortion as the "best" solution to their problems. This is especially significant when over 90 percent of those encouraged to abort by their Planned Parenthood counselor said that there was a strong chance they would have chosen against the abortion if they had not been so strongly encouraged to abort by others, *including their counselor.*

Of the Planned Parenthood patients, over 60 percent were still hoping to find an alternative to abortion when they went in for counseling.[13] Only 25 percent were already firm in their abortion choice before counseling, and all felt that their Planned Parenthood counselor did little or nothing to help them explore their decisions. Instead, 89 percent felt that Planned Parenthood counselor was strongly biased in favor of the abortion option.

In terms of describing the abortion procedure, Planned Parenthood counselors scored slightly higher than their counterparts at other clinics. Almost 17 percent of the Planned Parenthood clients stated that the abortion procedure was thoroughly described to them, 23 percent said it was moderately well described, while 68 percent still felt that the procedure was not described with any degree of depth or clarity. In the task of describing fetal development and the health risks of abortion, however, Planned Parenthood counselors were scored as being no better than abortion counselors in general. Ninety-five percent of the Planned Parenthood counselors gave little or no biological information about the fetus which the abortion would destroy, and over 80 percent of the Planned Parenthood counselors gave little or no information about the potential health risks which might follow the surgery.

Planned Parenthood counselors were scored slightly higher for encouraging their clients to ask questions; but when questions were asked, over 64 percent of these women felt their questions were not adequately answered or were trivialized. In fact, over three-fourths of the Planned Parenthood patients felt that they had been misled by their counselors and had been denied information which might have influenced their final decisions. Only 13 percent felt adequately prepared for the abortion and forewarned of its risks after receiving counseling at a Planned Parenthood facility.

Overall, only 19 percent of the women who were served by Planned Parenthood clinics or referrals registered high to very high satisfaction with the abortion services they received there, as compared to an 18 percent high satisfaction rate of those going to abortion clinics in general. Another 13 percent were moderately satisfied with Planned Parenthood abortion services, while the majority, 56 percent, were very dissatisfied.

The Physical Aftereffects of Abortion

The physical aftereffects of abortion range from those which are minor (e.g., headaches and nausea), to those which are very severe (e.g., chronic infections or a punctured uterus). But not all complications, particularly severe ones, are readily apparent. While some physical aftereffects show up immediately after the abortion and others a short time later, many complications may not appear until several years later (e.g., a slightly damaged uterus may cause miscarriages in later pregnancies, or a small infection may cause scarring of the fallopian tube and permanent infertility).

Of the 252 women surveyed, approximately one-half complained of suffering from at least one type of physical complication following their abortions. Moreover, at least 18 percent of those surveyed reported having suffered permanent physical damage traceable to the procedure.

Of the 47 percent who reported suffering from a complication, 40 percent said it was a very minor problem, 26 percent said it was moderately severe, and 35 percent claimed that it was very severe. Judging by the complications which were listed, it would seem that immediate and short-term complications were generally listed as the least severe type. Delayed or long-term complications often involving a reduced or a total fertility loss, were most likely to be listed by the respondents as being very severe. This trend, which subjectively evaluates delayed and permanent damage as being more severe than immediate complications, suggests that aborting women are able and willing to tolerate correctable mistakes. But when unforeseen and irreversible damage is done to their reproductive lives, this damage is more unforgivable and is therefore subjectively rated as being more severe.

Of the short-term complications, the most frequently identified was post-operative hemorrhage, noted by 15 percent of all the women surveyed. Infection was the second most likely complication, reported by 9 percent of those surveyed. Incomplete abortions were also frequently noted, which though correctable by a second abortion, carried additional risks, especially of infection. Other relatively minor problems included: clotting, cramps, irregular periods, chronic bleeding, chronic infections, exhaustion, loss of weight, pelvic inflammatory disease, and endometriosis.

Long-term complications were generally more severe and more permanent. Of the aborted women surveyed, approximately 6 percent were forced to undergo a total hysterectomy to remove a uterus that had been damaged or infected by the abortion procedure. Another 8 percent reported that post-abortion infection had left them sterile by blocking their fallopian tubes or through some other means. Yet another 4 percent contracted cervical cancer, which they attribute to the abortion.[14]

Besides suffering sterility from the above causes, many aborted women suffer a reduced ability to carry a later wanted pregnancy to term. Of the women surveyed, approximately 20 percent later suffered miscarriage of a wanted child. In addition, no less than 8 percent were diagnosed as suffering from cervical incompetence after their abortions. Other birthing problems and reproductive damage were also frequently reported.

Finally, several women reported that a fear of needing another abortion "forced" them to undergo tubal ligations, which they later regretted. In these cases, sterility was not directly caused by way of a post-abortion physical complication. Rather, post-abortion psychological trauma indirectly "forced" these women to submit to "voluntary sterilizations" which were often irreversible.

In Chapter Three we will examine the physical complications of abortion in greater detail. We will see that the complication rates reported by WEBA members are well within the rates reported by independent sources. In other words, WEBA members are not more likely to have suffered from abortion-related physical complications than is any other sample of aborting women in general.

The Psychological Aftermath

As with the physical complications, the psychological traumas caused by abortion vary from mild to severe, may occur immediately or may be delayed, and may take many forms. The main difference is that while physical complications affect only about 50 percent of all aborted women, psychological problems occur in the lives of almost all aborted women. This impact is not always readily apparent and may even be denied by many aborted women, but most psychiatrists agree that it is always there. The psychological and emotional complications associated with abortion will be thoroughly discussed in Chapter Four. For now we will concentrate on the subjective responses provided by this survey.

Of the 252 women surveyed, 94 percent said they had experienced negative psychological effects attributable to their abortions. This response rate is certainly higher than what would be reported from the general population of aborting women. One reason for this lies in the fact that by joining WEBA the women surveyed in this study have already recognized the problems they had following their abortions. Over 70 percent of the WEBA women reported that there was a time when they would have denied the existence of any negative reactions after their abortions. For some this denial stage lasted only a few months, for others it lasted over ten or fifteen years.

The evidence shows that denial is an almost universal reaction to post-abortion trauma. Just as most alcoholics are unable or unwilling to recognize their affliction, so it is with aborted women. But similarly, just as the ability to join Alcoholics Anonymous signals that an alcoholic has finally recognized his or her problem, so too aborted women do not join WEBA until they have stopped denying their problems and have begun to face them head-on. Furthermore, many of the psychological aftereffects of abortion are not obviously linked to that experience. A woman may be suffering from chronic depression, anger, bitterness, loneliness, or low self-esteem, yet never realize until undergoing psychotherapy that these problems stem back to her repressed abortion experience.[15] In fact, one of the most significant findings of this survey and of the testimonies which follow is that abortion is *typically* followed by a long period of denial and unrecognized negative reactions.

Because they are more actively coping with their abortion experiences than are the "average" aborters, WEBA members are more keenly aware of the emotional and psychological effects of their abortions. Rating the severity of their post-abortion problems, 73 percent said the negative impact was severe, 14 percent said it was moderate, 7 percent said it was minor, and 6 percent were unsure.

Asked to list what they felt were their most significant psychological reactions, over forty different reactions were reported. The most frequently listed reactions were guilt, depression, a lowered sense of self-worth, and self-hatred.

Depression and loss of self-esteem often lead to self-destructive behavior. Of the aborted women surveyed, 62 percent described themselves as having become "suicidal" as a direct or indirect result of their abortions. Approximately 20 percent reported that they actually made one or more suicide attempts.

Self-destructive behavior was also displayed in other ways. Nearly one-third of the women surveyed described themselves as drinking more heavily after their abortions, while 15 percent admitted that they became alcoholics. Allowing for overlap, 40 percent said that after their abortions they began to use or increased their use of drugs. Eleven percent described themselves as having become drug addicts.

Many of those surveyed reported that their abortion left them feeling extreme and chronic "anger" or "rage" at others. Short-fused, over 5 percent admitted engaging in "child abuse" or "child neglect," and several others reported "parenting difficulties."

For some of the aborted women, interpersonal relationships became difficult or impossible to handle. Anger, resentment, and even hatred was directed at the husbands or boyfriends who had been involved in the abortion. No less than 50 percent experienced "sexual coldness" or a "revulsion of sex" following their abortions. For some, this sexual coldness was directed toward the father of the aborted child; for others it was due to a fear of becoming pregnant and being "forced" into another abortion. Many women also reported becoming "promiscuous" after their abortions, even though they might also have experienced a loss of pleasure from intercourse.

Many reported that they had been unable to put the abortion out of their minds. These women struggled with constant thoughts about the abortion and were particularly distressed on the anniversary of the abortion and the would-have-been due date for the child.

Many others had frequent thoughts about the child, wondering what he or she would have been like, what mother and child would have been doing together now, and so on. About 30 percent of those surveyed indicated a strong desire to conceive a "replacement" or "atonement baby." One woman described herself as being under the "compulsion to be a perfect mother," in order to atone for the child she had destroyed in her abortion. Another woman felt a constant need to touch babies, while others were afraid to touch babies and would even break into tears whenever they saw one.

Over 40 percent of the women surveyed noted that they had experienced nightmares related to the abortion, and about the same number said they suffered from insomnia. Another 20 percent claimed to have undergone a "nervous breakdown" or a "complete mental breakdown."

Two women suffered from anorexia nervosa, the onset of which they attributed to their abortions. In contrast, at least one woman suffered from excessive weight gain after her abortion, as she tried to bury her guilt in food.

Other frequently reported symptoms were profound remorse, regret, grief, a sense of murder, fear of punishment, and a general sense of loss. Miscellaneous responses included bitterness, unforgiveness of others, unforgiveness of self, anxiety, fear of others finding out, loneliness, isolation, feelings of having been exploited, a feeling of helplessness, indecisiveness, and the inability to make decisions.

It should be noted that the list of psychological aftereffects to abortion discussed in this section was based on short, written responses—not a checklist of possible reactions. Therefore, most responses simply indicated what was at the top of each woman's mind, or what seemed to her to be the most severe problem she faced. If they had been given a checklist on which to mark off the aftereffects they experienced, it is probable that most would have indicated a broader pattern of reactions. With this in mind, it is clear that the percentages given above cannot be projected onto the population of aborting women as a whole. Instead, these percentages can best be described as minimum rates useful for understanding the range and severity of post-abortion sequelae, but not its scope. The scope of these problems will be discussed more thoroughly in Chapter Four.

With regard to their post-abortion psychological conditions, the women surveyed were asked "Did you require professional counseling and/or treatment?" In response, 37 percent felt a very strong need for psychological counseling. Another 6 percent felt a moderate need for counseling, and 49 percent said they did not "require" counseling. Eight percent answered with an "unsure" response. Several women, however, added a comment to this question, saying something like "I needed counseling, but none was available." Because of confusion as to whether the question asked if they actually *had* received counseling or whether they had *needed* counseling, some of these women answered negatively and others positively.

The duration of psychological aftereffects, regardless of severity, was almost always long. Approximately 82 percent said their post-abortion emotional and psychological aftereffects lasted for three years or longer. Eight percent began to feel "normal" again one to two years after their abortions, and another 8 percent felt relief only one to six months after their abortions.

For most of those surveyed, participation in WEBA seemed to have played a significant role in easing their post-abortion trauma. Approximately 48 percent stated that they have almost completely reconciled themselves to their abortion experience, 19 percent are still moderately troubled, and 26 percent are still faced with persistent post-abortion emotional problems.

Looking Back

Hindsight is always clearer than foresight. Thus, in retrospect, after facing the physical and psychological aftereffects, after struggling with ambivalence and doubts, after seeing their lives unimproved or even worsened, it is no surprise that the vast majority of the women surveyed rejected their original choice for abortion.

As we saw earlier, for most of those surveyed the choice to abort was unfirm, marginal, and filled with doubts. The vast majority were unsatisfied with the choice they had been "forced" to make, and many were looking for options, hoping for a better way out, even up to the final hour before their abortions. Afterwards, 93 percent felt that their self-images had been very much worsened by their abortion experience.

If they had known where their lives would have been today, over 95 percent of those surveyed said they would not have chosen abortion. Asked if their lives now are better or worse because of their choice, 66 percent said that their lives are worse because of their abortions, 8 percent said their lives were about the same, and only 5 percent said their lives were better. It should be noted, however, that those who said their lives are better almost always added a qualifying note. For these women, it was not the abortion which had improved their lives, but rather the realization of how wrong their abortion had been. After "hitting the bottom," they had "found God" or had otherwise "grown" to greater personal maturity. Thus, it was by repudiating their abortions that these women felt their lives had been indirectly improved by their abortion experiences. For them, evil had been turned into good.

Nearly all of those surveyed are no longer ambivalent about abortion. Instead, they all have a clear and negative view of abortion, but this view was seldom quickly achieved. For most, there was a long period of denial and rationalization. For almost 25 percent, their first abortion was followed by a second abortion, or even a third or fourth, until at last they were able to free themselves from the self-destructive, self-punishing cycle of repeat abortions.

Obviously, not all aborted women have yet reached this level of insight, this level of inner peace. Most have yet to cope with how they have been manipulated, exploited, and deceived for the convenience of others. That type of self-examination takes time, patience, and often requires help and support from others. In the Profile sections which follow, we will see what several of the women who participated in this survey actually experienced and how they finally found the inner peace they so desperately needed.

PROFILES ONE

Coerced Abortions

This is the first of nine Profile sections in this book. In these sections, twenty WEBA members describe their abortion experiences in their own words. While surveys can be useful for providing a rough statistical understanding of the abortion experience, such methods are always, cold and analytical. The case studies offered here, on the other hand, are very personal and subjective. Their value lies not in numbers and percentages, but in their human dimension.

The twenty testimonies gathered here only scratch the surface of what aborted women face. Just as all persons are unique, so too are the stories and insights of these women. Their experiences are not particularly worse or better than the "average" abortion experience. In fact, since completing this collection, we have come into contact with WEBA members who have stories to tell which make those recorded here seem mild. But that is the way with a topic such as this; each story of despair, pain, and regret seems worse than the next. Indeed, the one internal danger which WEBA members are constantly fighting against is the false pride of martyrdom, the one-upmanship which claims: "If you think that was bad, wait until you hear what I went through." But a search for only the most disastrous of stories and circumstances would be impossible, and to publish only the "worst" of abortion experiences would be unfair. Therefore, care has been taken to select "typical" stories as much as possible.

As we will see, not all aborted women experience the extreme external circumstances and complications which can be associated with abortion. Conditions and reactions vary. But most women do face the same *internal* doubts and dilemmas. It is this common internal experience, more than the external circumstances of abortion, which must be understood and dealt with. It is these internal feelings, feelings which go beyond words, which the reader should try to grasp when reading these stories. Only by putting oneself into the "shoes" of aborted women can one gain a greater understanding and sympathy for their needs.

Unlike other collections of abortion testimonies which are available, these stories are complete. Most other researchers have interviewed aborted women only a short time after their abortions. In these cases the women are often confused and still uncertain about their feelings, and they are always anxious to preserve their anonymity. The stories collected here, on the other hand, were all written from a long-range point of view by women who have a matured and reflective perspective on what they have experienced. They have gone beyond the sad ambivalence which most aborted women feel. They have reconciled themselves to what they have done, and they have come to a better understanding of both themselves and abortion. They have completed the cycle.

Eighteen of the twenty profiles included in this book were solicited from among the first fifty women who responded to our survey. The criteria we used for identifying those to be included here were largely subjective, loosely based on a "first come, first serve" basis. Since the goal was to provide a representative sample of as many different circumstances as possible, certain categories were ignored once two or three samples had been received. For example, since women who aborted because of pressure from boyfriends are "typical" according to the surveys received, such stories were not solicited once two or three had been obtained, even if "better" stories or more articulate women presented themselves. Because of this selection process, therefore, these twenty stories do not represent a statistically "average" sample. The last categories to be filled were those for abortions in the cases of rape and incest, to preserve the health of the mother, and for fear of a potentially handicapped child. Testimonies from women who faced these circumstances were the most difficult to find because they are the rarest reasons for abortion, accounting for less than 3 percent of all abortions in this country. However, because of their unique importance to the abortion debate, stories involving rape or incest were sought throughout the survey period.

After a survey was identified as being of potential interest, the woman was contacted by mail and asked if she would be willing to contribute her story to this book. Thirty-two requests were made, and twenty-eight women responded. Because of space limitations only twenty of these testimonies are included in this book.

Most of the women contacted for a detailed account of their abortion experiences submitted written versions of their stories. This was the method we preferred and urged, because it encouraged the greatest reflection and thus provided the most insights. It was also the easiest method to transcribe into final form. Four women submitted cassette tapes of their stories, and four others chose to be interviewed over the phone. These verbal testimonies were transcribed and edited and returned to the contributor for final approval. Because our goal was to let each woman describe her experience in her own words, very little editing was done to their stories except to remove redundant passages.

Once our sample of testimonies was collected, we tried to find a scheme by which they could be organized. Because there are so many ways in which these stories both overlap and differ, this was a formidable task. In the end, we decided to divide the testimonies into categories which would demonstrate the themes presented by the preceding chapters. Even under this system, most of these testimonies could have been placed in more than one category. But compromises were made, and the stories were divided into eight categories defined in the following ways: (1) those women who felt pressured or coerced by others into having an abortion; (2) those who were of a strong, feminist, pro-choice ideology and aborted with a firm belief that it was their legitimate right to do so; (3) those who made a "decision to be weak" and uncertainly accepted abortion because it seemed the easiest solution for all the people involved; (4) those, in contrast to the previous group, who made a clear and determined choice for abortion to satisfy their own needs; (5) those who aborted because of "health" reasons, either to preserve their own health or to prevent the birth of an unhealthy baby; (6) those who aborted because the pregnancy was the result of rape or incest; (7) those whose abortions involved deception and/or coercion by abortion counselors or social workers; (8) those who underwent illegal abortions before 1973.

The twenty stories in these eight categories all include common elements. Each describes the situation leading up to the abortion, how the decision was made, what feelings were experienced afterwards, and how the feelings of guilt and remorse were finally resolved. This last point, the self-reconciliation of aborted women, is unique to this collection of abortion testimonies. For most of these WEBA members, the discovery or renewal of religious faith became the cornerstone around which they rebuilt their lives and their self-images. Particularly for those who have publicly revealed their identities, it is from their religious faiths that they draw the strength to make this public "confession" in the hope that other women will be forewarned.

Before their abortions, very few of these women had strong religious beliefs. Most were religiously apathetic, if not agnostic. But in the years that followed, most felt increasingly isolated from others by the pain and doubts associated with their abortion experiences. The depth of this isolation is demonstrated by the need of so many to turn to the solace of religion. In discovering a religious faith, these women found a constructive way to deal with their abortion experience by placing it in a spiritual context. Thus, just as Alcoholics Anonymous encourages members to draw on the strength of a Higher Power outside themselves, so WEBA also encourages aborted women to draw on that same Higher Power, rebuilding their lives around the spiritual message of forgiveness, hope, and eternal life. For many WEBA members their greatest comfort comes from the belief that the children they aborted were not truly destroyed, but instead are waiting with forgiveness to be reunited with their mothers in the afterlife.

One last note: unless set off in quotes, all of the names used in these Profile sections are real. Many have publicly testified about their abortion experiences before; for others, this is the first time they have placed themselves under public scrutiny. For those who preferred to remain anonymous, the reader will quickly see that anonymity was most often retained to preserve the privacy of others, often their parents or children, rather than to protect themselves. Whether they have gone public or remain anonymous, all these women deserve our utmost respect and admiration for bravely sharing their painful stories.

Coercion

It will become increasingly clear throughout this book that women faced with problem pregnancies often face coercion from loved ones or civil authorities who insist that abortion is "the best solution" to their problems. This pressure to do the "practical" thing is usually exerted out of love for the woman and with the sincere belief that such paternalistic care will be appreciated later on. At other times loved ones will push abortion on a woman not out of concern for her so much as out of concern for themselves. In either case, the woman who gives in to such pressures suffers because her abortion is not the result of *her* free choice. Instead, she feels compelled to compromise her own values in order to please others, and this compromise always involves a loss of self-respect.

Perhaps the most powerful form of coercion which women face is the threat that families and boyfriends will withdraw their love and support. For example, WEBA member Sandra Morean was forced to choose between her husband and her unborn child:

> The more I thought about being pregnant, I realized there was a life in me, and I wanted to give birth to it. But my husband told me, "Either you have an abortion, or I'll leave you. You can raise it by yourself, because I don't want any more children." Not being strong enough to do what was right, and too afraid to go it alone, I gave in.

Another survey respondent describes the pressures she faced as coming from all directions:

> My family would not support my decision to keep my baby. My boyfriend said he would give me no emotional or financial help whatsoever. All the people that mattered told me to abort. When I said I didn't want to, they started listing reasons why I should. They said it would be detrimental to my career, and my health, and that I would have no social life and no future with men. Could I actually do it alone? I started feeling like maybe I was crazy to want to keep it.
>
> I finally told everyone that I would have the abortion just to get them off my back. But inside I still didn't want to have the abortion. Unfortunately, when the abortion day came I shut off my inside feelings. I was scared to not do it because of how my family and boyfriend felt. I'm *so* angry at myself for giving in to the pressure of others. I just felt so alone in my feelings to have my baby.

Two days later this same woman attempted suicide. Seven months later, at the time she responded to the survey, she was attempting to deceive her boyfriend into making her pregnant again in the belief that a second pregnancy could somehow make up for the first.

These two examples and the two profiles which follow demonstrate some of the forces which pressure women into having abortions. Coercion may come from the woman's family, the baby's father, physicians, welfare workers, or some other person with a measure of power and authority over their lives. Whatever the source of the pressure, these women feel that abortion was not really *their* choice. It was a choice which they accepted because they were scared, because they trusted others, because they wanted to please others, or even because they were made to feel that they "owed" it to others to "do the right thing." These women chose abortion not with a bold step of strength, but because they were unable to find a way to defend their own desires.

1) Cathe Birtwell

A California resident, Cathe has had three abortions. She was pressured into two of them by one boyfriend, and into the third by another boyfriend. Cathe says she aborted in hopes of gaining love and respect. But each time she aborted, she lost her baby, her boyfriend, and her own self-esteem.

I was twenty and I had been going with this guy for a long time when I got pregnant. We talked about it and he told me he would marry me. Then when I was ten weeks pregnant, I found out that his other girlfriend, who I hadn't known about, had also gotten pregnant. So he decided he would rather marry her than me. I was really crushed. Emotionally, I just couldn't handle it; and when I'm pregnant I get *real* emotional. Getting told "Go away, I don't want you," was just more than I could handle. I felt that the only way I could deal with it was to get an abortion. I didn't feel like I could talk to anybody. I just went into my shell and held everything inside.

By that time I was twelve weeks pregnant. I went to a doctor down in Sacramento. It was really awful. He treated me badly. He was rough, rude, and unprofessional. He said mean things and ridiculed me for being overweight. The way he treated me hurt a lot, on top of everything else.

It's amazing to me that I was able to have another abortion after that. It hurt so bad. Everything inside me hurt. And I want kids so bad, and I don't have any.

The guilt was really heavy. In order to deal with it and survive, I just had to harden my heart and convince myself that what I had done was the "best thing." I just kept pushing it down and covering it up. "Don't worry, don't think about it." I was trying to fool myself into being happy. I got really involved in trying to act happy-go-lucky all the time. My parents started calling me the "Bar-Fly," because I started going around to all the bars. Before this I didn't care to drink very much, but I took to drinking then because it helped to bury the hurt.

Anyway, the same guy I had been going with before broke up with the girl he had left me for—she had miscarried—and we got back together again. The guilt about my abortion was still there, but I just kept pushing it down and pushing it down. Then I got pregnant by him a second time. I've always been one who has tried to look at the positive side of things and see the best side of people, so I said, "It's O.K. This time everything will work out."

So I called him and he said, "I can't talk to you right now. I'm leaving town. Come to the fire station (where he worked) in two days and I'll be on duty and we can talk." So two days later I went in to talk to him and found out that he had gotten married that day. "O.K." I thought, "This is really great. Here I am again, in the same lurch!"

This second rejection was almost more than I could handle. And the fact that his marriage didn't last two weeks just made me feel worse. It was all more than I could bear.

I had had a vacation planned, so I took the money I had saved and went down to be with my sister, who was married and expecting a baby anytime. It was down there in Los Angeles that I had my second abortion. It was Valentine Day, and there I was alone—having an abortion. I was really low. Very angry and bitter.

It was weird. I didn't want an abortion. I didn't want all that guilt again. But all the people at the abortion clinic were real helpful and friendly and tried to make you feel like you were doing the right thing. Nobody else in my life had tried to help me. Everybody else would just look down their noses at me for being pregnant. It seemed like the abortion clinic was the only place to find help. I couldn't talk to my parents. I wasn't religious. And most of the people I was hanging around with at the bars weren't either, but they seemed to have a lot of compassion. To them, abortion was the "best thing" to do. There just didn't seem to be any other way to go but to get that second abortion.

Anyway, I went down and got the abortion; and when I came back I found out that I had been fired from my job while I was gone because I had been acting "too despondent and depressed." No one thought to ask why. So I had to try to go find a new job and try to explain to people why I was so depressed. Again I kept trying to pretend that I was happy-go-lucky. I kept thinking that it was not normal to be so depressed, so sad. I was trying to fake my way into being happy. But it kept eating away at me inside, and I just kept pushing it deeper and deeper trying to pretend that it wasn't there. I started drinking more and more. I got into some drugs but got out of that because I didn't like it. So I kept to drinking and hung around the bars because I felt accepted there.

Then, about two weeks after my abortion, I had a miscarriage. I had been carrying twins, and they had only aborted one. This really hurt, but I just pushed it down with all the other things I had buried in my mind and heart. I covered them up and started going out with another fellow.

My sister soon had a baby girl. She was beautiful, but I felt terrible. I just kept looking at her.

All my life I had been searching for the love I hadn't gotten from my father. I know now my father has always loved me in his own way. But I've always felt a lack, so I've always tried to give the men I dated what they wanted in order to get the love I wanted so badly. My feelings of insecurity and unworthiness kept me falling into the same pattern.

So I dated this guy for quite awhile, and then we broke up. His mother and sister had died in a car accident, and he really freaked out. He decided that it hurt to love someone, so he wasn't going to love anyone anymore. He rejected me and his brothers and his step-dad. He retreated from reality. It hurt a lot, to be pushed away again. But I knew that he was hurting so badly, I couldn't be mad at him.

So one night I saw that his car was at a bar he liked to go to, and I really wanted to go in and see how he was doing. I went in the bar and we talked and he seemed better. He seemed happier. And so he invited me to his house and we talked some more. One thing led to another and we ended up in bed together. This was the first time that I wasn't on birth control, so naturally I became pregnant again. (My first two pregnancies had resulted when I *was* on the pill.)

When we found out I was pregnant, we talked. He told me that his father had deserted him when he was a toddler, and he would never want to do that to a child of his. He said he wasn't ready to be a husband or father because he was still dealing with his mother's and sister's deaths. We talked and talked, and we came to the decision to have the abortion. It's funny, abortion always seems to be the first thing that enters the mind. And by that time I had really encased my heart for protection and thought, "O.K., I can do it again." My heart was really hard.

So I went to Planned Parenthood and made an appointment to have it done. Then I went to his house because we had agreed that he would go with me to have it done. It was like a scene from a movie: as I walked up to the front door, I could see through the window that all there was in the whole house was one crumpled piece of paper. Everything else had been cleared out. Gone. No goodbyes. Nothing.

I couldn't handle the rejection a third time. I was so angry, and I don't get angry very often—I get hurt, but I don't get angry. So I went down to Planned Parenthood fit for a rage. The only counseling they gave down there was a session of "How are you feeling about yourself right now?" stuff. And all these girls were sitting there with their boyfriends and husbands there to support them, and I was *so* mad and embarrassed! There I was again, going through it alone. Well, I was the last one the doctor was going to do, and so while I was sitting there the lady who had been talking to us said to me: "I know you're feeling bad. But when I had an abortion, my kids asked me if that wasn't killing a baby. And I told them that if you step on an acorn that's not killing an oak tree! It's just a seed. It's O.K. to kill a seed." So instead of following my conscience, which was telling me to get out of there, I sat there trying real hard to hang on to that and tried to believe that the baby wasn't alive.

The first two abortions I had no idea what they had done to my babies, and the third time they didn't tell me either. But this time, I was sick to my stomach for days. I had finally realized what I really had done. It was all I could think about. I had just killed my baby. Nobody could ever accept me if they knew.

What happened next was kind of strange to me. The church that I had recently started attending had about a thousand people, and I had met the pastor only one time, just "Hi, how are you?" But one day he called me and said, "I noticed that you haven't been in church, and I just wanted to make sure you were okay, and see if there was anything wrong." I tried to cover up what I had done and said, "Oh, no. Nothing's wrong. I'm just dealing with a little bit of guilt, and when I handle it I'll be back," knòwing I would never ever go back. And he said, "If you ever need anything, feel free to come talk to me. Remember, God forgives you no matter what it is you're feeling guilty about. Sometimes we feel that we have to punish ourselves before we can receive His forgiveness, and that just isn't true. It's there, all you have to do is accept it."

I had spent the money I needed for my bills for the abortion, and I was really desperate. I couldn't ask my parents for money because I would have to explain what I had done; so I went in to talk to the pastor. He didn't asked me what the problem was or why I had spent the money; but I had to tell someone, so I told him. I searched his face for any contempt or disgust, but there wasn't any—just so much compassion and love. It was the first time I ever felt accepted unconditionally. He said, "Your sins are no greater than anyone else's, and you are welcome here." He gave me the money and said, "This isn't a loan. It's a gift, accept it from the Lord. I hope to see you at church Sunday." But I thought there was no way I could go back.

But when Sunday morning came, I knew that I had to go. I sat there and cried through the whole service; and nobody sat next to me—I felt like everyone knew what I had done. When the service was over, a woman came up and asked if she could pray with me. I really didn't want her to, but finally said okay. I couldn't believe that without knowing details, she prayed for exactly what I needed: relief from guilt. Then she hugged me and left.

After that, I surrendered everything to Jesus. I felt Him lift the burden of my past off of me. It still blows my mind that He could forgive me, after all that I had done. Today He continues to restore me and has even showed me that my children forgive me, and that I will be together with them in heaven. Until then I am trying to help others that are in the same situation now by sharing my life and hope with them.

2) Gaylene "Hayes"

Gaylene was forced into an abortion when she was fourteen years old. Her California high school authorities and the local Planned Parenthood chapter worked closely together. They made Gaylene feel she had no choice in "the

36

matter." When she tried to ask questions about what they would do to her and her baby, they refused to answer. This loss of choice about her life led her to drugs, alcoholism, suicide attempts, jail, a probation farm, and a religious cult.

In my case, I was fourteen years old and somewhat serious over a young man. When I thought I was pregnant, I talked to the high school counselors, who said I should go to Planned Parenthood for a pregnancy test.

This was easy to do. I lived in a town with a high school population of 2,400. In addition, there were five other high schools within a thirty-mile radius. So Planned Parenthood had a well-organized operation for all of these schools. Every Tuesday a scheduled bus picked up students from all the area high schools and took them to the Planned Parenthood clinic. The bus had posters extolling the virtues and ideals of Planned Parenthood—have small families, intelligent people only have two children, etc. School counselors arranged for the visits and provided the students with passes to be excused from school for the entire day.

So on that Tuesday I took the bus to the large, modern Planned Parenthood clinic. All of us students were greeted by a pleasant receptionist, who sent us to our designated areas: boys with V.D. to one room, girls for pregnancy tests to another, etc. After we were seated, we were instructed to move to the adjacent chair whenever the person occupying the first chair went into the examining room. It was all so organized.

When it was my turn to go in, I was greeted by a doctor and nurse, who told me that my urine would be tested for pregnancy, and then they would phone me with the results. They were all particularly careful to find out when my parents would not be home, so as not to "embarrass" me or cause me any kind of "family problems."

So I returned to school and then rode my regular bus home. I sat by the phone for the entire hour that they were to call me. When they called and told me I was pregnant, they said I could return to the clinic the following week, and that they would "go from there." The word "abortion" was *never* used, nor was any reference made to abortion.

Two days later I finally had enough courage to see the counselor. He was sympathetic and understanding. He felt there was no need to worry my family. He also explained about having a child, how tough it would be on me and that I wouldn't be able to do what I wanted to do. He said the child would suffer because I was much too young to be a parent. He pointed out that the best thing for me to do was to abort the fetus at this stage so that no one would be hurt. No mention was made of talking to my parents about this or of carrying my baby to term. He indicated that adoption would be difficult and not an option for me. The cost (thanks to Planned Parenthood) was only $35, as opposed to thousands of dollars for raising a child. He said he would even pay the $35 if I couldn't.

So I took the bus again the following week, on a different day. Then there were college-age girls as well as women in their 20s and 30s. Looking back, I realized that there must have been a particular day of the week on the bus for abortions, for all of these women were taken to Planned Parenthood for that purpose. On the bus I felt as though I had no control over what was happening to me. I started to question what I was dong, but in my logic I'd refer back to what the counselor had told me, and then I would think he was right. But still today, I feel like *I* did not decide to have the abortion.

At the clinic we were ushered into a different room than the one we came in for pregnancy tests. The chairs were lined up in the same organized way though. We were given pamphlets which showed a uterus with a pink blob in it. The aide matter-of-factly told us that they would remove the "pink blob." She said that then we would no longer be pregnant, and that it was a simple surgical procedure. That's all she said.

Upon entering the surgery room, I was told to go behind a curtain, put on a hospital gown, and fold my clothes into a neat pile. When I climbed up on the surgery table, the nurse instructed me to move my hips down on the table. Since I was only fourteen, I really didn't know what she meant. So she grabbed my hips roughly and pulled my body down to the end of the table and fastened the straps around my feet. I asked what was going on, and she snapped that I had already been given the information. She said this was not the time to be asking questions, that I should have asked them sooner.

The nurse and doctor then acted angry with me. I had the feeling that I had done something wrong or that I wasn't cooperating. I was confused because I thought these people were the answer to my problems; but they weren't treating me with the consideration that

38

they had the other day when I'd had my pregnancy test. I didn't even know what they were going to do to me or my baby.

I was given no anesthetic. There was a needle nearby, but they told me that by the time the anesthetic took effect the procedure would be over. They gave me an option, but they made me feel as though it was unnecessary. The vacuum was very noisy. The doctor and nurse went about their work as a routine—almost as though I weren't there. It was very painful. I know it was only a short time, but when you're in pain it seems like an eternity.

When they were finished they rolled me out into a recovery room, where ten or fifteen other girls were lying on surgical beds. Some were sitting up, but most were lying down. A couple were crying, and I was sniffling because it hurt. I wanted to get back to school and put all this behind me, because the school counselor had said that everything would be all right after it was over. I just kept repeating to myself what the counselor had said.

After two to three hours of lying there and juice and cookies, we boarded the bus and were taken back to our schools. We went to the school counselor, and he gave us all a school pass for classes the next day. He asked how we felt and joked about how we shouldn't let this happen again.

My regular bus had already left, so I had to phone my mother. The counselor filled out a detention slip stating that I'd had to stay after school, and that was why I'd missed my bus. My mom asked me what I had done to be detained, and I said that I had mouthed off to a teacher. This was the beginning of a major barrier with my family.

The nurse from the clinic phoned me at home at the hour I had said that my parents wouldn't be there. She asked how I was feeling and if there were any problems. I was just glad it was over, and would just as soon have not heard from them again. They told me to get on contraceptives right away.

After the abortion, I turned to drugs. Before the abortion, I had tried pot, but only to the point of getting buzzed. But after it, I always tried to get bombed—totally loaded. On a few occasions I tried the needle—LSD. I continued with school but was kicked out after a series of being busted: for skipping school, drug dealing, and as an accomplice to robbery. I was sent to a probationary farm for nine months and had classes there. The strict environment helped my grades, but I continued my life of drugs and sex. Once I attempted suicide by taking all the aspirins in a huge bottle. They pumped my stomach, and I was very sick. I thought I would just as soon die.

While at the farm, my father died suddenly. I was allowed to go to the funeral; but at my mother's request, I was not allowed to return home.

I did go home from the farm at the end of the school year. I returned to my old ways, and by the beginning of December I was kicked out of school again. I attended an "alternative school" that had minimal requirements for attendance and curriculum. I was living from day to day, trying to stay as high and loaded at all times as possible, but I finally graduated from high school.

When I turned seventeen, I moved to another state for a year. I worked odd jobs and got into booze and heavy drugs. Finally, a friend phoned my mother and new stepfather and told them if they wanted to see me alive again they had better send me a ticket home. They did, and tried to have me dried out—with little success. Six months later they moved. When my mother left, she gave money to my sister for me, "for either a doctor, lawyer, or mortuary," because they were sure I'd need at least one of them.

At that point I started living in my car. A cult called "The Children of God" took me in. I straightened out for a year or two, but left them because of their sexual practices.

Then I went to live with my parents for awhile. It was the happiest six months of my youth. I turned twenty-one during this time.

I met the young man whom I later married, had a good job, and have kept pretty steady employment since then. But though we wanted to have children, I was unable to become pregnant. Tests have shown large amounts of scar tissue in my uterus. Frustrated, I started drinking heavily again. Six years later, during a drinking binge, I attempted suicide with a gun. I had it loaded and set up when a friend discovered me.

I went to the hospital for two weeks and finally came to terms with why I was trying to destroy myself: I had killed my own child, so I felt I didn't deserve anything. I know now that my Father in heaven has the same love for me as he has for my child.

Though I still have no baby of my own, my husband and I have adopted two wonderful older children. Best of all, I know that God has truly forgiven me. I want others to know about the pain and anguish a woman can go through from abortion, and I'd like them to know the forgiveness that Jesus has for us.

40

T   W   O

Evidence from the Pro-Choice Side

The women who contributed their stories to the Profiles sections of this book have all had this in common: they have all reconciled themselves to their abortion experiences by (1) openly admitting that they made a wrong choice; (2) claiming spiritual and/or personal forgiveness for themselves; and (3) working to save other women from making the same mistake. All of these women suffered emotionally and psychologically from abortion, and all of them complain that they were not adequately warned about the psychological impact of abortion. But were such warnings really necessary? Or are WEBA-like experiences uncommon? Are these women just the unfortunate few? Or are they typical examples of the 18 million American women who have had abortions since 1973?

In this chapter we will see that WEBA women are not simply the "unfortunate few." Instead, we will find that even the pro-choice literature helps to prove that abortion is almost always a negative experience. Whenever women who have had abortions are interviewed, even by pro-choice authors, they always report the same ambivalence and pain. Thus, the research of the pro-choice authors confirms that the WEBA-like experience is far closer to being the rule than the exception.

41

A. Passage Through Abortion

In 1973 sociologist Mary K. Zimmerman began a comprehensive study of how women experienced abortion. Published in 1977, her book *Passage Through Abortion: The Personal and Social Reality of Women's Experiences* summarizes the results of her survey, includes excerpts of her interviews, and dwells on her own analysis of the abortion experience. Though she occasionally lapses into pro-choice rhetoric and seems to rely exclusively on pro-abortion literature for her supplemental material, the core of Zimmerman's work is an impartial and systematic study of the short-term abortion experience.

Zimmerman's study was based in a Midwest city with two abortion clinics serving a population of approximately 165,000 people. With cooperation from both clinics, Zimmerman sent letters to women seeking abortions. The letter explained the nature and purpose of her study and asked for their participation. Attached to the letter was a short survey. Six to ten weeks after her abortion, Zimmerman interviewed each patient. During these interviews, Zimmerman followed a systematic outline of questions in order to elicit responses on a variety of topics. Forty such interviews were conducted, and these make up the body of her study. This number was selected as being sufficiently large to be significant, yet small enough to be manageable.

It should be noted, however, that certain restrictions surrounding the selection of these forty women biased the sample in several respects, a fact noted by Zimmerman herself.

First, women who had undergone previous abortions were excluded from the study sample. This exclusion was deemed necessary because repeat aborters are likely to report greater negative reactions than women who are "naive" about abortion and experiencing it for the first time. Zimmerman felt that this variation in reactions could not be "adequately handled and so it was eliminated."[1]

Second, women undergoing second or third trimester abortions were excluded in order to confine the study to those women undergoing suction abortions. This limitation was made in order to study reactions to similar abortion experiences. This limitation, however, eliminated some of the most negative abortion experiences from the sample, since late-term abortion procedures are more traumatic, both physically and emotionally, than vacuum curettage.[2]

A third bias was placed on this study's sample not by Zimmerman, but by the abortion clinic director, who told staff members "not to give the client [Zimmerman's] letter, consent form, and questionnaire if, in their judgment, it would be inadvisable clinically." In other words, if the patient was already displaying signs of being upset, guilty, or extremely ambivalent, she was screened out of the sample. This staff "screening" of clients not only prevented the study from including the "worse case" examples of the abortion experience, but also allowed the clinics to put their "best" clients forward. Thirteen percent of the women aborted during the timeframe of this study were eliminated from the sample at the option of the clinics. Most were under twenty-two years old and unmarried; and they were often accompanied by a parent with whom there were arguments and hostility, an indication that parental pressure was being exerted to secure the abortion.[3]

While these limitations may have been necessary for the purpose of standardizing the study in relation to first trimester, first abortion experiences, the fact that the results are thus biased cannot be overlooked. Over one-third of all abortions in the United States are repeat abortions, and nearly one-tenth are performed in the second trimester or later. In addition, the screening out of 13 percent of the "most sensitive" cases at "clinic discretion" must clearly have affected the study's final results.

Lastly, of all the women asked to participate in the study, 36 percent refused. How the characteristics of the women who refused to be studied would have affected the study is not known. However, it can be speculated that the women who were unwilling to participate in the study refused primarily because they wanted to "get it over with," and did not want to face the prospect of a later interview. This implies strong negative feelings prior to the abortion and suggests that strong negative reactions would have occurred afterwards as well. Thus the women who "screened" themselves out of the study were probably at a high risk of suffering post-abortion sequelae, and knew it. ("Sequelae" is a medical term meaning physical or psychological aftereffects.) Most of these women probably refused to participate in order to insulate themselves from any further association with a negative experience.

All of the "screening" mechanisms mentioned above suggest that compared to the truly "average" sample of aborted women, Zimmerman's study disproportionately represents the "best" patients under the most "ideal" circumstances. But with this strongly "positive" bias, Zimmerman's findings are disturbingly bleak and mirror the results of the survey described in Chapter One.

Contraceptive Use

Of the study group, Zimmerman found that 7 percent of the women had been consistent users of a "reliable" method of birth control (defined as either the Pill, the IUD, or the diaphragm). These women became pregnant by contraceptive failure. On the other hand, 80 percent were sporadic users of various contraceptives or had suddenly discontinued use of a "reliable" method just prior to becoming pregnant, often due to health reasons or because they were in transition periods between relationships. Finally, 13 percent were not using any method. Confirming numerous other studies, Zimmerman reports that almost all of the women studied were familiar and experienced with birth control methods. Abortion resulted not from ignorance, but from "carelessness" or "indifference." [4]

Reaction to Pregnancy

Upon first becoming aware of their pregnancies, 63 percent of the women studied initially tended towards abortion, 24 percent tended towards childbirth, and 13 percent were uncertain.[5] Zimmerman notes, however, that although:

> two-thirds of the women were displeased upon learning that they were pregnant . . . this does not mean that two-thirds of the women did not want the baby. In the final analysis, only a little more than a third explicity stated that they did not want the child. While all of the women studied eventually made the same decision about abortion, they did not all adopt the same stance on wanting the baby.[6]

In fact, 30 percent told the interviewer that there had been a strong desire to have and keep the baby, but they had felt that circumstances did not allow it. Another 33 percent deliberately ignored the question of whether or not they wanted the child. These women instead focused on the life constraints which "forced" them to abort. Whether or not they wanted the baby was a moot and dangerous question for these women. Since outside pressures were "forcing" them to abort whether they wanted to or not, any desires to continue their pregnancies were consciously ignored or denied. Some of the women in this latter group expressed joy and happiness about the pregnancy through indirect means. Thus, for no less than 30 percent of aborters, and possibly up to 60 percent or more, the abortion involved the destruction of a "wanted," or at least an "acceptable" child not out of "choice" but because of circumstances.[7]

44

EVIDENCE FROM THE PRO-CHOICE SIDE

The Decision

In 95 percent of all cases studied, the male partner played a central role in the abortion decision. A significant majority of the men agreed to, supported, or actively encouraged the abortion option. In 20 percent of the cases where the woman's initial decision was to abort, however, the male opposed the abortion. On the other hand, in another 20 percent of the cases, the woman's initial decision was to continue the pregnancy, but the man insisted upon the abortion and eventually the woman submitted. Thus, no fewer than 20 percent felt "forced" to abort by the man.[8]

Overall, Zimmerman records that 35 percent of the aborted women studied remained confused throughout most of the decision-making process. Many were not clear about what they would do until right before the abortion was performed.[9] Of the 65 percent who said that the decision to abort was clear, most saw it not as a choice but rather as their only alternative. In general, the choice seemed clear because all the persons with whom they consulted positively encouraged and supported the abortion option.[10] Altogether, over two-thirds of the women made statements suggesting that they had had "no choice" or had been "forced" to have the abortion.[11]

Reasons for Their Abortions

The two most frequent reasons given for the abortion were financial problems and being unmarried.[12] The expectation of financial hardship after the birth of the child was a major concern for both married and single women. For single women, refusal by parents to help support her and her child was frequently the overriding pressure to abort. In some cases, parents insisted on the abortion.[13] Being unmarried, having a partner unwilling to marry, or being unwilling to marry an undesirable partner are also major factors in abortion decisions, since the prospect of being a single parent appears overly burdensome, or even impossible.[14] "Almost all of the women studied, regardless of the exact configuration of circumstances, felt that the time was not right for a baby. Most wanted to become pregnant again in the future, but only when the circumstances were just right. Rather than deal with the problems that having the baby posed, they chose abortion."[15]

Disruption of Relationships

In 50 percent of the cases, the abortion was quickly followed by disruption and termination of the relationship with the man involved in the pregnancy. In 5 percent of the cases, a major disruption occurred with other family members.[16]

Their Ethical Views of Abortion

Fully 70 percent of the women studied expressed disapproval of abortion, seeing it as deviant and immoral.[17] But seeing themselves as forced by others, by their circumstances, or by society at large, they frequently attempted to deny responsibility for what they believed was an immoral act.[18] In other words, 70 percent of these aborted women felt forced to compromise their own values and ideals.

In order to avoid upsetting the women in this study, Zimmerman asked no specific questions concerning the nature of the fetus. But nearly 25 percent of the women interviewed stated that the aborted fetus was a life, a person, or a human being. In many of these cases, they admitted a sense of having killed or murdered another being. Another 25 percent expressed confusion about the nature of the fetus. In these cases the women generally believed the fetus was human but denied that abortion was killing. Zimmerman suggests that this contradictory stance was taken in order to maintain their self-images as moral persons. Finally, only 15 percent maintained that the fetus was not a person or human life, but even these women expressed themselves in terms of denial rather than with arguments to support their beliefs. For example, "I feel that it's something there, but I don't really feel that it's a life yet."[19]

Reaction to the Abortion Experience

Before evaluating the reactions of women to abortion, Zimmerman attempted to measure and define two classes of women receiving abortion: the affiliated and the disaffiliated. She defined affiliated women as those who were "well-integrated or 'tied in' to their social worlds. These women are clear about their obligations, expectations, and futures. They knew who they were and where they were going . . . a pattern characterized by persons who are securely rooted or enmeshed in social life." These women were more likely to be from a higher economic level and social class, had strong career goals, and were more likely to abort for self-serving, pragmatic reasons. Disaffiliated women were defined as "less firmly attached to their social worlds. They had fewer and weaker social ties, role relationships, and other forms of systematic social participation. They also appeared to have

less a sense of purpose [plans for the future] than the former group."
Because these women tended to be less certain about their futures and
less assertive, they were more likely to abort in order to please others
(i.e., their boyfriends or families).[20]

In her interviews, Zimmerman found that only 26 percent of the
"affiliated" women expressed such "troubled thoughts" as guilt, regret, sadness, and loss. In contrast, 74 percent of those classified as
"disaffiliated" expressed "troubled thoughts." Altogether, 48 percent
of the women studied described themselves as disturbed by the abortion.[21]

Even when taken at face value, these percentages indicate a
relatively high level of negative reactions to abortion. But when examined in the full context of the study, these figures clearly represent only
the tip of the iceberg. Two factors indicate that these are minimized
figures. First, Zimmerman's sampling limitations, plus the clinic's
"screening" of sensitive cases, eliminated several classes and situations
most prone to post-abortion depression. Second, Zimmerman's interviews took place only six weeks after the abortion. Other studies show
that the percentage of women experiencing post-abortion sequelae
increases with time. Many of those who reported few problems soon
after the abortion may face long-term distress from repressed feelings.
Indeed, Zimmerman notes that many of the affiliated women who
seem to be coping best with the abortion are able to do so primarily
because they are the most proficient at blocking it out of their minds or
at making it seem like an "unreal" memory.[22]

Whether such blocking out of the abortion feelings at six weeks is
sufficient for a lifetime is questionable. Indeed, the WEBA experience
strongly suggests otherwise. At six weeks the women in Zimmerman's
survey had not even faced the common triggering experiences for
abortion trauma, such as the date when the child should have been
born, the anniversary date of the abortion, the birth of a later child, the
death or miscarriage of a later child, and so on.

Despite its limitations, the Zimmerman study provides valuable
insight into the abortion experience and helps to confirm that the
thrust of the WEBA experiences are by no means "rare" or "unusual."

B.   The Ambivalence of Abortion

One of the most haunting tales about the experience of abortion was
published in May of 1976 on the Op-Ed page of the *New York Times*

under the title "There Just Wasn't Room in Our Lives Now for Another Baby." The author, Linda Bird Francke, writing under the name Jane Doe, was a professional journalist, feminist, and a pro-choice activist. When faced with an unplanned pregnancy which would have interfered with her and her husband's careers, the couple decided to have an abortion. But as the time for the abortion approached, Francke became increasingly ambivalent about their choice, and as she and her husband sat in the waiting room she desperately hoped for some escape from her predetermined course. Intellectually, she tried to concentrate on how small the fetus was, and therefore how impossible it was for it to be human. But she had borne children before, and the feel of her own body kept telling her that there was life growing within her.

By the time she entered the operating room, Francke longed for her husband to burst through the door and stop it from happening. When he failed to do so, she begged the doctor to stop. But the abortionist told her it was too late and completed the surgery anyway.

In the months following the abortion, her ambivalence continued. During times of relaxation when she had time to reflect on the beauty of the world, she experienced the common reaction of "visitations" from her aborted child. Her benign "little ghost" would come to her and wave. And she would tearfully wave back to reassure her lost baby that if only it returned, they would now make room for it in their busy lives.[23]

The *New York Times* account was published three years after Francke's abortion, only when the "guilt and sadness" associated with the experience had waned. Two years later, drawn once more to investigate her own mixed feelings about abortion, Francke published a book entitled *The Ambivalence of Abortion* in which she transcribed the reactions to the abortion experience of almost seventy women, couples, parents, and men.

Though Francke is a pro-choice activist who has marched herself into "blisters" in support of abortion rights, her book is not primarily intended to be a defense of the pro-choice ideology. In fact, when Francke's ideology comes into conflict with her own negative abortion experience, the result is often a confusing series of rationalizations. For example, Francke candidly acknowledges that she feels that she destroyed a life. Yet she still supports abortion, and would have one again herself, because there are "no neat answers," just a lot of bad options.[24]

Thus, despite Francke's pro-choice rhetoric, her book is not intended to defend abortion per se. Instead, she seems to have two other goals in mind. First, by painting such intimate portraits of the women forced to seek abortion, she attempts to convince anti-abortionists to leave these poor, troubled women alone. She is attempting to show that women do not take the decision to abort lightly. Their reasons are well thought out; the problems and obstacles they face are severe. Abortion is difficult enough as it is; women should simply be left alone.

Second, perhaps more importantly, Francke's book is intended as a form of group therapy for her fellow aborters ("See, others have gone through the same thing too.") and a cautious warning for future aborters. Indeed, if there is one theme that Francke returns to time and time again, it is to the warning that while abortion is an "undeniable right" it is an experience never "easy" to undergo or "easy" to forget. Instead, it is a choice which carries with it many unresolved and ambivalent feelings. She warns that everyone should know that abortion always involves a period of great stress for everyone involved, women, men, relatives, and even the doctors and nurses. To ignore the emotional risks of abortion, she writes, is blind foolishness.[25, 26]

Filled with so many varied interviews, *The Ambivalence of Abortion* is *must* reading for anyone who wants to understand the abortion experience, but it is not without faults and limitations. The weakest portions of the book are the introductory and concluding chapters in which Francke describes the history of abortion and argues the pro-choice line. These chapters are filled with factual errors, which probably occurred because Francke was overly dependent on the biased materials supplied her by pro-abortion foundations.[27]

The second major limitation of Francke's work is that she gathered her interviews primarily in abortion clinics, just before or immediately after her subjects' abortions, thus limiting the range of reactions. This is a serious problem, since studies show that the number of women who experience negative feelings about their abortions increases with time. On the other hand, this limitation is also one of the book's strengths. The immediacy of these interviews provides an intense view not seen in the settled, matured WEBA stories. These are women in the midst of their crises. They have not yet reconciled themselves to what they have done. They have not yet settled on whether it was right or wrong, only that it was necessary. As Francke herself points out, these women are frequently incoherent and inconsistent, struggling to understand and rationalize their actions.[28] Almost every testimony reflects deep-rooted ambivalence and unresolved doubts. In their stories, one sees women who have not yet realized how they have been exploited, who have not yet been able to admit their mistakes.

Besides the limitations of who and when she interviewed, Francke's interviewing style does not encourage stories which are easily analyzed. Unlike Zimmerman, a sociologist who carefully guides each woman through a regular routine of questions, Francke is a journalist who allows each woman to tell her story in her own way. This approach provides much more varied and interesting reading than Zimmerman's clinical study, but it is less patterned and consistent. Some women reveal themselves in intimate detail; others are brusque and short. Some go to great lengths to describe their feelings and emotions; others limit themselves to factual descriptions as to when, where, how, and why the abortion was obtained, but give no glimpse of their innermost feelings. Because the interview process was not patterned, each woman tells only what seems most significant to her at that moment, only what she is willing to reveal to this sympathetic and understanding reporter. But even for those who are most comfortable with Francke and her tape recorder, significant feelings, too sensitive to be revealed to oneself much less to a stranger, are probably held back. The interviews gathered by Francke, therefore, reflect only what the women were *willing* to share and what was currently at the "top of their minds." They are less circumspect than they are spontaneous.

Despite these limitations, *The Ambivalence of Abortion* offers a wealth of information. Though it cannot be considered unbiased or fully representative, the data which can be culled from these interviews substantially confirms this researcher's own findings which show that abortion almost always has a negative impact on women's lives. Examining the 49 interviews with women and couples which Francke includes in her book, the following facts emerge:

Sexual Coldness

Eleven women (22%) volunteered information which described how the abortion resulted in sexual coldness towards their mates, or men in general.[29] A few mentioned that having to abort their pregnancies made them angry at men, or even resulted in feelings of hatred towards all men. For others, sexual coldness was directed more inwardly. One woman said she felt her body "get cold and dry up" whenever her boyfriend approached her. Another felt guilt over the abortion whenever she and her husband made love. One woman slept with her boyfriend for three years after her abortion but never made love to him again. Others simply lost all pleasure in sexual intercourse or became fearful of sex believing they would be forced to go through a second abortion.

Desire for Pregnancy and Child

Twenty-two of those interviewed (47%) mentioned an initial happiness over the pregnancy or said that they had desired to keep the baby.[30] It is this tension between wanting the baby (or at least feeling a sense of duty to accept it) versus the practical necessities not to have a child, which is central to the emotional ambivalence towards abortion. In order to do the "practical" thing, women are forced to compromise their own values, deny their "impractical" desires, and submit to the humiliating but "necessary evil" of abortion.

Because of this conflict between wanting the child and rejecting the responsibilities of motherhood, many of the women interviewed told stories filled with confusion and contradictions.[31]

Frequently those who expressed a desire to keep the baby said they were aborting only out of a sense of duty to their boyfriends.[32] Others only aborted under extreme pressure from parents.[33]

Abortion as a Violation of the Body

Several of the women whom Francke interviewed described the abortion procedure itself as horrible and degrading. One woman equated the humiliation of it with brutal rape. For some, the pain of abortion helped to divert their attention from their moral dilemma. Their pain was seen as "payment" for what had happened. For others, the worst part of the abortion was the unnaturalness of the act, the emptiness felt afterwards, the feeling that the body was in a state of "limbo," lost and waiting to complete what it had begun.[34]

One woman whom Francke interviewed, though basically pro-choice in attitude, described abortion as a violent disruption of the female body's natural balance. This disturbance of the body's natural "ecology" has far-ranging effects. In short, this woman said, abortion is not allowing things to flow their natural way.[35]

Negative Feelings

Thirty-five of the women interviewed by Francke (71%) clearly expressed some type of negative feeling about their abortion experiences.[36] Some described their experience and its aftermath in extremely negative terms; others avoided details of their feelings but admitted to a general feeling of ambivalence, confusion, or doubt.

The most frequent complaint was from women who described themselves as feeling "guilty" or "dirty." Many said they felt they had killed or murdered their babies and expressed self-hatred because of what they had done.[37] Others reported looking at other children and imagining possible similarities to their own aborted children.[38] Guilt led one woman to attempt suicide with an overdose of tranquilizers.[39]

For some, feelings of guilt were not immediate. Instead, remorse came tumbling in during later periods of crisis. One woman, for example, reported a sudden onslaught of post-abortion guilt only when she faced problems with a later wanted pregnancy. Ordered to bed for five weeks to avoid miscarriage, she had nothing to do but think of her previous abortion. In the end, she miscarried anyway. In addition she soon learned that she was suffering from blocked fallopian tubes. From this period, her guilts and fears increased, ultimately requiring psychiatric therapy to deal with her repressed feelings.[40]

The desire to forget the abortion experience is common to almost every story. But Francke found, just as many WEBA members report, that even the most determined efforts to push the abortion out of one's memory often fail.[41]

For many, rationalizations were maintained only by a conscious effort. One woman stated that she just didn't want to think of it as a baby.[42] For others, their rationalizations only added to their confusion. A woman back for her third abortion insisted to Francke that she was well-adjusted to the first two, but then she went on to describe the symptoms of post-abortion syndrome, such as compulsive fascination with other people's children, anger, denial, and rationalization. No longer knowing what to believe, she said that she probably should go to a psychiatrist for help.[43]

Again and again the women interviewed by Francke reveal how difficult it is to balance reality against rationalizations, feelings against ideology. For many of them peace of mind is gained only at the cost of closing out all feelings and emotions. One woman, for example, described herself as feeling dead a lot of the time. Still another found relief only when she just stopped feeling altogether.[44]

For others there can be no rationalizations. These are the women who were originally against abortion but felt forced by circumstances to compromise their values. These women felt the sharp pain of their own hypocrisy and self-betrayal.[45]

EVIDENCE FROM THE PRO-CHOICE SIDE

Despite the limitations and biases mentioned earlier, Francke's interviews support our findings that for the vast majority of women, 71% in her sample, abortion involves negative experiences which women try desperately to forget, but rarely with success.

Positive Experiences?

But what of the other 29% of the women whom Francke interviewed? Is abortion an easy or even a positive experience for this minority? Probably not. Most of the fourteen interviews which do not contain negative comments about the abortion say little or nothing about the woman's feelings. Many of these interviews were taken just prior to the abortion, minutes afterwards, or only two weeks later. Most of these women had nothing negative to say because they had not yet had enough time to reflect on the experience or to face later situations which would recall their abortions. In these interviews, the women's minds were focused on the anticipation of the abortion to come or on the relief that it was finally over.

Despite these time limitations, Francke tries to use a few of these interviews to "prove" that for some women, at least, abortion is not emotionally damaging and thus is a good choice. For example, only two weeks after her abortion, one woman told Francke that she had not had any regrets or emotional problems. But, she adds, she had been so busy dealing with the physical complications since her abortion that she had not yet had time to notice any emotional reactions.[46]

Another interview which Francke numbers among the positive cases is too short to sustain her conclusion. Indeed, this interview is less than a hundred words long, and taken when the woman was on the recovery table, only minutes after the abortion was completed. She had four children already, was on welfare, and couldn't afford another child. She said she didn't feel any guilt, only fatigue. The abortion, she said, was "simple and the only thing to do."[47]

This is hardly one of Francke's more open and revealing interviews, and yet she lists it as one which proves that for some women there is little difficulty in reaching a decision and no appreciable trouble afterwards.[48] But obviously this woman felt forced into her abortion by her financial circumstances, felt no freedom of choice in reaching her decision, and had not yet had time to reflect on what had really happened. In the first few minutes after her abortion, she was holding to the relief she felt at having it over and done with. Her statements are hardly a convincing proof that abortion can be an easy or positive experience.

Another story selected by Francke to show that abortion is sometimes a "positive experience and a period of personal growth," seems anything but positive. Indeed, it is amazing that Francke can interpret it in that way. Interviewed two weeks after her second abortion, this woman said that during her first abortion she just couldn't stop crying. All she could think was that she was going to be a mother and that this child would love her and she was hurting it. She lay on the table and kept cradling her arms as if there was a baby there. She could "hear" it crying. She thought she was going crazy.[49]

Afterwards, this woman described herself as becoming promiscuous for a time; then she suddenly stopped when she realized she was becoming a "whore." A year later, she deliberately became pregnant a second time. Then, to punish herself and her boyfriend, she had her second abortion: she wanted to punish herself, and she was setting the boyfriend up to be a victim too.[50]

Her interview was conducted two weeks after this second abortion, one she described as equally painful—both physically and emotionally—as the first. But this woman concluded her story by saying that during the last week she and her boyfriend had been trying to talk, trying to let their angers and frustrations out: . . . "So that's the way I feel right now, this abortion's really been a positive one. And maybe it's going to be okay, now."[51]

From this *hope* to change her life, this resolution to try again, Francke concludes that this woman's second abortion was a positive experience and a period of personal growth. Though everyone would hope that this woman's bad experiences have motivated her to make constructive changes, her qualified hope that "maybe it's going to be okay, now" clearly indicates that she was trying to talk herself into a positive attitude, not that it had been achieved through her second abortion.

Several of the women interviewed by Francke insisted that they were emotionally unaffected by the abortion but were nonetheless extremely bitter towards the man, or men in general, and often displaced this anger towards the child. Though these women did not admit to any negative feelings stemming from their abortions, the intensity with which they denied doubts and regrets reminds one of fireworks being used to disguise tears.[52]

Even the few women who insisted that the abortion had a positive effect on their lives expressed discomfort, insisting that they didn't ever want to go through it again.[53] Strangely enough, Francke, often takes a woman's comment that she is taking greater precautions to prevent ever needing another abortion to mean that her first abortion was a positive experience.[54] Ironically, it seems any woman who resolves never to have another abortion is said to have "grown" from her experience. Only repeaters, she implies, have failed to grow. But this discrimination against repeaters implies that there is something wrong about abortion, that abortion is something to be avoided. For if abortion is to be avoided a second time, why shouldn't it be avoided the first time? If it is dangerous or irresponsible to undergo many abortions, why is it not also dangerous or irresponsible to undergo one?

In sum, if one reads the stories recorded by Francke looking for signs of pain, one will find them in every story—though often buried under tough and bitter words. On the other hand, if one reads her collection looking for women who are trying to cope with their pains, trying to reconcile themselves to what has happened, trying to avoid future mistakes, future abortions, one will find this common search for hope too. But pro-abortionists are too willing to ignore the former fact and emphasize the latter as proof that abortion can be a positive, growing experience. Though no one doubts that women who undergo abortions learn something from the experience, that does not mean that abortion is a desirable lesson. Indeed, it might very well be a lesson which should be avoided at any cost.

The testimony of WEBA women confirms this latter point of view. These women have learned from their abortion experiences; they have experienced growth, but it is growth which has been achieved by recognizing their errors and the evil of abortion, not by defending it. For many, abortion led them to the pit of despair where they found and accepted the forgiveness of God. Growth came not in defending the pit of abortion as their "right," their home, but in seeing the pit for what it is and crawling out of it. Growth came not because abortion is a positive experience, but because they were finally able to recognize and condemn it as a negative experience.

C.   In Necessity and Sorrow

A third powerful book which examines the abortion experience from a pro-choice perspective is *In Necessity and Sorrow: Life and Death in an Abortion Hospital* by Magda Denes.

As with Francke, Denes' book was an outgrowth of her own abortion experience. Three times she entered a private hospital with an appointment to abort her pregnancy. Twice she changed her mind and left in tears; the third time she stayed and was aborted. Two weeks after her abortion, Denes returned to the hospital and asked the director if she could conduct in-depth interviews with consenting patients, relatives, and staff. When informed that Dr. Denes was a university professor and a certified psychologist, the director gave his blessing to the project, feeling that it would help to shed light on an important topic.

During the "many months" that followed, Denes became a fixture at the hospital, quietly observing, befriending, interviewing, and observing. Her book is the story of her experiences, a diary of her reflections, and a summary of her interviews. It is often slow, frequently cynical, often morbid, but always revealing.

What was the motivating force behind Denes' book? Twice she walked out of the hospital before finally returning for her own abortion. In this ability to waiver and feel uncertain, she felt that she was among the lucky few. She had a secure home, secure finances, and a husband who would have supported her even if she had chosen not to abort. But she was forced to wonder about other women: "I wanted to know most urgently what lies behind the abortion myths," she writes. "What happens to women who are not as privileged as I and who can not freely choose but are rather compelled by circumstance to renounce their child? Do they grieve less, or more?"[55] This is the question that prompted her study; but after returning to the hospital to begin her study, it was the "now" of abortion, not its aftermath, which caught her eye.

The time and place to which Denes confined her research was very limiting. Her study began shortly before the 1973 Supreme Court decision legalizing abortion in all fifty states, and ended a short time later. The place was New York City, the abortion capital of the nation, where abortions were easily and legally obtainable since 1970. The place was a private hospital which specialized in providing second trimester abortions.

In addition to the limitations imposed by this time frame and setting, Denes' perspective of the abortion experience in this hospital was constrained by the position and rank with which the patients she met perceived her. By way of comparison, Zimmerman's approach was as that of a sociologist. She carefully and consistently interviewed aborted women under formal conditions, following a uniform outline. Francke, on the other hand, was less clinical, less formal. Hers was a reporter's style. She interviewed women in clinics around the country. She was out in the trenches, out among the people, "one of them," so to speak, and this position allowed for some startlingly candid interviews. But Denes had none of the advantages accorded to a "normal" woman. She was a "Doctor," no mere pedestrian. At times, as she herself points out, this rank became a barrier between her and the patients she interviewed. Cautious and circumspect, already filled with doubts and ambivalence, many were afraid to confide in a "shrink."

Like most of those with whom she worked at the hospital, Denes had an honest compassion for the patients. Furthermore, having been aborted herself, she clearly identified with them. Still, the patients soon became passing figures, one sad face after another, one sad story after another, and Denes' senses became dulled by the recurring dramas. Instead, the hospital and staff—always the same day after day—took on a greater reality and permanence both in her mind and in her book. It is this reality, the abortion hospital, which is the true focus of her book. The patients Denes talked with are seen only from the hospital point of view, what the counselors heard, what the doctors saw. There were still tears, doubts, terror, and most of all, determination to have it over with as soon as possible. But all these interviews were from the "before" point of view. She never followed up to see how the patients were reacting after abortion had sucked the life from their wombs.

Denes' book includes interviews with seventeen abortion patients: ten saline, seven D&C. The interviews are all relatively short and most are conducted *before* the abortion actually took place. But the stories follow what is, by now, a very familiar pattern. Many of the women were being pressured to abort by boyfriends, husbands, or parents. Since they all were second trimester aborters who had delayed their decisions, almost all had strong feelings of ambivalence. Some openly desired to keep the child; others were already plagued with guilt.

Some of the women Denes talked with openly discussed their feelings of guilt. For example, one woman who was being pressured to abort by her husband told Denes: "Like when you have an abortion, you just destroying [sic] a part of yourself; that's the way I feel anyhow. I just feel bad inside, that's all. I didn't really want to do it. It's a sin."[56]

But more typically, the women were simply trying to block out their negative feelings. As one woman told her: "I made up my mind to do it and like I could let it drive me crazy, any woman could, but you

57

can't, because you've got to live with it and there's really no sense in letting it drive you right off the edge.[57]

As a trained psychiatrist, Denes knows how to look beyond the words of those she interviews. She sees that words of bravery are used to disguise fears, words of calm to hide doubts. For example, when introducing the interview of one patient, she writes: "All that she says sounds honest and straightforward. It is only when she refers to the abortion that she lies, not so much to me as to herself."[58] But seeing through these self-deceptions does not mean that Denes criticizes them. Instead, she justifies denial as a necessary defense mechanism by which all people protect themselves from their worst sides: "Oh yes," she writes, "these people lie, they kid themselves, testify falsely, confess in bad faith, shirk responsibility, only pretend to honor, bracket the past, and invent their lives. And who among us does differently? Especially in times of crisis. Especially in times of irreversible choice."[59]

Self-preservation is the name of the game, and Denes clearly sees that sanity in the abortion clinic can be achieved only by a strict adherence to the rules of the game. Both patients and staff collaborate in this conspiracy of self-deception. Describing her interviews with both staff and patients, she writes: "Above all, this is a document on the evasions, multifaceted, clever, and shameful, by which we all live and die."[60] In the abortion hospital, she adds, "Reality is a matter of courtesy. A matter of agreement not to rock the tempest-torn boat."[61]

It is a primary task of abortion personnel, then, to assist patients in constructing and maintaining this tunnel-vision view of reality. It is their task to keep the patients from becoming afraid, doubtful. Thus Denes perceives the abortion routine as being designed to carry the patients along, to numb them against reality. This is done in often contradictory ways: busy them, push them, coddle them, ignore them. The routine minimizes questions, stifles doubts, and fans the hope that soon it will all be over with:

> As I sit watching these two women, I am overwhelmed by the bureaucratic banality of suffering. Obscure chatter, legal forms, repeated signatures, waiting, these are the structured anesthetic that oil the machinery of institutions.
>
> At this hospital, downstairs they wait, in this unit they bear witness, further up they are delivered. In between they endure the purgatory of routine and fear, of lab-tests and regrets and

reaffirmations of purpose. Until it is over. Until the crisis recedes, and the dull comfort of monotony asserts itself once more.[62]

In Necessity and Sorrow is filled with such commentaries. Denes' style is like that of a funeral dirge: solemn, sad, respectful of both the living and the deceased. Although she recognized the need for patients and staff to hide from the reality of abortion, she herself feels compelled to confront this reality in its most grisly forms. In this sense, her book is less an examination of others than an examination of herself. It is her own ambivalence towards her own abortion which she returned to the hospital to confront, and it is this confrontation which is most illuminating.

Some of the most disturbing portions of the book are those in which Denes cautiously and fearfully investigated the inner sanctum of the abortion hospital: the operating rooms. There she watched frightened, often sobbing women undergoing saline abortions. There she saw surgeons who were compassionate and cruel; efficient and mercenary. She heard tales of severe complications, near deaths, and even of aborted babies born alive. She saw contradictions, paradoxes, and pain:

> I am drawn to the [saline] unit, irresistibly, by my reactions of disbelief, sorrow, horror, compassion, guilt. The place depresses me, yet I hang around after working hours. When I leave, I behave outside with the expansiveness of one who has just escaped a disaster. I have bad dreams. My sense of complicity in something nameless grows and festers. I consider giving up the research, but it is unthinkable to not return to the saline floor without knowing more.[63]

After returning day after day, Denes finally began the process of interviewing doctors, nurses, and patients. But she still felt drawn to know the full truth. She needed to see it all for herself.

Half-heartedly, Denes makes several attempts to see a saline abortion through to completion, to see the laboring birth of the dead fetus. But she never quite succeeds in this task. Other duties call her, and somehow she seems to always miss seeing that unpredictable event. Finally, she writes:

> I decide to put an end to my stalling and spend an uninterrupted afternoon on the floor. Nothing happens, not even screaming.

Toward evening I turn in desperation to one of the nurses. "Isn't anybody going to give birth today?" Before she can open her mouth, her face tells me that I have spat in the soup. "Doctor, that is not what happens here." "I am sorry, I mean deliver the baby, I mean fetus. To hell with it, nurse, I am going home. Good night."

The next afternoon I return determined, regardless of where I am at the time of delivery, to look inside the buckets. . . .

Planting myself in front of the table . . . I remove with one hand the lid of a bucket. . . . I look inside the bucket in front of me. There is a small naked person in there floating in a bloody liquid—plainly the tragic victim of a drowning accident. But then perhaps this was no accident, because the body is purple with bruises and the face has the agonized tautness of one forced to die too soon. Death overtakes me in a rush of madness. . . .

I take the lid off all the buckets. All of them. I reach up to the shelf above this bucket graveyard tabletop and take down a pair of forceps. With them I pull aside in each bucket the placenta, which looks like a cancerous mushroom shrouding the fetus. With the forceps I lift the fetuses, one by one. I lift them by an arm or a leg, leaving, as I return them again, an additional bruise on their purple, wrinkled, acid-soaked flesh. I have evidently gone mad. I carry on the examination, whose sole purpose by now is to increase the unbearable anguish in my heart. I lift a very large fetus. . . . I look at the label . . . This is Master Atkins—to be burned tomorrow [in a hospital incinerator] who died like a hero to save his mother's life. Might he have become someday the only one to truly love her? The only one to mourn her death?

"Nurse, nurse," I shout, taking off my fancy gloves. "Cover them up."[64]

Like the woman who aborts again and again, determined to prove to herself that it doesn't really hurt, Denes forced herself to look at all the horrors of abortion again and again, hoping despite the tremors, to find the reasons why, the justifications, the apologies for this "evil necessity." Eventually, her purgation in this chamber of death achieved its desired effect:

In a month's time I acquire a sort of wooden torpor to the screams that periodically shatter the humdrum noises of the floor. Tears cease to unsettle me. I am unmoved by wailing. I take it for granted that we are in the business of death here, and the tenor of each day will be heartache. . . . I am shell-shocked, as it were, stunned by being spoken to. Staggered by these readily revealed dramas, whose plots are loneliness, whose resolutions are defeat.[65]

Numbed by the saline floor, Denes pressed on, forcing herself to face even greater shocks. On a superficial level, the D&C floor is more controlled and "civilized" because the abortions were quick, finished in minutes rather than days, and the patients were anesthetized. But the D&C procedure itself was more graphic and gruesome. But Denes was determined to witness it in full.

At the first D&C abortion she attended, the disorienting noises and smells drive her from the room, nauseated and shaken. She had yet to see anything. The second time was only slightly better. She remained at the patient's head for the whole time but again saw none of the procedure itself. By the third time, Denes was determined to witness everything. And she did.

Watching an abortion at the surgeon's end of the table, Denes' first reaction is one of shock at how the patient is put to sleep, spread-eagled, and violated with cold impunity. It is coarse, degrading, and even defiling. But it is not until the fetal parts are removed that all her feelings are deadened by the enormity of what she sees:

He pulls out something, which he slaps on the instrument table. "There," he says. "A leg.". . . . I turn to Mr. Smith. "What did he say?" "He pulled a leg off," Mr. Smith says. "Right here." He points to the instrument table, where there is a perfectly formed, slightly bent leg, about three inches long. It consists of a ripped thigh, a knee, a lower leg, a foot, and five toes. I start to shake very badly, but otherwise, I feel nothing. Total shock is passionless.

"I have the rib cage now," Holtzman says, as he slams down another piece of the fetus. . . . "There, I've got the head out now. Also a piece of the placenta."

I look at the instrument table where next to the leg, and next to a mess he calls the rib cage but that I cannot recognize, there lies a head. It is the smallest human head I have ever seen, but it is unmistakably part of a person. My vision and my hearing though disengaged, continue, I note, to function with exceptional clarity. The rest of me is mercifully gone.[66]

After this, Denes left the hospital completely "exhausted," but she returned again and again. Forcing herself to witness these terrors again and again, Denes soon discovered the deadening comfort of repetition. Her dearly bought callousness was tested one day when she watched the most morbid of spectacles without a quiver of distaste. On this day, one of the nurses lost her wedding ring in the operating room, so she and another staff member pawed through a bag of blood and fetal parts hoping to recover it. At first, the scene did not arouse Denes' normally keen sensibilities. She writes:

> I am all for them. It is frightful to lose one's wedding ring. The event is completely divested of its larger context. Hours later when the scene reasserts itself in my mind, I do not recognize myself. Is inhumanity a habit? Is indifference the result of the attrition of meaning? If so, one must watch the self like an enemy.[67]

If numbness to abortion was what Denes had been seeking, then that is what she found. By the end of her stay at the hospital, she was so benumbed by the months she has spent in this abortion hospital that she was indistinguishable from the rest of the shell-shocked staff. Together, she and other members of the abortuary sit in the hospital's cafeteria and find hysterical laughter in jokes about a menu of "fetus-stew" and "mince meat pie."[68]

Ironically, one of the few incidents which Denes describes with joy is when a young girl fled the clinic, running from her pressuring parents:

> There are exceptions. One is a young girl barely sixteen. She is scrawny, Puerto Rican, uneducated, poor, and headstrong. Some say she is crazy. I love her as she takes off down the corridor, screaming, her white gown flying in a blaze of glory. "Let me outta here. I won't do it. It's my baby." Six weeks pregnant—afflicted with an abstraction, one might say—she leaves triumphant, with two sulky parents who have been hastily summoned by Dora.
>
> Will this madness cost her her life? . . . I have no opinion except to observe once again that the question of which life,

whose life, is a frequent and unanswerable dilemma in this hospital. To note also that after her departure, all the women—patients and nurses—set their faces a little tighter.[69]

All these others, it would seem, are struggling against the same "crazy" impulse to flee. But they are all too strong, or too weak, to take that other route.

The glue that holds it all together, the hospital, the staff and the patients, is weak and precarious. It is always on the verge of collapse and always maintained by sheer willpower, by the collective agreement that what must be done, must be done. There is no room for questions:

> The most threatening pitfall in this hospital is a creeping conviction of absurdity. Daily, terror and desolation dictate decisions, the meaning of which are obscure to everyone. This life against that. Why? That life against this. Why again? Because patients can speak, and fetuses are mute?
>
> Things happen. Situations arise. We do what we can, which is not much. Will, God's or otherwise, appears an obsolete notion. The most frequent gesture is a shrug. The most prevalent phrase is "I don't know."[70]

But this game of denial and the tunnel-vision it breeds, Denes sees, has a high cost. There is insensitivity. There is forced isolation, because to come too close is to shatter the illusion. For example, she records an incident in which a frightened patient asks a nurse for the time when a clock is in plain sight. When the nurse answered "Quarter past four, dear," and ignored this subtle plea for attention and reassurance, Denes wants to shout and expose these pained masks, these silent absurdities, but instead she remains silent, thinking. "To uncover reality here would mean to turn this place into a madhouse. Therefore I am silent, and clutch my stomach, and go for a walk down the corridor."[71]

What does Denes think of all these games of denial? "Sometimes acquaintanceship with reality makes people sane, at other times it drives them mad," she writes. "Who is to say what is the right path? Certainly not anyone with a heart."[72] Oddly, this rhetorical question seems to argue that isolationism can be substituted for compassion. She could just as well say: "Who are we to interfere? Let them make their own mistakes. Whether the path they choose leads to sanity or madness, it is the path they choose alone."

Though Dr. Magda Denes is personally committed to the prochoice philosophy, her book, like Francke's, is never embraced by the pro-choice movement. It is too dark, too questioning, too disturbing. Despite the author's pro-choice perspective, *In Necessity and Sorrow* is a powerful indictment of abortion. It is an indictment which Denes did not want to make, but an indictment which cannot be avoided by one who would report the facts she observes. Denes herself is unsettled by the tone of her writing. Despite her intellectual belief in abortion, her writings had taken on a dark nature of their own:

> On reading it, my book appears to me boobytrapped. It seems a mined object ready to explode in utter destructiveness at the slightest corrupt or careless touch. For in fact I am for abortions. My rage throughout these pages is at the human predicament. At the finitude of our lives, at our nakedness, at the absurdity of our perpetual ambivalence toward the terror of life and toward the horror of death.[73]

The reason both Denes' and Francke's books are so anti-abortion—despite the opposite leanings of their authors—is simple. When one studies the effect of abortion on women in an intimate and personal way, it is never an encouraging story. What emerges is always much more sorrow than joy, much more guilt than relief.

The pro-abortion/pro-choice philosophy is admirable only when stripped of its reality, only when worshiped as an ideal, believed in the abstract. When examined from the viewpoint of women filled with despair, dread, guilt, and denial, pro-choice rhetoric is cold and uncomforting. When examined from the viewpoint of torn limbs, saline-burnt bodies, scarred uteruses, and infertility, it is a mockery.

Denes herself finds little reason to cling to her pro-abortion stance other than for the abstract ideal of "choice." With a candor unusual for a pro-choice advocate, she readily admits that abortion is "a type of murder," that its victim is "alive and human." But she sees abortion on demand as justifiable murder because it "saves the life" of the woman, or at least "saves" her from an unwanted burden.[74]

In sum, speaking as one who has been there, Denes favors abortion on demand purely on the grounds that women should be given a choice. Yet she is discomforted with that choice, for even under ideal circumstances, even if abortion on demand were "provided free by the state, [and] supported with mercy by the church," she believes that such a pure freedom to abort would only accentuate the horrors, doubts, guilts, and other problems which are *inherent* to abortion. "For if we remove abortions from the realm of defiance of authority," she writes:

> . . . if we permit them to be acts of freedom as they should be, their meaning, private and collective, will inescapably emerge in the consciousness of every person. . . . I think it is a far, far lighter task to regard oneself as a martyr and to battle the world than to know the private sorrows of unique commitments and the heartache of self-chosen destiny. I wish, therefore, to be taken for what I am. A proabortionist with a bad secular conscience.[75]

D.   Other Testimonies

Aside from this book, the three books discussed above provide the widest collection of interviews with abortion patients available today. They are not, however, the only sources wherein aborted women provide testimony about their experiences. Bits and pieces are scattered far and wide. Individual stories can be found throughout the general media, in pro-life publications, and in pro-choice publications. To gather all such stories would be an impossible task, but a brief review of some of them supports our finding that abortion is never an easy experience for the women involved.

Looking first to pro-choice literature, one can hardly miss *Our Bodies, Ourselves*, compiled in 1973 by the Boston Women's Health Book Collective. Written from a feminist perspective, this book covers a wide range of women's health topics and includes sections on female sexuality, lesbianism, reproduction, and abortion. The abortion chapter is devoutly pro-choice, but there is a reluctant admission that although abortion brings a relief from immediate problems, "Even the most positive feelings afterward tend to be mixed with negative ones."[76]

As examples, the Boston Women's Collective prints a few quotations from aborted women, such as: "I began my mourning during my short pregnancy. I feel there has to be a mourning in some form for the life that was never allowed to continue." Another reports: "I was so relieved not to be pregnant any more that I didn't think I had any sad feelings at all. Then a few days later, on my way to a friend's house, I saw a young couple walking a new baby and I burst out crying right there on the street."[77]

Besides the few brief testimonies such as these, *Our Bodies, Ourselves* contains the complete abortion testimonies of two anonymous feminists. Both resemble the "typical" stories of ambivalence encountered so far. The only difference is that each ends her story with an appeal to feminist ideology and the glories of self-determination.

The first of these stories recounts an illegal abortion in 1967. At first, the woman was pleased to learn she was pregnant, but then she went through a process of trying to talk herself out of having the child. This impulse seemed to stem from a feminist belief that reproduction is a crude, secondary function of the female body, and a binding and enslaving one at that. From this viewpoint, then, every pregnancy should be regarded with suspicion. One's "biological" yearnings to keep the pregnancy should be weighed against the more important needs of the woman's "rational" being. Thus, this woman chose to suppress her strong desires to keep the pregnancy and instead chose to prove her "rational control" over her own life. To her, her pregnancy was the test case which would determine whether she was a feminist, free and independent, or a weak-willed victim bound by her biology and the conventions of a "male-dominated society."[78]

In order to fight her "biological" impulses and proceed with the abortion, she writes, "I shut myself down emotionally" and even years later, "my total emotional reaction to it escapes me." But she ends her tale with pro-choice bravado, telling women that there is no reason to feel guilt over abortion despite "societal taboos," because "it is my nature and my right to determine my destiny as a woman.[79]

The second story, also intended to reinforce the pro-choice philosophy, is even more ambivalent than the first. This time it is the story of a legal abortion by a married woman, a mother, who was in the process of returning to college. Her plans were upset, so:

> I kept hoping for a miscarriage. The idea of abortion—the word—came in and out of my head but was quickly dismissed. I felt strongly that abortion was not a choice for me. I, as a person I thought I had begun to know, did not have the freedom to make that choice. I had believed abortion was every woman's right, but those were hollow, liberal thoughts for me. It's so easy to be liberal when you're comfortable. For me abortion was a whole life-death question that I could not bear to settle.

. . . It's important to say that my husband was adamantly opposed to a third child, which didn't help me at all in making a decision. We argued bitterly—I defending anything he was against.

. . . I kept getting very entangled in the sanctity of life: this fetus was growing within me whether I was awake or asleep, all the time. When does one have the right to destroy a life, potential or real? When is life real? . . . . [I was] confused by the realization that I could consider aborting a fetus. Fetus—to me a child.

I was completely muddled—and I had nowhere to go. But friends kept helping and supporting—women supporting no decision, just me as I was.[80]

At this point, her friends convinced her that she had to take responsibility for making her own decision. She learned, as all aborting women do, to shift away from the moral question, "Is it a life?" to the practical question, "Do I want a child?" For this would-be feminist, facing this practical question was a challenge to be a "mature woman" and "make your own decision" independent of past "conditioning" or social norms.

I had to take on the responsibility of saying "I want to have this child, and I will accept that" or "I do not want another child and I must accept the responsibility for aborting this fetus." I had to say that I was real, that my life was real and mine and important. Those feelings were very hard to come to. I don't think I believe in them fully even now. . . . [But] there was a certain strength in knowing that I could make a choice that was mine alone and be entirely responsible to myself. On the strength that I had begun to feel as a woman, I made the decision to have an abortion. There was no decision of right or wrong or morality—it simply seemed the most responsible choice to make. It is still upsetting to me— the logic of it all—but somewhere within me it is still very clear, and I'm still very sure of that decision. . . .

I was very sure of my decision that day [of my abortion], much more than at any other time, but my emotions were some- what shut down. Perhaps it was in self-defense. I had questioned my decision so many times that I just had to stop. . . . What in reality happened was that I had become a person I control— someone who is able to say "This is the way my life must go."

In retrospect, my feelings are very contrary and complex—some high, some low. I do not feel guilt—almost rather guilty over my astonishing (to me) lack of guilt. I have felt at many times very strong and sure in my identity as a woman—a very real person.[81]

Like the first story, this testimony is intended to teach aspiring feminists, modern and independent, that abortion is bearable if one fixes one's eyes on the ideal of self-determination—no matter who must suffer to achieve it. Abortion, then, is seen as the "badge of honor" by which women reclaim control over their own lives.

Despite the bravado of these testimonies, the doubts and ambivalence which these women feel is clear. Their closing remarks about the virtues of the "freedom to choose" may have been necessitated by the editorial slant of the volume to which they contributed their testimonies; but it is more likely, as Denes put it, that they are "evasions, multifaceted and clever," intended to convince themselves more than their readers.

Quite honestly, these two stories from *Our Bodies, Ourselves* are the most "positive" abortion testimonies one can find. Clearly, abortion is *never* free of sour doubts and pains. Those who are "completely satisfied" are few and far between. But even when such "satisfied" aborters are encountered, their claims of being untroubled by their abortions must be taken with a grain of salt, since such women have far more reason, if only to reinforce their own self-images, to hide negative feelings and insist that the decision to abort was good and right. To admit otherwise is to open the door to reevaluation, doubt, self-reproach, and despair.

Periodically, letters from aborted women will appear on the editorial pages of the popular press. The pain they describe almost always follows the same pattern. For example, a letter which appeared in the *Tampa Tribune* said in part:

I am 34, married seven years. I had an abortion not quite four years ago. The pain of the knowledge of what I did is permanent, deep and fresh again when I least expect it. A word about a child, Mother's Day, a song—can literally rip me apart. There is never any warning. In the middle of the happiest moments, something will trigger a sadness for my action.

I can't make you feel how I feel or how I felt. I would be writing for hours. Even if I talked to you, you could not know the pain I've set myself up for. It's not just babies that abortion kills. It's mothers too.[82]

Occasionally, stories of grief over a past abortion turn up in the most unexpected places and at the most unexpected times. For example, during an interview on the Donahue show, actress Shelly Winters was discussing the love affairs in her life when suddenly she blurted out: "You know, I find myself agreeing with the Catholic Church on some issues. You all will probably not like me for this . . ." and she proceeded to tell the audience that despite her reliance on contraceptives, she had had two abortions in her life. "I am a very lonely woman," she confessed, "I would give up everything—my money, my academy awards, my career—if only I could have those children now." With that, she broke into uncontrollable sobs. As the audience roared with sympathetic applause, Donahue switched to a commercial.[83]

Another great star who lived in the shadow of an abortion was Gloria Swanson, America's sweetheart in the 1920s and 1930s. Remorse over her abortion experience was so central to her life that her autobiography, *Swanson on Swanson*, begins and ends with lamentations over her aborted child. After having aborted to preserve her reputation and career, Swanson writes: "I could never view my life or my career in the same way again." Even fifty-four years later, she was still crying "fresh tears out of guilt." Near the end of her life, at 84 years of age, she writes that "the greatest regret of my life has always been that I didn't have my baby, Henri's child, in 1925. Nothing in the whole world is worth a baby, I realized as soon as it was too late, and I never stopped blaming myself."[84]

The trend is clear to anyone who looks. The negative, WEBA-like abortion experience is the rule rather than the exception. Many aborted women will deny it by hiding their emotions and telling little or nothing of their experience. Others may hide it behind the anger and bitterness they feel toward other persons who were involved, especially against the male. But most will admit they are troubled; they simply don't know what else to do other than to try to forget it and move on.

Most of all, the stories of aborting women are stories of isolation and despair. What they are saying is that they did not really need a "solution" to *avoid* their problems; rather they wanted love and support to *face* their problems.[85] As one WEBA woman said: "The responsibility of carrying a child for nine months—and even of raising that child, if one chooses, for twenty years—is far less than the responsibility of having taken another's life."

The Granberg Study

The purpose of this chapter has been to illustrate that the negative reaction of WEBA women is typical of nearly every aborted woman's experience. Even the evidence gathered by pro-choice authors confirms this view. The titles alone, *In Necessity and Sorrow* and *The Ambivalence of Abortion*, are evidence that the consensus of women who have been aborted is very negative.

But if the case against abortion is still in doubt, we offer one last item of evidence to support our contention that the vast majority of aborted women regret their decisions. Ironically, this evidence is again supplied by a pro-choice source.

In 1981, Planned Parenthood's *Family Planning Perspectives* published an article by Donald Granberg entitled "The Abortion Activists." In this article, Granberg unearthed figures which, if properly interpreted, indicated that the "outbreak" of previously aborted women banding together to denounce abortion was not unpredictable. What these figures really reveal, though carefully disguised behind a pro-choice bias, is that aborted women are much more likely to become anti-abortion activists than pro-choice activists.

In this study, sociologist Donald Granberg compared the membership characteristics of the nation's two largest organizations supporting and opposing abortion—the National Abortion Rights Action League (NARAL) and the National Right to Life Committee (NRLC). Surveying approximately 450 members of each group on a broad number of questions, Granberg was able to contrast many of the opinions and characteristics of each group.

Most of Granberg's results were unsurprising. He found, for example, that NRLC members were more likely to have larger families, were much more likely to think religion was important in their lives, and were much more likely to reject sexual activity outside of marriage. NARAL members, by contrast, preferred smaller families; held religion to be moderately or minimally important, if at all (40% listed themselves as being atheist or agnostic); were much more permissive about all forms of sexual activity; and were more likely to belong to higher social and economic classes.[86]

In terms of favoring abortion for any given circumstances, of course, the two groups held diametrically opposed positions. Notably, however, 73 percent of anti-abortionists approved of abortion when necessary to save a woman's life. Pro-choice advocates, on the other hand, showed less than absolute support for freedom of choice than their rhetoric would suggest, with only 58 percent approving of abortion as a means of sex selection, though 85 percent also claimed a woman should be able to obtain an abortion "for whatever reason." This hostility towards the use of abortion for sex selection suggests that many NARAL members place at least a minimal value on the unborn life when compared to "trivial" reasons for abortion.[87]

But the most unexpected, and least analyzed, result of the Granberg survey was the response of women members from each group to the question of whether or not she had ever had an abortion. In response, 32 percent of NARAL's female members reported having had an abortion compared to 3 percent of NRLC's female members.

Granberg carefully twists these figures to reach the pro-abortion conclusion that "women who have abortions tend to strongly support the availability of legal abortion for others." He admits however that "it is recognized that the bulk of women who have had abortions do not join any organization on either side of the abortion controversy. Many of these women, no doubt, feel a real and sometimes abiding ambivalence about the abortion."[88]

Granberg's focusing upon the *percentage* of aborters in each group is, in fact, a ploy for hiding an uncomfortable truth which his statistics would otherwise expose. Percentages are useful only in relationship to a whole, and when the percentage of aborters Granberg discovers in each group are applied to the whole groups from which they were drawn, an entirely different picture emerges.

According to the *Encyclopedia of Associations*, NARAL has a total membership of 156,000, whereas NRLC has a total of 12 million members.[89] It is in this fundamental difference in the size of the organizations from which he draws his survey sample that his deception is revealed.

Granberg himself finds that 78 percent of NARAL's members are female, compared to a 63 percent female membership in NRLC. Therefore, based on Granberg's own figures, 32 percent of NARAL's female members have had abortions yielding a total of 39,000 aborters. On the other hand, 3 percent of NRLC's female members yields approximately 245,000 aborters.[90]

In other words, *women who have had abortions are six times more likely to work against abortion than for it.*

A few more points should be made about this comparison of the number of aborters working for and against abortion. Those who have joined NRLC were probably motivated by remorse and guilt over a previous abortion. It can be assumed that few, if any, had their abortions after joining the pro-life group. The NARAL women, on the other hand, were not asked whether they had joined the pro-choice group before or after their abortion, a missing factor which would be helpful for understanding the motivation behind their pro-choice activism. It is possible that many of these women had their abortions *after* becoming involved with NARAL. In these cases, the abortion decision reflected on prior political feelings, perhaps the abortion was even seen as a "badge of honor" reflecting one's commitment to the cause, proof of one's liberation and freedom. For others who aborted before joining NARAL, it is possible that for some the vocal defense of abortion was a way of denying underlying feelings of guilt and psychological distress—a reaction reported by several WEBA members. By joining an organization which loudly proclaims that abortion is moral and good, they surround themselves with people who will confirm their choice and reassure them of their integrity.[91]

Summary

Even studies done by pro-choice researchers show that the abortion experience is almost always negative and is often harshly disruptive of one's life. It is never a trivial act; it will always continue to be a major part of a woman's life.

The WEBA-like experience recorded in this author's survey and in the Profiles included in this book are a close match to the "typical" abortion experience. The only "atypical" aspect of this sample of aborting women is that the vast majority of this group has come, or is coming, to terms with their abortion experience through a radical renunciation of abortion. They are freeing themselves from ambivalence and guilt by openly admitting their ambivalence and guilt. In a society which urges women to hide and suppress their post-abortion feelings, this is a radical approach.

PROFILES TWO

Feminists Who Abort

Despite the claims of some abortion clinics, abortion is *never* "as simple as having a tooth pulled." No matter how much a woman believes in women's rights or the rhetoric that her unborn fetus is only a "potential life," she cannot deny or ignore the fact that during an abortion her body becomes a battleground where a life force within her is destroyed. Furthermore, this destruction is an irreversible event which alters the future of her own life forever.

For some feminists, a negative abortion experience will draw them deeper into feminism, where they hope to find answers to the uneasiness they feel. They may even hope to become abortion reformers by drawing on their abortion experience to bring more compassion and caring to family planning and abortion clinics. Some may find this satisfying, at least for a time, but many others eventually become disillusioned with the pro-choice rhetoric and seek peace through renunciation of their abortions and even turn to pro-life activism.

Approximately 30 percent of the WEBA members surveyed were pro-choice advocates before their own abortions. Many were active feminists, and many are now pro-life feminists. Their changes of view are a result of their abortion experiences.

3) Karen Sullivan

Karen became pregnant when she was twenty-two. Unmarried, career-oriented, and a proponent of "free choice," she chose abortion as the best way to preserve her lifestyle. Afterwards, she worked as an counselor for a feminist health collective in California until she became pregnant a second time. The birth of her son compelled Karen to reevaluate her abortion experience and eventually led her to become a pro-life activist.

At the time of my abortion, I was living in California. I had recently moved there to be near my boyfriend, who was attending the University of California at Berkeley. I didn't know anyone there; so when I found out I was pregnant, I went straight to Planned Parenthood. It was from that organization that I had received my contraceptives a year earlier.

The counselor, a man, painted a bleak picture of parenting alone, and never told me that I would be eligible for WIC, foodstamps, welfare, and medical aid should I carry my baby to term. Instead, the counselor told me that I had to explore my career goals before having a child.

I gave my decision much thought; in fact, I was obsessed with it. I was very pro-choice in my philosophy. Although I wasn't active in any feminist organizations, I felt the feminists had it all together, and I was very sympathetic to their pro-choice reasoning. Within one week I decided to go ahead and have the abortion.

On the day of the abortion, my boyfriend took me to the Choice Clinic in Los Gatos, California. At the time our relationship was very shaky and tense. While we were there, we were situated with four other women, and were "counseled." Actually, we all just sat there, nervous and tense, looking at each other and trying to convince ourselves that we did really want to have an abortion. A few minutes before we were to be ushered in to have the abortion, we were offered five or ten milligrams of Valium. I didn't take any, because I wanted to be wide awake and conscious of what was happening to me.

I was twelve weeks pregnant, so they performed a suction abortion. They inserted dilators into my cervix, one after the other, until the largest one was as big around as my little finger. It was really, really painful. I wasn't told that it would hurt that bad. They turned on the suction machine. I could feel the baby being torn from my insides. It was really painful. Not having had any pain killers, I felt all of it, completely and totally. Three-quarters of the way through the operation, I sat up. To my right, and down, I saw the tube that led out of me, from the vacuum aspirator, and it led into a glass cylinder. In the cylinder I saw the bits and pieces of my little child floating in a pool of blood. I screamed and jumped up off the table. They took me into another room and I started vomiting. They responded by offering me Seven-Up and cookies. It all was just repulsive to me, and I just couldn't stop throwing up.

I stayed there for a couple of hours, and then Mark, my boyfriend, took me home. While we were saying our feelings about all this to each other, I begged him to stay with me: "Please don't leave me, I don't want to be alone tonight." He said he had homework and that he had to leave, but that he would check back with me the next day or the next week, but sometime soon. I haven't seen him since. It's been four years, and there's been no word or sight of him since.

A few days afterwards, I began to feel relief. There was no tummy, no shame, and I wasn't pregnant anymore. I felt pretty good. But I did not escape the aftermath of abortion. I had nightmares and recurring dreams about my baby. I couldn't work my job. I just laid in my bed and cried. Once, I wept so hard I sprained my ribs. Another time while crying, I was unable to breathe and I passed out. I was unable to walk on the beach because the playing children would make me cry. Even Pampers commercials would set me into fits of uncontrollable crying.

I tried to establish a post-abortion counseling group for women and hung a notice of a meeting on a bulletin board at a women's health collective. But nobody showed up at the meeting, so I just dropped it.

After that, I joined the women's health collective and began working as a women's health counselor. It was a feminist clinic, and they were really anti-men. There were a lot of lesbians working there. And because of my grief, I submitted myself to counseling with a therapist who was homosexual and living with another woman. And I couldn't figure out why her counseling didn't help me—now I know, but at that time I didn't.

Her counseling tried to get me to the point where I could deny my grief, where I would be "healthy" enough to not ever admit that abortion was wrong, but to say, "Hey, I had an abortion. No big deal." To get to the point where I could counsel other women to have abortions would be to have "arrived," that I could cope. But I never got there. By her standards, I guess, I was a total failure. She never ever dealt with my guilt. I was a walking, talking pile of guilt; but she never ever dealt with that. Her response was like, "Guilt is just something imposed on us by our religious, male-dominated society, and we women have to fight against it." I was just supposed to "take control of my life" and deny my guilt. I was in counseling with her for about six or seven months.

But counseling which tells you to have the abortion and then forget about it just doesn't work. Even at an early stage of pregnancy a bond is formed between the mother and the child, a physical bond, of course, and a psychological bond. It is natural for mothers to bond with their children. Abortion puts an unnatural halt to the natural bonding. Eventually, nature will strike back.

All this time I continued to work at this pro-abortion facility dedicated to presenting an alternative to regular health care. There's safety in numbers. I didn't feel really awful about my abortion as long as everyone where I worked was patting me on the back. But I never really came to believe in their philosophy; I never really "arrived." I just never could bring myself to talk anyone into an abortion.

I got pregnant again while I was working there. I conceived my son the very week that my aborted baby should have been born. It was no accident; I set out to get pregnant. My son is an "atonement baby" for the child I lost. I had felt that by my abortion I had taken something precious out of the world, and so I wanted to put something back into it. At first, though, I had a strong impulse to terminate this second pregnancy. But luckily a friend made me aware of what I was doing: "You're going to have abortion after abortion. Your life will be hell." My friend convinced me that I was running scared and that I didn't hate my baby. Now I love him for who he is, though he was definitely conceived out of my grief for my first baby.

At the counseling center, though, my becoming pregnant by a man was like a "sin" to them. You see, they were very hostile towards men, very anti-male. So for anyone who was working there to become pregnant was like a betrayal, since it was proof that you had "known" a man. Abortion, to them, was the way you killed the "thing" the man had made in you; it was a reaction against men. For this reason, when counseling women they definitely pressed for abortion as the "best solution." (My lesbian therapist had had a child by artificial insemination, but that was OK with them.)

I was already on the outs with them then, just by being pregnant. But halfway during my second pregnancy, when I felt the baby move inside me, I really began to feel funny about all this abortion advocacy. I certainly wasn't what you'd call a pro-life person, but when I got "caught" praising a woman for choosing not to abort, that was the last straw. I was fired.

I had my baby and moved to Arizona. By this time the full impact of what I had done hit me. I felt like a criminal, like I was the worst person on this entire earth. But I still wasn't pro-life or anything. Then one Sunday, about a year ago, I had the impulse to go to the Grace Lutheran Church, though I had never been there before. But I went, and there I heard a woman speaking about abortion and pro-life, etc., and something just clicked in my mind, "Yes." At this time I was still really struggling with my own abortion; but with all the love and support of the pro-life people, I began to get over it. Then I heard about WEBA and decided "I want to get involved with that." And ever since I became involved with the right-to-life movement, my whole life has changed. Now I'm able to use my own experience to help other women avoid abortion. There's a lot of hope in that.

4) Carol St. Amour

Carol has had two abortions. She has little or no memory of her first, but her second abortion eventually drove her to severe depression, alcoholism, heroin, and violence against her husband.

My story begins almost a year before the abortion, because of the circumstances and people who touched my life and led to the decision. I was divorced and struggling to raise two children; my daughter born out of wedlock when I was eighteen, and a son from my first marriage.

I was working as a bartender at a local pub when I met Jim. He managed a local band and was a very handsome, intelligent and determined man. He showed up at my apartment one night, claiming that he and his wife were through. Our love affair began.

As the months passed, it turned into a family-type relationship. He was helping to raise my children and loved them the best he knew how. We talked of marriage but made no definite plans. I felt insecure, because his ex-wife kept interrupting our happy home. I felt bitterness toward his former family, but I tried to remain supportive.

77

Several months after this I started having difficulty with birth control. I had an IUD, but had trouble with it, and had to have it removed. I tried the pill, but after one week my breasts swelled and had lumps everywhere. So I discontinued use, and became pregnant. I was very satisfied, nearly ecstatic about our baby. I saw it as a bond between our children, and it gave me a sense of belonging and a purpose in our relationship, besides my being a sympathetic ear to Jim's previous marital problems.

After I left my doctor's office, when I found out I was pregnant, I stopped and talked to the wife of one of the members of the band that Jim managed. News spread quickly, and the band members were all very excited for us.

Jim, however, didn't feel that way. At first he was very quiet about it and didn't speak to me for over a week. When I pressed him about it, he stated he did not want me to have the baby; and that if I did, he'd leave me. I was crushed. I was a very open-minded, pro-choice feminist . . . but this was *his* child, too. So I talked to a friend about abortion alternatives, and she said, "Well, you can always have more children, but there's only one Jim. So if you love him, . . ."

So I weighed the costs, and wanting very much to please him, plus being fearful of his leaving me, I made an appointment to "discuss" this with my doctor. Upon my arrival at the doctor's office, and sharing Jim's reaction with him, the doctor made arrangements to have the pregnancy terminated the following week. The place was Women's Medical Services. I found out later that the doctor operated this place outside his Ob/Gyn practice.

This was to be my second abortion. The first time had been a D&C in 1975. I was asleep during it. I guess that's what kept me a pro-choice person after my first abortion: I didn't really know what an abortion was until I experienced the horrors of it while wide awake.

Now it was 1979. I went in on a Thursday for the insertion of a laminaria, and returned the next day for the "procedure." Jim took the day off work (big of him, huh?) to go with me. He was the only guy in the lobby of about fifteen girls. There was a *heavy* silence there. I had an inward battle going on inside me that only God and perhaps other women who have had abortions could possibly understand. It was like the cartoon of the person who has the devil on one shoulder and the angel on the other: one is whispering, "You're doing the right thing, life will be better, he'll love you more for it . . ." while the angel is saying, "Leave this place, you'll be OK, he's not worth it, it's your baby, a part of the man you say you love. . . ."

Finally I was ushered into a room, given a gown to put on, and given five milligrams of Valium—big deal. I remember the assistant's very cold, businesslike manner, not too talkative. I wasn't impressed by any of the people working there—there was no compassion or counseling, just an attitude of "let's get it over with; there are many patients to deal with." I was instructed to get up on a table, put my legs in the stirrups, and relax (easy for them to say).

My "doctor" came in, dressed in a surgical gown. The doctor began inserting this and that, and then the machine started. The noise was unforgettable—I can still hear it, even now. I grabbed at my chest and closed my eyes and started praying. Then I felt this gripping pain—it hurt so bad that I cried out. The doctor told me to "shut up" because there were "other girls" and the "walls were thin."

The ride home was short. Jim asked if I was all right, and I lied and said I was. We got home at 1:00 PM, and I went right to bed and cried all day and night. This depression worsened as several weeks went by. Jim's compassions and concern began turning into anger, as I started lashing out at him—"I want my baby back!"

One night Jim's band was playing at a local club, and he insisted that I go with him. Up until that point I hadn't left the house. I reluctantly went. I was beginning to enjoy myself as we slow-danced, and I laughed for what seemed the first time in months.

Then something happened that I should have expected, but had forgotten about: these people still thought I was pregnant. One of the wives came up and said, "You must be thrilled! When's the due date?" I about died, and had to think fast. My emotions about it all were rushing again; and as I looked at Jim, I could honestly say that I hated him. First the abortion and now this! I knew I'd have to lie to protect his rapport with our peers. I sadly told her that I had miscarried. We left shortly thereafter because I couldn't handle the sympathy these people were giving me—Me, a murderer!

Our relationship was like a roller coaster ride; but we were married in December, eight months after the abortion. Now I believe that on his part he married me out of pity and guilt. The eight months leading up to our marriage were filled with knockdown, drag-out fights. During this time I began drinking heavily and doing drugs, mostly amphetamines.

I hated myself and Jim so much that I could no longer keep it inside. I was very pathetic, instigating fights between us, saying things like he loved his ex-wife and children more than me and our dead baby. We went for secular counseling during this time. Our therapist said that I was experiencing a mourning period and overwhelming grief. To me it was a baby, my baby. To Jim it was a products-of-conception blob, a problem. He understood my feelings, but he couldn't handle it.

In November, during a bitter fight, I grabbed a 12-inch butcher knife and cut up his good brown suit, stabbing at it and crying. He began hauling things out of the house, leaving and taking his possessions with him. I was furious. We began throwing things at each other, spitting, name-calling. As I watched him load *our* car with his things, something clicked in me that I wanted to kill him. I lunged at him with the butcher knife, and he hit me as a full-grown man would hit when fighting with another man. He picked up an oxen yoke from the porch (I collected antiques) and used it as a baseball bat on me. It knocked me off my feet and drove me six feet into the house. There I lay, I couldn't move. My kids were running around screaming, crying, and attacking him, hitting him for hurting me.

That was the end of our marriage—I went downhill from there. I neglected my children because I was too busy at bars with other men, looking for love or free drugs. It finally came to the destructive drug heroin. I enjoyed the drug and that scared me enough to stop. I closed down the day-care center I operated in my home because I couldn't cope with looking at babies anymore. I packed up my kids and moved to Virginia Beach where my dad lived. There I read my daughter's Bible and asked God to save me and help me. After three months in Virginia and reading the word of God, it was impressed on me to go back to Michigan and make amends. I asked Jim to forgive me, which he did. But he was happy now and wanted nothing to do with me.

I became involved in a pro-life, Christian fellowship and formed a chapter of WEBA in December of 1983.

Soon after, in March of 1984, following months of symptoms of physical illness, a friend forced me to see a doctor. After the abortion I had vowed never to see a doctor again. My friend sought out a pro-life doctor, put me in a car, and drove me to my appointment. I was informed that I had cervical cancer. It was a new mountain to conquer, as it was a severe case of invasive cancer that was inoperable. I underwent a series of radiation treatments and radium implants.

It was a traumatic experience, but I survived it. There is now a study being done by a medical/psychological team at an Ohio medical school to investigate the increase of cervical/uterine cancer in aborted women. Their suspicions are that the psychological aftereffects, such as I have suffered from abortion, have triggered this cancer growth. Only time and research will tell, but I believe in my heart that the two are definitely related.

Anyway, the radiation treatments left me hopelessly sterile for life. Not only that, but I must take progesterone ten days each month and estrogen daily. I am thirty-one years old and experiencing mid-life crisis. My strong desire to have another baby is heartbreaking, but I'm learning to cope and compensate by saving others.

As a feminist—and former "pro-choicer"—I believe that the feminists have gone too far in supporting legal abortion. I know that my body is not my own when I am pregnant. That baby is its own person.

Where was the feminists' protection of my rights at the doctor's office and the abortion clinic? No feminist was encouraging my male chauvinist pig boyfriend to take a walk. None of my feminist friends offered to *really* help me. No, they rallied to *his* side. Nobody was there for me but the Lifegiver, and for that I am thankful.

P.S. July 23, 1984: Today I had to go see my oncologist (cancer specialist) because the radiologist found another "spot" on my cervix. I was led into an examination room and told to undress from the waist down. After the nurse left the room, I started looking around, checking things out. To my shock and complete loss of control I saw, two feet from my left foot, a suction aspirator machine! I freaked out. I had a total flashback of the abortion experience. I began crying uncontrollably, got up, dressed, and ran out into the hall, hyperventilating. I found the nurse and was near hysteria as I explained why I couldn't go back in there. She understood, and tried comforting me, reassuring me their office did not do abortions but that the machine was used for other purposes. She took the machine out of the room. I returned shaken and surprised at my lack of self-control. I wonder . . . will it ever end?

5) Deborah Hulebak

Deborah underwent four abortions. With each abortion she became more hardened and more angrily pro-choice. Of the four, only the decision to have her first abortion was very difficult. In that case she wanted to keep the baby but was pressured by her doctor into accepting an abortion for eugenic reasons.

My story begins in January of 1972. I was eighteen years old. I had been married for only a few months when I found that I was pregnant; it was my first pregnancy. My husband was in the military, so I was receiving medical care from the military doctors in Palo Alto, California.

When I found out I was pregnant, I was really excited. The thought of being pregnant had always appealed to me, and I was really anxious to start a family. I'd always just loved children, so my initial feeling was overwhelming joy. But when the doctor told me I was pregnant, he immediately asked me, "What are you planning on doing?" I guess I misunderstood the question, because my initial reaction was, "Well, I was going to go home and call my husband and tell him."

But then it occurred to me that the doctor was not thinking in those terms. The look on his face was very sober, and he said, "Had you considered abortion?" And my heart fell to the floor. It was as if he had come into my hospital room after I had delivered the baby and said, "Your baby is dead." I felt as if he had just signed my baby's death certificate. I told him, "No, I'd never thought about it."

The look on my face prompted the doctor to explain about the medication I'd been taking for thrombophlebitis (blood clots in my legs), coumadin, an anticoagulant. He said in a very matter of fact way, "This drug causes birth defects." In this whole conversation, I don't remember saying anything. I had so many thoughts; it seemed like he did all the talking. But I remember very clearly what he said: "I would be running a risk if I even gave you a fifty-fifty chance of having a normal child."

My immediate answer was "No. I will not even consider an abortion." He wanted to know why not, and I'm sure I said something like, "I just don't want to do that. This just can't be the only answer—there has to be another answer."

He said, "Why don't you go home and think about it, and let me know what you decide in a few days." I remember feeling greatly eased by that, and I went home.

I don't remember a lot of emotions; you know, I find that I seem to have blocked a lot of this out. I do recall calling the doctor and telling him that my husband had just received notice that he was to be stationed in Vietnam; and at that point, I would not consider an abortion. My reason to the doctor was that I did not expect my husband to return from Vietnam alive, and that I wanted to have this baby, regardless of how it would turn out. I felt very confident in my decision that I did not want that abortion.

The doctor was very concerned about my decision not to have an abortion and literally pleaded with me not to have the baby. He begged, "Please reconsider this. I don't know why you would want to do this to yourself and your husband. The baby would be a burden to you." He had no respect for my decision and kept saying things like, "You have *got* to be kidding. There is *no way* you can carry this baby to term. There are so many dangers involved. You're a fool to think of not aborting." Before I hung up he said, "I want you to consider it again carefully, and call me if you change your mind." In the years since, I've suspected that the doctor was so adamant with me about the abortion because he was afraid that if the baby did have birth defects, I'd hit him with a malpractice suit.

I did change my mind and made the decision to go ahead with the abortion. I'm not sure what prompted it, other than that my husband called me a couple of weeks later and informed me that he would not be going to Vietnam. Instead, we were going to be stationed in Germany. I also gave some thought to the fact that though my husband wanted children he didn't want them right away. This compounded my fear. I remember thinking, "If I have a deformed child, he's going to blame me. He's going to say that it was my fault, because I could've gotten rid of the kid but didn't."

Looking back now as a 31-year-old adult and mother of three children, assuming these things make me more mature, I would say that the primary reason for my decision came from a seed that the doctor had planted in me. It was his mannerism, his firm belief that I should have that abortion. He was so serious that it frightened me: I felt fear at *not* having the abortion. I felt justified because the doctor was so determined for me to have the abortion. That really played the biggest part in my decision.

After informing the doctor of my decision, the first thing they did was another examination, to verify that I was pregnant. Then I had to receive some "supposed" counseling from two psychiatrists. (This was 1972, and abortion-on-demand was not yet legal.) I remember that the psychiatrist asked me why I was having the abortion, and I told him it was because my baby would be deformed. That was about it. He never dealt with my thinking or my emotions. For example, he never asked, "Do you think you're going to be really upset when you find out that your baby is dead?" or "Do you realize that you're killing a child? How do you feel about killing this child?" They never referred to this baby as a baby; they never referred to my maternal instincts, to missing my child. . . .

They did ask me how my husband felt about this, and I said I didn't know, that I didn't think he cared. And the truth of the matter was that he didn't care. He and I never really discussed the abortion that much, except when we were in Germany together six months later. A couple of nights I would wake up with nightmares about the abortion, and he would comfort me. Other than that, we never really talked about it.

Anyway, they put me in the hospital, and I had to be on anti-coagulants because of my blood clots, and I had to stay three days. After the abortion, I remember waking up as I was being wheeled to my room. I heard my mother's voice saying, "That's my baby." And I could hear crying in her voice. I looked up and saw my mother and her best friend standing over me. I felt something soft next to my cheek and looked over and saw that they had brought me a stuffed animal. Bless her heart, I'm sure she was thinking that I would need something to replace that baby. But you know, I never thought of that. At that point, there was no baby; there had never been a baby; it was never referred to as a baby to me. But I remember the pain in my mother's voice and the tears in both women's eyes as they stood over me.

And then it occurred to me, for a split moment; I felt cheated, deprived, angry, hurt, and alone. At that moment no one could comfort me. I didn't cry then, but I did later. I'm not sure if they were tears for me or for the baby, but I think they were for me, because I felt like such a rotten person.

When I left that hospital, I put up a wall within myself with a big sign on it that said, "Don't ever think about this experience again. What you did was the right thing to do. Don't ever think about it again." I used to think that wall was put there by God to protect me, it was Him comforting me saying, "It's OK." But now I know that that wall was put there not only by the Enemy, but also by those doctors and nurses, the medical staff. They put it there to protect themselves; they instill those thoughts in you: "Don't think about it, don't dwell on it."

After that, I joined my husband in Germany. My life went to alcohol and hard drugs, all the time. I was so distraught and terribly depressed, and I had to be hospitalized for depression. When he was scheduled to return to the U.S., I came back ahead of him. I was so unhappy. He was abusing me quite severely; and I wanted to get away for awhile, to try to start a singing career.

Looking for love, I had an affair with a married man. His wife and I got pregnant at the same time. *She* got her baby; he gave *me* $300 for an abortion. This abortion triggered me into coldness about abortion, for it was done in anger. At the time, the first one was justified because of the possible birth defects. But this one was a lot easier. I was saying to myself, "You're real tough. You can do this and it won't hurt a bit."

After this second abortion, I developed an extremely serious uterine infection and had to be hospitalized. The doctor couldn't even examine me the first day. He said, "There is so much blood and pus in there that I can't even get in." I was on antibiotics for a week.

In addition to drugs and alcohol, I now found myself being very promiscuous. I had always been insecure and needed a lot of attention. I needed to be popular and needed to be accepted. I hated school; so the only way, in my mind, to get attention was through sex and drugs and partying. I had never had a "solid" father in my life. I realized that by sleeping around I got attention and affection. I soon found myself in need of a third abortion. By now, though, I was "tough" enough that I could laugh about having it.

I talked real openly about abortion. I was pro-choice, and I talked to other women about the value of having an abortion. During my first abortion, I would have said that "No, I don't think abortion is right. But in my case, since this baby might be deformed, it's OK." But with each successive abortion my attitude got worse and worse. I became increasingly pro-choice, to the point where I would say to other girls, "Big deal if you get pregnant. You can have an abortion. I've had three and it hasn't hurt me a bit!"

I found that in talking to other women about abortion, their decisions to abort satisfied something in me. It made me feel better about what I had done. It was almost like I was gloating in their misery. If I'd had an opportunity to work at a counseling center to counsel women before their abortions, I would have done it. It would have strengthened my own decisions to abort.

I did have an opportunity to get close to this situation. In between my second and third abortions, I worked in a hospital lab, doing blood work. You knew when these patients were having abortions, because it would say right on the labels "AB," which stood for "abortion." Sometimes I'd be tempted to ask them why they were having their abortions. I remember thinking that if I should ask them, part of my heart would be saying, "Wait! Think about it!" But then another part of me would be thinking, "Yes, that's the best thing."

Working there also gave me the chance to see the effects of an abortion. I walked into the lab one day and saw these big plastic bowls with lids on a table. As I walked toward them, the lab technician said, "I don't think you want to look in there." So I picked it up and looked in underneath, and I saw a baby floating in there. It had little legs, fingers, toes, eyes. It shocked me, but I set it back down. I was so hardened at that point that I just didn't let it get to me. But I know it did something to me; I've never been able to get that picture out of my mind.

There was one girl who came in for abortion blood work, and just started crying. I asked her what was wrong, and then asked, "Are you pregnant?" She just started crying harder and said, "I don't know what to do." I don't remember counseling her one way or the other, but I do remember saying, "Maybe you better think about this some more." She left, then came back a couple weeks later. She said, "I decided to keep the baby, and my boyfriend and I are getting married." I remember feeling happy for her, but there was also something in me that felt a little defeated, too. It was like *"She* got to do it, but I didn't." I was envious, because she'd been braver than me.

I think I acted that way out of bitterness. I was trying to cover up my true feelings. When I think back now, in between abortions, I can recall actually talking to my aborted babies. I'd comfort them and tell them that I loved them. I'd tell them that it just wasn't the right time in my life to have them. I cried sometimes, thinking about it. But you know, until I received my healing and was forced to bring all this sadness back to the surface, I never remembered these sad times. I only remembered making myself think, "It's easy to have an abortion. I'm tough enough to do it."

Anyway, my lifestyle didn't change. In between my abortions, I did give birth to one child, a daughter. But when I became pregnant a fifth time, I went ahead and had my fourth and last abortion.

I've thought about why I kept doing that to myself, getting pregnant and having abortions in an endless cycle. I feel like I did it because I had to prove to myself that I was right. I had to prove to myself that it didn't hurt, that I could go through it over and over again and it wouldn't hurt. The more I did it, the less it hurt, physically and emotionally. I deadened myself to pain—and to right and wrong. Until finally, with the last one, it didn't hurt at all. It was one of the "quickies" at the clinic. You go in, pop a Valium, take a shower, hop up on the table, they suck it out, and it's "adios, hope we never see you again." On the way out the door, they hand you a brown paper sack full of birth control: foam and prophylactics and things. The father of that baby, I even swindled out of him an extra three hundred dollars, to keep my mouth shut. I went out and bought myself some new clothes after the abortion, that same afternoon. And then I got drunk that night.

I started to think about my life then—something clicked in me. I began to realize that everything I had done—the abortions, drugs, affairs, depressions—had all been a result of the circumstances of my first abortion. After that, I couldn't make any decisions at all. I knew that all the sex and drugs were wrong, but my mind was so clouded with negatives that I wasn't in any position to get my life straightened out. I just went with the flow of everything around me. I don't want to totally blame the doctor and other people involved with my first abortion, because I know that in the end I made that decision. But my decision to abort distorted my ability to make other decisions.

It's amazing how you can think that you know all the answers, and that what you're doing is right and good. And then ten years down the road you look back at your actions, and you realize that you were just living a bunch of lies, and that each lie just seems to compound the other ones and force them deeper and deeper into my subconscious. It has taken me so long to admit and discuss this. God has healed me, and God is using my stories to heal others; and maybe, prayerfully so, He's using my stories to prevent others from doing what I did.

Thinking along those lines, I started to recover. I married my high school sweetheart, the only man I ever really loved, and the man I knew the Lord wanted me to marry. We tried to conceive a child. I had a miscarriage; then I had an ectopic pregnancy, which resulted in the loss of twins. At that time I asked my doctor if this was all related to my abortions, and he very hesitantly suggested that it was. But he was reluctant to talk about it. What he did tell me was, "Your right fallopian tube is nearly destroyed. I can't tell what the left one looks like, but I can tell you that there is no guarantee that you'll ever successfully conceive a child." They then had to remove the right tube, and didn't leave me much hope about the left one.

Fortunately for me, I had just received the Lord. Jesus made it possible for me to conceive my second and third children. But before I conceived the second child, I had yet another miscarriage. Then again before my third child, I miscarried.

Please go public with my story. I have nothing to hide. In fact, I have everything to share. If my stories, no matter how badly they hurt or embarrass me, will prevent one baby from being destroyed, it's worth that to me; it's worth a lot.

T H R E E

The Physical Risks of Abortion

Abortion is a surgical procedure in which a woman's body is forcibly entered and her pregnancy is forcibly "terminated." Because it is intrusive, and because it disrupts a natural process (pregnancy), abortion poses both short-term and long-term risks to the health and well-being of the aborted woman. Abortion is never without risks.

A few abortion advocates continue to insist that abortion is so safe as to be virtually "risk free," but such claims are exaggerations resulting from some blind belief in the slogans and clichés fostered by the early abortion reformers.[1] In contrast to these few abortion zealots, most defenders of abortion, particularly those in the health fields, admit that there are inherent risks to abortion. Within the medical profession the intense debate is not over whether there are risks or not but over how often complications will occur. Some claim the risks are "acceptable," while others insist they are not.

Answering the question "How safe is abortion?" is crucial to any public policy on abortion; but it is even more crucial to the women facing the abortion decision. Unfortunately for hundreds of thousands of women, their "safe and easy" abortions proved to be neither safe nor easy. Even more outrageous is the fact that almost none of these women were given a realistic assessment of the risks of abortion.

A Systematic Cover-up

Maintaining abortion's image of "safety" is important to groups supporting abortion for a variety of reasons. Obviously, for abortion referral agencies, abortion counselors, and the abortionists themselves, financial success depends upon their ability to assure clients that abortion is "safe." For population control groups that encourage abortion, achieving their long-range goals for population control depends on their ability to promote abortion as a "safe" and even "preferable" alternative to childbirth. And finally, the ideological success of the pro-choice philosophy in feminism depends on the "desirability" of abortion. After all, if abortion is found to be dangerous to women, its legalization can hardly be claimed as a triumph for "women's rights." For these reasons and others, abortion providers, population controllers, and pro-choice feminists are all anxious to believe that abortion is safe, and they are even more anxious to spread this belief to the general public. They support the contention that abortion is "relatively" safe by citing national statistics which report a "low" incidence of abortion-related deaths. But are these statistics accurate? Probably not.

In the first place, accurate statistics are scarce because the reporting of complications is almost entirely at the option of abortion providers. In other words, abortionists are in the privileged position of being able to hide any information which might damage their reputations or trade.

How can this be so?

Federal court rulings have sheltered the practice of abortion in a "zone of privacy." This prohibits any meaningful form of state or federal regulation other than broad "general requirements as to the maintaining of sanitary facilities and . . . minimal building code standards . . . ."[2] As a result, any laws which attempt to require that deaths and complications resulting from abortion be recorded, much less reported, are unconstitutional.[3] Thus the only information available on abortion complications is the result of data which is *voluntarily* reported. Since abortionists want to hide their failures, underreporting of complications is the rule rather than the exception.[4]

The deliberate underreporting of abortion complications occurs primarily for three reasons: 1) Abortionists are seeking to protect their personal and professional reputations; 2) By minimizing the existence of unfavorable records, abortionists can minimize the availability of damaging evidence in the event of malpractice suits; and 3) Abortionists want to maintain the general myth that abortion is safe.

THE PHYSICAL RISKS OF ABORTION

But even assuming that abortionists were totally willing to report complications, underreporting would still occur for other reasons:

1) Most outpatient abortion clinics do not provide follow-up examinations. Without these, the clinics simply assume there are no complications unless they receive a complaint. Other clinics do provide post-abortion exams, but these are usually brief and superficial.

2) Even if a post-abortion exam is insisted upon, conditions which may develop into long-range complications, such as sterility or an incompetent uterus, are not easily detectable without prolonged surveillance.

3) Many women hide their identities when seeking an abortion and may fail to return for a post-abortion exam even when one is available.

4) Over 60 percent of the women who need emergency treatment following an outpatient abortion go to a nearby hospital instead of going back to the abortionist. In these cases, an abortionist may never know that a complication occurred.[5]

5) When women are treated for long-term complications such as infertility, they may hide their past abortion experience or simply not realize that it is relevant.[6]

What all these factors add up to is simply this: complication records from outpatient clinics are virtually inaccessible, or nonexistent, even though these clinics provide the vast majority of all abortions. Even in Britain where reporting requirements are much better than in the United States, medical experts believe that less than 10 percent of abortion complications are actually reported to government health agencies.[7]

When treatment for a complication takes place in a hospital, however, the records are much more likely to be contributed to the health agencies which compile national health statistics; but this still does not mean that the records will be completely accurate. Instead, complications due to abortion are often listed under other categories. Sometimes this is done to disguise the cause of death. In one case, for example, a 21-year-old woman died only a few hours after a saline abortion, and her death was creatively listed as due to "spontaneous gangrene of the ovary."[8] The reason for the cover-up is relatively obvious—abortionists don't want to be held legally and financially responsible for the complications and deaths which are a natural result of "routine" abortions.

In many cases, even physicians who are not involved with performing abortions contribute to the cover-up. There are primarily two reasons for this: loyalty to one's patient, and loyalty to one's profession. Examples of the first category occur when young women who have been aborted want to hide the cause of their hospitalization from their families and friends, even when they are in danger of dying.[9] Thus, what begins as an attempt to avoid embarrassing a woman and her family ends up as an omission of facts in the hospital's official records and, subsequently, as a distortion of national abortion statistics.

Secondly, there exists in the medical profession, as in most professions, an unstated code of "brotherhood" which discourages pointing fingers at the mistakes of other physicians. Therefore, in keeping with the general rule of the fraternity, "see no evil; speak no evil," the physician attending an abortion complication at a local hospital is quite likely to simply treat the condition and avoid recording that it was the result of an incomplete abortion performed by his colleague down the street.

All of the above factors have been mentioned to explain the lack of complete records on abortion complications in America. Political and financial motives, as well as respect for personal privacy, all hinder the reporting of these statistics. With these factors in mind, it should be remembered that the figures which will be cited in the following sections are *minimum* complication rates based on partial studies. They reflect only what is voluntarily reported, not what is actually happening.

Abortion Morbidity

The rate of complications following a medical procedure is known as the morbidity rate. For the reasons cited above, the morbidity rate due to abortion in America is unknown, though a few hospital studies have been done. But while the rate of complications is uncertain, the variety of complications which occur is well documented.

Over one hundred potential complications have been associated with abortion. Some of these complications can be immediately spotted, such as a puncture of the uterus or other organs, convulsions, or cardiac arrest. Other complications reveal themselves within a few days, such as a slow hemorrhage, pulmonary embolisms, infection and fever. Still other complications are long-term in nature, usually the result of damage to the reproductive system, and may result in chronic infection, an inability to carry a subsequent pregnancy to term, or sterility. These latent complications may not be apparent until a later pregnancy is attempted or until the uterus is so infected as to require removal. Thus, an abortion recorded as complication-free in a short-term study might in fact have caused long-term damage. Thus, as many investigators have discovered, short-term studies of abortion complications reveal only the tip of the iceberg. Indeed, the longer women are kept under surveillance after an abortion, the higher are the reported rates of latent morbidity.[10] Women who may appear physically unaffected by an abortion after a one year follow-up may be found to be severely effected by the abortion as many as ten to fifteen years later.

Because of the large number of possible complications, it is difficult for any medical study to check for them all, especially the more elusive ones. Furthermore, because of the great time variation between short-term complications and long-term complications, no major scientific studies have been done to tabulate both.

After noting all of these qualifications, a few general observations can be made. First, every type of abortion procedure carries significant risks. Second, the earlier the abortion is done, the lower is the rate of immediate and short-term "major" complications. Third, every type of abortion procedure poses a significant long-term threat to a woman's reproductive health. Fourth, the younger the patient, the greater the long-term risks to her reproductive system.

Overall, the rate of immediate and short-term complications is no less than 10 percent. This figure is based on a *reported* 100,000 abortion complications in 1977, when the total number of legal abortions in that year was approximately one million.[11] This 10 percent morbidity rate, it should be remembered, is an undisputed *minimum* rate for immediate and short-term complications. It does not include unreported complications or long-range complications such as infertility. As we will see, the evidence indicates that the actual morbidity rate is probably much higher.

Immediate and Short-term Risks

Suction Curettage

Almost 90 percent of all abortions are performed by suction curettage, commonly known as vacuum abortions. In this procedure, the vagina and cervix are forcibly dilated with progressively larger tapered cylinders called dilators. Dilation provides the abortionist with the necessary "working room" through which he inserts the abortion instruments, in this case a cutting instrument attached to a high powered vacuum (29 times more powerful than a home vacuum). With this device, the abortionist dismembers the "products of conception" (i.e., the unborn child and its placenta) and simultaneously vacuums out the pieces. Abortionists insist that in skilled hands suction curettage is the safest form of abortion. Many physicians disagree.[12]

According to two independent studies, the immediate or short-term complication rate for vacuum abortions is approximately 12 percent.[13] The reported "major" complication rate (strictly defined to include only life-threatening complications) is 4000 per million. Obviously, defining "major" complications in restrictive terms would make abortion appear safer than it really is.[14] Considering both immediate and long-term complications, a major German study found that the total morbidity rate for vacuum aspiration abortions exceeded 31 percent.[15]

Because the abortionist operates blindly, by sense of feel only, the cutting/suction device is potentially deadly. Perforation of the uterus is one of the most common complications (this can occur during dilation or evacuation) which leads to severe hemorrhage and can occasionally result in damage to other internal organs. In a few recorded cases, abortionists have inadvertently sucked out several feet of intestines in a matter of only a few seconds.[16]

Another common complication results from failure to extract all the "products of conception." If a limb or skull is left in the uterus, or if a portion of the placenta remains intact, severe infection may result, causing severe cramping and bleeding. Treatment may require another dialation followed by mechanical curettage and antibiotics. If the infection becomes too advanced or is persistent, a hysterectomy will be necessary to remove the diseased uterus.[17]

Third, as with all forms of abortion, suction curettage results in a high incidence of embolisms. An embolism is an obstruction of a blood vessel by a foreign substance such as air, fat, tissue, or a blood clot. Usually, such a blockage is minor and goes unnoticed and is eventually dissolved. But if the block occurs in the brain or heart, it may result in a stroke or heart attack. If it occurs in the lungs, it may result in a pulmonary thromboembolism. This condition may occur anywhere from two to fifty days after an abortion and is a relatively frequent major complication. In one group of abortion-related deaths, pulmonary embolisms were the second most common cause of death. Because of the nature of embolisms, these abortion fatalities are unpredictable and often unavoidable. This risk, like most others, is seldom revealed to women during counseling at abortion clinics, even though it is widely known in medical circles. Pulmonary emboli are reported to afflict about 200 aborted women each year.[18]

Fourth, due to the rich blood supply around the uterus during pregnancy, local and general anesthesia during abortions are particularly risky. Anesthesia complications during first trimester abortions are fairly common and unpredictable. When an adverse reaction to anesthetics occurs in an outpatient abortion clinic, there is generally little equipment and expertise available on the site to deal with the emergency. Convulsions, heart arrest, and death are not an uncommon result of these circumstances. In one study of 74 women killed by legal abortions, anesthesia complications ranked as the third leading cause of death. The officially reported rate of anesthesia complications is 20 per 100,000 first trimester abortions.[19]

The nine most common "major" complications resulting from vacuum abortions are: infection, excessive bleeding, embolism, ripping or perforation of the uterus, anesthesia complications, convulsions, hemorrhage, cervical injury, and endotoxic shock.[20] "Minor" complications include: minor infections, bleeding, fevers and chills, second degree burns, chronic abdominal pain, vomiting, gastro-intestinal disturbances, weight loss, painful or disrupted menstrual cycles, and Rh sensitization.[21]

A word about the last item: only 42 percent of aborted women receive Rh screening prior to their abortions; and even for the minority that are tested, the analysis of the blood samples are often rushed and inaccurate.[22] Unless a woman with Rh negative blood receives a Rho-Gam injection immediately after the abortion, sensitization may result. In a later "wanted pregnancy" this sensitization may endanger both the life of the mother and her child, a complication which could no longer be considered "minor."

Dilation and Curettage (D&C)

Dilation and curettage is very similar to suction curettage but is used primarily in late first trimester and early second trimester abortions. It differs from suction abortions in that instead of vacuuming out the "products of conception," the abortionist manually dismembers the fetus and scrapes the organs out of the uterus and into a basin. Because it uses sharper instruments and involves more scraping, D&C abortions typically result in much greater blood loss and a higher rate of overall complications.

The types of complications associated with D&C abortions are virtually the same as with vacuum abortions, but are approximately 20 percent more frequent.[23]

Saline Abortions

Each year there are between 100,000 and 150,000 second and third trimester abortions. Most of these are saline abortions. The rate of "major" complications associated with saline abortion is reported to be about five times greater than for first trimester suction abortions.[24]

In a saline abortion, also known as a "salting out," a concentrated salt solution is injected into the amniotic sack surrounding the baby. This solution burns the skin of the fetus and slowly poisons his system, resulting in vasodilation, edema, congestion, hemorrhage, shock and death.[25] This process takes from one to three hours, during which the distressed unborn kicks, thrusts, and writhes in its attempts to escape. Twelve to forty-eight hours after the child dies, the mother's hormonal system shifts in recognition of this fact and she goes into natural labor. Normally, within 72 hours after the injection, she will deliver a dead fetus.

The technique of saline abortion was originally developed in the concentration camps of Nazi Germany.[26] In Japan, where abortion has been legalized since the 1940s, the saline abortion technique has been outlawed because it is "extraordinarily dangerous."[27] Indeed, in the United States saline abortion is second only to heart transplants as the elective surgery with the highest fatality rate.[28] Despite this fact, state laws attempting to prohibit saline abortions because of their great risk to aborting women have been declared unconstitutional by the courts.[29]

Severe infections and hemorrhages are extremely common following saline abortions. In addition, seepage of the salt solution into the woman's blood system may result in life-threatening coagulation problems. Incomplete abortions and retained placentas occur in from 40 to 55 percent of all cases, the correction of which requires additional surgery. Furthermore, infections or uterine damage incurred during saline abortions frequently require removal of the uterus.[30]

Prostaglandin Abortions

In a technique similar to saline abortions, the chemical prostaglandin is injected into the amniotic fluid. But instead of killing the unborn outright, this method induces intense contractions of the uterus and causes forced labor. Usually the child dies during the trauma of premature labor, but frequently it does not. This results in one of the most disturbing "complications" of prostaglandin abortions, a live birth.

When prostaglandins were first introduced, there was great hope among abortionists that this new technique would be safer than saline injections. But when six women died and a large number of "aborted" babies were delivered *alive*, the enthusiasm for prostaglandins dwindled rapidly.[31]

Frequent complications associated with prostaglandin abortions include spontaneous ruptures in the uterine wall, convulsions, hemorrhage, coagulation defects, and cervical injury. Incomplete abortions are also very common. In these cases the decay of retained tissue may result in severe infections, prolonged hospitalization, additional surgery, and in many cases the need for an emergency hysterectomy.[32]

In sum, rather than replacing saline abortions, prostaglandins have simply caused a debate within the aborting community as to which method is the most dangerous. Oddly enough, however, although the evidence seems to indicate that prostaglandins are slightly less dangerous, most abortionists continue to prefer saline abortions. The reason for this is simple. Live births following prostaglandin abortions are extremely disturbing to both the medical staff and the mothers. In other words, a higher priority is being placed on killing the fetus than on providing the safest way for a woman to be rid of her pregnancy.[33]

The Living Complication

Except when dilation and curettage is used, second and third trimester abortions always run the risk of producing a live born aborted baby. These premature infants generally die within a few minutes or hours. Some, however, live for days, and a few live to adulthood.[34]

Besides the extraordinary trauma which a live birth abortion poses for a woman, live births constitute the most difficult ethical and legal dilemma faced by abortionists. Is a physician who is being paid to kill an unwanted fetus one moment, required to attempt to save an unexpected baby the next? According to Dr. Robert Crist, a Kansas City abortionist, "the abortion patient has a right not only to be rid of the

97

growth, called a fetus in her body, but also has a right to a dead fetus."[35] But when witnesses reported that they saw Dr. William B. Waddill choke and kill a live born baby which resulted from a nonlethal saline abortion, the physician was subjected to trial for murder.[36]

Though most doctors do not actively attempt to kill live born babies following an abortion, most do attempt to ensure death through neglect. Following most second and third trimester abortions, abortion staffs make a conscious effort *not* to discover whether the child is alive or dead. Any signs of movement or breathing which might be noticed are dismissed as "reflex," unless movement and crying reach a level which cannot be ignored. One abortionist describes his policy this way:

> At the time of delivery, it has been our policy to wrap the fetus in a towel. The fetus is then moved to another room while our attention is turned to the care of [the woman]. She is examined to determine whether complete placental expulsion has occurred and the extent of vaginal bleeding. Once we are sure her condition is stable, the fetus is evaluated. Almost invariably all signs of life have ceased.[37]

Wrapping the fetus in a towel accomplishes two things. First, it conceals all "signs of life" which may be disturbing to the patient and staff. Second, if the premature baby is not already dead, the towel will prevent the baby from getting the oxygen it needs to survive.

Most abortionists will do anything to avoid treating a live born aborted baby.[38] One of the most shocking examples occurred in Pine Bluff, Arkansas, where an abortion resulted in a kicking and screaming baby:

> In the examining room after the abortion, the doctor wrapped the baby in a towel and laid it aside while he finished caring for Marie. The infant continued to squirm and cry.
>
> Soon afterward, Marie left the doctor's office for a friend's house nearby. The physician then placed the child in a sack and gave it to one of the two friends who had accompanied Marie. . . .
>
> In a few minutes, the woman with the sack arrived at the house where Marie was waiting. She said the doctor had told her to "take it along with you, and pretty soon it will stop moving."
>
> After Marie fell asleep, the friends kept their death watch over the aborted infant until they decided to seek help.[39]

In this case, even after prolonged neglect, the baby survived. Marie, filled with guilt, is glad that her child lives.

Live birth abortions occur in the United States at a rate of 400 to 500 times per year, literally an every day experience.[40] The number may be higher, since (1) there is no effort to determine if a child is live born, and (2) most abortionists avoid reporting live birth abortions. Dr. Williard Cates, chief of abortion surveillance at the Center for Disease Control in Atlanta, describes the cover-up this way: "It's like turning yourself in to the IRS for an audit. What is there to gain? The tendency is not to report because there are only negative incentives."[41]

In order to avoid the "complication" of live births, abortionists are experimenting with more deadly techniques for second and third trimester abortions. One new technique involves the injection of a poisonous dose of digitoxin directly into the unborn child's heart. As with most experimental abortion procedures, women are generally not informed that the procedure is untested.[42] These new techniques may solve the "abortionists' dilemma," but they may also pose unforeseen dangers to the health of women.

Long-range Risks

A high risk of infection is common to all forms of abortion. Infection may result from bacteria and viruses introduced into the womb during the abortion or from the decay of damaged uterine tissue or unremoved "products of conception." In one series of 1,182 abortions which occurred under closely regulated hospital conditions, researchers found that 27 percent of the patients acquired post-abortion infections resulting in fevers lasting three days or longer.[43] The infection rate from outpatient "abortion mills" is probably much higher.

Many infections are dangerous and life-threatening, and severe pain will typically prompt the patient to seek emergency treatment. But the majority of infections are of a milder order. These lesser infections will cause only minor discomfort, if any. Eventually a woman's body will overcome these milder infections, but long-term damage may still result.

Mild or severe infections may extend from the uterine lining to the fallopian tubes or to organs adjacent to the uterus. Scar tissue left by the infection may block the fallopian tubes, resulting in total or partial infertility and an increased probability of ectopic pregnancies. If a chronic infection results, a total hysterectomy may be required several months or even years after the abortion.[44]

Studies have shown that a woman's risk of an ectopic pregnancy dramatically increases following an abortion. One study suggests that the risk increases 100 to 150 percent, another study suggests a 400 percent increased risk, and a third indicates an 800 percent increased risk.[45] Since the legalization of abortion in 1973, there has been a 300 percent increase in the occurrence of ectopic pregnancies in the United States.[46] Other countries with legalized abortion have witnessed the same effect.

Treatment of an ectopic pregnancy requires major surgery to remove the impregnated fallopian tube before it bursts. For every 100,000 cases of ectopic pregnancy, 300 women die due to rupture and hemorrhage.[47] These deaths are always listed under the "maternal mortality" category rather than as "abortion deaths," even though abortion may be the root cause of most ectopic pregnancies today.

If the scar tissue caused by post-abortion infection is severe enough to completely block the fallopian tubes, total sterility will result. Women who undergo just one induced abortion are three to four times more likely to suffer from secondary infertility than non-aborted women.[48] Numerous studies have found that 3 to 5 percent of all aborted women are inadvertently left sterile by the operation.[49] If a woman is also infected by a venereal disease at the time of her abortion, the risk of being rendered sterile is even greater.[50]

After infection, cervical damage is the next leading cause of post-abortion reproductive problems. Damage to the cervix may occur during the "scraping out" in a vacuum or D&C abortion, or during the "expulsion" in a saline or prostaglandin abortion. But undoubtedly, it is during the forced dilation of the uterus in vacuum and D&C abortions that most cervical damage is incurred.

Normally the cervix is rigid and tightly closed throughout the pregnancy. Only at the time of birth does it begin to naturally soften and open. But in an artifically induced abortion, no such natural change occurs; the cervix is hard and "green," designed by nature to resist intrusion and to protect its charge. In this context, it is clear that abortion is an attack not only on the unborn, but also on the woman's reproductive organs, which are designed to protect the child. Thus, during the forcible dilation which occurs in all early abortions, a tremendous stress is placed upon the woman's "green" cervical muscles. This stress virtually always causes microscopic tearing of the muscles, and occasionally results in severe ripping of the uterine wall (a "major" complication). According to one hospital study, 1 in 8 suction curretage abortions required stitches for cervical laceration.[51] Another study indicated that laceration of the cervix occurred in 22 percent of aborted women. Again it should be remembered that in outpatient abortion clinics, such lacerations are frequently not noticed, much less treated.

In any case, whether the dilation damage to the uterine muscles is microscopic or macroscopic, this damage frequently results in a permanent weakening of the uterus. This weakening may result in an "incompetent cervix" which, unable to carry the weight of a later "wanted" pregnancy, opens prematurely, resulting in miscarriage or premature birth.[52] For this reason, the chance that a later "wanted" child will die during pregnancy or labor is at least twice as high for previously aborted women.[53]

Cervical damage is extremely frequent in young women pregnant for the first time, because the cervix is much more rigid in women who have not previously given birth.[54] This fact is particularly unnerving since nearly 60 percent of all abortions are for first pregnancies. Most of these women will later seek a "wanted" pregnancy, but because of cervical damage they may instead face the traumas of repeated miscarriages and premature births.

According to one study, the risk of a second trimester miscarriage increases tenfold following a vaginal abortion. Similarly, the risk of premature delivery also increases eight to ten times. Though normally only 5 percent of all babies are born prematurely, this rate jumps to 40 percent among women who have had abortions.[55] In another study of first pregnancy abortions, a researcher found that 48 percent of the women studied suffered from abortion-related complications in later "wanted" pregnancies. Women in this group experienced 2.3 miscarriages for every one live birth.[56]

These figures reflect the increased risks for the average woman undergoing an abortion. But when the woman is only a teenager, the frequency and severity of the damage is even worse since a teenager's "green" cervix is still growing and changing. This fact is best illustrated in a comparative study done by Dr. J. K. Russell. In this study, Dr. Russell tracked the reproductive lives of 62 pregnant teenagers. When first pregnant, 50 of the girls had abortions, 11 gave birth and 1 miscarried. Of the 11 teenagers who gave birth, 9 later became pregnant with "wanted" children and delivered with no complications and a 100 percent success rate. Among the 50 girls who had undergone abortions, there were 47 subsequent "wanted" pregnancies. Of these 47 "wanted" pregnancies, 66 percent ended in defective births (including 19 miscarriages and seven premature births). Only 34 percent of the pregnancies among the previously aborted group ended with a full-term delivery of a healthy child.[57]

Induced abortion may cause not only cervical incompetence, but also cervical rigidity. Permanent damage to the uterine wall may result in the faulty placement and development of the placenta during later pregnancies. A 1981 study at Vanderbilt University found that after a single abortion the risk of placenta previa in later pregnancies increases seven to fifteen times.[58] Abnormal development of the placenta due to uterine damage increases the risk of fetal malformation, perinatal death, and excessive bleeding.[59]

Due to uterine damage, previously aborted women also face much more difficult and dangerous deliveries in later pregnancies. Aborted women face at least three times more labor complications than non-aborted women.[60] Previously aborted women require longer periods of labor during all three stages of labor; they are more likely to require manual or instrumental assistance to complete their labor; they are more likely to suffer from retained and adherent placenta following delivery; they are more likely to experience rupture of their uterus during labor; and they are more likely to suffer from severe hemorrhage at parturition and experience substantially greater blood losses than their non-aborted sisters.[61] In short, abortion places women and their future children at much greater risk during both their pregnancies and their deliveries.

Finally, there is a large class of long-term complications which is only now being investigated. For example, a recent study performed by California researchers found that the risk of breast cancer doubled among women who abort their first pregnancy.[62] Two known studies are now underway to determine if there is a link between abortion and the high incidence of cervical cancer among aborted women.[63]

The explanation for increased breast cancers and cervical cancers among aborted women lies in the unnatural disruption of their changing bodies. Early in pregnancy, the breasts and uterus undergo a rapid growth and change. Suddenly disrupting these changes before their completion may render these cells susceptible to "neoplastic stimuli" (tumor initiation) or might hasten the growth of cells which are already malignant.

Only the future will reveal how many other side effects result from abortion. But already it is clear that because of its many immediate and long-term complications, legal abortion is perhaps the leading cause of gynecological and obstetric emergencies in the United States.[64] This is reflected in the trend in medical malpractice insurance toward creating a new "ultra-risk" category for surgeons who perform abortions.[65]

Evidence from Other Countries

As we mentioned at the beginning of this chapter, the American "experiment" with abortion has yet to provide any comprehensive data. The abortion industry has everything to gain by withholding data, and nothing to lose. Most of the data that is available comes from hospital supervised abortions, which are not representative of the "average" clinic abortion; and even these studies are usually narrow in range and scope.

But though information about abortion complications is generally obstructed in the United States, this is not always the case in other countries which have had longer experience with legal abortion. In particular, many European nations have socialized medicine, including Britain and Sweden, and in these cases government control provides a more systematic method for the gathering of abortion statistics than is available in the United States—though this does not necessarily mean that these governments provide an impartial tabulation and release of these statistics.

Overall, however, the foreign experience with abortion complications seems to confirm the worst fears about its health risks in America. Abortion proponents in this country typically ignore foreign data or insist that such figures are not representative of the "better health care" in America. But in fact, medical care in many European countries is regarded by medical authorities as superior to that in America. In addition, because many of these countries have socialized medicine, most of their abortions are performed in hospitals, with little regard for cost, and the patient is hospitalized for two to three days in order to watch for complications and treat them promptly. Since Americans rely primarily on outpatient abortion clinics, the abortion complication rate in America is probably much higher than that experienced in these other countries.[66] Here are a few examples.

Japan

Japan has had the most experience with legal abortion. It was first legalized there as part of the population control measures established during the American occupation following World War II.

According to one Japanese study, women undergoing abortions experienced the following complications: 9 percent were subsequently sterile; 14 percent suffered from recurring miscarriages; 17 percent experienced menstrual irregularities; 20–30 percent reported abdominal pain, dizziness, headaches, etc.; and there was a 400 percent increase in ectopic pregnancies.[67]

England

In Great Britain the high complication rate associated with abortion has been a major subject of concern among physicians. Records at one university hospital revealed a 27 percent infection rate among aborted patients; 9.5 percent hemorrhaged enough to require blood transfusions; 5 percent of early vacuum and D&C abortions tore the cervical muscle; and 1.5 percent perforated the uterus. Anticipating the counterargument that more skilled abortionists would have fewer complications, the author of this study made special note that: "It is significant that some of the more serious complications occurred with the most senior and experienced operators. This emphasizes that termination of pregnancy is neither as simple nor as safe as some advocates of abortion-on-demand would have the public believe."[68] In other words, abortion is an inherently risky and intrusive operation, and even the most skillful surgery will result in complications.

Another detailed British study found that many complications are easily missed without repeated follow-ups. The authors stated that "the prevalence of morbidity following induced abortion . . . depends on how long the women concerned are kept under surveillance after the operation. *The longer the surveillance, the higher the morbidity reported.*" [emphasis their own] Two meticulous studies cited by these investigators revealed 35.6 percent and 36 percent of aborted women suffer from abortion-related complications.[69]

Sweden and Norway

Swedish and Norwegian studies indicate an incidence of total sterility following 4 to 5 percent of all abortions, a figure which is less than half the reported rate in Japan.[70] Assuming this conservative 4 percent figure is applicable in America where 1.5 million women are aborted each year, one would conclude that 60,000 women per year are inadvertently rendered sterile by abortion. Most of these women are aborting a first pregnancy and will later be seeking a "wanted" pregnancy in vain.

Hungary

First trimester abortions have been allowed in Hungary under increasingly permissive laws for about thirty years. During the course of this time, the rates of miscarriages, premature births, low birth weights, and damaged infants have increased in proportion to abortions provided, despite continually improving health care. Perinatal mortality alone has doubled since abortion was made easily available.

These figures have led Hungarian health authorities to declare that "the cause-effect correlation between first trimester induced abortion and subsequent difficulties in pregnancy has been established beyond a doubt." And for this reason the Hungarian government has passed a law with "numerous restrictions for women seeking abortions early in their reproductive life, but without restriction for those who, having borne two or three children, had presumably completed their families. The officially stated purpose of the new law was to avoid the negative effects of induced abortion upon subsequent gestations."[71]

Czechoslovakia

Under socialized medicine in Czechoslovakia, abortion is legal up to twelve weeks after conception. Vacuum curettage is used and the patient is kept under observation in the hospital for three to five days, ordered to take bed rest for one week at home, and paid by insurance for her lost wages. More ideal conditions could hardly be expected, but the complication rate is still high. According to a thirteen-year study done at a university hospital in Prague:

> Acute inflammatory conditions occur in 5 percent of the cases, whereas permanent complications such as chronic inflammatory conditions of the female organs, sterility and ectopic pregnancies are registered in 20–30 percent of all women. . . . A high incidence of cervical incompetence resultant from abortion has raised the incidence of spontaneous abortions [miscarriage] to 30–40 percent.[72]

In sum, the Czechoslovakia Deputy Minister of Health states that, "Roughly 25 percent of the women who interrupt their first pregnancy have remained permanently childless."[73]

Why The Truth Remains Buried

The morbidity rate from induced abortion is undoubtedly high. Some abortion advocates may continue to argue about the particulars, just as tobacco companies continue to insist that the dangers of smoking are exaggerated, but the trend of the evidence is certainly clear. Compared to childbirth, the morbidity rate of abortion is astronomical. For childbirth, the overall maternal morbidity rate is approximately 2 percent.[74] But as we have seen, the reported immediate complication rate, alone, of abortion is no less than 10 percent. In addition, studies of long-range complications show rates no less than 17 percent and frequently report complication rates in the range of 25 to 40 percent. One public hospital has even reported an overall complication rate following abortion of 70 percent![75]

The extraordinary degree to which this evidence has been suppressed and ignored is shocking but instructive. When contrasted to the regulation and publicity surrounding other potentially dangerous activities, the silence surrounding abortion morbidity is deafening. For example, the FDA frequently bans drugs for fear of complications which are much less documented or severe than in the case of abortion. Similarly, the Surgeon General requires each pack of cigarettes to carry a warning of the potential dangers of smoking, and the newspapers and magazines are full of health and safety warnings about automobiles, toys, acid rain, saccharin, etc. But except for some minor activity within anti-abortion groups, virtually nothing is being done by the abortion industry, the government, or the general press to warn women considering abortions about its high rate of short-term and long-term risks.

Indeed, the Supreme Court has given abortionists "super rights" which allow them to use any abortion technique they desire, no matter how dangerous it may be, and the Court has made abortion clinics immune from any requirements for minimal standards of counseling.[76] According to this latter "constitutional right," abortion clinics are allowed, and even encouraged, not to tell their clients any of the risks associated with abortion. Instead, patients are to be kept in ignorance and thereby "protected" from "unnecessary fears" which may lead them to reevaluate the desirability of the abortion option. The Court guarantees "freedom of choice" but denies the right to "informed choice." *Abortionists can legally withhold information*, or even avoid their clients' direct questions, in order to ensure that the patient will agree to an abortion which will be, they assume, "in her best interests."

All this silence has led one British surgeon to complain that:

There has been almost a conspiracy of silence in declaring its [abortion's] risks. Unfortunately, because of emotional reactions to legal abortion, well-documented evidence from countries with a vast experience of it receives little attention in either the medical or lay press. This is medically indefensible when patients suffer as a result. . . . [The] termination of pregnancy is neither as simple nor safe as some advocates of abortion-on-demand would have the public believe.[77]

Why is there such widespread silence about the dangers of legal abortion? Wasn't abortion legalized in order to *improve* health care for women rather than to encourage them to take unnecessary risks?

The answers to these questions are complex. We will deal with them at length later on. For now it is sufficient to say that there are very definite pro-abortion forces in this country who seek to encourage increasing numbers of abortions without regard to the risks which women will face. These include government and private agencies who seek to promote abortion as a means of population control, groups which promote abortion particularly among the poor for eugenic reasons, and clinics and doctors who perform abortions for financial gain. Obviously, none of these truly pro-abortion groups wants to admit to the dangers of abortion; they would rather be inclined to contribute to a cover-up.

But perhaps more important to the present discussion is the large number of people who do not want to know about the dangers of abortion. These people do not advocate abortion for its own sake, they are simply "pro-choice." But they create and maintain the social attitude that abortion is the "easy way out"—for mother, child, relatives and friends, and even for society as a whole. These people never encourage abortion for reasons of social engineering or personal gain. Instead, they support the option of abortion with paternalistic advice like, "It would probably be the best thing for everyone, honey."

This "pro-choice" option allows the paternal friend and society at large to avoid the costly, time-consuming, emotional involvement which would otherwise be necessary to deal with these mothers and their "unwanted" children in positive, creative ways. Abortion is a convenient "band-aid" solution to real problems, a half-hearted solution promoted by those with a half-hearted concern. Thus, many pro-choice advisors simply *want* to believe abortion is safe because they want to have a "solution" to offer women with problem pregnancies which does not involve a demanding personal relationship with the woman and her child.

Finally, abortion, like most evils, is tempting. Because it promises to solve so neatly a potentially major problem, many women themselves want to believe in it, too. Abortion is a promise too valued to allow it to be tarnished by facts.

But if there are really so many complications from abortion, why aren't they more apparent? Why haven't more aborted women complained before now? There are many reasons for this.

1)   Many women have tried to tell others about the physical damage they incurred from abortions. But they usually find themselves ignored and turned away: "You're just the exception. Everyone knows that abortion is safe. Unfortunately, you were the victim of an accident, but don't be bitter and say it happens all the time." If people don't want to hear, they won't hear. Furthermore, educated Americans tend to place far greater credibility on statistics than on personal testimony. Unfortunately, however, it is the abortionists who control the statistics.

2)   Most abortionists require clients to sign forms relieving them from responsibility for complications—after they assure women that complications are rare, of course. What most women do not know, however, is that these release forms are not legally binding.[78] Abortionists require these forms to be signed only to intimidate and bluff women into submission, if and when complications develop. These release forms are only an extra tool in the abortionists' arsenal of deceit.

3)   In most cases abortion is a personal or family secret. Only in the most radical feminist circles is abortion something that women talk about with aplomb. This air of secrecy and shame compels a majority of abortion's victims to be silent about the complications they experienced. Few are willing to air their grievances in public, especially if the complications are "minor" and can be "fixed" or endured. Like the abortion itself, the complications are something many women simply try to put out of their minds.

4) Especially with regard to the long-term complications, most women simply cannot be sure that their problems relate to the original abortion. Even if a gynecologist knows that a woman's problems may be abortion-related, he may not tell her so—if only to avoid rubbing salt into her wounds.

5) Many women view the complications as punishment which they "deserve" for having undergone an abortion in the first place. For this reason, they remain silent about both their "sin" and their "punishment."

6) Finally, although it is the women who experience the pain and complications of abortion, it is the abortionists who keep and control the statistics. In other words, the party which suffers least, and indeed has the most to gain, also has complete control of the information.

The Underreporting of Abortion Deaths

On June 14, 1977, Barbaralee Davis underwent a routine suction abortion at the Hope Clinic for Women in Granite City, Illinois. After the customary period of observation in the clinic's recovery room, she complained of weakness and was sent home with instructions to rest. Alone in her bedroom, she slept and quietly bled to death. Her body was found less than twelve hours after the abortion. After the incident was reported in the local press, Michael Grobsmith, chief of the Illinois Department of Public Health's Division of Hospitals and Clinics, commented on the death by saying: "It's unfortunate, but it's happening every day in Chicago, and you're just not hearing about it."[79]

One year later, during an investigation of only four Chicago-based clinics (in a state with over twenty abortion clinics), the *Chicago-Sun Times* uncovered twelve abortion deaths that had never been reported.[80] Even when abortion-related deaths such as these are uncovered, they are generally not included in the "official" total since they were not reported as such on the original death certificates.[81] If there are this many unreported abortion deaths in one city from only a few clinics, in a state with regulations as strict as any allowed by the courts, how many more are there across the country?

As with other abortion complications, there is no accurate mechanism for gathering statistics about abortion-related deaths. The Supreme Court's abortion cases have struck down all requirements for reporting abortion-related complications and deaths on the grounds that such reporting might discourage women from seeking abortions.[82] This new freedom allows abortionists and others to disguise abortion deaths under other categories when filling out death certificates.[83] Even the Center for Disease Control, a data bank for U.S. health statistics which is strongly pro-abortion in its editorial opinions, admits that the reported rate of deaths due to legal abortion is being deliberately kept low through selective underreporting.[84]

But though there are no precise figures for the number of deaths from legal abortions, there is no doubt that the figure is much higher than the officially reported totals. On one occasion, for example, Dr. Lester Hibbard, chairman of the Los Angeles County Medical Society Committee, which is charged with keeping track of maternal deaths, told a newspaper reporter that there had been only four abortion-related deaths officially reported as such. But, Dr. Hibbard added, he *personally* knew of at least four other deaths which had followed legal abortions but had not been reported as such on the death certificates. Furthermore, he said he was certain that these unreported abortion deaths were only the tip of the iceberg.[85] According to one estimate, less than 10 percent of deaths from legal abortion are reported as such.[86]

The degree to which abortion deaths are underreported is hinted at in the results of a 1974 survey which asked 486 obstetricians about their experience with complications resulting from legal abortions. Of the doctors surveyed, 91 percent had treated patients for complications, 87 percent had hospitalized one or more patients, and 6 percent (29 doctors) reported one or more patients having died from a legal abortion.[87] It can be assumed that these doctors witnessed these deaths between the years 1968 and 1974, since 1968 was the first year in which abortion became legal in some states. Therefore, extrapolation of this 6 percent sample rate to all 21,700 obstetricians in the U.S. in 1974 would indicate a probability of 1,300 patient deaths due to abortion-related complications during the six-year period between 1968 and 1974. But the actual number of deaths from legal abortions reported for that period was 52, only *5 percent* of the projected figure.[88] In order for the reported figure of only 52 deaths during this period to be accurate, the 486 doctors surveyed in this study must have coincidentally seen *over half* of all the nation's deaths from legal abortion—a very unlikely coincidence. Finally, this projection of 1,300 deaths between 1968 and 1974 is based on a survey of obstetricians only. Aborted women who died under the care of general practitioners or other health professionals would not be included in this survey, so the actual mortality rate, and cover-up, could be even worse.

What should be clear is that there is a major flaw in the mortality statistics for legal abortion. It is quite possible that only 5 to 10 percent of all deaths resulting from legal abortion are being reported as abortion-related. Even if 50 percent were being accurately reported, that extra margin of risk is far greater than women are being led to believe. Indeed, based on the *reported* abortion deaths alone, abortion is already the fifth leading cause of maternal death in the United States.[89]

The most common causes of death from legal abortion include: hemorrhage, infection, blood clots in the lungs, heart failure, and anesthetic complications.[90] These can occur after any type of abortion procedure and are generally unpredictable. Some of these deaths result because outpatient clinics are seldom equipped to handle an emergency. But more frequently the death occurs *after* the patient leaves the clinic. According to one study: "43% of abortion deaths occurred on the day of the abortion, 4% on the second postabortion day, 22% on the third day, and 30% thereafter."[91] Obviously, fifteen minutes or an hour in a clinic recovery room (usually under the supervision of a staff person without medical training) is not sufficient to ensure that an abortion is "complication free." Without daily follow-ups, infections, blood clots, and slow hemorrhages will continue to take their toll.

Furthermore, it should be noted that abortion actually increases the chance of maternal death in later pregnancies. Medical researchers Margaret and Arthur Wynn, who favor abortion on request, state in their comprehensive study of the effects of abortion on later pregnancies that: "Any patient who has had a previous history of an abortion should be regarded as a high risk patient."[92] This is because abortion dramatically increases the risks of ectopic pregnancies, cervical incompetence, miscarriage, and other complications of pregnancy. These conditions increase the risk of death for both mother and child in later pregnancies. But despite the fact that abortion is indirectly responsible for these deaths, deaths resulting from these conditions will be included only under the maternal mortality column; they will *not* be proportionately attributed to abortion.[93]

Finally, the present claims for a low abortion mortality rate in the United States should be compared to experience prior to *Roe v. Wade* when states with permissive abortion laws were allowed to require reporting of abortion-related deaths. Of course, this did not guarantee that all deaths would be reported, but failure to report might result in legal problems and even the revoking of a physician's license. Under these conditions, Oregon reported 13.9 abortion deaths per 100,000 legal abortions compared to only 8.4 maternal deaths per 100,000 live births. Maryland reported 40.5 deaths per 100,000 legal abortions as compared to 23.1 maternal deaths per 100,000 live births.[94] According to these pre-*Roe* state statistics, the mortality rate for legal abortion is nearly twice as high as the overall maternal mortality rate.

The only state which claimed an abortion mortality rate lower than the maternal mortality rate was New York. There, a public health official, citing the official records, claimed only 5.3 deaths per 100,000 abortions. But these New York figures are widely recognized as invalid because only 32 percent of all the abortions performed were included in the follow-up. Any deaths among the other 68 percent would not have been recorded. Indeed, even among the abortion-related deaths that were reported, at least seven known deaths were arbitrarily excluded from the "official" total for strained, technical reasons. In addition, a large number of other known deaths which had occurred after the patients had flown back to their homes out of state were also excluded from the "official records."[95]

In contrast to New York's "official" safety record for abortion, a 1971 study done by Dr. Joseph J. Rovinsky concluded that the actual abortion mortality rate in New York was no less than 38 per 100,000.[96] Indeed, by 1972, the year prior to *Roe v. Wade,* the *reported* number of women who had died from legal abortions exceeded the number dying from illegal abortions by almost two to one.[97] Only after all requirements for reporting were struck down did the number of reported deaths from legal abortion even begin to level off.[98]

The experience in other countries also confirms that abortion mortality rates, even during the first trimester, are invariably larger than their respective maternal mortality rates. For example, in Sweden the death rate for legal abortion is 39 per 100,000, and in Denmark the reported death rate is approximately 30 per 100,000. These rates are more than double the maternal mortality rates of these countries.[99] Canadian figures list 36 deaths per 100,000 abortions.[100] And in one British study at Glasgow University, fifteen deaths were found in a series of 20,000 legal abortions yielding an unexpected fatality rate of 75 per 100,000.[101]

In sum, what can we say about abortion mortality rates? First, not all abortion-related deaths are reported as such. Indeed, circumstantial evidence indicates that only a minority of abortion deaths are reported as abortion-related. Second, for the average, healthy woman, *abortion is far more risky than childbirth.*[102]

But it should be remembered that in terms of practical decision-making for the individual, mortality rates for both abortion and child-birth are virtually meaningless. As Dr. Thomas Hilgers points out:

> If a woman achieves pregnancy and carries it through to term with the delivery of the infant, her chances of surviving that pregnancy are 99.99 percent. In fact, her chances of surviving that pregnancy are higher, at all age levels, than her chances of simply surviving the next one year of life.[103]

Likewise, the chances of surviving an abortion are only slightly worse or slightly better, depending on whom you believe. The vast majority of pregnant women will survive either childbirth or abortion.

In terms of a pregnant woman's decision-making, comparing the *complication* rates of abortion and childbirth is far more important than the mortality rates. When judging the comparative health risks of abortion versus childbirth on the basis of morbidity rates, it is an indisputable fact that the risk of long-term complications following an abortion is ten to twenty times greater than the risk of *any* complications following childbirth.[104]

The question which women considering abortion must face is not so much a question of their survival as it is a question of how *well* they will survive. Since abortion is frequently damaging to a woman's reproductive system, women who may wish to have children at a later date are especially at risk.[105]

Summary

This chapter has dealt with the subject of physical complications related to abortion. The subject is complex because so little is known. The reporting of abortion complications is not required by law and there are numerous motives for not reporting them. All evidence seems to confirm that *underreporting is the rule rather than the exception.*

But even assuming that all complications and deaths from legal abortion are reported, the safety record of abortion is dismal. The *reported* rate of immediate complications following induced abortion is fully 10 percent. The frequency of late complications is not documented in American statistics, but based on foreign experience, long-term complications can be expected in from 17 to 50 percent of all aborted women. Most of these long-term complications result in partial or total infertility, and an increased risk of ectopic pregnancies, miscarriages, and premature births. These risks are especially high among young women who have not yet had their families.

The evidence overwhelmingly proves that the morbidity and mortality rates of legal abortion are several times higher than that for carrying a pregnancy to term. But this fact has been largely suppressed in America for political and population control reasons.

All of these points, of course, are open to dispute to the degree that it is impossible to prove the cause of any health problem. Just as tobacco growers and cigarette companies continue to claim that the "causal link" between smoking and lung cancer has not yet been "proven," so do abortion providers insist that the dangers of abortion are still "uncertain."

But one thing is certain. Despite the legalization of abortion, complications and deaths continue to occur, and little or nothing is being done to warn women about the possibility of such negative results. No one doubts that legal abortion is marginally safer than illegal abortion, but neither is there any doubt that decriminalization has encouraged more women to undergo abortions than ever before. Risk goes down, but numbers go up. As we will see in later chapters, this combination means that though the odds of any particular woman suffering ill effects from an abortion have dropped, the *total* number of women who suffer and die from abortion is far greater than ever before.

Before looking at that comparison, however, there is another area of post-abortion complications which needs to be examined. These complications are not physical, but they are certainly no less painful.

F   O   U   R

The Psychological Impact of Abortion

Even more so than with physical complications, the psychological damage caused by abortion is practically impossible to quantify. Once again, the lack of comprehensive studies in America is due in part to obstructionism by abortion providers who keep few, if any, records.[1] But even assuming that complete records were kept, psychological complications are never easily quantified. By comparison, it is much easier to count scarred uteruses than scarred psyches.

As with physical complications, there are two distinct levels of dispute. On one level, some abortion proponents have confused the issue with numerous unscientific opinion papers insisting that psychological problems associated with abortion are a myth, but these efforts are so obviously biased that they tend towards the ludicrous.[2]

But even when more objective studies are done, the biases of researchers may still be evident, particularly in the ways in which they define "significant psychiatric sequelae" (aftereffects). For example, studies done by abortion advocates typically count only women *hospitalized* with mental breakdowns as victims of post-abortion sequelae, whereas anti-abortion researchers will always include women treated on an outpatient basis as well. Thus, while both pro- and anti-abortion researchers agree that some women are not capable of dealing with post-abortion sequelae, they disagree as to whether psychological discomfort alone, even when bearable or intermittant, should be considered "significant."

Besides the dispute over defining "significant" sequelae, the process of documenting the rate of post-abortion sequelae is further complicated by delayed reactions. A woman that a six-month post-abortion survey declares "well-adjusted" may experience severe trauma on the anniversary of the abortion date, or even many years later. This fact is attested to in psychiatric textbooks which affirm that: "The significance of abortions may not be revealed until later periods of emotional depression. During depressions occurring in the fifth or six decades of the patient's life, the psychiatrist frequently hears expressions of remorse and guilt concerning abortions that occurred twenty or more years earlier."[3] In one study, the number of women who expressed "serious self-reproach" increased fivefold over the period of time covered by the study.[4]

Often the delayed trauma from a previous abortion will rise in association with other causes for anxiety, including such incidents as the death of a loved one; the failure to conceive or the loss of a "wanted" child; the birth of a niece, nephew, or grandchild; or seeing a child or young adult who would be about the same age as the aborted child.[5] Miscarriage of a "wanted" baby is a particularly common occasion for renewal of post-abortion anxieties. If and when the woman learns that the miscarriage may have been due to a previous abortion, the guilt and anguish can be overwhelming. In this sense, physical complications from abortion often contribute to psychological sequelae as well.

On an even longer timescale, it has been observed that latent anxieties over a previous abortion frequently surface only with the onset of menopause.[6] This may be due to a woman's renewed awareness of her reproductive system and the realization that there will be no more opportunities to replace the pregnancy that was "lost."

Obviously, then, the validity of studies on post-abortion sequelae are heavily dependent on the stage of the post-abortion period which they examine. Surveys which are taken within the first few weeks after an abortion invariably show lower rates of emotional distress than those which are taken months later. One reason for this is that a short-term follow-up may record the patient's temporary relief or happiness at having the dreaded procedure finally over with, or at having the cause of the temporary embarrassment removed.

A second, similar reason why short-term studies are skewed involves what psychiatrists identify as emotional paralysis, a post-abortion "numbness," which in itself may be an adverse reaction meriting psychiatric treatment.[7] Like shell-shocked soldiers, many aborted women are unable to truly express their emotions. Their focus is primarily on having survived the ordeal, and they are at least temporarily out of touch with their inner feelings.

Third, short-term studies are of little use because many women, even those who are not "numbed" by their experiences, are simply unwilling to expose their emotional turmoil. The wounds of abortion, at this point, are too fresh, too tender to be probed. For this reason, a superficial post-abortion survey will record only what the patient *wants* to feel rather than what she really feels. As one abortion counselor admits:

> Abortion is very emotional for everyone. The women think, Let's get it over with fast. They don't open up in counseling as they should. . . . So the trouble doesn't come out till afterwards and they just keep it all in. Post-abortion counseling doesn't do any good either, because if the woman has any regrets, admitting it will feed her guilt feelings even more. . . ."[8]

The tendency to conceal negative feelings can be further accentuated by the desire of the aborted woman to say what she thinks the interviewer wants to hear. If the woman thinks the counselor wants to hear her say she feels "fine," she may say so just to avoid being considered "abnormal" and thus exposed to further probing questions.[9]

These insights were confirmed by a Canadian study, which found that short-term studies using questionnaires or routine post-abortion exams always underestimate the actual rate of negative responses. These psychiatrists found that women who answered the questionnaires responded much differently when professionally interviewed in detail. One reason was that women saw questionnaires as cold, and so they answered coldly, unemotionally, "without reaching down within themselves and searching for their inmost feelings." On the other hand, when women were questioned with psychotherapy techniques, they were encouraged to grasp their emotions, understand them, and express them.[10]

Furthermore, no matter how a survey is structured, timing limitations will always exist. For example, in one study conducted by a university hospital interviews with women four weeks after abortion reported that 94 percent of the women expressed "satisfaction that [the] right decision was made." But a six-month telephone follow-up found that the "satisfaction" rate had dropped to 85 percent.[11] No further follow-up interviews were done to see if the downward trend would continue with time. Indeed, the "long-term," six-month follow-up was still extremely short since most of the aborted women had yet to face the original delivery date or the anniversary date of the abortion—both of which, we now know, can trigger latent reactions.

The final difficulty in recording post-abortion sequelae lies in the ability of women to express the root cause of their mental pain. Even assuming a willingness to discuss their post-abortion misgivings, some women are simply not consciously aware of their inner conflicts. This is because denial and suppression of negative feelings is a common reaction to abortion. In one report, a psychiatrist treated fifty women who had come to him for problems which were supposedly *not* abortion-related. But after prolonged therapy, it was discovered that their disabilities stemmed from long-buried reactions to previous abortions. On a conscious level, each of these women believed that she had effectively resolved herself to her previous abortion. Each woman believed that the psychological turmoil which had led her to seek treatment was due to other situations in her life. But in fact, they each revealed under therapy that it was unresolved conflicts associated with their abortions, hidden at a subconscious level, which were precipitating the new problems in their lives. It was only after recognizing their repressed grief that these women were able to make progress towards improving their emotional and mental states.[12]

Women such as these who suffer from abortions at a subconscious level are "walking time-bombs," waiting to explode over situations seemingly unrelated to their previous abortions. In such cases, obviously, superficial surveys or questionnaires investigating abortion sequelae will not reveal this subconscious disorder created by abortion.

Given all these variables and uncertainties, a complete quantification of post-abortion sequelae is virtually impossible. But though it can be debated as to how frequently the impact of abortion is "severe," the personal testimony on both the pro-choice and pro-life sides demonstrates that the abortion decision and its aftermath are seldom, if ever, trauma-free. Doubts, discomfort, ambivalence and tears are the rule rather than the exception, as even many pro-choice advocates admit.[13]

Psychologically, the ideal abortion is at best a neutral experience. No one looks forward to having an abortion, and even those who claim to be untroubled by it are generally anxious to avoid repeating the experience. The only positive feeling commonly expressed after abortion is an overwhelming feeling of relief. But even then, the relief which is felt is often as much relief at having the "ugly" abortion procedure over with as it is relief at no longer facing the "unwanted" pregnancy. Indeed, studies show that many women who express relief after abortion are simultaneously experiencing the mixed reactions of guilt, shame, fear, loss, anger, resentment, depression, and remorse.[14] Women experience so many emotions following an abortion that the only safe thing to say is that it takes a long time for a woman to sort through them all.

With these points in mind, it should be indicated again that the figures from the studies which follow are *minimum* rates of psychological distress among aborted women.

Statistical Reports

As we mentioned earlier, the reported ranges for "severe" post-abortion sequelae vary by a wide degree. In a survey of available studies, the Royal College of Obstetricians and Gynecologists in England observed that, "The incidence of serious, permanent psychiatric aftermath [from abortion] is variously reported as between 9 and 59%."[15] Naturally, the percentage is higher if one includes the "non-serious" and "non-permanent" aftermath.

The following is an assortment of figures given in various studies. The standards and definitions used in each study were different, and so the results cannot be added together or compared in any meaningful way. But the general trend strongly supports our own survey findings which show that significant post-abortion sequelae are common.

- A European study reported negative psychiatric manifestations following legal abortions in 55% of the women examined by psychiatrists.[16]

- In the *American Journal of Psychiatry*, researchers reported that of 500 aborted women studied, 43% showed immediate negative responses. At the time of a later review, approximately 50% expressed negative feelings, and up to 10% of the women were classified as having developed "serious psychiatric complications."[17]

■ In one of the most detailed studies of post-abortion sequelae: "Anxiety, which if present after an abortion is felt very keenly, was reported by 43.1% . . . Depression, one of the emotions likely to be felt with more than a moderate strength, was reported by 31.9% of women surveyed . . . 26.4% felt guilt, . . . [and] 18.1% felt no relief or just a bit. They were overwhelmed by negative feelings. Even those women who were strongly supportive of the right to abort reacted to their own abortions with regret, anger, embarrassment, fear of disapproval and even shame."[18] In another paper, the same group of psychiatrists reported that when detailed interviews were performed, every aborted woman, "without exception" experienced "feelings of guilt or profound regret. . . . All the women felt that they had lost an important part of themselves."[19]

■ Another study of aborted women observed that 23% suffered "severe guilt." An additional 25% were classified as suffering from "mild guilt" and exhibited symptoms such as insomnia, decreased work capacity, and nervousness.[20]

■ One research project contacted 84 women who had received legal abortions two years previously and visited them in their homes. Four of the women were embarrassed and distressed and were unwilling to talk about it, 22 expressed open feelings of guilt, 9 were classified as consciously repressing guilt feelings, and 10 were classified as having suffered "impairment of their mental health."[21]

■ One doctor reports: "Since abortion was legalized I have seen hundreds of patients who have had the operation. Approximately 10% expressed very little or no concern . . . Among the other 90% there were all shades of distress, anxiety, heartache and remorse."[22]

■ In a Canadian study it was found that up to 14% of aborted women later seek psychiatric help to cope with the abortion, and up to 10% of these were hospitalized.[23]

Even the most biased pro-abortion surveys admit that severe post-abortion psychological trauma does occur. But these investigators insist that disabling sequelae are rare, occurring in only five percent of all aborted women. One researcher even claims that "disabilitating" psychiatric problems occur in "only" one percent of aborted women.[24] But dismissing even a one percent rate of disabling sequelae with an "only" is obviously unjustifiable when the number of women undergoing abortions each year has reached such large proportions. If "only" one percent of 1.5 million women suffer severe disabling psychic trauma from abortion, that means that each year 15,000 women are so severely scarred by post-abortion trauma that they become unable to function normally. Since this one percent figure is by far the lowest claimed anywhere in the literature, the actual rate of disabling sequelae is probably much higher.

An Inside Look

Statistics can be looked at and argued about ad infinitum. But they are really valid only as indicators. The real issue is not exactly how many women suffer, but that they *do* suffer. The first several chapters of this book revealed how women themselves feel they have been affected by abortion. In this section we will take a closer look at some of the major categories of post-abortion sequelae, and at how these reactions are analyzed by psychiatrists.

Guilt and Remorse

Feelings of guilt are among the most common reactions to abortion. Sometimes the feelings of guilt are vague. Other times they are quite specific, as when a woman states, "I have murdered my baby." Often the belief that abortion is murder exists even before the abortion, yet the woman proceeds despite her qualms.[25]

Many studies have shown that unapproving attitudes towards abortion are very prevalent among aborters. Zimmerman's study, as discussed earlier, found that fully 70 percent of aborting women expressed general disapproval of abortion.[26] Another study which concentrated on unmarried adolescent aborters found that 34 percent believed abortion was wrong except for the "hard" cases such as rape, incest, or saving the mother's life. Yet despite their moral disapproval of abortion in general, many young women tend to rationalize themselves as "exceptions" to the rule.[27] This "exception" clause was enunciated by one girl who after an abortion said: "It's murder, but it's justifiable murder."[28]

Cases like these demonstrate a conscious awareness of a moral compromise. Those who submit to an abortion, even though it violated their consciences, feel that they have "copped out," betraying their values and themselves.[29] As one woman said: "We were convinced that the abortion was the best thing rather than the right thing. If you asked me how I felt about abortion, I would say I was against it. I feel very hypocritical."[30] All of this, of course, represents a severe attack upon the self-images of aborted women. It makes them feel that they are "too weak" to live the way they would want to.

Traumatic feelings of guilt from abortion have been recorded decades after the fact. Such "blood guilt" does not easily dissipate with time. Those who mention God in speaking of their guilt express two points of view. Some believe that they are forgiven by God but cannot forgive themselves. Others believe that God is punishing them through infertility, miscarriages, or through other emotional conflicts in their lives.[31]

This view that guilt feelings arise from within runs counter to the claim by some abortion advocates that guilt over abortion occurs solely because of the Christian "hang-ups" of Western civilization. If society approved of abortion, they claim, women wouldn't feel guilty. But this claim is hard pressed by the evidence from Japan, which is not a Christian culture and has had abortion-on-demand for several decades. Yet surveys there show that guilt feelings are still prevalent. According to one survey, 73.1 percent of Japanese women who have had abortions report "anguish" about what they have done.[32] Furthermore, 59 percent felt that abortion is something "very bad," 16 percent felt it was considerably bad, 17 percent felt it was somewhat bad, while only 8 percent thought it could not be considered bad. Repeated Japanese surveys showed that slightly over half believed that abortion "is bad, but cannot be helped."[33]

Guilt, it would seem, is crosscultural, rising from interior discomforts rather than from exterior expectations. Though abortion proponents will continue to claim that guilt is a social "hang-up," such claims do nothing to alleviate the pain and doubts of those who are afflicted by remorse.

Finally, it should be noted that psychiatrists believe that feelings of post-abortion guilt may eventually cause psychotic conditions if the woman's personality is not well enough integrated to handle the stress.[34]

Broken Relationships and Sexual Dysfunction

Abortions almost always result in changed attitudes toward sexual partners, usually for the worse. This fact, though never mentioned in abortion counseling, is recognized by both sides of the controversy. Pro-choice advocate Linda Bird Francke notes that almost every relationship between single people broke up either before or after the abortion.[35]

Women who have abortions, if not actually abandoned by their partners, often *feel* abandoned. This results in anger at boyfriends or husbands whom they feel failed to support or help them continue with the unplanned pregnancy. They may resent their partner for his unwillingness to "want" the baby.[36]

Women frequently feel that their partners forced them to have their abortions. Sometimes this is literally true; often it is more symbolic. Any hesitation on the part of the father to accept the pregnancy, or a statement such as "I'll go along with whatever you decide," is perceived to imply a preference for abortion, if not an insistence on abortion. Indeed, any failure on the male's part to be happy about the pregnancy may be interpreted as negativism. Since the father's attitude is a leading determinant in a woman's abortion decision, such negativism, whether real or imagined, may be the decisive factor in the abortion decision, and thus a continuing source of resentment within the relationship.

Confusion and resentment, on the other hand, can also develop on the male side of the equation. Conditioned to believe that abortion is solely the "woman's choice," many men hesitate to express their doubts about abortion, or even their excitement about being a parent. They believe that to be good partners and "liberated" lovers, they should express only support for her decision, no matter what she decides.[37] In such cases, the man may unwittingly add to the pressure to abort. Failing to urge childbirth, the man leaves the woman feeling isolated or forced to bear the weight of the decision alone. In the meantime, the man himself may inwardly feel frustrated and angry about being "helpless" to prevent the abortion.[38] Such failures to communicate openly about the abortion decision are due in part to the pro-choice rhetoric of our age. When either partner remains silent about his or her ambivalence, seeds of resentment are planted which will later emerge as a severe strain on the relationship.[39]

Sometimes women interpret the post-abortion silence and withdrawal of their partners as coldness and insensitivity, when in fact the male, too, is suffering from feelings of remorse, guilt, and loss.[40] Though each partner may have anticipated grief over the abortion, each becomes determined to accept the abortion and overcome their grief for the sake of the other. Suffering separately, they are unable to share their remorse openly without falling into accusations. One suspects that if these couples had been able to freely communicate their mutual doubts about abortion in the first place, many would have decided against it. But the choice of abortion is not an easy topic to talk about. Indeed, many deliberately hide their feelings simply because .they don't want to talk themselves out of "the practical thing to do."

Another seed for future conflict is planted when a man deliberately thrusts the weight of the decision upon the woman because he is unwilling to accept responsibility for it. This may be done because the man feels that abortion would be "convenient," even though he consciously believes it to be morally wrong. In such cases, the male may want to "wash his hands" of responsibility by insisting that it is "her body and her decision." By abandoning her to make the decision alone, he can rationalize his own innocence on one level, while on another level his isolation pressures her towards the abortion—pressure which might be increased by complaints about how *she* became pregnant. In other words, he wants the abortion, but he wants to deny responsibility for it, too.

In cases like these, however, the woman is usually aware of the duplicity, at least on a subconscious level. Though the feeling of isolation may drive her into the abortion option, she will seldom emerge without resentment towards the person who forced her to make the decision alone.

The overwhelming weight of evidence indicates that abortions performed with the hope of saving a relationship seldom succeed. If either person is unhappy with the abortion choice, or if either accepts it merely out of compromise, bitterness and resentment inevitably develop.

Abortion, it seems, always underscores the weaknesses in a relationship. As an act of conditional love which reflects an unwillingness to accept an inconvenient child, abortion also implies that the love between the adults, too, is conditional. It implies that the relationship is viable only as long as each partner is *convenient* to the other, only as long as their separate aspirations and careers are compatible. Thus the question of "should we have a child?" slips quickly into "should we continue this relationship?" Choosing to keep the child reaffirms the relationship; choosing to abort calls the relationship into question. Especially when it is the first child of a couple's union which is being aborted, the abortion symbolically represents an unwillingness to make a deeper commitment to each other. By denying the union of their flesh, the couple denies any long-range commitment to each other.

One woman, very conscious of how a child increases the bond between parents, deliberately chose abortion as a means of keeping open the possibility of divorce, even though she actually wanted a child.[41] And in still another case, a woman chose abortion out of spite for her partner, not because she was unwilling to bear the child.[42] In a case like this, the fetus is not seen as part of her body, but as a part of *his* body which is to be punished, destroyed, and expelled. Abortion is used not as a tool for liberating herself, but for wreaking vengeance on him.

Sometimes resentment is aroused over who "caused" the pregnancy, with each blaming the other for having failed to take proper contraceptive measures. Or if contraceptives were used, the couple may blame the failed contraceptive. In either case, abortion is something they feel compelled to undertake because of the contraceptive failure. Again, the abortion is not seen as an act of free choice, but as an unwanted "necessity." Abortion thus makes both man and woman feel like victims of the system, rather than liberated human beings.

In short, some level of discontent about the abortion decision always exists. And once it enters a couple's lives, its memory is a source of conflict within the relationship which can be renewed at any time. Particularly when one knows that the abortion is a sore point for the other, references to it and accusations become a weapon to belittle and hurt the spouse in later conflicts, months and even years later.[43]

Abortion strains relationships on a sexual level too. Frigidity is a common problem following an abortion, possibly because avoiding sex seems like the best way to avoid repeating the abortion experience. According to two studies, sexual coldness was expressed by 33 percent of aborted women within nine months after their abortions, and an additional 14 percent developed sexual coldness four to five years later.[44] Post-abortion shock may also result in impotence on the part of the male, sometimes only with the woman he had impregnated, other times with all women.[45]

Because abortion disrupts the woman's natural reproductive cycle, it may cause her to experience confusion about her sexual identity. Fears of infertility are common, and many women feel compelled to "prove" their sexual femininity. In these cases, rather than becoming frigid, aborted women may become promiscuous, even to the point of seeking replacement pregnancies. But even the replacement pregnancies may be aborted in a cycle of approach-avoidance conflict, causing still greater inner conflict, anger, and a sense of self-destructive martyrdom.[46]

Psychiatrist Theodore Reik has suggested an analogy for understanding the psycho-sexual trauma of abortion. For the woman, Reik suggests, abortion has an unconscious meaning comparable to that of castration for a male. It is an assault on her fertility and sexuality which may embitter her towards her partner.[47] This analysis would seem particularly accurate in the case of a woman who contacted the Pregnancy Aftermath Hotline in Milwaukee, Wisconsin. Distressed about a previous abortion, she told the hotline counselor that she felt the abortion had "castrated" her, leaving her with the feeling she was an asexual "amputee."[48]

Depression and a Sense of Loss

Depression and a sense of loss are extremely common after abortion. These "post-abortion" blues generally fade within a few months, but prolonged, deep depressions are not uncommon. Some of these deeper depressions may be unmanageable, causing an inability to concentrate or work. Some women report feeling completely immobilized by their emotional state and unable to "get interested in anyone or anything since the abortion."[49]

Uncontrollable crying is often part of post-abortion depression. Daily crying may continue for years, sometimes lasting for hours or days at a time.[50]

Most women report a "sense of loss" following their abortion. They feel empty. They feel they have lost the "family I could have had." Those who report this symptom describe a number of related reactions such as the inability to look at other babies or pregnant mothers, or a jealously of mothers. Many consciously seek a replacement pregnancy. This sense of losing a child may be exasperated by the perception of lost relationships, either the loss of a boyfriend or a deteriorating marriage.[51]

One study into the factors which motivate women to become surrogate mothers found that a disproportionate number of these volunteer mothers had previously been aborted. According to the author of the study, Dr. Philip Parker, "Some women said they wanted to be surrogates to atone for the guilt associated with previous abortion. . . ."[52]

Another psychiatrist has noted that the frequency and degree of severe depression associated with abortion is far higher than with miscarriage, even though the loss in each case is comparable. He suggests that while a miscarriage is regarded as an unfortunate accident resulting in disappointment, regret, and a sense of loss, an abortion is the result of a premeditated choice. He adds, "Even more important is the woman's realization that she is responsible for a decision which must sacrifice some important goals and values (motherhood and the value of life) in order to sustain or attain other beliefs or achievements (career, self-determination, independence.)" Though legalization has reduced the sense of guilt coming from society, it has been "at least partially replaced by an intrinsic awareness of responsibility" which increases self-accusation and self-guilt in making this compromise between conflicting values.[53]

Deterioration of Self-Image and Self-Punishment

Abortion often creates feelings of low self-esteem, feelings of having compromised values, having "murdered my child," and so on. The damage abortion inflicts on a woman's sense of confidence and self-respect is even worse when these traits are already weak. For such an "unaffirmed woman," the "consequences of induced abortion . . . consist always of a deepening of her feelings of inferiority, inadequacy, insignificance, and worthlessness."[54]

Rather than having their egos strengthened by a society which says "You can be a good mother—you can succeed," many women are encouraged to abort by a society which insists "You can't afford a child. You're not mature or stable enough to raise children. It is better to abort the child than force it to live under your inadequate care." Thus the offer of abortion becomes an implied criticism that deflates an already weakened ego. According to psychiatrist Conrad Baars, encouraging such women to abort "constitutes psychic murder."[55]

If we seek to protect and promote the mental health of women facing problem pregnancies, Dr. Baars points out, we should concentrate on offering positive, affirming support, not abortions. To affirm an unaffirmed woman, he argues, "means to accept her in her helplessness and thus also to recognize that she is not guilty of her psychic inability to welcome the child in her womb." True acceptance and love allows her to be dependent; it does not force her to feign independence or self-sufficiency. The offer of positive, life-affirming aid (affirming the value of the mother's life as well as that of her unborn child) can often be the beginning of new psychic strength and freedom. With such optimistic support, a woman faced with a problem pregnancy will no longer feel trapped by her situation and condition, no longer feel threatened by her unborn child. "But to advise her, or to insist, that she have an abortion," he concludes, "is tantamount to conveying to her that she is indeed the inferior, inadequate, and worthless person she had always felt she was, a person who could or would not even give the child within her its own life. . . ."[56]

Psychoanalysis of women experiencing post-abortion trauma has in some cases found that a woman's perceptions of parental rejection during her own childhood, particularly rejection by her mother, may prompt her to re-enact that rejection towards her own unborn child. Thus, believing that her own mother harbored infanticidal desires towards her, the woman acts out these fears by aborting her own child (a substitute victim with whom she subconsciously identifies). Abortion, in this type of case, represents a form of self-punishment by which the "rejected" woman confirms the feelings of her own rejection and low self-esteem.[57] Ironically, young women from a home environment in which they felt rejected may have sought a pregnancy in order to prove their self-worth, express their maturity, or to produce a person whom they could love and who would love them in return. But once the pregnancy is achieved, the cycle of self-punishment and self-rejection is directed at the unborn child and leads to a desire for an abortion, further self-rejection, lowered self-esteem, and so forth.

Whether it is the result of having compromised their own values or having further weakened their poor self-images, many aborted women develop patterns of self-destructive behavior in order to punish themselves for their "unworthiness." Such self-destructive behavior, called symbolic suicide, may include abuse of alcohol and drugs. Some may become obsessed with food and try to "eat their way into oblivion" or "to fill" the great emptiness they feel inside themselves. Still others may develop anorexia nervosa in a subconscious attempt to starve or "fast" themselves to death.[58]

Sometimes, accepting the frightening ordeal of abortion may itself be an act of self-punishment by the young woman seeking to atone for feelings of guilt about becoming pregnant. Pregnancy resulted from a desirable "sin," and so abortion is seen as the "pain payment" owed as penance for the illicit pleasure of intercourse. In a study of the decision-making process of abortion, Dr. Howard Fisher, a professor of psychiatry at the University of Minnesota, concludes that there is substantial evidence to believe that abortion is a symptom of underlying emotional disturbances, and a "symbol of failure." In such cases, he adds, the "physicians [may be] merely accomplices in self-destructive behavior."[59]

Suicide

Feelings of rejection, low self-esteem, guilt and depression are all ingredients for suicide, and the rate of suicide attempts among aborted women is phenomenally high. According to one study, women who have had abortions are nine times more likely to attempt suicide than women in the general population.[60]

The fact of high suicide rates among aborted women is well known among professionals who counsel suicidal persons. For example, testifying in support of parental notification prior to abortion for teenagers, Meta Uchtman, Regional Director in Ohio of a national organization called Suiciders Anonymous, reported that in a thirty-five month period the Cincinnati chapter of Suiciders Anonymous worked with 4,000 women, of whom 1,800 or more had abortions. Of these, 1,400 were between the ages of 15 and 24, the age group with the highest suicide rate in the country. She also pointed out in her testimony that there has been a dramatic rise in the suicide rate since the early 1970s when abortion was first legalized. Between 1978 and 1981 alone, the suicide rate among teenagers increased 500 percent.[61]

Other Sequelae

The ways in which post-abortion sequelae are manifested are as numerous as the number of women who are aborted. Symptoms of inner distress are filtered by individual personalities and thus are displayed in personalized manners. We have explored some of the most common reactions and attempted to explain some of the underlying psychologies. We will now briefly mention some of the most commonly reported "minor" symptoms.

Many aborted women express extreme anger and rage. This may be directed at family, husbands, boyfriends, or even other children; the latter may result in child battery. In the case of Renee Nicely of New

Jersey, post-abortion trauma triggered a "psychotic episode" which resulted in the beating death of her three-year-old son, Shawn. She told the court psychiatrist that she "knew that abortion was wrong" and "I should be punished for the abortion." Unfortunately, Shawn became the second victim of her frustrations.[62]

Similarly, abortion may sometimes distort maternal bonding with later children. For example, WEBA member Terri Hurst reported that after her first child was born, "I did not understand why her crying would make me so angry. She was the most beautiful baby, and had such a placid personality. What I didn't realize then was that I hated my daughter for being able to do all these things that my lost [aborted] baby would never be able to."

Post-abortion anger is often directed towards the abortionists or abortion counselors "who didn't give me the other side of the picture." Women are angered that they were not forewarned about the emotional problems they would face."[63] Feeling that they were misinformed or deceived by abortion clinic personnel, many women feel that they have been "used" for the profit of others.

Sleeping problems are often reported. Some women complain of nightmares concerning the abortion, often involving the "return" of the aborted child. Others experience insomnia, often mixed with depression and crying.[64]

The experience of a "phantom child," is not uncommon when a woman imagines her aborted child as old as it would have been if it had been born. This may include seeing "her baby" whenever viewing other children of that age group.[65] Similarly, some women become obsessed with the "would have been" birthdate, or the date of the abortion itself; and others report frightening "flashbacks" of the abortion procedure as late as six years after the fact.[66]

General feelings of helplessness, isolation, loneliness, and frustration are expressed. Some describe their situations as "hopeless."[67] Others claim they are "going crazy." Still others express fear of or a preoccupation with death. Many report they are unable to escape or resolve their conflicts. One woman told an abortion crisis center that she wanted "to get in a car and drive and drive and get out and start life over again."[68]

Suppressed feelings of remorse over abortion cause some women to suffer from psychosomatic illness. One study found that self-induced diseases among aborted women included abdominal discomfort, vomiting, pruritis vulvae, dysmenorrhea, frigidity, headaches, insomnia, fatigue, and ulcers.[69]

Abortion has also been identified as the cause of psychotic and schizophrenic reactions. Symptoms frequently include extreme anxiety and feelings of paranoia.[70]

Who Is Most Likely To Suffer?

Though it is impossible to predict what type of post-abortion psychiatric illness any particular woman is likely to face, there are general guidelines for identifying women who may be most susceptible to severe post-abortion syndrome. These guidelines have been developed by many psychiatrists who have done extensive work in the treatment of post-abortion sequelae.

According to a report by a group of psychologists headed by Dr. C. M. Friedman:

> The literature on abortion and our clinical experience both indicate that there is a greater likelihood of postabortion psychiatric illness in situations in which any of the following elements are present: coercion, medical indication [including abortings to save the life or health and eugenic abortion of a possibly handicapped child], concurrent severe psychiatric illness, severe ambivalence [i.e. when the woman wants a baby, sees this preborn as her baby, or feels she is its mother], and the woman's feeling that the decision is not her own [i.e. is required by needs and circumstances outside of her control].[71]

Note that this list of "worst candidates for abortion" includes women who would need abortion for the "hard" cases: to save her life or health, in cases of rape and incest, and to prevent the birth of a handicapped child. These specific categories, representing less than three percent of all abortions, will be discussed in detail in the next chapter. But their inclusion here demonstrates what can be considered a general principle: *The more difficult the circumstances prompting abortion, the more likely it is that a woman will suffer severe post-abortion sequelae.*

In other words, the more one sympathizes with the conditions surrounding a woman's problem pregnancy, the more one should discourage the "easy" escape of abortion, if only for the woman's own mental well-being. Why these rules-of-thumb are valid will become clearer during the following discussion.

Excluding the "hard" cases, Dr. Friedman's "worst candidates for abortion" list includes any woman who feels pressured into the abortion, whether by her sexual partner, her family, social norms, or economic hardship. Second, any ambivalence, any desire to keep the child "if things were better" is also a strong warning flag for future problems. The common link between these two categories is the woman's feeling of having compromised herself. In the first case, she aborts not because *she wants to*, but because abortion is the compromise solution demanded by circumstances or the "needs" of others. In the second instance, abortion compromises her own values or desires. She aborts despite her desire to keep the child, despite her moral uncertainties, and in so doing she betrays herself.

A team of psychiatrists which followed over 500 case histories of post-abortion sequelae observed that, "In all of the cases of postabortion illness we have presented, there were compromises in the decision-making process."[72] Writing in the *American Journal of Psychiatry*, these authors report that whenever a woman makes the decision to abort, *any compromise*, whether the compromise is in complying with the wishes of others or in setting aside one's own values, *opens the door to later psychiatric problems*. Thus anyone who encourages a woman who is showing signs of uncertainty to choose abortion may unwittingly be pushing their loved one toward self-compromise and a subsequent loss of self-respect.

All of the above warning signs for post-abortion sequelae hold true for young women and especially for teenagers. Because of their limited experience, their greater dependence on others, and their youthful idealism, teenage women are extremely vulnerable to coercion, deceit, and compromised decision-making.

The greater psychological impact of abortion on young women was disclosed in a study which found that nearly one of every three young women who aborted "showed moderate to considerable decline in psychosocial functioning five to seven months post-abortion, as measured from the base-line of reported adequate prepregnancy status." Describing the psychic deterioration which teens experience after an abortion, the authors write:

These young women, at initial follow-up, were suffering with a variety of specific symptoms of maladaptive behavior including mild to moderate depressive episodes, a variety of new physical complaints for which medical attention had not been sought, . . . difficulty in concentrating in school, withdrawal from previous social contacts, lower self-esteem explicitly related to the pregnancy and abortion experience, a newly begun promiscuous pattern in relationships with men, and regression to more infantile modes of relationships with parents. These difficulties did not predate the pregnancy.[73]

A similar study has found that less than one-fourth of aborted teens were able to achieve a healthy psychological adaptive process. Many of the remaining three-quarters who faced prolonged disturbances fell into a vicious cycle of "replacement pregnancies."[74] Many of these young women will complete the cycle by undergoing a second abortion, then another pregnancy, and another abortion, and so on, reenacting their own torn emotions, the conflict between the desire for a child and their desire to be unburdened.

Unfortunately, the problem of post-abortion sequelae among young women is increased by their greater tendency to "bottle-up" their emotions after an abortion experience.[75] Thus, even though teens are likely to be most deeply affected by abortions, they are also likely to be the least expressive about their doubts and pains. Some are emotionally "numbed," others conceal their inner pain as part of the veil of secrecy surrounding the abortion. Others strive to conceal their grief, especially from parents who might have encouraged or pressured them to choose the abortion, out of fear that expressing any complaint afterwards would only drive a further wedge between them and their parents.

It must also be remembered that when a young woman (or man) engages in intercourse, she is seeking much more than just physical pleasure. (Indeed, young women frequently complain that such intercourse is pleasureless and "done only for the guy.") In the broader perspective, intercourse is just a symptom of the young woman's search for love, fulfillment, and maturity. Abortion destroys not only the consequences of intercourse, but also disrupts this larger search for meaning. When a young woman is encouraged by her boyfriend, friends, parents, or society to abort rather than to give life to her child, she is being told that her search for love was wrong. Instead of receiving support to act with courage and compassion, she is told to "do what is best for yourself," meaning to place selfishness ahead of love. Instead of being encouraged to accept the consequences of her choices and to mature through the responsibilities of parenthood, she is encouraged to "mature" through infantile destruction. Thus she is made to participate in desolation rather than growth; she is exposed to the fear of death rather than the joy of life.

Dr. Baars echoes these concerns, noting that the psychological threat of abortion is greatest for the uncertain, unaffirmed "girls who are in a desperate search for someone to love them." He writes:

When they [the unaffirmed women searching for love] learn from personal experimentation that this cannot be found in sexual promiscuity, they often desire to have a child of their own, in the expectation that the child will give them what their parents failed to provide. No one can be blind to what must happen, and is happening these days all too often to unaffirmed youngsters, when other grown-ups prove to be just as pseudo-affirming or denying as their own parents, in their eagerness to persuade or force them to have an abortion. Such conduct constitutes psychic murder of these already deprived girls, and unless they are so fortunate to be helped by affirming persons, they will become the victims of malignant depression.[76]

Aborted Women: The Destruction of Self

Very few women can approach abortion without qualms or walk away from it without regrets. It is this ambivalence towards abortion, to use Francke's title term, which is the gateway to post-abortion sequelae. For most women, abortion is not just an assault on their womb; it is an assault on their psyche.

As we have seen, some women are literally forced into abortion by lovers, families, friends, or even by their physicians. Others slip into the abortion decision, restraining their doubts and questions, simply because it is the most visible and presumably the "easiest" way out of their dilemma. For these women, pro-abortion clichés replace investigation; blind trust supplants foresight. They assume abortion is safe because that is what they are told, and that is what they want to believe. They naively hope that they will have the strength to deal with the aftermath of abortion—even though they are choosing abortion because they feel they lack the strength to handle an unplanned pregnancy.

Unfortunately, abortion does not build psychic strength; it drains it. And so the aborting woman is even less able to handle post-abortion sequelae than she would have been able to handle the unplanned birth.

The abortion mentality, the institutional system of birth control

134

counselors, abortionists, and clinics, all contribute to this faulty deci-sion-making. As we will see later, abortion counselors are cosmetic figures who only reinforce the abortion choice, acting to support the woman's decision against the rebellion of her instinctive fears against such an unnatural procedure. Rather than urging the woman to con-front her decision, reconsider it, and be prepared for its consequences, the counselors work to maintain the "safe and easy" myth and encour-age the woman to believe in abortion's tempting lie: "Soon it will all be over."

In response to the many pressures they face, most women tend to rush their abortion decision in an attempt to avoid becoming "too attached" to the idea of having their baby. Unfortunately, this rush to decide frequently occurs during the period in which most women, even those whose pregnancies are planned, experience some ambivalence toward childbirth.[77] This ambivalence occurs in part because it always takes time to become accustomed to a major change in one's life. But also, there is always a downswing in a woman's hormones during the early months of pregnancy. Because a pregnant woman is experiencing a major hormonal disturbance, "depression is to be expected during the 2nd and 3rd months [of pregnancy], often the time the pregnancy is verified and a decision made."[78] This natural, hormone-induced de-pression may be easily misinterpreted to mean hostility towards child-birth, parenting, or even one's sexual partner.

The shock of an unplanned pregnancy, combined with the swing-ing moods caused by the woman's shifting hormones, may make a woman particularly vulnerable to outside pressures. According to one study:

> Her ambivalence [towards her pregnancy] may lean one way or the other according to the attitudes she perceives: with love, help, and support she is more likely to overcome her negative feelings to accept and love her child. But the reverse is also true: the percep-tion of hostile reactions towards her pregnancy may reinforce her negative feelings and push her towards abortion.[79]

The authors add that these negative pressures may come not only from spouses and family, but from those subtle social campaigns against the poor:

> Unfortunately, hostile attitudes towards women with problem pregnancies are currently being reinforced . . . by antinatalist

campaigns. Such campaigns encourage a sense of shame and guilt about procreation, especially among the poor, and, in their haste to lower the birth rate, promote an antichild attitude. This attitude in turn contributes to the withdrawal of previously existing forms of social support for pregnant women.[80]

Thus we see again that a woman may choose abortion in an attempt to please others rather than herself. This view is supported by the theories of Harvard psychologist Carol Gilligan, a pro-choice feminist specializing in the moral decision-making processes of women. According to Gilligan, the conventional theory of moral development which says that moral consciousness is formed by a process of rejecting peer pressure in favor of one's own vision of right and wrong, is not applicable to women. Instead, she argues, women "base moral decisions on what will please others—a kind of moral development no worse than the 'independent' male version."[81]

Gilligan strains in her attempt to use this model as a justification for abortion; but if true, her theory only shows how easy it is to pressure a woman to abort "in the best interest of everyone concerned." In one of her examples, she praises a woman who after evaluating the desires of her boyfriend and parents (who all want the abortion) decides that the "loving" thing to do is to have the abortion even though she personally wanted to keep the baby very much.[82] Only Gilligan's pro-abortion bias can account for her blindness to the fact that this girl is submitting to a compromise against her own best interests, her own desires, and her own preferred choice. What she has been given is not the freedom to choose, but the "freedom" to be pushed.

But the knowledge that one is being pushed into an abortion is no defense. Indeed, it can simply become another excuse for the woman to shift responsibility for the choice onto those who urge it. Like a hot potato, everyone passes off the responsibility. Parents and boyfriends believe the final choice is the woman's responsibility; the woman thinks it was theirs: "They forced me to do it." From within all these mind games, the woman may view herself as the "martyr," giving in to the wishes of others, accepting the undesirable. Thus many women accept abortion not only as self-punishment, but as a means of gaining virtue (martyrdom) through submission.[83]

In sum, the choice for abortion is usually an unwanted choice made in despair. It is a "fight or flight" reaction to a seemingly insurmountable problem, a reaction which curiously combines the destructive violence of the fight instinct and the denial/avoidance attributes associated with the instinct to flee. These observations were confirmed at a symposium on the psychological apsects of abortion held on October 31, 1978 in Chicago. By the end of the conference, the psychiatrists who had gathered there concluded that:

> Without question, abortion is psychologically a symbol of the despair which seems to be endemic to modern society. It is a totally negative response to environmental pressures. Without benefit of an affirming love, abortion is always an empty response—a gesture of denial.[84]

They continue by pointing out that "carrying an unwanted child to term" is far less traumatic than abortion, and they imply that helping a disturbed woman give birth to a child is often an aid to overcoming her emotional or mental problems. They conclude by saying, "In the final analysis . . . life is better than death, and that psychotherapy which affirms life is by far the best. Abortion is a defeatist answer, a psychic retreat for those who have given up looking for answers."[85]

Abortion is an act of despair not only on the part of women, but also on the part of the society which has given up trying to give them authentic help. What began with the abortion of unwanted children,

> . . . before long becomes de facto "social abortion." Women who seek abortion . . . find themselves "socially aborted" long before they seek the medical abortionist. They are aborted, rejected and unwanted by those close to them—their husbands, parents, and friends. By the time these women reach the abortionist (who at least identifies himself), they are already isolated and afraid; they feel literally trapped.[86]

It is these feelings of isolation and abandonment which cause despair, which cause the abortion alternative to appear to be the *only* alternative. For these women the feelings of loss and abandonment do not end after they have given in to the "practical need" for abortion. Instead, for many, the experience prompts the final and most wrenching of abortions—"self-abortion," that is, the loss of their self-worth, the loss of their dignity. Instead of giving birth to life, their abortions give birth to feelings of self-hatred and self-punishment. For many

137

women, the destruction of their "fetuses" marks also the destruction of their self-respect. Abandoned by others, the aborting woman feels forced to abandon her child, and finally even her self.

Who Is Least Likely To Suffer?

Because the list of those most susceptible to the psychological impact of abortion is so long (including the youthful, the dependent, the coerced, the ambivalent, the frightened, the poor, the emotionally unstable, and the ill-informed), it may in fact be easier to describe the smaller category, the opposite set: those who are in the least danger of suffering from post-abortion sequelae.

According to Professor Peter Peterson of the Hannover Medical School, while those who are most likely to suffer psychological distur-bances are "motherly women," those with the least chance of becom-ing disturbed, he notes, are women "with little motherliness."[87]

All the published evidence seems to agree with Dr. Peterson's assessment. More precisely, the women least likely to experience post-abortion sequelae are aggressive rather than nuturing. They are likely to be self-centered and property-oriented rather than people-oriented. For such women, abortion is not experienced as something which is "forced" upon them by circumstances. Instead, abortion is truly an act of self-determination for these women, simply the cutting down of another obstacle on the road to success.

In his treatise "Psychic Causes and Consequences of the Abortion Mentality," psychiatrist Conrad Baars explains that such women with "little motherliness" have never truly believed that they themselves were loved or "affirmed" for who they are. Instead, these women feel that parents and friends "love" them for their actions rather than for themselves. Not having experienced and internalized love from others, such a person seeks to become "self-affirmed" by proving:

> . . . to the world and to himself that he *is* significant, worthwhile and equal. This self-affirming person does this by using his "mind" to plot and manipulate others in trying to amass material goods, riches, power, fame, status symbols, and the like, which he expects will give him the feelings his parents failed to give him.[88]

Lacking the confidence of a person who feels loved, the self-affirmed rely on pseudo-confidence which they display as ag-gressiveness—an aggressiveness born of inner doubts and an exagger-

138

ated need to "prove" themselves. The result is that the self-affirming person struggles on an unending treadmill, blindly trying to gather more and more pseudo-happiness (material success) as a substitute for true happiness (affirming relationships outside of his or her self). The self-affirming person is thus trapped in a cycle of accumulating rather than giving, practicing self-love rather than love of others.

Depending only on self-love is self-consuming, and thus the self-affirmed person is unable to truly affirm (love) others. Since all they do and think is centered around affirming their own self-worth, the self-affirmed are extremely manipulative of others. Other people become objects for manipulation rather than persons honored for their own sake. For example, in sexual encounters the focus is always on the self rather than the other. Thus intercourse becomes an act more of mutual masturbation than of mutual love. Since each concentrates on proving themselves in such intercourse, the self-affirmed frequently prey upon each other, often by mutual consent.

According to Dr. Baars, these self-centered, self-affirming men and women are incapable of truly loving and affirming each other or their children. Their children, like all other persons, are only objects used to prove themselves to the world. Their children exist only to please them, and they have no claim to more than the self-affirmed parent is willing to give. Coming from this perspective, then, the self-affirmed "are the first to demand the right to abort the child they know or sense they are incapable of loving."[89]

Thus it is these self-affirmed women (and men) who find it easiest to choose abortion when it advances their self-interests. But even then, many self-affirmed women will suffer post-abortion ambivalence.[90] But although many, or even most, of the self-affirmed will be troubled by ambivalence or guilt, at least some of this group will emerge from an abortion relatively unscathed.

As a class, then, the self-affirmed represent those with the best chance of being unaffected by abortion. They suffer least not because they are more psychologically stable, but because they are already so psychically crippled. The abortion experience is unlikely to breach their defenses precisely because those defenses have been in place for so long.

Rather than denying the humanity of the unborn, self-affirming women might accept that a human life is destroyed, but they simply rationalize the death as "necessary" or justified. As one woman put it: "No one shrinks from what abortion means: the irrevocable ending of

. . . [a] unique human being. To be unequivocally, all-out for life, any life, is quite satisfying to the soul, but it's an ethical indulgence I cannot afford. The bottom line is, someone's rights are going to take precedence. I vote for the woman."[91]

Similarly, another feminist philosopher insists that women should never agree to be the "victim" in an unwanted pregnancy. If there must be a "victim," and she agrees there always is, then it might just as well be the unborn child, who by virtue of its lower social standing is logically less valuable.[92]

Self-affirmed women such as these are simply unwilling to sacrifice any of their own immediate ambitions or their own material possessions for the sake of an unwanted responsibility. They are addicted to the pseudo-happiness of their own plans, careers, and possessions—the "things" in their lives upon which they depend for their self-affirmation. Like all addicts, they are unable to trust that there is a greater happiness to be found in a human relationship, particularly a future relationship with an unseen child.

In sum, the women least likely to suffer from post-abortion sequelae are those for whom most people have the least sympathy. They are the self-affirmed women for whom abortion is not a dire necessity, but an act done purely for the sake of convenience. They abort not for health reasons, nor out of economic necessity, nor even to avoid social embarrassment. (Indeed, since she is self-affirmed, such a woman would be the first, if it suited her, to deliberately seek a child out of wedlock, through artificial insemination, or by a "one night stand." She cares not for social norms, or for the well-being of a child raised without a father, only for her own desires.) Instead, the self-affirmed woman aborts to prevent a disturbance in her lifestyle or career. If married and with children already, abortion is chosen simply because "We don't want any more." The self-affirmed woman may abort simply to avoid being "tied down."

It is circumstances such as these for which most people have the least sympathy, but it is the women and men who abort for these reasons who are the most active and vocal in demanding "freedom of choice" in order to protect their lifestyles. Conversely, it is the women who feel compelled by necessity to abort who are least active in demanding the right to abortion. Indeed, the latter abhor abortion (that's what makes it traumatic for them,) and submit only because they see no other alternative. To them abortion is "ugly" and "dirty." It is not a convenience or a "right" which they cherish; it is an awful

140

"necessity." But it is these latter women, those with whose circumstances we all sympathize, who are most likely to experience post-abortion trauma. By allowing and even encouraging them to compromise themselves, society abandons these women to the "ugly necessity" of abortion which carries with it guilt, despair and loss.

In the final analysis, then, every woman pays a psychological price for abortion. Those who abort out of "necessity" pay through post-abortion trauma. Those who abort for the sake of convenience have already paid by buying into the abortion mentality, the "me first" philosophy which has crippled their ability to affirm others and to recognize or accept unconditional love when it is offered to them.

This observation is substantiated by the testimony of Dr. Julius Fogel, a psychiatrist and obstetrician who has been a long-time advocate of abortion and has performed hundreds of abortions himself. Although he approaches abortion from a "pro-choice" perspective, Dr. Fogel is deeply concerned about the "psychological effects of abortion on the mother's mind." According to Dr. Fogel:

> Abortion is an impassioned subject. . . . Every woman—whatever her age, background or sexuality—has a trauma at destroying a pregnancy. A level of humanness is touched. This is a part of her own life. She destroys a pregnancy, she is destroying herself. There is no way it can be innocuous. One is dealing with the life force. It is totally beside the point whether or not you think a life is there. You cannot deny that something is being created and that this creation is physically happening. . . . Often the trauma may sink into the unconscious and never surface in the woman's lifetime. But it is not as harmless and casual an event as many in the proabortion crowd insist. A psychological price is paid. It may be alienation; it may be a pushing away from human warmth, perhaps a hardening of the maternal instinct. Something happens on the deeper levels of a woman's consciousness when she destroys a pregnancy. I know that as a psychiatrist.[93]

Clearly, if a psychological price is not paid after the abortion, it was probably compromised away long before.

Summary

Abortion is never simply "over and done with." The experience is always tainted by a lingering ambivalence and is often the source of severe psychiatric disabilities. Pro-abotionists do not deny that post-abortion sequelae occur, they simply insist that they are usually bearable. Several sources place the rate of severe post-abortion sequelae, defined as requiring psychiatric hospitalization, as high as 10 percent. Observable sequelae of a less serious nature occur in 55 to 90 percent of all aborted women.

Not surprisingly, most reactions include aspects of guilt, depression, self-punishment, and feelings of loss and emptiness. Many women deny their inner doubts, but psychiatric evidence indicates that all aborted women continue to face unresolved conflicts about the abortion, at least at some subconscious level.

The women most likely to suffer post-abortion sequelae are those whose situations are most sympathetic, those who are "forced" by social or economic conditions, or those who want a child some day but "not just now." Those least likely to suffer are those with "little motherliness," who abort purely for convenience and have no doubts about what they are doing. These "self-affirming" women are chronic exploiters, used to manipulating people as objects, and so are easily inclined to think of the unborn as disposable property. These self-affirmed women may recognize the humanity of the unborn child, but their worldview is self-centered, and so is insulated from compassion for the child or for anyone else.

Given the great psychological and physical risks posed by abortion, it is clear that the responsible physician, one interested in his client's overall health, would be extremely reluctant ever to recommend or perform an abortion.

PROFILES THREE

Decisions to Be Weak

For some women, the choice to have an abortion is never truly made. Instead, buffeted by the pressures they face and the advice of well-meaning friends, they feel themselves carried by some outside momentum toward the unwanted but seemingly inevitable solution of abortion. One survey respondent writes:

> I didn't want to kill my child; I just made the decision to be weak and not care about any of it. . . . I made a decision not to make a conscious choice at all. In fact, Planned Parenthood and all the abortion mills tell you that you have No Choice but to get an abortion. This is the irony of the "pro-choice" rhetoric.

Similarly, when Kathleen Trueland Smith became pregnant as a junior in high school, she too found it easy to abdicate responsibility for her decision to her parents.

> I reasoned that I had already disappointed my parents once by getting pregnant, so I didn't want to disappoint them again by having the baby. By this time I was in such an emotional state that I turned off all logical thinking processes. I let my parents take over; it was so easy to have them make the decisions for me.

Often women faced with unplanned pregnancies find that they lack the courage which is necessary to assert their desire to keep the baby. They desperately pray that someone will step into their lives and give them the encouragement they need to "do the right thing." For example, even as she was sitting in the abortion clinic, Renate Penney was looking for even a small word of hope: "I waited for someone to talk to me. I wanted someone to tell me not to do this. Anyone. But no one did. And it was done."

Thus, just as a despondent person will threaten suicide in the hope that someone will reach out and care, so too do many women threaten abortion hoping to be talked out of it. But instead, they all too often discover that others are only going to encourage the dark option of death. One WEBA member writes:

> I called a priest who was counseling me and said, "I want to get an abortion." I couldn't believe I would ever say such a thing. He put me in touch with a woman who had had an abortion and she escorted me to a clinic. No one *ever* counseled me about financial and emotional help—nothing. If that is pro-choice—where is the *choice!* I could have been counseled and led to find a "joy in living and procreation"—instead I was allowed to run from life.
>
> Those two people had a chance to intervene in my life. Instead they were passive wimps.

By not choosing, or by letting others choose for them, some women hope to avoid responsibility for their abortions. But while this strategy may help to divert blame for negative feelings which occur after the abortion, it does not prevent those bitter feelings from occurring. Indeed, these women experience a great sense of exploitation, and they suffer an even greater loss of self-esteem.

What most women faced with problem pregnancies want is nothing more than encouragement and love. Instead they are given abortion—an act of despair and lovelessness.

6) Carolyn Walton

When Carolyn became pregnant under difficult circumstances, she went into a state of "shock." She didn't know what to do. But her well-meaning relatives did. They took over her decision-making for her, and had her undergo an abortion at a Cleveland clinic. The trauma of her abortion made her lose complete control of her life. She found herself abusing drugs and alcohol, sterile from abortion complications, and dangerously suicidal.

Ten years ago I found myself pregnant, divorced, and virtually alone. The first emotion was that of sheer panic. I only had a small income and was working two jobs. I had a four-year-old daughter to support. The baby's father immediately retracted his marriage proposal as soon as he found out I was pregnant. I had no money, no medical insurance, and didn't realize that there were places to turn to for help.

As I turned to friends and relatives for advice, the whole matter became more confusing. Advice poured in from all sides. I felt like I was being put through the third degree. "What is a divorced women going to do with such a small income? You already have one child to feed. How will you pay the hospital bills?" As I think back, not once did anyone just put their arms around me and ask my feelings or allow me to even have time to have any. Just some positive love and support would have been a relief. A relative that had had an illegal abortion 25 years before talked to me about abortion. After all, it was now legal and "safe." She had never been able to have children because of her abortion, but strangely enough, advised me to have one anyways! I felt like I was in a tailspin. There was no time to think.

My relatives went about their business of making all the arrangements while I remained in a total state of oblivion. I felt like someone on the outside looking in. It was as if it was happening to someone else. I don't blame anyone, they only did what they thought was right; that is why educating people about what's really right is so important.

Anyway, I was soon whisked off to Cleveland and dropped off at some friend's house. The next day I was again dropped off at the abortion clinic. My heart told me I was wrong, but my mind, like a robot, did what it was told. After I got inside (alone), I paid my $200 and was given a pregnancy test and given a locker (just like in a gym). I was given a paper gown and told to put it on. The place was cold and the people formal. No compassion, no understanding. It was like a busy assembly line.

I then waited in a small room until my name was called. I was taken to another room and told to get up on the table, put my feet in the stirrups and scoot down. It was so cold—I shivered and have never been so scared or felt so alone. I was soon to find out that the "painless" procedure I was promised was anything but painless. As my baby was ripped from my body, the pain became unbearable and tears streamed down my face. I was told to be still, it would soon be over. After the abortion, I walked to another room and was allowed to lie down for thirty minutes, after which I was told I could leave. I went to my locker, got dressed, and was told to see my family doctor in six weeks. I asked if I could use a phone to call my ride and was told they had no phones for public use, but there was a pay phone down the street I could use.

I walked down the street. It was November, and very cold. As I walked back to wait for my ride outside the clinic, I felt cold, nauseous, dizzy, alone and empty. When my ride picked me up, she had a friend with her. They were going to a steak house for lunch and I had to go along. You would have thought I had just gone to get my eyes checked for all anyone cared.

Later that day another relative took me home and dropped me off in front of my apartment. It's amazing how everyone was there to give advice before the abortion, but afterwards I was on my own.

What was to follow was more like a nightmare than reality. I began having nightmares about my murdered baby. I began drinking more and more until I was up to five bottles of alcohol a week. I sometimes went so long without eating that when I would try to eat, I would vomit. I finally went to the doctor and found out that I had an infection from the abortion. He started treatment, but it didn't help. I told him about the nightmares and my nerves, and he gave me tranquilizers—no comfort, no counseling—just pills.

So I started taking tranquilizers to help me sleep, and pep pills to keep me going during the day. Four times I deliberately overdosed, trying to commit suicide. I don't think I really wanted to die, I only wanted someone to care, to help, to listen. I wanted the pain to go away. The doctor continued to try treatment after treatment on the physical problem. But to no avail. I finally changed doctors and had to have surgery because the infection caused by the abortion had destroyed the cervix and the uterus. This helped for a short time.

I finally met the man I am now married to; with his love and support, I started to put my life back together. We started to attend church and I came to find Christ as my Savior. I then knew I was forgiven, but it took time before I was able to forgive myself. I was finally alive after being dead and living in hell.

But the physical problems caused by the abortion started cropping back up. More infections and more damage. I changed doctors again. I had a D&C. I was filled with tumors by this time and had endrometriosis. A hysterectomy was inevitable, but we put it off as long as possible. But March 15, 1984 it finally came to pass. *Everything* had to be removed, for it was totally destroyed. It took ten years of constant problems, but the abortion finally took its final toll.

As I look back, if I had had love and support, and above all, the true facts, I would have never even considered an abortion. The pain never goes away; it's always there.

I really believe WEBA needs to be heard. We have a right to be heard. The thought of anyone going through what I went through (although I know that there are literally millions who have) is heartbreaking to me.

7) Alice Gilmore

Sometimes women are pushed into abortion by circumstances, and they find themselves in and out of the abortion clinic without really understanding what has happened to them. Such was the case for Alice Gilmore. Though naive about abortion before she walked in the door of the Kansas City abortion clinic, Alice spent the next six years experiencing the traumatic physical and psychological problems caused by that abortion.

I was eighteen years old when I first became pregnant. A few weeks later I went to the doctor so I could be sure, but I was very naive about what to expect. My boyfriend was not encouraging; he said he was too young to be a father. So I went to a girlfriend, who suggested that maybe I could have an abortion. She gave me the name of a place that did abortions.

So I called them, and they told me what to do to prepare myself. I didn't even know what abortion really was. So I went up there the next day—it all happened really fast—and the woman at the reception desk asked me the reason for terminating the baby. I said that "I would like to keep it, but I can't." She said, "Well then, you don't want it, do you?" I said, "No, I want it; but I can't keep it." I had no support from anybody at that time. She wrote down anyway that I didn't want the fetus. That hurt me really bad at that time, because I did want my baby.

She didn't mention any alternatives whatsoever. In fact, everybody that I talked to was very rude to me. It seemed like they were all angry. I went to this other room for counseling, or what they called counseling; but it wasn't really. They didn't give any alternatives, either. Their counseling was to tell us about what they were going to do. Then they showed us pictures of ways to prevent birth next time. They wanted us to get an IUD; they said that was the best thing to get. So they sold me an IUD, and they put it in me after the abortion.

The doctor told me I was almost four months along. I asked the doctor, "Is the baby alive?" He said "No." I never had prior instruction in school as to the development of a baby, so I didn't know any better. All I had to go on was what he told me; and that's all he said.

From there, I had to get ready. There were two or three of us sitting in this room, right next to where we would go in and lie down. Although we couldn't see what was going on, we certainly could hear. There was a girl in the next room crying very loud. Then it was my turn; I went in and laid down on the table. They gave me my choice of a local or gas. They made a big point of telling me that the gas cost $50 more. "If you don't want to pay it, you get a local." But I didn't have the extra money.

So they gave me the local, and it made me feel sick. I told them "I'm going to be sick." And the doctor said, "Oh, she's going to be sick. Get her something." The nurse said, "All right, all right." They were very, very rude about it. They were not nice at all. They acted like I was an inconvenience to them. So the nurge got a bowl and laid it next to me.

So the doctor started and said, "You'll feel a little pinch; it will be very, very minor." But it hurt an awful lot! It felt like they were pulling my insides out. I don't think I've ever felt that much pain.

Afterwards, I just felt badly, and I had a lot of pain. I felt no relief at all. I didn't realize why I felt bad. My boyfriend took me home. It wasn't long after I got home that I knew—it just hit me—that I had killed my baby. That's what I said to myself: "I killed my baby."

After the abortion I started to bleed a lot. They had told me that I would bleed for about six weeks, and that unless I had clots bigger than an inch across, not to worry about it. I went way past the six weeks; I bled for over a year. I bled a whole lot for the first nine months. I didn't go to the doctor, because I was ashamed, especially at first. And secondly because the clots weren't very big, half an inch across, but never an inch. I was bleeding so bad that I couldn't get away from the bathroom for more than fifteen minutes. I had to have double protection to keep the blood from going through my pants.

I also began to feel a great deal of pain during intercourse. This lasted for many years. From what I've been able to learn since, I probably had a torn cervix. And I still have pain now.

I also became very, very depressed. I had a lot of trouble concentrating; I couldn't keep my mind off the abortion. I cried a lot. I don't think I ever got out of the depression. I used to laugh a lot; I used to be known in school as the class clown. But afterwards I could never laugh. People tried very hard to make me laugh; but I just couldn't laugh, even at something very funny. I went through a complete personality change.

A lot of times I wanted to die—I was very, very lonely. There was no reason to live, not really.

I had six years of depression after my abortion. I developed into a really weird person. I hated myself; I had no self-confidence. My boyfriend started to feel really guilty, too. Right after making love I'd say, "I killed my baby." And he started feeling really bad. Things started going downhill. He started lying to me, and going out behind my back.

Two years after my abortion we broke up. I met my husband-to-be the next day. We started to live together, and I got pregnant right away. I guess I was a very lenient-type girl; I grew up with no love. I told my boyfriend, "I won't have another abortion. I already went through that once; I won't go through it again." He said, "I wouldn't ask you to." He was very good about it; he wanted to marry me right away when he knew I was pregnant. I kept saying, "No, I don't know you. I don't love you."

We lived together while I was pregnant. He wanted to marry me, but I kept saying no. Finally I told him to quit asking me, and I would let him know when I was ready to get married. Two months after my son was born I decided that he wanted me and the baby, so we were married.

Several years later I started reading the Bible, especially the New Testament. For a long time my husband ridiculed me because he hadn't been born again, yet. But later we both became active in a

Christian church. It was only then that I could start to forgive myself, but that was the hardest part. I knew the Lord had forgiven me, but I couldn't forgive myself. Within myself, it took about a year and a half to completely heal.

I really feel sorry for women who have had abortions. It's never a good thing, not even in the case of incest. I've been through incest with my natural father—though I never became pregnant. Even in the case of incest, abortion is wrong. It would only hurt the girl more, physically and emotionally.

PROFILES FOUR

Decisions to Take Control

While many women abandon their decision-making power to others and are pressured into abortion, others make a clear and independent choice on their own. For these strong-willed women, the choice for abortion is a choice to control their own destinies. These are modern, liberated women. They are assertive and they know what they want. And one thing they do not want is an unplanned pregnancy which will disrupt their plans for their futures. Unfortunately, they seldom realize that the short-term solution of abortion will eventually be just as disruptive, if not more so.

8) Donna Merrick

Donna was just finishing nursing school and was looking forward to her career when she discovered she was pregnant. Despite the desperate pleas of her boyfriend, Donna aborted their child. Today her sense of guilt includes her mistreatment of both her baby and her boyfriend.

I found out I was pregnant on my twenty-first birthday. For a fleeting moment I let myself kind of giggle inside. I had always had my sights set towards being a mother, and I figured that's where I would eventually end up. I had just graduated from nursing school, and I enjoyed nursing. Yet I wanted to get married. I wasn't too crazy about myself, and I wanted somebody to love me, hug me, and tell me I was OK. I'm sure I'm not the only one who's ever been through anything like that.

When I found out I was pregnant, then, it was almost like everything that "little girl Donna" had been looking forward to and playing house about had finally arrived: I was *pregnant*. But I didn't let myself consciously think that I was going to be a mommy, because that would have led me to think that I was also going to kill this child that was going to make me a mommy. Still, I did give a squeal of delight, subconsciously thinking, "Oooh I'm pregnant—how neat! I can do it!" I mostly remember experiencing a shudder of joy—what a contradiction in terms.

So when the nurse on the phone said, "Yes, Donna, your test was positive, you are pregnant," all I said was "Oh." Then she said, "Do you want to terminate?" And I said "Yes." She set up an appointment for the following week. I was in New Hampshire, as a summer nurse at a camp. I had to drive to Springfield, Massachusetts to the doctor's, where I also got my abortion.

One reason I chose to abort was simply because I didn't want to tell my parents that I had made a mistake. I knew they would have loved me through the entire thing, should I have decided to bring the baby to life; and I knew they would have supported me if I had still decided to abort after I told them. My parents were like that, unquestioningly supportive. We just didn't have a communicative relationship. But in my mind I felt that I needed to attain certain goals to keep them pleased with me. That was something I needed, to have them pleased with me. Becoming pregnant definitely did not fit into the scheme of things.

I remember thinking about this friend I had in nursing school who had problems with her ovaries. She wasn't sure if she could conceive, so she allowed herself to get pregnant on purpose to see if she could get pregnant. Then she went and had an abortion. I remember thinking at the time that that was a really stupid thing to do. The way she used her boyfriend, that's what I thought about, too. I looked up to her; I was trying to learn from her. The blind leading the blind, I suppose. . . .

Anyway it was July of 1974 when I found out I was pregnant. I drove into town and told my boyfriend about it. It shocked me, but he looked at me and asked if he was the father. It took me back for a minute; I was almost insulted. But I said, "Of course you're the father." He asked me what I was going to do, and I told him I was going to have an abortion. Then he asked me not to do it. He wasn't very forceful about it at first; I think he saw in my face that I was more or less resigned to having the abortion. But then he did try to talk me out of it, saying he was ready to get married, even though we'd been seeing each other for a month, maybe, at the most. In fact, he begged me to marry him. I remember that night when we were in bed; he put his hand on my tummy and he cried, because he didn't want me to have the abortion.

But I wasn't ready to get married, or I didn't think I was. I'd just graduated from nursing school, I had a (supposedly) "glorious" future ahead of me, and I was determined not to be so old-fashioned or inhibited as to get married right away. I wanted to fit in with the intelligent, free-thinking people. I respected those people and looked up to them because I felt I had never been one of them, and I was trying very hard to be like that. So at the time abortion seemed the best option.

My boyfriend didn't want me to have the abortion, but he didn't know what else to do. We talked about homes for unwed mothers, but they left such a lousy taste in my mouth. Just saying "homes for unwed mothers" made me think of girls with long, stringy hair sitting in dark, dingy rooms just waiting for their babies to be born, so they could go back home and walk around with their eyes to the ground for the rest of their lives, knowing what they had just done. I certainly didn't want to face that prospect. I was a chicken. Abortion is not a courageous decision; it is a cowardly decision. It is a decision to sweep your mistakes under the rug and not face up to them. It needs to be realized that for an unwed mother to give life to her unborn child is a courageous and noble decision.

Anyway, by the time I got around to telling my boyfriend about my planned abortion, I really hadn't thought much about his feelings. I didn't think that he had much to say about it. I didn't really think about whether I should involve him in the decision or not. So, I was the only one to make the decision. My boyfriend was brought up a good Catholic, desperately wanted to have children, and knew that abortion was wrong. He tried to convey that to me.

But I can't remember any kind of reason that I would have accepted. I think that's a characteristic of women who have made a decision to abort, especially in the circumstances that I was in.

Anyway, my boyfriend agreed to take care of me after I had the abortion. But he would not go with me, though I don't remember

153

asking him. I guess I thought it was something I had to do on my own. I think it had something to do with my "coming of age," that I could do this all by myself, and be stalwart, and not be affected by it. In my heart of hearts, though, I was dying to have him with me through the whole thing. I was so scared; I had no idea what was going to happen to me. We hadn't touched on abortion in nursing school.

When I went to the clinic, then, I was by myself. In the waiting room were three or four other scared-looking women, like myself. There wasn't a smile on any of their faces. It was very quiet. Some of the girls had their boyfriends there. I kind of envied them; they were all hugging up to each other like scared little kids.

While we were all sitting in the waiting room, a counselor called us in one by one. When it was my turn, I wasn't sure what to expect. I remember that it was very traumatic for me to go through the "counseling" session. The woman wasn't what I would call one of the most compassionate people in the world. One of the things I remember most vividly was that the counseling was very demeaning. She asked me was I using birth control when I got pregnant, and I said no. She asked me if I had ever used birth control, and I said yes. Then she burst out with, "Well how in the world did you get pregnant?" She made me feel like a jerk all over again; I felt stupid enough as it was, without her hammering on me.

I was sitting there trying desperately not to cry; I remember just wanting to scream. I felt so stupid and I felt so ashamed throughout that whole session. I felt so much guilt and shame that I was just trying to sit on it, instead of allowing myself to cry. I never cried through the whole thing. I was very calm and cool and in control; I wanted to be in control.

I think that's a characteristic of women who have set their minds to having an abortion. Once they've made the decision, it's almost tunnel-vision; making a decision feels so good. That's because being pregnant at this time is an uncontrollable aspect of your life. To make the decision to abort is taking control of this situation that is horrifying to you at this time in your life. That's how the repression of feelings begins. If you let yourself cry, you may become hysterical and uncontrolled; that is *not* the name of the game.

Anyway, the only other thing the woman asked me was, "Have you considered adoption?" I said, "No, I don't think I could do it." "Oh," she said, and that was the end of that.

Of course she asked me what kinds of plans I had for my life, and why I didn't want to get married, and how my boyfriend felt about it. I told her that he didn't want me to have the abortion. She asked me how I felt about that. I answered that I wasn't happy that he didn't want me to have the abortion, and that I wished he would support me. Nothing was said about the baby.

So after we all got counseled (and verbally whipped—that's how I felt), we walked into the hospital, into the day surgery rooms, which were next to the delivery rooms. I laid down on the table and put my hands behind my head, determined to be 'cool' until the end. That's how I needed to cope with it. The doctor and nurse walked in and saw me like that. The doctor made some comment that made me feel very ashamed for lying there with that nonchalant attitude. They gave me some Demerol IV. I was conscious, but I didn't feel very much pain. I felt cramps and pinches, and the doctor told me how each step would feel, and what he was doing. Then he turned on the suction machine, and it was all over.

I went back to my boyfriend's apartment. I felt so relieved and so pampered. He had a pitcher of ice water next to the bed, and he had the blankets turned back. But he wasn't there; he didn't want to be there. I went to sleep, but only for awhile. I had to be back to camp that night. My boyfriend came back and was concerned about me being able to drive during the hour-and-a-half trip. But I had to be back, so I waved good-bye.

That was the last time I ever saw him. I came back to his apartment three weeks later to pick up some things I had left there, and he wasn't there. When I asked his roommate where he was, he said my boyfriend wasn't going to come, that he didn't want to see me. That was the end of the relationship; he couldn't face me.

That's where I remember feeling guilty. At that time I was angry and very, very hurt. I knew this man loved me; he did. I had told him I loved him, though not enough to get married. I expected him to come crawling after me and keep pursuing me; that's what I wanted. But it never occurred to me then that he just couldn't look me in the eyes, knowing what I had done to his child.

That's been one of the hardest things for me to deal with, following the abortion. I began to realize it about two or three months later when I returned to his town to see some other friends. It happened to be the day he was getting married. The things that had transpired during those three short months were that he broke a leg, dropped out of nursing school, got engaged, and rejoined the Army. It blew me away to find that out; his many years in the Army had not been a happy time in his life. I knew that something must be wrong, and that he was in a bad state of mind. I felt completely responsible for all of these things.

I tried to get on with my life, and moved in with my sister in Philadelphia. I began to work in a nursing unit there; and ironically enough, I got a job in a nursery, working with premature babies.

But I became very promiscuous after that. I got introduced to the periphery of the feminist movement. I would read *Cosmopolitan* magazine from cover to cover every month, because it told me that the lifestyle I had chosen was the right one, a noble one, a fulfilling one. I needed a fix of that, somebody to tell me that what I was doing was OK. I didn't feel very fulfilled, though. I'd go to clubs at night, and I'd be with a different man every night. Every morning I'd wake up and they'd be gone, and I'd feel dirty, physically and emotionally. It was just a vicious cycle. But I hung on to my *Cosmopolitan* magazine like my Bible.

About a year after my abortion I found myself thinking that I was pregnant again. I was panic-stricken. I confided in my sister, who I had told that I had had an abortion, that I thought I was pregnant. She asked me what I would do; and I said I didn't know, but that I knew I couldn't have another abortion. She didn't ask me why, and I didn't know why, either. I just knew that it had made me feel bad, and I didn't want to do it again. But I have a feeling that if I really had been pregnant at that time, which I wasn't, that without other options, I would have had another abortion. I wasn't ready to deal with myself responsibly yet.

Though I didn't want another abortion, I didn't see anything wrong with other women having abortions. I went along with the thinking that a woman should have a right to choose, a right to her own body, and on and on. I felt that way quite strongly.

When I met the Lord, it was about two or three years after my abortion. I hadn't really connected my promiscuity or increased drug use with my abortion, but now I know it was all hooked together. When I met the Lord, I knew right away that what I had done was wrong. It was the first time I'd ever consciously admitted it to myself: my having the abortion was a bad thing to have done. It was a great relief to admit it. I knew that the Lord had forgiven me for it and that He still loved me. I realized that there isn't anything in our lives that the Lord will allow to go to waste. God is big enough to even use abortion to bring people to Him.

About three years later, living in New Mexico, I saw Nancyjo Mann on television, and I really started to think about my abortion. I wrote to her, and she called back and told me I was the first one she had ever heard from in New Mexico, and would I consider directing a chapter here. After much thought, I accepted. It has been a tremendous healing process for me because I've been able—I've been forced, actually—to look at what abortion does to women, at what causes women to have abortions, and at what they go through afterwards.

I feel that women are being deceived when they go in to have an abortion because they aren't being shown pictures of what their child looks like. Women are being deceived before they get to that place in that they're being sheltered from this truth. Women are being deceived about the procedure they will undergo. I wasn't told that it would be a blind procedure, that the physician cannot see inside my uterus. Women should see pictures representing the child inside of them, and they should know beforehand the side effects of abortion. They should know that there may be as much as a twenty-five percent chance of her never having another child. Can she live with that? That should be included in the counseling. Without it, that's deception; women aren't being allowed to make a truly informed decision about their abortion.

9) Monica Harshbarger

Monica had a legal abortion in Colorado in 1971. Though she was afraid that a baby would spoil her teenage fun, she soon found that the complications she suffered from the abortion weren't worth all the "fun" in the world.

In 1971, at the age of seventeen, I became pregnant. I had been a pretty rebellious teenager, and I went through a lot of emotional turmoil at that time. I now know that most of that was due to the fact that my parents divorced in my early teens. I lived with my mother, but I loved and missed my father more than I knew, or at least was willing to admit at the time.

157

I guess I fell in with the wrong group of kids when I was in junior high school and high school. We were experimenting with drugs and casual sex. Oh, we knew about birth control, thanks to our local Planned Parenthood. But it is my belief that teenagers are not responsible enough to handle any form of birth control. I now know that abstinence is the only sure form of birth control.

When I discovered I was pregnant, I was devastated, and could think of no one but me, and my life. No one else mattered because I was having fun, and I knew it all. A baby would have spoiled that. I didn't think I could give birth to a child and give it to someone else. I knew at seventeen that I was not capable of raising a child.

I had heard that abortions were safe and easy. My best friend had had one, and she was fine. She has since had four more; how sad. Needless to say, she is not my best friend now, but we are friends, and I feel terribly sorry for her. She tries so hard to bury her guilt, and justify them.

Anyway, I truly believed that what I was carrying at that point, the first trimester, was a blob of tissue. No one ever told me any different at any time before my abortion. I went to my mother with the news of my pregnancy and told her that I wanted to have an abortion. She tried to talk me out of it, not because she knew how developed my baby was, but because she believed it was a life, and because of her love and concern for me. But I was determined, and no one was going to change my mind. Then, as now, a parent had no legal influence over their minor child when it came to abortion or birth control. My father was the one who paid for the abortion; my mother wouldn't.

My friend's sister was a nurse, and she gave me the name of her Ob/Gyn. Abortion was liberalized in Colorado several years prior to the 1973 Supreme Court decision, for the "health" of the mother. I now know what a generalization that is: it can mean anything. For me it meant a half an hour in a psychiatrist's office, telling him that I did not want to have a baby. He recommended in favor of the abortion.

I then had a physical examination by the Ob/Gyn. My mom went with me, I think in hopes of changing my mind. After the exam, we met with the man who called himself "doctor." He never informed us about the development of my baby. He never informed us of the dangers, the possible complications to me.

I returned the day before my abortion for the insertion of a laminaria tent to start dilation. I returned home, and the next morning

I checked into a Denver-area hospital. (Before 1973, all abortions were done in a hospital.) Mine was a twelve-week suction abortion.

I remember lying on the stretcher outside the operating room, everything so sterile and so white. Everyone pretended to be so compassionate. You know, I believe I even had a crush on that man who took my baby, he was my savior! What a fool I was then. . . .

I believe I had a moment of hesitation: "Am I doing the right thing? I can't turn back now. And it really is for the best." Then they came and rolled me into the operating room.

They put me to sleep. I spent the night, and then left the next morning. I was a bit numb, but relieved. It was over. Now I could get on with my life.

The next Friday night, I was out at a party, having a good time, when I went into labor. It was the most horrible pain I would ever experience. My mom picked me up and rushed me to the emergency room. There I underwent a second suction abortion to remove the parts left behind the first time. When the pain was gone, I was relieved. The doctor told me that either I had had twins, and he had only gotten one the first time, or that my uterus was tipped, and he hadn't reached all the fetal tissue. Whatever it was, I didn't care.

I'm sure I justified my abortion to other women after I aborted; I know I did. I was pro-choice, pro-abortion. Justification is where it's at for aborted women who refuse to admit their mistakes and accept the truth. I guess a lot of women are scared to admit their mistakes, or talk about it, because they are scared of how it will affect them. Often, after telling my story to a group, I will have a woman come up to me with tears in her eyes, thanking me for having the courage to tell what she has been unable to tell. They are my sisters. And you watch us; pretty soon that fear and doubt will turn into strength and determination, and we will put an end to this degradation.

Anyway, I didn't think about that procedure consciously until six years later, when my daughter was born. I say "consciously," because when I met my husband-to-be, a couple of years later, at nineteen, I had a strong wish to have a baby. When we were married, I was twenty-two. I went off the pill immediately, in hopes of conceiving a child soon. After a year or so of trying to conceive, without luck, I went in for some rather uncomfortable fertility tests. We discovered that my fallopian tubes were blocked with scar tissue. My tubes were cleared, and then I became pregnant. How lucky I was!

During my prenatal visits I can remember crying each time I heard my daughter's heartbeat. But I still did not consciously recall my abortion. Finally, the time for delivery came, and my water broke. I was in labor for twenty hours, but my uterus did not dilate. They had to take her C-section.

When the nurse handed me my baby for the first time, that is when it hit me: what had I done when I was seventeen?! Danielle, my daughter, was such a beautiful miracle. From that day on I started to read and study about the unborn child and abortion. I have been a completely dedicated, pro-life activist ever since.

I will never know if my physical complications—blocked tubes, incompetent uterus, extraordinarily heavy menstrual periods, endometriosis (scar tissue in my uterus), pain in intercourse—were the result of that abortion. When I tried to recover the medical records of my abortion from that office, I was told that they had been destroyed in a fire in 1972, one year after my abortion. But I believe these are all abortion complications.

Emotionally I have felt a lot of guilt and remorse since finding out that my baby was completely formed at the time of the abortion, and I felt horrible pain. I have trouble telling my story; at times I will break down while telling it.

One other thing: only several years ago did my mother finally unburden herself to me. I wish she'd had the courage when I was seventeen to tell me her story. She had become pregnant when she was seventeen, also, and was taken by an uncle to an abortionist. She got up and ran out because she could not go through with it. She stayed in a Catholic convent home until she gave birth to a little boy, John. She kept him there for two years in hopes that something would work out so that she could keep him. Knowing it was hopeless, she finally gave him up for adoption. We found him a couple of years ago. He's thirty-seven now, and his name is Jerry. This was really a thrill for me. I really wish that adoption did not hold such a stigma. It is the greatest show of a mother's love and the best alternative for a lot of young girls today.

F   I   V   E

The "Hard" Cases

In the last two chapters we have seen that abortion is fraught with many risks, both physical and mental, short-term and long-term. Thus, because of her limited knowledge and experience, the woman seeking an abortion has never possessed an unconditional "right to abortion." Instead, the legal responsibility for the abortion decision, as is clearly stated in *Roe v. Wade*, rests with the attending physician.[1] It is the physician/abortionist's responsibility, at least according to the Court's theory, to determine whether or not an abortion is actually in the "best interests" of the woman's health (where "health" is broadly defined to include her psychic, emotional, social, or even her economic well-being). Using his intimate knowledge of the woman's physical, mental, and socio-economic "health" needs, only the "conscientious physician" is able to weigh the "health" advantages of abortion against its health risks. Though the Court guarantees that any woman has the right to *request* an abortion, her physician, at least in theory, must make the final decision. Indeed, a physician would be obliged to refuse to do an abortion in any case where he knew such "treatment" would be detrimental to the woman's life or health.[2]

Abortion in practice, however, is much different than abortion according to the Supreme Court's legal theory. In actuality, there is little or no consultation between the woman and her physician. The vast majority of professional abortionists operate in clinics on an "assembly line" basis. They see themselves as providing a "service" to women, not as their counselors or co-decision-makers. Thus, abortionists consistently ignore their responsibility to weigh the woman's "health" needs against her "health" risks. It is, they presume, *her* responsibility to determine her "health" needs; it is *her* "choice."

Because of their personal interest in making money, abortionists not only ignore their own responsibility to evaluate their patients' overall "health" needs, but they also routinely deny patients information about the health risks of abortion. To this end, abortion clinics have actively fought, and beaten, all informed consent requirements.[3] Their rationale is that such information would scare women away.

This system is perpetuated, in part, because the "conscientious physicians," upon whom the court models its abortion theory, simply do not control the abortion industry. The "conscientious physician" who is the family's doctor may indeed be intimately aware of both a woman's overall "health" needs and the risks associated with abortion; but if he recommends against abortion, the woman only has to go and find a slightly less "conscientious physician." In fact, most women are unlikely to undergo the potentially embarrassing "consultation with her physician" in the first place. Instead, the vast majority of women seeking abortions go straight to the local abortuary where an anonymous physician will simply perform the procedure without questioning her reasons or remembering her face.

Despite this dismal reality, we must in all fairness ask when, if ever, the "conscientious physician" would recommend abortion in consultation with his patient. Specifically when, if ever, do the "health" benefits of abortion outweigh the "health" risks? Since the Court ruled that mental, emotional, and socio-economic "health" are to be considered when justifying abortion, these same criteria should be considered in refusing abortions. Obviously, a physician who justified an abortion on psychiatric grounds, while aware that the abortion was likely to cause greater psychiatric disturbances than it would alleviate, would be negligent in his duty to protect the woman's overall health. In "treating" only a patient's short-term emotional distress with an abortion, he might well be accused of profiteering at the expense of her long-term mental health. Such lack of circumspection would, of course, fall short of the judicial model of the "conscientious physician."

Considering the information from the last two chapters, a "conscientious physician" would certainly hesitate to recommend or perform an abortion on a teenager, for example. In weighing her temporary emotional distress against the high probability of permanent reproductive damage, combined with the high likelihood of post-abortion psychological sequelae, a "conscientious physician" would be obliged to try to convince the young woman that her long-range health needs would best be served by carrying the child to term. If her emotional or socio-economic well-being was threatened by premature parenthood, the "conscientious physician" would be obliged to advise adoption as the best alternative for preserving her "health," as broadly defined by the Court. Similarly, a "conscientious physician" who was asked to perform an abortion for emotional or psychiatric reasons would hesitate if any of the signs indicating a high probability of post-abortion sequelae were present: ambivalence, feelings of helplessness, coercion, compromised decision-making, and so on.

Indeed, as we have seen, the risks of abortion are so great that truly "conscientious physicians" would almost certainly confine their approval of abortion to only life-threatening circumstances. At the very least, one would expect "conscientious physicians" to limit their approval to only the "hard cases" which have been the mainstay of the pro-abortion rhetoric: (1) cases where abortion would save the mother's life, (2) cases where the mother is afflicted with a severe mental disorder; (3) cases where the diagnosis indicates a high probability that the child would be born with a handicap; and (4) cases where the pregnancy was the result of rape or incest. But even in these "hard cases" the physician would be obliged to weigh the risks of abortion and completely inform the woman of those risks.

In the next two chapters we will examine the risks of abortion in these "hard cases." We will find, however, that even in the most sympathetic of circumstances, the threat abortion poses to a woman's overall "health," as broadly defined by the Court, far outweighs the potential benefits. Indeed, we will find that these cases are the *worst* conditions under which to have an abortion. This finding is in keeping with the maxim presented in the last chapter: *The more difficult the circumstances prompting abortion, the more likely it is that the woman will suffer severe post-abortion sequelae.*

Abortion to Save a Woman's Life or Health

The occasional need for therapeutic abortions has always been used as the cutting edge of arguments supporting abortion on demand. Indeed, abortion to save the life of a mother has enjoyed strong public support and has always been legal. No anti-abortion group, to our knowledge, has ever sought to ban abortions necessary to save the mother's life. The only conflict which arises over this specific issue is in the area of diagnosis: When is a pregnancy truly life-threatening?

Life-threatening conditions which are agreed upon by all are ectopic pregnancies and cancers or tumors which require removal of the uterus during pregnancy. In such cases, the destruction of the unborn is not the *intended* result of the operation, but only a side effect which occurs when removing the impregnated fallopian tube or cancerous uterus. Such lifesaving surgery is not even properly classified as an "abortion." Even the most rigorous of religious ethics allows "abortions" in these cases.

The consensus begins to falter, however, when therapeutic abortions are recommended in cases where the mother is suffering from other maladies, such as heart or kidney disease, which *may* worsen as the pregnancy progresses. Dispute occurs in these cases because the death of the mother is only a possibility rather than a certainty. Professional opinion is split over whether or not abortion is ever advisable under these circumstances.

The evidence that abortion in such marginal cases is "therapeutic" is unconvincing, since the vast majority of these diseased women, if not aborted, will survive and carry their pregnancies successfully to term. Furthermore, since these women are already weakened by disease, they are also more susceptible to complications associated with abortion. Though childbirth poses extra risks for these women, so does abortion. In many such cases it has been found that "therapeutic" abortions are in fact far more dangerous than childbirth.[4]

According to one obstetrician, "After many years' work in several large gynecological hospitals, I have never yet seen a woman's life in danger, necessitating abortion." In contrast, he adds, "I have seen two extremely sick women offered abortions because of serious heart-lung disease; both refused, and both delivered normal children, normally. When a doctor declares that the patient's life is in danger because of pregnancy and an associated disease, that is his clinical opinion. There is no absolute indication for a legal abortion in such circumstances."[4a] Similarly, Dr. David Decker of the Mayo Clinic states that there are "few, if any, absolute medical indications for therapeutic abortion in the present state of medicine."[5]

It is important to note, at this point, that in this "gray" area surrounding therapeutic abortions, disagreement is generally confined to medical debates rather than political action. No anti-abortion group or religious body is seeking criminal sanctions against abortions in these cases where honest medical judgement varies and abortion *may* be indicated as lifesaving treatment. Instead, pro-lifers seek only to educate physicians and the public about alternative treatment options and to encourage that every attempt be made to save the child as well as the mother (for example, the Caesarean delivery of a premature infant rather than its abortion by D&C). These educational efforts are intended only to remind both the doctors and patients who face such dilemmas of the seriousness with which the moral questions should be addressed. At the same time, anti-abortionists would seek through education to prevent the "stretching" of such exceptions to include less serious indications.[6] In any case, less than one percent of all abortions presently done are medically indicated—a figure agreed upon by both sides of the issue. And as medical science improves treatment for these diseases, the "need" for therapeutic abortions will continue to decline.[7]

As a matter of fact, the only reason that therapeutic abortions are an issue of debate is that prior to 1973 elective abortions were often disguised as being "therapeutic" when physicians were actually performing abortions for social reasons, sometimes merely because the woman requesting the abortion was a wealthy or preferred customer. The granting of "therapeutic" abortions when no medical indications actually existed was widely practiced prior to total legalization, a fact admitted to by the doctors who performed them.[8] For example, Dr. Alan F. Guttmacher, a pro-abortion advocate who was later to become president of Planned Parenthood, wrote that during his period of practice at Mount Sinai Hospital (1952–1956), 85 percent of all the "therapeutic" abortions performed "at least bent the law, if they did not fracture it."[9]

Pro-life cynicism towards "therapeutic" abortions, therefore, does not reflect insensitivity to the health of women. Instead, pro-life advocates recognize how quickly the terms "therapeutic" and "health" can be distorted from their original meanings. For this reason, the typical amendments and legislation proposed by anti-abortionists avoid using the distortable terms of "therapeutic" or "health" exceptions, and allow exceptions only when an abortion is "necessary to save the mother's life." This wording is consistent with the original meaning of therapeutic abortions and would allow abortions even in those few

165

"gray" areas where the health threat is potentially fatal even to a lesser degree. In such marginal cases, it is extremely doubtful that a physician or the diseased woman would be prosecuted, much less convicted by a jury, if they acted in "good faith," seriously believing that the pregnancy presented a threat to the mother's survival. In sum, some abortions performed for medically questionable reasons will probably always exist, but certainly these few cases are preferable to the present state of wholesale abortion on demand.

Finally, it should be noted that therapeutic abortions pose the same psychological risks associated with elective abortions, perhaps more so since the women who are told they "should" have an abortion for health reasons are generally being asked to abort a wanted baby. It is not uncommon for such women to insist on carrying their babies to term even at the risk of their own lives. Such decisions reflect great bravery and love for their unborn, but obviously these standards should not be imposed on all women whose lives may be threatened by their pregnancies. In any case, it is clear that most women faced with the recommendation for a therapeutic abortion do not make the decision lightly, and so this option is unlikely to be abused on their part. Unfortunately, the same cannot be said for all doctors, for in some cases it has been recorded that doctors have urged "therapeutic" abortions in order to cover up their own mistakes, malpractice, or incompetence.[10]

In brief, no one is claiming that abortions which are necessary to save a mother's life should be made illegal. In such cases the "conscientious physician" might be justified in recommending an abortion, but should fully advise the woman of the risks. In every case, the physician should be sensitive and supportive if the mother wishes to accept the risks of pregnancy in order to save her child. As in any other case, if any overt or subtle coercion is used to convince the woman to accept a therapeutic abortion, there is a high likelihood that the woman will experience long-term psychological complications.

Psychological Indications

Before 1973 abortion laws were commonly circumvented through claims that "psychiatric indications" warranted a "therapeutic" abortion. Obstetricians willing to perform an elective abortion for a preferred patient would refer the woman to psychiatric colleagues sympathetic to abortion on demand who would give their approval for the abortion on mental grounds. Sometimes women were even coached on how to claim that the "unwanted" pregnancy had made them suicidal.[11] It is estimated that 80 to 95 percent of the "therapeutic" abortions performed during the 1960s were thus certified as "psychiatrically necessary."[12] Today, less than one-tenth of one-percent of abortions are performed for psychiatric reasons.[13]

This abuse of "therapeutic" abortions on psychiatric grounds was a source of embarrassment to both obstetricians and psychiatrists. It was such a thinly veiled deception. All involved admitted that the true basis for approving such "therapeutic" abortions was not psychiatric but rather socioeconomic—an area in which neither the physician or the psychiatrist had expertise or training beyond a rudimentary level.[14] Many of the professionals who advocated abortion admitted that these abortions did not promote medical or psychological welfare, but insisted that they were "therapeutic" in a sociological way because they prevented "unwanted" children, reduced the "surplus" population.[15]

In 1971, for example, Dr. Seymour Halleck, a Wisconsin psychiatrist, wrote:

No psychiatrist, if he is honest with himself . . . can . . . describe any scientific criteria that enable him to know which woman should have her pregnancy terminated, and which should not. When he recommends an abortion, he usually lies. It is a kind lie, a dishonesty intended to make the world a little better, but it is still a lie.[16]

Prior to 1973, then, the use of abortions as psychiatric "therapy" was a common alibi but, in general, rarely sincere. This does not mean, however, that psychiatric problems *never* existed. Indeed, it can be argued that the only time women seek abortion is when they are experiencing psychic distress.[17] The real question then is when, if ever, does abortion alleviate or "cure" psychological disorders? Only if abortion is identifiably beneficial to a woman's mental health could it be justified as therapeutic. If it hurts her or is only neutral and has no positive effect, then it is not therapeutic.

The answer to this question is very well known and commonly accepted by professionals on both sides of the abortion debate. Within all of the psychiatric literature available, there is not one psychiatric condition for which abortion is a recognized cure.[18] Instead, the evidence overwhelmingly indicates that true psychological problems are generally complicated and aggravated by abortion rather than alleviated by it.[19]

167

For example, suicidal tendencies would seem to be the strongest indication for abortion on psychiatric grounds. Abortion would save the woman's life, it could be argued. But though the diagnosis of women as "suicidal" was a common ploy, it was a recognized falsehood for two reasons. First, "suicide is one of the most difficult things to forecast in any patient."[20] Any psychiatrist who routinely predicts suicide is practicing voodoo rather than science.[21] Second, all the evidence shows that the suicide rate among pregnant women, including women with unwanted pregnancies, is only one-sixth to one-tenth of the rate among non-pregnant women. This has led some psychiatrists to suggest that pregnancy somehow serves a psychologically protective role.[22]

Explanations as to why pregnancy reduces suicide attempts are many. Some suggest that the woman received more attention from society when pregnant than when not pregnant. Others suggest that physiological changes and heightened instincts manifest themselves in greater maternal protectiveness. Still others suggest that the truly suicidal woman may find in her pregnancy a positive reason to at least postpone suicide.[23] Finally, it is worth noting that in the few cases in which pregnant women do commit suicide, the "push" is caused by the stress between the man and the woman rather than merely rejection of the pregnancy.[24]

Though pregnancy weakens suicidal impulses, there is strong evidence that abortion dramatically *increases* the risk of suicide.[25] According to one study, the rate of suicide among aborted women is nine times higher than among an identical population of non-aborted women.[26] In at least one reported case, an eighteen-year-old committed suicide three days after having a suction abortion because of guilt feelings over having "killed her baby." Later examination of the clinic's records revealed that she had not actually been pregnant. The "abortion," therefore, had been unnecessary.[27] In conclusion, abortion is far more likely to drive an unstable woman to suicide than is pregnancy and childbirth.

But suicide is only a measure of the most extreme negative reactions to abortion. Not fatal but no less serious is the deepening of psychological problems among mentally ill women for whom abortion was deemed "therapeutic."[28] The evidence is compelling, universal, and undisputed. According to Dr. Fred E. Mecklenburg, Professor of Obstetrics and Gynecology at the University of Minnesota Medical School and member of the American Association of Planned Parenthood Physicians:

There are no known psychiatric diseases which can be cured by abortion. In addition there are none which can be predictably improved by abortion. . . . [Instead], it may leave unresolved conflicts coupled with guilt and added depression which may be more harmful than the continuation of the pregnancy.

Furthermore, there is good evidence to suggest that serious mental disorders arise following abortions more often in women with real psychiatric problems. Paradoxically, the very women for whom legal abortion may seem most justifiable are also the ones for whom the risk is highest for post-abortion psychic insufficiency. . . .

When abortion is substituted for adequate psychiatric care— and there is ample evidence to suggest that this is already happening—then there is a distinct danger of minimizing established psychotherapeutic principles. Unfortunately, it is the distressed woman who ultimately faces the dulling impact of this minimization. She is the one who cries for help, and she is also the one who is turned away.[29]

Similarly, an official statement from the World Health Organization reads: "Thus the very women for whom legal abortion is considered justified on psychiatric grounds are the ones who have the highest risk of post-abortion psychiatric disorders."[30] And an article in the *World Medical Journal* observes that: "[Abortion] is a bad way of treating true psychiatric disease. . . . Investigation shows that there is less psychological trauma associated with normal birth than there is with a legal abortion."[31]

If all this is true, one might ask, why have psychiatrists ever supported abortion on therapeutic grounds? The answer, in part, is because psychiatry is an inexact science. There was a period in which some psychiatrists experimented with "therapeutic" abortion as a means of alleviating symptoms of distress. It was hoped that by eliminating one external problem they could concentrate on other areas. It was only after long periods of study that it became apparent that abortion was almost always a negative or, at best, a neutral form of "treatment."

Second, abortion was often encouraged not for the patient's welfare but for the convenience of the psychiatric hospital and staff where she was confined. In a 1947 article, for example, therapeutic abortion was recommended for selected cases where the patient was institutionalized. According to the authors, abortion "may be advisable owing to the inability of the patient to care for the child and the problems *inherent to management, confinement, and labor.*" [italics added][32] In other words, childbirth would not be detrimental to the patient, but it would be very inconvenient for everyone else!

When all the evidence is added up, then, psychic weakness and mental disorders must be considered as *contraindications* for abortion. The "conscientious physician" should therefore refuse to abort any woman on psychiatric grounds, since it is very likely that such an abortion would only aggravate her psychiatric condition in the long run. On the other hand, those women who least "need" an abortion are most able to cope *without* one. Bearing an "unwanted" baby is a "tragedy" to which the mentally healthy woman quickly adjusts.

This may seem like a neat little Catch-22 invented by anti-abortionists, but it is a fact confirmed not only by medical experts but by common sense as well. For example, the succesful woman who is confident, competent, secure, independent, able to handle all challenges and overcome all odds, would hardly be suddenly incapacitated by an unplanned pregnancy. While an unplanned child might certainly be inconvenient for such an "all-together" woman, it would hardly be unmanageable. Any woman who is capable of adjusting to abortion is just as capable of adjusting to the birth of an unplanned child.[33] Given that her mental health and well-being would survive either event, her claim to "convenience" is unconvincing when weighed against the child's claim to life. If society chose to infringe on this "all-together" woman's convenience and place a higher priority on preserving the life of her unborn child by making abortion in such cases illegal, her health does not suffer in any way. She would adjust, no worse for the infringement, and perhaps later she will even be grateful for the unforeseen joys of her "unwanted" child. At the very least, society would be richer for having added one more member raised by such an "all-together" parent, or by loving adoptive parents.

On the other hand, the mentally distressed woman, for whom every new challenge is psychic agony, will find the adjustment to childbirth no worse than the adjustment to abortion. Indeed, all the evidence shows that abortion will hurt a psychically weak woman far more than the bearing of an "unwanted" child, an event with positive, often strengthening overtones. Thus, for the psychically weak woman, abortion should be actively discouraged.

THE "HARD" CASES
Eugenic Abortions

The abortion of unborn children diagnosed as potentially handicapped is frequently placed under the category of "therapeutic abortions." But selective abortions are not in any way therapeutic for the mothers and are certainly not therapeutic for the aborted children.[34] The correct term for such abortions is *eugenic* abortions, where eugenic, in this case, means identifying and eliminating persons with "inferior" genes or those who are deemed capable of only an "inferior quality" of life.

Unfortunately, once the way is opened for the killing of any "defective" or "diseased" person merely for "the relief of suffering and burden to family and society," there is no telling where eugenicists will draw the line to limit the liquidation of the "unfit." Is it all right to kill a handicapped child who has already been born? And if a handicapped child can be killed as an "act of mercy" to relieve the burden it would impose on family and society, should elderly persons who are handicapped by age be "aborted" so as to relieve the burden they pose on their families and society? And what about the comatose? The insane? The neurotic? Those with criminal behavior patterns? The stupid? The ugly? Those of the "wrong" sex?

There are, in fact, many respected scientists and philosophers who advocate all these eugenic options in order to create a more "perfect" human race with a high "quality of life." But while this eugenics philosophy lies at the core of the pro-abortion movement, an examination of this complex subject goes beyond the scope of this book. For now, we will ignore the moral questions and the future implications of eugenics, and we will confine ourselves to the medical and psychological problems involved with eugenic abortions.

The greatest difficulty behind eugenic abortions is identifying which fetuses are "defective." One method promoted by genetic counselors is to examine the family history of parents to identify the probability of inherited diseases, such as hemophilia and muscular dystrophy. This technique is always uncertain. It provides only a probability of the risks that the child is affected by the disease. In most cases where the parents are considered carriers of a recessive disease, the odds are one-in-four that the child will be affected. If the disease is sex-linked and affects only males, for example, then tests can be performed to determine if the fetus is male or female. But even if the fetus is of the sex which is at risk, there is at most only a one-in-two chance that it will be affected.[35]

171

Thus, of all eugenic abortions prescribed on the basis of genetic history, one-half to three-quarters of the unborn children destroyed are not affected by the disease. *More normal children are killed than "handicapped" children.* The only reason that such gambling with lives occurs is because the eugenic creed of genetic counselors holds that the risk of aborting normal fetuses is worth the opportunity to prevent a "defective" child from being born.[36] Eugenicists rationalize this slaughter of unafflicted children by insisting that many of these children are not truly "normal." Many are "carriers" of the disease and so should be eliminated in order to prevent the risk of these "carriers" producing "defective" children in the next generation.

Genetic counseling alone, then, is a rather haphazard way of preventing handicapped children. Its recommendations lead to the abortion deaths of more normal children than abnormal ones. But in a very limited number of cases, prenatal diagnostic tools are available for confirming whether or not a suspected defect does in fact exist. This reduces the number of normal fetuses sacrificed on the altar of "racial purity," but it also leads to other problems.

Amniocentesis is the primary tool used for identifying candidates for eugenic abortions. Rather than using the "hit and miss" approach of blanket abortions in suspected cases, amniocentesis attempts to ascertain whether or not the suspected defect actually exists. Because of its greater accuracy, this diagnostic tool has often been called the "search and destroy" method of eugenic control. The number of defects which can be identified by amniocentesis, however, is still very limited. It is primarily useful for identifying three possible disorders: Down's syndrome; neural tube defects, such as spina bifida; and children of the "wrong" sex.

Sex selection, however, is still a comparatively rare use for amniocentesis in the United States. And certainly it is never promoted by doctors for that purpose unless a sex-linked genetic disease is suspected. Instead, advanced maternal age is the most frequent reason for which doctors recommend amniocentesis. Statistics indicate that the risk of having a child with Down's syndrome is 1 in 1000 for women under age 35, 1 in 290 for women aged 35 to 59, approximately 1 in 100 for women 40 to 45 years of age, and 1 in 40 over age 45. Therefore, it is a common practice for some physicians to urge amniocentesis for women over 40, and some doctors even urge it for all women over 30. The second most frequent reason for recommending amniocentesis is when there was a previous birth of a Down's syndrome child, in which

172

case there is a 1 to 2 percent chance that another such child will be conceived.[37]

Finally, amniocentesis is frequently recommended in cases where the mother has previously delivered a child with a neural tube defect such as spina bifida or anencephaly. If a previous baby had been born with such a defect, there is a 3 percent chance that a subsequent baby might have a similar condition. Amniocentesis is fairly accurate when there is an "open" neural tube defect, but since approximately one-third of these defects are "closed," a negative result of the amniocentesis still leaves a 1 percent risk that an undetected neural tube defect exists.[38]

Amniocentesis generally poses minor health risks to the mother, but the risk it poses to the unborn child is almost always greater than the risk of there being a genetic defect. One recent study, for example, found a 1.5 percent rate of spontaneous miscarriage after amniocentesis.[39] Thus, a forty-year-old woman undergoing amniocentesis faces a greater risk of miscarrying a healthy child because of the procedure than she faces for having a Down's syndrome baby in the first place.

Dr. Hymie Gordon, Chairman of the Department of Medical Genetics at Mayo Clinic in Minnesota, seriously questions the medical appropriateness of amniocentesis for identifying rare fetal defects because the risks and limitations of the test pose undue hardship on the parents. In a letter explaining the limitations of amniocentesis, Dr. Gordon writes:

[Amniocentesis] must be done between the 16th and the 18th week of pregnancy. At this time, the uterus is quite small, and much of the space inside the uterus is occupied by the baby's head. Even with the help of ultrasound, accidents have happened.[40] A conservative estimate is that there is a 2 percent risk of either damaging the baby, tearing the uterus, introducing infection, or precipitating a miscarriage.

Even if the procedure itself does no harm, it is not always successful. Quite often it is not possible to obtain an adequate specimen of fluid either because the volume is insufficient or it has been contaminated with blood from the mother. There is a risk of at least 5 percent that an adequate specimen will not be obtained and then the procedure, with its risks, must be repeated.

Even if an adequate specimen is obtained and sent to the laboratory, there is a substantial risk that the cells will not grow.

173

The cells in the amniotic fluid are the decaying cells from the baby's skin (dandruff) which simply have washed off. They are not healthy growing cells. Accordingly, there is a substantial risk—10 percent at minimum—that the cells will not grow.

Finally, errors in laboratory diagnosis are made. Because the cells are not "healthy," they often have secondary changes in them (such as mosaicism) making it difficult to be certain whether there is truly an abnormality in the baby. Some errors have been reported, [an inaccuracy rate of .6% was reported by an NICHD study[41]], including mistakes in determining the baby's sex. I have little doubt that many other errors have gone unreported.

Thus, adding up the risk of the procedure itself, the probability of not getting an adequate fluid specimen, the failure of cells to grow, and the possibility of a laboratory error, I estimate that there is *at least a 15 percent probability that the procedure will be harmful or unreliable.* This probability must be contrasted with the risks of birth defects in the babies who are being studied. If a woman is 40 years old, there is a risk of 1 percent that her baby might have the Down syndrome. . . . In my experience of many dozens of such cases, the smallness of the risk is seldom explained to the parents, nor are the disadvantages of the amniocentesis adequately explained. It is my experience—with, at most, two exceptions during the past five years—that when these indications and disadvantages are explained correctly to the mother and father, they elect not to have amniocentesis. . . .

The great majority of women who have come to me for a "second opinion" have not been informed adequately. . . .[42]

In an attempt to evaluate the "likely human consequences" of amniocentesis, a British study concluded that the amount of screening necessary to abort 523 anencephalic children and 555 spina bifida children would result in 120 dead or harmed normal infants—63 accidental abortions of normal infants and 57 others suffering severe to mild harm from the procedure.[43]

Though the physical health risks posed to women undergoing amniocentesis are considerably smaller, the emotional and psychiatric costs are very significant. First, it must be remembered that amniocentesis can be performed only in the second trimester, and the results will be known only late in the second trimester or sometime during the third trimester. Since the mother did not previously elect to abort, the baby is obviously wanted—though there is clearly a strong desire to make sure that the child is healthy. Adjustments and plans are already in progress, and the parents are anxious to have the child. Exaggerated warnings about the risk of defect only create anxiety, and the delay of four to six weeks waiting for results can be excruciating.[44] One woman waiting for the results writes:

> Those of my friends who have had an amniocentesis report terrible fantasies, dreams and crying fits, and I was no exception: I dreamed in lurid detail of my return to the lab, of awful damage. I woke up frantic, sobbing, to face the nagging fear that is focused in the waiting period after amniocentesis.[45]

If being put into the position of waiting six weeks or more for bad news is not bad enough, there is also at least a 10 percent chance that the test results will be inconclusive and another test, and another wait, will have to be endured.

In the vast majority of cases, however, the worry is all over nothing—the test results are negative. How can eugenicists who advocate such screening justify putting 99 couples through the expense and scare of amniocentesis for every one child identified? Is identifying the opportunity to abort one handicapped child worth subjecting 99 women and 99 normal babies to the risk, the pain, and the worry of amniocentesis?

And in the 1 percent of cases where the test is positive, what does the woman face? She is faced with the pressure to abort, "in the child's best interest." But this is a child she had previously looked forward to with enthusiasm. Well along into the second trimester of her pregnancy, she has already felt the child move and has already begun to form a close maternal bond to it. At such a late date in the pregnancy, the humanity of even a handicapped unborn baby is no longer even debatable—for months now it has been able to feel pain and recognize sounds and shapes, and it has developed personality patterns such as sucking its thumb or fingers, and it even has favorite tastes.[46] The mother in such cases does not have the luxury of aborting an abstraction of "fetal material." For her the child and its humanity is very real. It is only the rhetoric which obligates her to abort "for the child's sake" that can ease her sense of guilt.

Not surprisingly, then, the rate of psychological sequelae following eugenic abortions is extremely high. In most cases the woman feels no sense of free choice, but rather an obligation to do what others tell her is "best." Typically, it is the eugenic-minded physician who first identifies the risk of handicap, first recommends amniocentesis, and first urges the option of abortion.[47]

Because the aborted child was wanted and the abortion is seen at best as "mercy killing" of an innocent child, the incidence of severe depression following a selective abortion is about 92 percent among the mothers, and 82 percent among the fathers. "These patients exhibited more depression than that described in the literature for women undergoing abortion on psychosocial grounds." One woman in the study declared that aborting her handicapped child was the "worst thing that ever happened to me."[48]

The risk of marital stress following a eugenic abortion is also very high. And researchers found that in all of the cases studied, the families had "received excellent counseling regarding the genetic and technical facets of amniocentesis" but had received no warnings about the psychological aspects of the procedure (perhaps because the physicians did not want to mention any negative aspects which would dissuade them from undergoing the tests, much less the abortion).[49] The severity of psychological sequelae following eugenic abortions is confirmed by at least two follow-up studies done by abortionists themselves![50]

In addition, since eugenic abortions are almost always late-term, the physical risks of abortion are many times higher than for childbirth. In fact, the odds that a forty-year-old woman will suffer a severe complication from abortion are more than twice as great as the odds that she will have a child with Down's syndrome.[51] Certainly a "conscientious physician" who was concerned enough about a 1 percent risk that the patient will have a Down's syndrome child, should be even more concerned about the minimum 2 percent risk of the woman suffering a severe complication from a second trimester abortion. Obviously, if the physician is more concerned with the woman's health than he is with killing handicapped babies, he would advocate that her own health needs are best served by carrying the child to term.

Finally, the use of amniocentesis as a way of targeting for eugenic abortions presumes that handicapped infants should be destroyed. The presumption that anyone can decide whether or not another's life is worth living is frightening indeed. But there is much more groundwork to lay before this major premise of eugenics can be adequately discussed. For now, however, it is sufficient to turn to a second presumption which lies behind the "search and destroy" mind-set of some physicians. This second presumption is that even if handicapped children would want to live, it is better for the parents if they do not. It is argued that even if abortion does not benefit children, then at least it saves parents from the "undue burdens" of raising handicapped children. But what do the parents who have been in that position think?

The fact is that not a single organization of parents who have mentally or physically handicapped children has ever endorsed abortion of the handicapped.[52] Indeed many organizations, such as the Spina Bifida Association, are not only vigorous in discouraging abortion of potential spina bifida victims, but their members also have a standing offer to adopt the newborn babies themselves, if necessary. These parents find the raising of handicapped children so worthwhile that they are willing to raise not only their own, but the handicapped children of others as well.[53]

Returning to our original question, then, we ask, Would a "conscientious physician" ever urge abortion of a handicapped child? No, not if he or she were considering only the health and welfare of the mother. Abortion in such cases is always more dangerous and traumatic than childbirth. Thus, any physician who urges the abortion of a handicapped child is letting his personal biases, and perhaps his personal devotion to the eugenics philosophy, supercede his obligation to protect his patient's health. Such a physician would not truly be a "concientious physician."

Summary

The need for abortion in order to save a woman's life is extremely rare, and no pro-life organization objects to such lifesaving procedures when such conditions actually exist. Pro-lifers do not seek to prohibit abortion in these cases, but they urge caution to prevent this legitimate exception from being distorted to include non-life-threatening conditions under the ambiguous title of "health."

The use of "therapeutic" abortion as treatment for psychological problems was a Pandora's box which led to much abuse and hypocrisy. In fact, it is a well-established principle in the field of psychology today that the existence of true psychological problems is a contraindication for abortion. No psychological condition has ever been cured or alleviatd by abortion; instead, it is found that abortion frequently worsens mental disorders and increases emotional stress. The recommendation for therapeutic abortion in cases where the woman is suffering from mental disorders is tantamount to malpractice. Psychiatric testimony suggests not only that mentally ill women should not have abortions, but also that mentally stable women do not need them. Truly stable women are capable of adjusting to an unplanned or even an unwanted pregnancy quite quickly, especially if given the emotional and economic support which is necessary.

Finally, the recommendation for the eugenic abortion of handicapped children is motivated by prejudice against the handicapped rather than by the health interests of the mother. Furthermore, the testing procedures which precede eugenic abortions are both emotionally and financially costly, pose a minor health threat to the woman and a significant health threat to the child. Promoters of eugenic abortion willingly destroy many normal infants in their rush to prevent the birth of the handicapped. It is a game of odds which unfortunately ends in the killing of human beings, both "normal" and handicapped. Such deaths never promote the mother's physical health, but almost invariably damage her emotional and mental well-being. Indeed, the physical health of these mothers is endangered by these second trimester abortions, and psychological sequelae are almost always present as parents grieve over the killing of a wanted child which happened to be "defective."

PROFILES FIVE

Victims of Therapeutic Abortion

10) "Tammy Conrad"

Tammy was forced into an abortion by the doctor treating her for mental instability. Institutionalized in Kansas at the time, Tammy saw no way to escape his decision. Thus she succumbed to the abortion "to preserve her mental health" and to "protect" her baby from the risk of "deformities" which they said would occur because of the drugs she was receiving. Since her abortion eight years ago, Tammy has become a nurse and has learned that her abortion was unnecessary on both counts.

The best way to start my story would be to give you a little history leading up to it. I was very young when I had my first experience with sex. I had been raised under the auspices that sex prior to marriage was immoral. I had not entered the relationship that I was in, at thirteen years of age, with the idea of becoming sexually active. But apparently the guy I was seeing, who was twenty-one at the time, had other ideas. One evening he pressed me up against a wall, in a barn of all places, and forced my hand into his pants. When I withdrew it, he forced it back in, pushed me down, told me that I wanted it as much as he did, and unclothed me. He took what he wanted, and left.

I got up and walked home. The whole thing bewildered me. I just could not understand how a person could feel so filthy and used by what had been built up to be such an earthshaking delight. But I felt that I had deserved what I had gotten, since I had been seeing this person on the sly; and I never told anyone I had been raped.

This happened in the early 1970s when "do your own thing" while "everybody's doing it" was really big. I see today, at the ripe old

179

age of twenty-six, what a hideous monster of a society has been bred from that logic.

In the course of a year I met someone else, also twenty-one. He was a kind and gentle person, and he did sort of care about me. But he was heavily into drugs and should have known better than to be seeing a fourteen-year-old child. I did not fear him, but I did not allow him to come close to being intimate with me. When he was busted and sent to prison, I was so upset that I quit eating. I did not believe anyone could love me or care for me as the person I was. In an attempt to do a complete bodily overhaul, I nearly starved myself to death.

During the next four years I was heavy into drugs, always trying to propel myself upward, speeding, freaking, the life of the party. I'd take downers to highlight the experiences in between, as well. Somewhere around sixteen years of age I became sexually active, almost with a zeal to be in control of a "relationship." I essentially became a little whore. I was hurting terribly all the while and would have given anything for a real relationship.

On graduating from high school in the spring of 1976, I finally called my psychologist, whom I had been seeing for three years, and asked to be admitted to a hospital for psychiatric treatment. Upon entering a Catholic hospital, I became the victim of Freudian psychology. My brains were essentially scrambled on Rorschach, MMPI, etc.

At a point where I had been fully stripped of every fragment of mental and physical integrity, I felt this strange sense of something not being as it should be, aside from the fact that I had become a walking, zombified, stuporous shadow of a person as a result of the antipsychotic drug therapy that had been inappropriately prescribed. (I am a nurse now and feel at liberty to say that I was not crazy, out of kilter or sync maybe, but not a lunatic.) Actually, what was not quite right was that I had missed a period or two and was generally feeling poorly. Down to the clinic for pregnancy evaluation, and yes, there was indeed a pregnancy there.

There was this warm, sad, shivery, amazed, sparkly feeling all throughout my body—me pregnant. There was a baby inside of me! I'd probably have to adopt it out. No, I couldn't do that—this was *my* baby. But what would be best for the baby? What would my parents think? But here I was, trapped in this hospital, and everybody knew. There was absolutely no way that I could just quietly exit and figure these things out.

The next day my psychiatrist called me into his office for a conference about my pregnancy. He established with me that under the circumstances, considering my emotional status, I probably should not carry this pregnancy to term. He said there was also the great potential that the psychotropic drugs I was on would cause fetal defects. He also assured me that there was hardly anything in my womb.

I sat there, numbed and empty to the core. I had nothing to say and felt the perfect fool for thinking I could get away with being pregnant and giving birth. The doctor explained that, though this was surely a very difficult "decision," I really had no choice under the circumstances but to have an abortion. He was very kind, telling me he would take care of all the arrangements, and would even tell my parents. My parents, though totally against abortion, were also convinced by the doctor that abortion was the only way to go in this situation. This shows the awesome power of the medical community in influencing life and death decisions.

Since Catholic hospitals do not do abortions, this psychiatrist referred me to an abortuary 100 miles away. My mom drove me there. A very simplistic and brief explanation of the procedure was given, and I was escorted into the examining room. The abortionist came in, said some rather crude things, and sat down between my legs. He started prodding and poking and dilating, then suctioned out what felt like my entire lower anatomy, without ever speaking to me. Just before leaving, he told me to stay on my feet as much as possible (why, I still do not know). The attendant stayed with me for a few minutes, told me to get my clothes on, and then left. That was the last I saw of them.

On returning to the Catholic hospital, the abortionist's instructions were followed to the letter. I'm not sure whether I was being punished or what. I was hurting terribly, mentally and physically, and every time I'd sit down to rest or try to go to my room to lie down, a nurse or aide would come over and say ever so sweetly, "You must be up and about, you know." I walked in circles until ten o'clock that night. I had cried all the way home from the abortuary, yet did not feel at liberty to cry here in the place that was supposedly helping me. No one ever asked me how I felt about having the abortion before the fact, and no one acknowledged my grief and despair after the fact.

Within the next year, after leaving the hospital, I began to seriously consider a life of prostitution. Then, after a nearly successful suicide attempt, I met my then-to-be husband. He explained to me how Christ can and does forgive sins, even mega-sins. I struggled with that, as I had never forgiven myself for the slaughter of my baby, and I

181

finally begged Him to forgive me. Jesus forgave and completely healed me of my long-term depression as well.

After marrying, my husband and I conceived our beautiful son. At first I had great difficulty in dealing with him. I did love him and very much still do, but my guilt and grief over slaughtering my first baby drove me to think that I didn't deserve this son. For four years I could not read to him without crying. I even entertained thoughts of putting him in the fireplace. Thankfully, I now live in Jesus.

I have since forgiven myself for everything, but continue to search out the truth of abortion. The medical literature, for instance, in all studies done regarding the drug I was taking, cannot substantiate that there is or ever will be fetal malformations or developmental problems as a result of taking that drug. I also visited with a neonatologist about my situation; he just shook his head and agreed with the literature. Either my psychiatrist had been very ignorant, or he had merely told me what he did to facilitate my thinking toward what he thought to be the only valid way to go: abortion.

11) Martha Wenger

Pregnancy had always been a difficult condition for Martha to bear, as she suffered from hypoglycemia, thyroid and nerve problems. She'd already had two children and lost two chidren when she discovered in 1977 that she was pregnant for the fifth time. Hysterical and terrified at the prospect of pregnancy on top of her illnesses, Martha chose to have an abortion for health reasons.

I have always had bad health, mostly problems with my legs, thyroid, bad nerves, and other things. I had very difficult pregnancies when I had my first two children. I also had a miscarriage and a stillborn.

By the time I got pregnant again, several years had passed, and my children were in school. I found out that I had high blood pressure, which I hadn't known before, so I was afraid to have any more children. Without knowing I was already pregnant again, I made arrangements to have my tubes cut and tied. During the waiting period, my doctor gave me a medicine to thin my blood, and I broke out all black and blue. The doctor told me that it was a reaction, and that it wasn't helping me.

They took me off the drug, and I went back in to have tests. That's when they told me I was pregnant. I got hysterical and started crying. I hadn't wanted any more children to begin with, and I had thought I was through. I just got so big when I was pregnant, I couldn't even drive a car. I knew my children would have to walk quite a distance to get to the bus stop for school. I panicked because we didn't have a house big enough to hold any more children. I just felt the situation would not allow it. All these thoughts kept upsetting me.

Right there in the doctor's office I became really hysterical. I had been on nerve pills, but not that day. I cried and cried. I was scared and nervous and sick, and kept hollering at the doctor, "I just can't have this baby." She was a good doctor and was worried, thinking I was about to go crazy.

That's when she said something about abortion, but added, "I don't do that, but I can recommend a place for you to go." I knew then that she wasn't for it, but she didn't offer me any pros or cons about it, either. She didn't tell me anything. It was like I was out on a limb. Because I was hysterical, she wanted to get me out of there. She filled out a paper and said, "Here's where to go."

And so I went home. I got my stepmother and father and told them the story. I kept crying, "I just need help, somebody to give me some advice." Everything seemed to be falling apart. They just couldn't stand to watch me because they'd seen all my sickness and all the problems I'd been through. They felt about abortion like I did—it was okay in a life or death situation. They felt that with my health problems, I shouldn't have any more children, and it would be okay. They didn't say anything at this point; they were just upset and went home. As they left, I was thinking I didn't even have money for this thing; money was tight for us at that time.

Then my stepmother came back and said, "Look, here's money. Your father says go ahead and have it done. He can't stand to watch you suffer anymore." But they both wanted to make sure that whatever I would do, I would never regret it later. I felt then, "Well, they're okaying it, so it can't really be too bad. This is a health situation."

I'd always been told, too, that until the baby moves, it's not really alive. You know, the same old thing you always hear. But I still didn't feel comfortable with it. If it was wrong, I was counting on someone to tell me, somebody to say something; but nobody did.

So I went ahead and had my stepmother take me down to the clinic. I went in there, and it was very cold, and there was a lot of fear in there. It was just awful. The people there didn't tell me a whole lot of anything until I got in the room and had it done. Even then, all they said was, "This will be simple and won't take long, because you're not very far along. It will be very quick and there won't be any pain."

But that's not true, because it hurt badly. Though quick, it was very painful. As soon as it was done, I started to cry. It was like an overwhelming, depressing feeling: there was just no way to fight it, the tears just poured. There was such an empty feeling—it was just awful.

They didn't give any counselling or anything, before or afterwards. They just wanted you to wait for awhile, and then get up to go.

I just cried and cried all the way home and all day long. I was in a deep depression. My husband just took one look at my face and I looked so bad, he turned around and walked out to work in the yard. He said all he saw was "hate on my face."

The whole procedure toughened me; I became a tough person. It was like, "I don't need anybody. Leave me alone and it won't hurt." I became hateful. I got to where "I'll make it alone" was how I lived. I had no compassion.

After that, if someone ever mentioned the word "abortion," it was like the floor dropped out from under me. It made me feel like a murderer. I could never use the word *abortion*. I would always say things like, "I had the baby taken from me." I just couldn't say that word.

A lot of women, I think, don't know what they'll be going through until it's all over. They think they're getting rid of a problem, but they don't have any idea of the problems they'll face afterwards. I didn't know better, or I would never have done it.

It was a year later that I became spirit-filled and claimed the healing God has given me. I was healed from the hypoglycemia, the thyroid condition, leg pains, nervous condition, the whole works. I haven't taken a nerve pill since then, not a one, even though I had become more reliant on my pills after the abortion.

But you know, even after I was healed, it took two years to get over the abortion. I felt awful. I knew God would forgive me of anything, but I couldn't forgive myself. It was like a nightmare. I turned it over to the Lord, but I still didn't feel a real peace. Finally, I prayed for inner healing and received it. God is a big God: He gave a new life to me.

184

12) "Sarah Logsdon"

Sarah's baby had been conceived despite the presence of an IUD, a sometimes dangerous circumstance for conception. The baby continued to develop despite Sarah's subsequent hospitalization, blood loss, and intake of anesthesia. Convinced that all these factors had deformed her child, Sarah chose to have an abortion for eugenic reasons.

Let me provide some background first. I was raised an atheist. My mother, who taught me her atheism, is German. She lived through the Holocaust of World War II, not as a Jew in the concentration camps or even as a Nazi, but as a victim of the times. The horrors of war made her question her belief. The scenes of burning babies, bombs, endless parades of death, hunger, cold and fear finally turned her heart cold to God. She came to rely on herself.

I went to college, received a B.S. in nursing in 1975, and later that year met and married my husband. We had everything going for us. Our first son was born in 1977. Following that, I had an IUD inserted.

In January 1979, I passed out one night. My first thought was, "I'm perforated." IUD's have a nasty habit of killing women, you know. In a hospital room, my husband and I found out that I was bleeding to death internally from a ruptured ovary; I was two weeks pregnant. Talk about a shock! I was twenty-eight years old at the time and in excellent health. Neither my husband nor I smoke, drink, or have ever experimented with drugs of any sort. There are no hereditary defects in either of our families. Knowing what I did as a nurse—that IUD's can cause limb reduction deformities, blood loss means an oxygen deficit and brain damage, surgical anesthesia can cause problems, and the fact that I left the hospital with the blood volume of a canary—I had talked myself into believing that I was going to have some kind of monster. The doctors all said I'd lose the baby.

Three months passed and I was still pregnant. I couldn't believe it. Some days I was happy, some days I cried. Thoughts came into my head seemingly out of nowhere: "Get rid of this baby, it's defective. There are enough idiots running around. You don't have a right to produce someone who will just end up being a vegetable. What kind of

185

life is that? People don't want to be burdened with imperfect weeds. Only the strong survive in this society." These are some of the hideous thoughts that raced through my mind. I thought I was going crazy; I know now that I was.

Against my husband's will and better judgment, I sought an abortion. Planned Parenthood was happy to refer me to a butcher in San Antonio. You see, by this time four months had elapsed, and the type of abortion I needed at this stage was not performed in Austin. The only counseling I was given at the office of the doctor who performed the abortion was to bring cash, no checks. How's that for business? The nurse informed me that Dr. Moore had done thousands of abortions; I guess that was supposed to reassure me. I was fully aware of what the D&C procedure consisted of and what the unborn child looked like at that stage of development. The thought of having a defective baby (and I don't even know for sure if the baby was defective) was enough to drive me to kill. That says a lot about my morally bankrupt condition.

As for the abortion experience itself, . . . After so many thousands of bodies, it becomes a boring routine carried out for profit. Abortion is anything but private: strangers peering at your most hidden parts, laughing, poking and tearing out a child growing under your heart. There's nothing private about that. Everything was so sanitary, so cheerful. Everyone had their little plastic smiles on. Music was piped in and the sun was shining through the windows. Death's pallid hue came over my little one and it was over. Or so I thought.

The hours, the days, the months, and the years that followed brought more and more pain and heartache. My husband and I grew distant, apart. We once shared so much. Love, trust and happiness were replaced by guilt, shame, fear, hate, blame, isolation, rejection, depression. You name it and we experienced it. Things just weren't the same. We fought over anything and everything. We blamed each other. After awhile, we didn't talk much at all and didn't talk about the abortion in any way. There was an unspoken agreement between us that I had committed a great evil.

We existed like this for five years. Three other children were born to us in the meantime, all perfect and healthy. But the pain persisted. That kind of emotional anguish is a torture so heartbreaking that there can be only one answer. Only one person can forgive a deed so horrible: the Lifegiver Himself.

Through all this darkness and pain and mental agony, we have finally found peace through the forgiveness of Jesus. Many women and their husbands (or boyfriends, parents and others) will never experience that peace. They will go on hurting in a place that no psychiatrist or drug can reach. Hopefully, WEBA will someday touch their lives.

S   I   X

Hostages of Rape, Victims of Abortion

Rape is a powerful word. It elicits strong and often contradictory responses, feelings of both horror and sympathy. Because people readily sympathize with rape victims, but also recoil from thinking too deeply about its effects on women, rape has been the "exception" to abortion restrictions which abortion proponents have most vigorously defended. "Should a woman who is pregnant from rape be *forced* to carry the child of her brutal attacker?" they asked. It was difficult for anyone to answer "yes" to such a question.

But after admitting to the possible justification of abortion in cases of rape, society has been forced by logic to expand this exception into a general license for abortion on demand. Once rape was accepted as an exception, the question became: "Should a woman be *forced* to bear an *unwanted* child, regardless of how she became pregnant." Indeed, the Supreme Court used this same expansive argument to strike down a Georgia law which generally prohibited abortion but allowed it in the case of rape. The Court argued that by allowing abortions in *some* cases, the states were revealing a lack of commitment to protection of the unborn. Therefore, if abortion was allowable in some cases, such as with rape, there was no justifiable reason to "arbitrarily" forbid abortion under other "compelling" circumstances. After all, once it was

188

admitted that a woman should not be "forced" into carrying the child of an unwanted rape, on what grounds could she be forced to carry the child of any unwanted father?[1]

Once the wedge of the rape "exception" was inserted into the fabric of abortion legislation, the remaining restrictions of abortion were torn apart. If abortion is allowed when a man forces himself upon the woman, then it follows that abortion should be allowed when an unborn child "forces" his or herself upon the woman. Through such arguments, the seemingly noble and compassionate "exception" in cases of rape was quickly distorted to devalue the unborn and lend sympathy to the abortion of any "unwanted" child.

The rape issue was used by pro-abortionists as a wedge by which they gained sympathy for abortion, but they also used it as a smoke-screen to confuse the central issue which was abortion on demand. Once abortion in the case of rape was allowed, the ambiguities surrounding rape were used to expand abortion access even further. For example, does the rape exception include "statutory rape," where any minor under the age of seventeen is considered "raped" whether she agreed to intercourse or not? Does the rape have to have been reported? Or can a woman claim the right to abortion due to rape months later, only after confirming that she is pregnant? Because the rape "exception" was so difficult to pin down, any legislation which allowed the exception could still be attacked as insufficient. Since legislatures had already committed themselves to alleviating "rape" victims from unwanted pregnancies, looser and looser legislation was necessary to ensure that every "victim" would have the opportunity to have an abortion.

Abortion proponents used the public's natural sympathy toward rape victims and the ambiguities surrounding the definition of such "exceptions" on abortion restrictions to convince the public that: (1) at least some abortions are justified; and (2) the issues are too complex to understand, much less to restrict through legislation; therefore (3) it is best to leave the abortion decision to women and their physicians.

But the failure of the pro-abortion rape argument lay not only in trying to turn a sympathetic "exception" into a general rule of toler-ance towards all abortions, but more importantly, they also failed in their diagnosis of the rape victim and her needs. As we will see, the pro-abortion argument—which was presumptuously and falsely pre-sented on behalf of rape victims—took only a shallow and paternalistic view toward the women involved. It automatically assumed that abortion was the "best" thing society could offer these victims of violence. The evidence is to the contrary.

Rape Pregnancies in Perspective

Rape is indeed a serious problem. Approximately 78,000 forcible rapes were reported in 1982 alone. This figure is even more appalling when it is recalled that 40 to 80 percent of all rapes are *not* reported.[2]

But despite the large number of rapes which occur, pregnancies resulting from rape are exceedingly rare. There are many reasons for this. Perhaps most significant is that even when penetration occurs, ejaculation may not, because the rate of sexual dysfunction among rapists is extremely high. Three studies found, respectively, that 39, 48, and even 54 percent of victims were not exposed to sperm during the course of rape. Another study found that 51 percent of rapists experience erective or ejaculatory dysfunction during sexual assault.[3] Still other investigators, having found that approximately one-third of rapists suffer from sexual dysfunctions, commented: "Thus, a significant portion of those who are labeled 'rapists,' and in popular mythology have excessive sexual appetites, are incapable of achieving orgasm in the rape situation."[4]

Besides the sexual dysfunction discussed above, some rapists are infertile due to low sperm counts, previous vasectomies, or other abnormalities. In addition, rapists occasionally use condoms themselves, an event which occurs in approximately 1 percent of rapes.[5]

Temporary or total infertility among rape victims is another major reason why the rate of pregnancies resulting from rape is so low. First, a victim may be naturally sterile. She may be too old or too young to be fertile, may already be pregnant, or may be infertile for other natural reasons (42 percent of rape victims in one study were in this category). Second, the victim may be taking oral contraceptives or have an IUD in place or have had a tubal ligation prior to the rape and thus have been artificially infertile (20 percent of rape victims were in this category, according to the same study). Thus, only a minority of rape victims are potentially fertile.[6]

Beyond natural and artificial infertility, some rape victims are protected from pregnancy by what might be called "stress" infertility— a form of temporary infertility which occurs in reaction to extreme stress. This occurs because a woman's menstrual cycle (controlled by hormones) is easily disturbed by emotional stress and may thus act as a natural form of birth control. Ovulation may be delayed; or if the cycle has already passed into the leutal phase, menstruation may occur prematurely so as to prevent fertilization and/or implantation during the period of stress. This is Nature's way of minimizing the number of offspring born into a hostile (stressful) environment. Thus the extreme trauma associated with rape frequently serves as a temporary and natural form of birth control.[7]

After subtracting the number of rape victims who are not at risk of becoming pregnant because of the reasons cited above, the risk for the remainder of rape victims is still much less than the natural limits of fertility under even optimal circumstances. The chance of conception resulting from a single act of unprotected intercourse between fertile, consenting individuals is estimated at only 3 to 4 percent. According to the American Medical Association's magazine *Prism*, even on the day of ovulation "the chances are ten to one against conception."[8]

When all of these factors are considered, it is understandable why pregnancies resulting from rape are extremely rare. In fact, one study found pregnancy resulting from sexual assault occurred in only .6 percent of 2,190 victims; three times that many were already pregnant at the time of the attack.[9] Other studies find the rate to be even lower, especially when rape victims receive prompt hospital treatment which includes pregnancy preventive care. In a series of 3,500 rape cases treated in hospitals in the Minneapolis-St. Paul area over a ten-year period, there was not a single case which resulted in pregnancy.[10]

Despite the odds, however, some pregnancies from rape do occur—but certainly not as frequently as pro-abortionists have at times implied. When this happens, what is already a psychologically difficult situation is further complicated when abortion is offered as the "best" solution. What must be remembered is that women in these rare circumstances are not "victims of pregnancy," they are victims of rape. In the vast majority of these cases, the victim's problems "stem more from the trauma of rape rather than from the pregnancy itself."[11] Abortion, which is itself always a psychologically stressful experience, may only further aggravate the woman's situation and should be approached with great care, not just a careless "fixing" or "hiding" of the external results of the rape.

The Psychology of Women with Rape Pregnancies

To the rape victim, rape is anything but external. It is a deeply traumatic experience that results in "guilt, anger, fear and a myriad of other, often overwhelming emotions [which] require ventilation."[12] Rather than being used as a separate category for justifying abortion, rape should properly be considered under the more general category of "psychological indications." All the reasons against abortion on psychological grounds, therefore, are also valid in the case of rape. As in any other emotionally stressful situation for which abortion might be recommended, abortion in the case of rape is a "cure" which only aggravates the "disease." As with other "psychological indications for abortion," the evidence actually shows that rape is a strong *contraindication* for abortion. This becomes clear when one considers the victim's psychological state, not simply her physical condition.

Rape is a "sudden, shattering intrusion which can leave the victim with deep and lingering emotional, psychological, and physical scars." These internal feelings are "aggravated by a society which often sees her as the guilty party. . . . Believing that she is somehow tainted, dirty, and dehumanized, and knowing that many will view her either as pitiful and helpless or as disgusting and defiled, she often takes great pains to conceal the fact of the assault [a fact which accounts for the low rate of reported rapes]."[13] The myths that raped women are "at fault" because they have "attracted" attacks, or because they have failed to thwart the attacks, are the attitudes most at odds with the healthy emotional recovery from rape. These attitudes, internalized by many rape victims and reinforced by family, friends, and society, are a source of continual pain for rape victims.

One reason why these "blame the victim" attitudes prevail is that most people continue to believe the myth that rape is a sex crime, and therefore, since the woman may "attract" the rapist, she is at least partially at fault. But this is simply not true. All researchers agree that the rapist is not driven by sexual urges, but by tendencies toward violence.[14] It is not primarily the woman's sexuality which invites attack, it is her vulnerability, the ease with which she can be overpowered. He displays his power in a situation which he can control because he finds himself generally powerless—or, to use a more symbolic word, impotent—in the world at large. Thus rape symbolizes an easy victory for the rapist. It proves his "superiority" over his victim.

Rape, then, is no more a sexual act than child battery is a disciplinary act. Unfortunately, society all too easily accepts the myths that both rapists and child beaters simply "lose control" or "go too far."

Because the myth of rape as a sexual (sensual) act continues to dominate public opinion, this myth plays a major role in shaping the mental state of the rape victim. According to this myth, rape is at least partially "the woman's fault." Such "blame the victim" attitudes frequently encourage the victim to engage in self-blame. "Despite its irrationality a sense of guilt is common, a consuming search for some flaw or characteristic which has caused the victimization. Anger, finding no legitimate outlet, may be turned inward, being nurtured by self-blame and often released as self-punishment."[15]

Frequently the victim's feelings of self-blame are encouraged by the reactions of family and friends, though these reactions are often subtly or unconsciously conveyed. First, anger may be directed at the woman by her husband, boyfriend, or family as a result of the accusatory premise that "nice women don't get raped." Second, because friends and family are uncomfortable in discussing the incident, or themselves feel embarrassment through association, they may take great pains to avoid or conceal the tragedy. Such "brush it under the rug" attitudes, however, only isolate the victim and aggravate her negative reactions:

> Often relatives and friends try to dissuade her from thinking or talking about it (the assault) in the mistaken belief that she will become more emotionally distressed. However, if others refuse to listen, the patient may conclude that they are embarrassed and ashamed and want to punish her for what has happened.[16]

Third, the attitudes of others, particularly her spouse, may imply that as a victim of the "sexual" attack of a "defiled" man, she herself is "tainted" and "dirtied." This revulsion may be conveyed by physical aloofness from the "unclean" victim and serves only to aggravate her feelings of humiliation and devaluation. Thus, the belief that she is "ruined" may become a central aspect of the victim's own self-image.

For all of the above reasons, proper care for rape victims must include not only psychological counseling for the victim, but also for her friends and family as well. Both the victim and her "significant others" need to be freed from the binding myths that rape is "sexual," that the victim is in any way at fault, or that the victim is "tainted." This task becomes even more important in the rare cases in which the attack results in pregnancy, or when there is even the suspicion of a rape pregnancy.[17]

Besides facing all the "normal" traumas associated with rape, the pregnant woman is faced with additional pressures because of her pregnancy. The social abhorrence of rape that rejects the victim as "unclean" also rejects the "tainted offspring" which is the evidence of the crime. The child is not only considered an illegitimate "bastard," but it is often viewed with all the revulsion associated with the rapist. Again the "rape is sex" myth rears its head and promotes the attitude that any pregnancy resulting from rape is the result of "ugly" or "sinful" sex, and so the child itself must be "ugly" or "sinful." Thus, in a society fixated on the stigma of rape, the child is never considered as an innocent entity, a second victim deserving of consideration. Instead, the pregnancy signifies "only a blot to be removed."[18]

It can be seen again, then, that the recommendation of abortion under such "unsavory" circumstances may be promoted for the convenience of society (which is already inclined to reject the rape victim), rather than for the welfare of the mother. Indeed, the entire abortion/ rape debate never included the pregnant victim's opinions or surveyed her needs. Instead, it was simply presumed that the rape victim would want an abortion, would need an abortion, and would benefit from an abortion.

The failure to study the needs of pregnant rape victims was due to two factors. First, the emphasis in rape studies has traditionally been placed on evaluating the characteristics of rapists. Only in the last ten years has there been a shift towards studying the needs and emotions of the rape victim and to the evaluation of effective forms of counseling.[19] Second, since the number of pregnant victims is extremely small, representing only a tiny fraction of all rape victims, the special needs of impregnated victims have not been addressed in detail. Instead, most of the literature merely maintains the myth that an abortion is to be recommended as soon as possible.

For the above reasons, the psychology of the pregnant rape victim received little attention until Dr. Sandra Mahkorn, an experienced rape counselor, investigated the issue in a report published in 1979.[20] In studying the case histories of 37 pregnant rape victims who had been counseled by various social welfare agencies, Dr. Mahkorn found that 28 women chose to continue their pregnancies, 5 chose abortion, and the outcome of the remaining 4 could not be determined. (A finding which clearly contradicts the presumption that most rape victims desire abortions.) Of the 28 who went to term, 17 chose adoption, 3 chose to keep the child, and details for the remaining 8 were unknown. Of those who refused abortion, the most common reason was their belief that abortion was simply another act of violence, immoral, or killing.

One woman said that she "would suffer more mental anguish from taking the life of the unborn child than carrying the baby to term." Others felt that the child had an intrinsic meaning or purpose, making statements such as: "All life has meaning" or "This child can bring love and happiness into someone's life."

The majority of the pregnant victims stated that their primary problem was the need to confront and deal with "feelings or issues related to the rape experience," though a significant minority (19%) placed primary emphasis on the need to confront and explore feelings about the pregnancy, including feelings of "resentment," "hostility towards the child," and "denial of the . . . pregnancy."[21]

When asked what conditions or situations made it most difficult for her to continue her pregnancy, the most frequent response was social pressure—the opinions, attitudes, and beliefs of others about the rape and pregnancy. Statements included, "family pressure [to abort]," attitudes of "boyfriends," and the belief that "people will not believe that she was raped or that it could have been prevented." Such feelings of being rejected because she is "unclean" aggravate self-rejection and the need to "cover up" what has happened. Under such pressure, abortion may seem the only solution because it will conceal the crime and "cleanse" the woman of rape's stains.

Though anger over the attack was occasionally displaced towards the child, Mahkorn's study revealed that such negative attitudes consistently changed to more positive ones as the pregnancy progressed. The overwhelming majority of the women investigated had a positive view towards the child by the time of delivery as well as much improved self-images. None moved toward more negative attitudes, a fact which prompted Dr. Mahkorn to write:

> The belief that pregnancy following rape will emotionally and psychologically devastate the victim reflects the common misconception that women are helpless creatures who must be protected from the harsh realities of the world. . . . [This study illustrates] that pregnancy need not impede the victim's resolution of the trauma; rather, with loving support, nonjudgmental attitudes, and empathic communication, healthy emotional and psychological responses are possible despite the added burden of pregnancy.[22]

Dr. Mahkorn's study also led her to the conclusion that encouraging abortion as the "solution" to a rape pregnancy is in fact counterproductive, because abortion serves only to reinforce *negative* attitudes. Her observations are worth quoting at length:

> Because it is likely that the victim already harbors feelings of guilt as a result of the assault, medico-social pressures which encourage and result in abortion could compound the woman's feelings of guilt and self-blame [over the abortion itself]. . . . Perhaps as a result of their own biases and an unwillingness to deal with the more emotionally difficult complications of a pregnant rape victim, many physicians suggest abortion in this case as one would prescribe aspirin for a tension headache. . . . While on the surface this "suggestion" may appear acceptable and even "humane" to many, the victim is dealt another disservice. Such condescending ["quick-fix"] attitudes on the part of physicians, friends and family can only serve to reaffirm the sense of helplessness and vulnerability that was so violently conveyed in the act of sexual assault itself. At a time when she is struggling to regain her sense of self-esteem, such a "take charge" attitude can be especially damaging. Often the offer of such "quick and easy" solutions as abortion only serve those who are uncomfortable or unwilling to deal with the special problems and needs that such complications as pregnancy might present.
> . . . The central issue, then, should not be whether we can abort all pregnant sexual assault victims, but rather an exploration of the things we can change in ourselves, and through community education, to support such women through their pregnancies. The "abortion is the best solution" approach can only serve to encourage the belief that sexual assault is something for which the victim must bear shame—a sin to be carefully concealed. . . . too often the pregnancy receives the most attention and the anger, guilt, fear, and lower self-esteem related to the assault fail to be addressed.
> . . . *[T]he attitudes projected by others and not the pregnancy itself pose the central problem for the pregnant victim.*
> By no means am I attempting to conclude that pregnancy as a result of rape is a simple matter. Such a conclusion would indeed be naive. This study does seem to suggest, however, that even though emotionally and psychologically difficult, these burdens can be lessened with proper support. [Italics added][23]

Clearly, many of the pregnant rape victim's problems stem from society's abhorrence of her condition. Revulsion towards the rape is carried over to the victims, both mother and child. But it is not the victims who are tainted by rape, it is the attitudes of society which are tainted by superstition and prejudice. The cure, then, is not abortion, but acceptance. Dr. Mahkorn writes: "Perhaps true liberation for the rape victim means the freedom to publicly acknowledge what has happened without fear of rejection. Perhaps true liberation means the freedom to carry a pregnancy to term with the realization that, like herself, the child is an innocent victim."[24] Feminist Mary Meehan agrees:

> Psychological support, especially from the woman's family and friends, is enormously important. They should stand by her and say clearly that, no matter what the circumstances of conception, there should *never* be any embarrassment about bringing a child into the world. There should never be anything but pride in that.[25]

As noted by Dr. Mahkorn, the child of rape must also be considered a victim of the crime. The child did not ask to be created any more than the woman asked to be attacked. The child has done no wrong, and abortion certainly does not undo the father's crime. Nowhere would the old proverb "Two wrongs don't make a right" seem more appropriate. Even convicted rapists are not punished by execution. Does it make sense that the innocent child of rape should be condemned to death in his place? Does it make sense to heap violence on top of violence, especially when the woman's body and psyche is made the battleground for both attacks? Does it make sense to tell the victim of violence to participate as the perpetrator of another violent act?

Rape and *abortion* are both harsh, cruel words. They are words so filled with revulsion that people don't like to think about either the acts or the victims involved. The world would no doubt be better without both, but unfortunately people are afraid to confront either. It is better, somehow, to try to ignore them, put them out of mind, pretend that they never happened.

Given such rejection of reality, it is not surprising that abortion is unlikely to relieve the anxieties of the rape victim, but instead it is much more likely to add to and complicate her emotional trauma. As with most abortions, the pregnant victim feels forced by circumstances to submit to the "corrective" violence of abortion. But as we have seen, the lack of free choice, the sense of being compelled to choose abortion, is a major indicator for the occurence of severe post-abortion sequelae. This is no less true in the case of rape, where the victim is struggling to regain control over her life but is being told that there is only one thing she can do—abort.

Indeed, the emotions surrounding rape and abortion are so nearly identical that abortion is almost certain to reinforce negative attitudes. Like rape, abortion accentuates feelings of guilt, lowered self-esteem, feelings of being sexually violated, feelings of having lost control or of being controlled by circumstances, suspicion of males, sexual coldness, and so on. Abortion of pregnant rape victims, then, tends only to reinforce these negative feelings and does nothing to promote the inner reconciliation which is so desperately needed. Encouraging a woman to vent her displaced anger in "revenge" against her unborn child only impacts negative and self-destructive attitudes into her psyche.

Abortion at best only hides a physical symptom of the rape; in its place, the woman is burdened with the memory of a child who was the victim of her "justifiable homicide." For the majority of pregnant rape victims who wisely choose to give their children life, the choice for childbirth is the choice to triumph over the rape. It is a choice which says: "This rape will not dictate my life." It is a choice which wrestles something good from what seems to be so inherently evil. Instead of remembering only her fear and shame, her choice allows her to remember her courage and generosity.[26] As Mary Meehan writes:

> It seems to me that honesty requires us to say that it is unjust that a woman must carry to term a child conceived through rape, *but that it is a far greater injustice to kill the child.* There is no way to avoid injustice in this situation; the best we can do is reduce it. The first injustice, which lasts for nine months of a life, can be relieved both financially and psychologically. But the second injustice ends a life, and there is no remedy for that.
>
> To say that good can come from evil is not to accept the evil itself. A young prolifer put it well when she said: "The answer to rape is not abortion, it is stopping rape.[27]

Returning to our original question, then, would the "conscientious physician" ever recommend abortion in the case of rape? Probably not.

He would recognize that what the woman really needs is emotional support through the rape. He would recognize that her confidence and sense of self-worth need rebuilding, not the added emotional dilemmas of abortion.

Incest

"Rape and Incest . . ." Hand in hand, these two words were the Trojan horse of abortion reform. But as with rape, abortion proponents appealed to the emotional abhorrence of incest to gain support for abortion while ignoring the real needs of the victims. Abortion was simply *presumed* to be the best answer—at least best for society if not for the women, girls, or children. Through abortion, they suggested, we could cover up these embarrassing victims of our sick society; we could destroy the "unclean" offspring of our sexual perversions. But in fact, just as with rape, there is no psychiatric evidence, nor even any theory which argues that abortion of an incestuous pregnancy is therapeutic for the victim—it is only more convenient for everyone else.

Setting aside the paternalistic attitudes with which society presumes that abortion is best for the incest victim, we must ask, what do these girls themselves want? It takes little investigation to find that almost all incest victims actually desire to keep the baby, and the majority do! Those who do abort do so under pressure from the impregnating relative who is seeking to cover-up his crime, and even in these cases, the victims abort only with resentment.[28]

The reasons why incest victims desire to keep their children are as complex as the issue of incest itself. But in brief, the pregnancy is desired by some because it offers a way to expose and escape the incestuous relationship. For others, the unborn child represents the hope for establishing a truly loving relationship as opposed to the exploitive one in which they are entangled. For others, giving birth serves as a means of claiming maturity and "winning" respect from their parents.

Incest can only be understood as a family pathology. The relationships between the husband, wife, and children are often strange and twisted. One investigative observer put it well when she said: "Reading the literature on incest is like trudging through a sewer."[29] Every member of the family touched by incest is embroiled in psychological turmoil, though the young victim is undoubtedly the most vulnerable and confused. As with any complex phenomenon, generalization about incest is a poor substitute for close study of its many and varied forms. Due to space limitations, only a brief overview of "typical" incest patterns is offered here in order to illustrate some of the underlying psychologies involved in an incest pregnancy.

Most cases of incest involve the male parent and a teenage or even a pre-teenage daughter. Though the perpetrator is frequently the girl's natural father, incestuous relationships with stepfathers are much more common. Incest with other men, such as uncles and brothers, represent only a minority of cases.[30]

Frequently the incestuous father will begin to sexually "train" his daughter for use at a very young age, as early as seven or eight, and will continue the relationship until she runs away, marries, or until the illicit union is exposed to outside authorities and intervention takes place. There are various motives that attract the offender to incest. Some involve sexual perversions; others are moved by the inadequacies of their marital relationships or by their own low self-esteem. Since the young daughter is sexually ignorant and naive, whereas the father is "sophisticated" and occupies a position of authority, she becomes the easy sexual "conquest" which he needs. Sexual excursions with his daughter are an easy escape from marital problems. Because of her youth and dependency, it is easier to dominate and control his daughter than to overcome conflicts with his wife. As in the case of rape, there is much more at stake than mere sexual satisfaction. Power and control are key elements of the incestuous relationship.

Obviously, the daughter exposed to incest is the victim of many psychological games and deceits. Even though she may never consent to the incest, she is made to feel obligated to submit to it. She is likely to feel guilty (often without understanding why), isolated, afraid, and at a loss as to how to change her circumstances. But though she may recoil from her father's advances and may dread repetitions of their sexual contact, it is also very likely that she has a sincere love for her father and a strong need to be loved by him. Though she may find their sexual relationship confusing or even repulsive, at least she finds in it some sense of the attention and love she so desperately needs. Though she would much rather be a daughter than a sex object, the latter form of attention is sometimes accepted as a meager substitute.

Incestuous daughters almost invariably feel that their mothers are bad mothers and fear that they, too, will be bad mothers. They feel estranged from their mothers and expect little support from the mother in escaping their incestuous relationship. Indeed, it is quite likely that the mother will be aware of the incest but will refuse to believe it or will fail to act. The daughter's attempts to hint at what is happening and to seek help are likely to be rebuffed and ignored by a mother who simply does not want to believe it. Sometimes, such denial can be taken to extremes. In one case, the mother had repeatedly seen her nude husband in bed with her daughter during a two and a half year period but ignored her "suspicions" until pregnancy occurred. In yet another case, where an incestuous pregnancy was ultimately reported by an outside party, the mother had simply "reassured her four daughters that father was merely trying to show affection by manipulating their breasts and vaginas."[31]

Because it involves so many strained relationships, the pathology of incest is usually shrouded in a "conspiracy of silence." The daughter is too ashamed to discuss it and doubts that there is any aid to be found; the mother denies what she doesn't want to believe; and, of course, the father seeks desperately to conceal it. All know what is occurring, but they will not admit it to each other, much less to the outside world. Until this denial is overcome, breaking the incestuous pattern is impossible. Until the incest is exposed, it is unlikely that the family will seek treatment.

The person who most wants to get out of the incestuous situation is the victim, the daughter. Through friends, teachers, doctors or relatives, she may eventually drop enough hints to arouse suspicion and action. Failing that, she may simply "wait it out" until she is old enough to move away, or she may seek other more immediate avenues of escape: running away, early marriage, or pregnancy.

Though the daughter wants out, it should be remembered that she would prefer to break the incest pattern in a way that would allow her to maintain or regain the love of her parents. Pregnancy is an avenue which offers to fulfill both of these requirements.[32]

Abortion of an incestuous pregnancy, then, not only adds to the girl's guilt and trauma, it also frustrates her plans for escape and attention. Abortion perpetuates the "conspiracy of silence" by covering up the incest, or at least its results, and continues the family pattern of denying reality. Indeed, it seems that the positive opinion which the daughter maintains towards her incestuous father turns negative only when he insists upon an abortion or denies his paternity and thus frustrates her needs for acceptance and escape.[33] Even though nearly half of all incestuous fathers press for abortion if a pregnancy occurs, resistance to abortion is generally very strong, with only a quarter of the daughters finally submitting to abortion.[34]

Fortunately, incestuous pregnancies are actually quite rare, a fact which is especially surprising considering the lengthy period of exposure. American studies involving a total of almost 2,000 cases of incest report a pregnancy rate of only 1 percent. According to one counselor, incestuous relations cause cessation of menses (apparently because of the emotional trauma) during the years of contact, but the ovulation cycle resumes once the girls enter therapy. Older studies indicate a higher pregnancy rate for incest, which may be explained by improved public awareness and more effective response to the daughter's "help" signals. In a comprehensive article entitled "The Consequences of Incest," psychiatrist George Maloof suggests that "Pregnancy is often a desperate measure taken to end the incest, and has been probably utilized more in the past when the community was less sensitive to reacting to a possible incest situation and when treatment programs which allow families to work together were not available."[35]

Leaving aside the issue of the unborn child's right to live (valid though it is), abortion of an incestuous pregnancy is undesirable primarily because it would probably be against the young girl's will. In addition, because the pregnancy was desired in order to expose her circumstances, it is usually not revealed until well after the first trimester. Thus, a late term abortion would expose the girl to health risks even greater than those associated with most teenage abortions.[36]

The problem the pregnant incest victim faces is not the pregnancy, it is the psychological pain of incest. Again, as with rape, it is the discrimination and superstitions of those around her which make the pregnancy difficult, not the pregnancy itself. Unlike the case of rape, most incest pregnancies are actually desired, at least at a subconscious level, in order to expose the incest. As a study of the experiences of girls with incestuous pregnancies showed: "Problems in accepting the pregnancy and birth of the child seemed related more to the negative reaction of friends and other relatives and to tensions which developed between the parents or between mother and daughter as a result of the pregnancy."[37]

As Dr. Mecklenburg notes, abortion in cases of incest is unproductive.

Furthermore, the incestuous relationship requires psychiatric care. With proper management, the outcome of incest may not always be as traumatic as was previously believed. . . . Incest is basically a family pathology. Treating it as such, there is evidence

that there may be gain for all concerned when the family cooper-
ates in treatment. Aborting an innocent unborn child will neither
correct the pathology nor mend the hurts. The problem exists
with or without pregnancy, with or without abortion.[38]

Dr. Maloof goes further, insisting that abortion is counterproductive for incest victims because it represents only a "further assault upon
their sexual integrity." Childbirth allows the victims of incest to "take a
step toward accepting responsibility for their sexual acts and thereby
toward freedom from the self-destructive effects of both incest and
abortion." But adoption, he believes, should be strongly recommended in incest cases, so as to facilitate repair of what is already a
severely torn family structure: "Only after having the child adopted can
there be some assurance that this new life will not simply become part
of the incestuous family affair. The family can be consoled by the
knowledge that they have broken their incestuous pattern. . . ."[39]

In conclusion, Dr. Maloof writes:

If the only way we can help the little Debbies [incest victims] is to
kill their babies and take away their fathers, are we not taking
away the people for whom she cares the most? If her mother rallies
to her side only to get rid of her father and child, isn't the pattern
of avoiding problems being perpetuated? . . . Are we reenacting
the maternal rejection felt by the daughter which predisposed the
incest situation, so that the daughter is dramatically demonstrating
what she feels the mother has done to her? Are we indirectly
killing the daughter who feels her child is an extension of herself?
Whatever else we may be doing by an abortion of an incestuous pregnancy, we are promoting mental illness by not allowing the girl to accept the consequences of her own acts. . . .
Accepting the pregnancy can be the first step to accepting the
incest and making the changes to alter the family pattern so that it
can be more productive rather than withholding and destructive.[40]

Finally, we must again return to the question which has prompted
this investigation. When, if ever, would a "conscientious physician"
abort an incestuous pregnancy? If he took time to talk to her and
understand her needs and desires—as opposed to the needs and desires
of her embarrassed parents—Never.

203

For the Hardest "Hard Cases"

As we have seen, all of the classical "hard cases" used to argue for abortion, when examined closely, are actually among the worst circumstances under which a woman could have an abortion. Accordingly, there is little or no reason why a "conscientious physician" would recommend abortion in these cases. Therefore, if abortions are ever again made illegal, there is no compelling reason to allow for "hard case" exceptions.

But, at least in theory, some unforeseen circumstances may arise when the risks a pregnancy may pose to a woman are far greater than the possible aftereffects of an abortion. But while such exceptional circumstances may be grounds for a lively debate, the possibility that such "hard cases" exist does not justify abortion on demand. If such cases ever occur, they should be tried and judged on an individual basis.

If the compelling conditions which led to the abortion are truly as extreme as the physician contends, and an "exception" for an abortion was justified, or even nearly justifiable, it is doubtful that any jury would convict him or that any judge would pass a heavy sentence. There is room within every law for "hard case" exceptions that are truly that, rare exceptions, not excuses for widening the door to exploitive abortions for convenience.

An interesting idea to limit therapeutic abortions to "good faith" exceptions is the proposal to forbid obstetricians and psychiatrists who approve of or perform therapeutic abortions from accepting any fees for their services. This "no fee" abortion alternative would clearly prevent profiteering and/or the caving-in to an unreasonable patient's demands. Without money to corrupt recommendations for therapeutic abortions, one can be sure that physicians would be very cautious and reserved in their offers to perform them.[41] Some pro-lifers might not like such exceptions, but they would certainly find such a "no fee" scheme more tolerable than the present system of profiteering and abortion on demand.

Summary

In the last two chapters we have carefully looked at the "hard" cases used to justify abortion. We have found that abortion proponents have used these "hard" cases to elicit sympathy for their cause, but they have failed to consider the real desires and health needs of the women who face these difficult circumstances. In fact, the urging of abortion on women in these cases is most often a paternalistic attempt to conceal their problems, rather than to aid them through their difficulties.

The "exceptions" of rape and incest, which in fact represent special cases, involve psychiatric stresses which are ill-treated with abortion. The evidence shows that pressures to abort in these cases arise primarily from outside sources, from the superstition and prejudice that friends, family, and society hold against these "tainted" women. When the desires of the victims are examined, it is found that the vast majority of women pregnant from rape or incest actually desire to carry their children to term. Psychologists confirm that this is a healthy response and is the most productive path these women can take in reestablishing their self-images and renewing control over their lives. It is the social pressure to hide (abort) these pregnancies which needs to be eliminated, not the innocent children who are "conceived in sin."

These "hard" cases all support our contention that the more sympathetic the circumstances indicating abortion, the less likely it is that abortion will solve those problems. Indeed, in what are generally very difficult psychological circumstances, abortion almost invariably tends to aggravate and complicate the woman's problems. Therefore, a truly "conscientious physician" would be obliged to strongly recommend against abortion, especially in these "hard" cases.

PROFILES SIX

Abortions for Rape and Incest

13) Jackie Bakker

Victimized by a violent rape in California in 1968, Jackie found herself pregnant soon after. Confused and frightened, she followed her parents' urgings for an abortion. However, she discovered that "the aftermath of the abortion continued for a long time after the memory of my rape had faded." Her story explains her deep, longlasting regret over her decision to abort.

Sixteen years ago, at the age of nineteen, I became pregnant as a result of a violent act of rape. The rape happened on a Friday night, around 10 PM. My girlfriend and I had been walking down Sunset Strip, looking for a place to have a cup of coffee. Two men approached us, telling us that they were photographers, and that we would make great models. My girlfriend decided to walk off with one guy, claiming she would be right back. The other man hung around me, trying to convince me to go with him. After an hour, she still hadn't returned. The man suddenly pulled me close to him, showed me a knife under his coat, and whispered, "If you want to see your girlfriend again, you'll come with me quietly." I followed him to his car, afraid to resist. He drove to an office building, took me to the basement, locked the door, and pulled my clothes off. He then violently raped me.

My friend was brought there soon after, and we were let go. She had also been raped, but didn't become pregnant. In fact, when I learned I was pregnant, my boyfriend and all my friends—including her—deserted me. They all acted like I was the "plague."

Anyway, I felt very "dirty" and "used." The very first thing I did after the rape was to go home and douche with vinegar, then take a hot shower and scrub hard with soap. That didn't seem to do any good, because I still experienced those bad feelings.

At first, in the early months of pregnancy, I ignored all the indications my body was giving me that I was pregnant. Finally, as I approached my fourth month, I saw a doctor. Upon learning that I was indeed carrying a child, my first reaction was to have an abortion. I felt I had all the best reasons for having one. First, I was carrying the child of a man who had committed a violent crime against me. I couldn't stand the thought of carrying "his child" and being reminded of the rape. I transferred all my negative feelings onto the baby, and hated it. The movie *Rosemary's Baby* was popular at the movie theater; and after seeing the rape scene in the movie, I thought for sure I had been raped by Satan himself. I began to think of my child as a devil baby.

Second, I had just had my first interview with a major airline company and had plans of becoming a stewardess. It was becoming more and more difficult to hide the fact that I was pregnant.

Within a week of learning that I was pregnant, my roommate convinced me that abortion was the "only answer." She had had an abortion several years before; she said she had no regrets and hadn't noticed any bad effects. She knew of a doctor who would give me one and set it up for me. I remember I had to go to his office blindfolded. After he checked me, he decided against doing the abortion. His examination had revealed that I had a bad case of strep throat, and he worried about the infection traveling down into my uterus.

Unable to cope with the circumstances, I returned home to live with my mom and dad. By this time I was nearly five months pregnant and beginning to accept the idea of carrying my baby to term. I was feeling my baby moving and began to experience love and acceptance for this child that was also part of me. However, my parents were very concerned about my circumstances. I had left home just one year before, a healthy, pretty teenager, optimistic about life. But I had returned home, tired, pregnant, and feeling hopeless and confused. They wanted so desperately to have their daughter back to normal. They tried to be supportive in every way they could, but they couldn't handle the thought of a baby being born as a result of a rape. So they consulted with their family doctor and a local family planning clinic and

207

were told of a new law just passed in California permitting a legal abortion in the case of rape. After testifying about my rape to the district attorney, who did two weeks of research on my case, permission for a legal abortion was granted.

I spent three days in the hospital, where a saline abortion was performed. I don't remember the doctor explaining very much to me about what would take place. I only remember going into labor in a room all by myself, so scared and alone. It seemed to take forever. Finally, after eighteen hours of labor, I knew it was time to push. I screamed, and a young nurses' aide ran into my room with a bedpan. I delivered my baby girl all by myself into a bedpan. I was in shock as I looked at the baby that people had told me was just a blob of tissue; she was really so large and developed. It was as if I was waiting for her to start crying, still hoping she was alive.

I soon discovered that the aftermath of the abortion continued a long time after the memory of my rape had faded. I felt empty and horrible. Nobody told me about the emptiness and pain I would feel deep within, causing nightmares and deep depressions. They had all told me that after the abortion I could continue on with my life as if nothing had happened.

As the years hastened by, the pain and regret of my abortion became buried deeper and deeper within. But even after becoming a Christian, I justified my abortion to myself because of my circumstances.

It wasn't until after learning that I had cancer of the cervix that the guilt of my abortion surfaced. I had been married for quite some time, and had been blessed with two beautiful sons. But now that I desperately wanted another child, hopefully a little girl, I was unable to. It had been diagnosed by several doctors that I needed an immediate hysterectomy. I became bitter toward God, thinking He was punishing me for my abortion. My husband reassured me by saying "We can always adopt." But after the operation, he seemed to change his mind.

During that period of time, I went through a deeper time of depression and loneliness than I had experienced immediately after the abortion. I kept thinking I would never have the daughter that I longed for. Finally, after what seemed like years of waiting, my husband and I began the process of adoption. I remember praying every night with my sons for the protection of our little Hope, the little girl I could picture in my mind so vividly, the little girl I had had reccurring dreams about for years. God honored our prayers and saved her life when her mother almost had her aborted. Today, Hope is a lively, healthy, imaginative little girl.

It took thirteen years for a complete healing to take place. But the strangest thing was that, as a Christian, I found that though I could forgive the man who raped me, I couldn't forgive myself for having the abortion. I had nightmares for years afterward, always hearing a baby crying in the distance, even when I wasn't sleeping. I thought I was going insane at times. I was so upset during my pregnancy with my first son, and had nightmares so frequently, that in my fifth month I started premature labor and nearly miscarried.

After being fully healed from my abortion, I began to do research on the effects of my abortion. I became aware of how victimized I had been, and of how victimized all women are. For example, the room- mate who had advised me to have my abortion after having one herself, still remains childless after years of frustrating efforts to become preg- nant. She didn't notice the effects resulting from her abortion until she tried to become pregnant again.

In my case, I feel my parents were also victims, in believing the lies they were told about abortion. They were told that a saline abor- tion was less dangerous than childbirth. But in reality, I've learned that saline abortions are so dangerous that they are no longer permitted in some countries. Now I've also heard that doctors are discovering there may be a link between abortions and cancer of the cervix. My parents were told that if I were made to continue with my pregnancy and give birth to a child I didn't want, I might flip out. But after being with a woman in labor who was releasing her baby for adoption, I believe that my experience of eighteen-hour labor and delivering my dead baby by myself was much more harmful emotionally to me.

I've discovered that no one has the control to have a baby exactly when they want to. People said to me that I couldn't love a child that was a product of a rape. But studies have proven that a woman will not have negative feelings towards a child just because she didn't accept the pregnancy. I have had the wonderful experience of knowing a beautiful young woman who gave birth to an adorable little girl, a product of rape. Her daughter is very much loved and accepted, and her mother is so grateful she didn't abort her daughter.

I feel that society has the wrong attitudes toward rape and abor- tion. Two wrongs *don't* make a right. With rape, that's one time that a woman is victimized; but to have to go through an abortion on top of it, I became a victim twice. The baby was the innocent party. She should not have been looked at as "the product of a rape" but rather as one of God's creations, created in His image. Women facing unplanned pregnancies—especially when rape or incest is involved—need crisis counseling. They need to talk to someone who has been there, to realize that adoption is an excellent solution.

During the past several years I have had the privilege of counseling young women facing difficult pregnancies. It isn't easy sometimes, knowing the decision some of them will make. However, it all seems worth it to me when I am able to experience with her the miracle of a new life coming into the world.

14) Debbie "Nelson"

Debbie chose abortion twice: the first was in Washington, under pressure from her husband; the second was in California, because the child had been conceived during a rape. But as Debbie's story emphasizes, no matter what the circumstances, the physical and emotional aftereffects are traumatic.

I have had two abortions. The first was when I was sixteen years old. I had been married for three months when I realized I was pregnant. My husband was opposed for financial reasons to our having a baby, and said I should have an abortion. Being newly married and only sixteen, I felt that I had to prove I could hold my marriage together.

The abortion was done in a hospital, under general anesthesia. When I woke, I was crying. I didn't understand why, but I knew that I felt a tremendous loss. When I was taken back to my room, I began bleeding heavily. I told the nurse that I had never bled like that before, and she said, "Well, you've never had a baby before." At the time I didn't understand that comment. Now I know the point she was trying to make.

My second abortion was three years later. I was working in a hotel as a maid; and while at work, I was raped at gunpoint. I was taken to the emergency room immediately, but a D&C wasn't done, thus I conceived of that rape.

When I suspected that I was pregnant, I went back to the doctor who had tended me in the emergency room. I remember sobbing and crying so hard when he told me the pregnancy test results were positive. In that moment of shock, the doctor told me that my only choice in a situation such as this was abortion. He was very kind. He held my hand and comforted me, then made a phone call to make an appointment for me with an abortion clinic.

The feelings that I had experienced with my first abortion came back to me, but I thought that this would be different. After all, I had been raped and couldn't possibly love this child. The doctor told me abortion was safe, easy, and painless. Having been asleep the first time, I had no reason to dispute this.

When I got to the clinic (I think it was three days later), I was asked to sign a form releasing the doctor and clinic from any responsibility in the event of complications. I asked what complications this was referring to. I was told that as with any surgical procedure, there was always the slight chance of problems—but that this very rarely happened.

I was awake this time. They used the suction method to kill my baby, and the pain was horrendous. I hadn't expected to feel the emotional trauma this time, but it was worse than before. I was taken to a room to rest and couldn't stop crying. The "oh-so-rare" physical complications began immediately. I began hemorrhaging and cramping severely and was given an injection to lessen the bleeding, and I was told to go home to bed.

One week later, while at work, I began hemorrhaging again. I went back to the clinic and was told that I had probably retained some of the tissue, but that it would pass. After three months of bleeding off and on, I went to another doctor, who was outraged at my condition. He did an emergency D&C to remove the retained placenta, then he told me that my uterus had been significantly damaged by the abortions and their subsequent infections. He said there was much scar tissue in my uterus and that any future pregnancies would probably be difficult.

In the years to follow, I was divorced and remarried; and I became a Christian, a mother, and a nurse. It was when I went through nurse's training that the reality of what I had done became clear to me. While studying fetal development, I realized that I had been lied to. At eight weeks, those "clusters of cells" had a remarkable resemblance to a baby. They had hands and feet, a heartbeat and brainwaves, which meant that those babies did indeed feel the pain of their horrible deaths.

I now have two little girls. During both of my pregnancies I had a condition known as placenta previa. Both were high risk pregnancies followed by very difficult labors and deliveries. Eight months after the birth of my second daughter, at the age of twenty-three, I had to have a hysterectomy. The damages done by my abortions were so severe that my childbearing days were over. All of this occurred because of my two "safe and legal" abortions.

Had I been told the truth about the risks that I was taking with my body and about the developing persons inside of me, I know that I would not have made the decision to destroy life. There are those people who can deliberately take the life of another person, but that is not my nature. Yet I must live with the truth, because that is what I have done.

I still feel that I probably couldn't have loved that child conceived of rape, but there are so many people who would have loved that baby dearly. The man who raped me took a few moments of my life, but I took that innocent baby's entire life. That is not justice as I see it. My first marriage ended in divorce, so the reality is that my first abortion was done for the convenience of two very selfish people.

15) Edith Young

Edith is thirty-eight years old. When she was twelve, she became pregnant as the result of rape/incest by her stepfather. To cover up the incident, her parents procured an abortion for her without telling her what was to happen. The emotional and physical scars of her incest and abortion experiences are still with her today.

Where do I begin? Rape, incest, and abortion. For most people, these things will never happen to them or to anyone they know. When reported in the media, rape/incest is usually called by the watered-down term of child molestation or sexual abuse. By any name, it's still a tragedy. Abortion, though legal, is also a tragedy. Both take away from the victim things that cannot be replaced.

My remembrance of most of the occurences are very vivid, even though they happened twenty-six years ago. These events began in 1960, and their effects continue still in 1986.

When I was eleven and a half years old, I began my menstrual period. Shortly afterwards, I became the victim of rape/incest. Rape, because it was violent and by force. Incest, because the perpetrator was my stepfather, who by marrying my mother had assumed the position of my father.

Several times before the attacks my stepfather entered my room and laid on the floor beside my bed. In the beginning, he didn't touch me or say anything to me. He'd pretend to be asleep, but I knew he wasn't. My mother, who was home during these times, would come to my room and make him leave. All she ever said to him was, "Leroy, get up and come out of here." She didn't say anything to me. She'd just leave, too.

One night she didn't leave as usual. Instead, she lifted my covers, opened my legs, and asked if he had messed with me. I told her "No." I began to be afraid after this. Questions started going through my head: Messed with me how? What was he supposed to do to me that made her look between my legs? Oh, God help me, what's going on?

Not knowing what to expect, I started getting my two younger nieces to sleep with me. I felt safe with one on each side. But mom stopped them from sleeping with me immediately, while my stepfather continued to enter my room. Often I have felt that I was set-up for all that was to happen to me—so conveniently being left alone with no assurance of protection. Frequently, while mom was working, I was left alone with him. My sister and brother would be out, unaware of what was happening. They were both older than me, my sister by ten years and my brother by two. I also have a brother who was about five at this time. I can't remember much about him except I resented him. He is the only child my mother and stepfather had together.

Although there were several, the attack I remember most vividly is the first one. There was no one home but us, maybe my younger brother was in bed, and I had also gone to bed. My stepfather entered my room the same as before, *except* this time he did not lay on the floor but started to climb onto my bed. I was terrified. I didn't know what he was going to do, but I knew I had to get away. In the struggle, I knocked over a table lamp. He grabbed my leg, pulled me back onto the bed, yanked my clothes off, then he began to sexually attack me. I recall screaming, "No! No! Get away! Leave me alone! Someone help me!" But it was all to no avail. There was no one to help me, no one to rescue me. So he continued, obviously sure he had time to do what he wanted, with no fear of being caught. This attack continued for what seemed to be forever. I was wondering to myself, "How could he do this to me? How could he be enjoying this? It hurts so bad. Why doesn't somebody help me? Why don't I die? Help! Help! Help!"

When he stopped, he threatened to hurt me and the rest of my family, including my natural father. He walked out as if what had happened was so natural. It meant nothing to him. But it meant something to me. I was left alone, crying softly so no one would hear me, and I was so scared. I didn't move for a long time.

Mom came home, checking me as usual. I could tell from the look on her face that she knew, after all I was bleeding. Nevertheless, she said nothing. She didn't even ask the usual, "Did he mess with you?" Instead, she left my room and got into bed with him. This was the last night she checked me.

From that night on, terror reigned in my life. I was being sexually abused, threatened by him, and betrayed by mom's silence. Even though she knew, I was still left alone with him, therefore the attacks continued. In the midst of these attacks, I tried to deny what was happening to me. But I have learned that denial is temporary, reality is forever.

I told no one about what was happening. Who could I tell? Mom and he were considered "upstanding" members of the community and church. People were always commenting on what a wonderful job they were doing in raising us. Several times I wanted to shout the truth, especially when I had been attacked the day before. But fear kept me from saying anything. What if I told and no one believed me? I would have to go home with them. Would he make good on his threats? What would mom do? She hadn't stopped him. I believed silence on my part was both my protector and friend.

One night in January of 1961, mom and I walked to the doctor's office not far from where we lived. I didn't know why we were going. He was an elderly man with a kind face. He examined me and told mom I was about three or four months pregnant. I knew being pregnant meant having a baby, but I said nothing until the doctor asked me, "Who did this?" I replied, "My stepfather." Of course mom denied the truth. She said, "It was some old boy she's been messing with." Her answer was so strange to me. I had better not look at a boy, let alone have one for a boyfriend. I didn't have any desire for one, the thought terrified me. We left his office and went home.

214

ABORTIONS FOR RAPE AND INCEST

Within a couple of days mom started giving me some large red pills. I didn't know where she got them, but I took them for a few days. Every day she would ask if I had started bleeding. She didn't explain anything, she just kept asking over and over, "Are you bleeding?" Suddenly I realized I was no longer being attacked sexually. Relief didn't come though. There was a constant fear it would start again. When the pills didn't bring about any bleeding, I was taken to another doctor.

As we entered the office, I noticed no one was there but us. He led me to where the examining table was. I was too scared to talk. He said things such as "Hi," "How are you?," "It won't take long." As I laid there, I looked around, asking myself, "What won't take long?" It was an ordinary doctor's office; he saw patients every day. My eyes wandered toward the foot of the table. I saw a red rubber tube in his hand. This was inserted into my vagina, there was a tug, then the tube was removed. I got off the table and joined my mother in the other room. We went home.

I had to stay in her room, in *their* bed. Again she began to ask if I felt or saw anything. I was told to use the basin whenever I felt *something* coming. I was alone when I began to feel "something." I got the basin and out "something" came. The "something" was a baby girl. Yes, "something" was unquestionably a girl, my daughter. I saw her with my eyes, after she came from inside my body, lying there dead, in a cold white basin. What happened to her? I don't know, but I'll never forget her. She had a face, hands, arms, legs, and a body. Everything I had, she had. After seeing my baby, I don't remember what happened. Did I scream, call my mother or what? I really don't remember.

Mom came in the room, told me to lay down, while she got me some bath water. She bathed me in the tub as if I had become as helpless as the baby in the basin. Maybe for the moment I was. Almost with every stroke, she made me a promise—promises she has never kept. For a while I believed things would get better if she would just keep her promises. I believed the confusion, fear, and pain would disappear. However, all the stroking and promises in the world could not erase what I had experienced. It was like being in a dream world where all the dreams are nightmares. I thought I would awaken and find the nightmare was over. But it was not a dream, and the nightmare continues. . . .

There weren't any more sexual assaults, but my mother started

215

beating me for any and everything. It seemed as if my mere existence was excuse enough. Mothers are supposed to love and protect, not betray and destroy.

It was when I was in the tenth grade (fifteen years old), taking nursing courses, that I began to fully realize what happened to me. Imagine the shock when I understood what took place that day. The day I passed "something," my baby, my daughter, Lori Ann, into a basin. My textbook said, "life begins at conception." Reality really sunk in. A life had ended that day. Murder had been committed.

After this revelation, I started drinking. Liquor was easy to get. My stepfather drank all the time, so I began stealing his hidden alcohol. I did not worry about being caught; in fact, I didn't care. Alcohol helped me through the next few years. Drinking made existing easier; it distorted reality enough to go on while truthfully my life was in a turmoil. Yet no one knew it. I was an honor roll student. In fact, I was in the National Honor Society in high school. From the sixth to twelfth grade I sang in the school choir. In high school I participated in intramural sports and was the captain of the girl's basketball team.

They stayed together approximately twelve or thirteen years after the abortion. How she could continue to stay with him, I'll never understand. . . . I tried to kill him a few times. Once by making him move when his nose was hemorrhaging, by throwing something out of his reach. Three times I attempted to stab him, but mom intervened each time. How I hated her for that. During those attempts I was upset by my failure to kill him. Now, I'm grateful to God that I didn't succeed. Living with the memory of sexual attacks, pregnancy, abortion, and beatings are more than enough without adding murder.

When I was a senior in high school, mom decided she didn't want me around anymore. I moved in with my natural father. You may have been wondering where he was during this time. He and mom separated and divorced when I was about three or four years old. I saw him often enough. Since he was included in the threats of my stepfather, I did not tell him about the attacks. I had vowed to never tell him. All I kept thinking was, what would he do? Would he be killed like my baby? Would it kill him to know? Would he kill them and end in jail? I was so afraid to tell him, and I only just recently did. It was a few days after he turned seventy-seven years old in September, 1986. After serving as Delaware State Director of WEBA, a press conference was to be held, and I didn't want him to read about me or hear it from someone else. Telling daddy was one of the hardest things I have ever had to do.

God's timing was perfect. Our national president, Lorijo Nerad was there to support me. Daddy wept when he was alone, but he said he was sorry; he didn't know.

The Lord has blessed me with three living children. I became pregnant before I moved out of my mother's, while I was a senior. The school's answer was adoption. Arrangements were made without my knowledge or consent. Refusal was made in not so polite terms by me. The pregnancy was not too bad; I carried my son full term. My third pregnancy, I had to wear a maternity corset. Without it my abdomen felt as though it was being torn apart. Ironically, this daughter was born on January 22, 1973, the day abortion was legalized. With my fourth child, also a girl, my water had to be broken by the doctor.

Throughout the years I have been depressed, suicidal, furious, outraged, lonely, and have felt a sense of loss. I have felt, and at times still feel, that my mother and stepfather owe me something. What? I don't know. Maybe a sincere, "I'm sorry." Even if my daughter had been put up for adoption, instead of killed, some of the pain would not be present. Often I cry. Cry because I could not stop the attacks. Cry because my daughter is dead. And I cry because it still hurts. They say time heals all wounds. This is true. But it doesn't heal the memories, at least not for me.

I've suffered many physical problems and continue to do so. Ever since the abortion I've suffered chronic infections of my tubes, ovaries, and bladder. The pain from my menstrual periods was nightmarish and continued from the time of my abortion until my partial hysterectomy in November, 1982. In April of this year, I again had surgery. There was a growing, bleeding cyst on my left ovary. On my right side, there was a massive amount of adhesions, and the ovary could not be found. Twenty-five years have gone by, but the consequences of the abortion are still going on.

As you can see, the abortion which was to "be in my best interest" just has not been. As far as I can tell, it only "saved their reputations," "solved their problems," and "allowed their lives to go merrily on."

My daughter, how I miss her. I miss her regardless of the reason for her conception. You see she was a part of me, an innocent human being, sentenced to death because of the selfish, sexual gratification of another and the need to "save reputations." She was a unique individual whose life was exterminated.

Yes, the abortion occured before the ill-fated legalization of abortion in 1973. Not in a back alley, but in a sterile office, on the examining table of a doctor, much like the abortion mills of today. Everyone is still living except for my daughter and both doctors.

In situations like mine, emotions are something you are expected to control no matter what. I wasn't allowed to cry, scream, react, or grieve. These things are also true of women who have abortions today. Whatever the reason, a baby is killed and his/her mother is left to face the reality of that decision, often alone.

In the past, incest was not spoken of. It, like abortion, was taboo in our country. But a few years ago when incest stories became a common headline for reporters, I wondered what was happening psychologically to the many women who have been victims of incest. What changes were they going through? Now I wonder what's going to happen to the millions of women who have had abortions when reporters finally get the guts to write as honestly about abortion as they did about incest. All the legalities in the world will not remove the reality that a baby is a baby. For many women the aborted baby is the only one they ever had a chance to have. For many more, abortion is the start of physical and/or emotional complications.

The attacks, the abortion, and my baby in the basin frequently return in my dreams. There have been a countless number of nights when I've gone without sleep just so I wouldn't dream. I still have these sleepless nights—not for me, but for the millions of babies who are still dying. I lose sleep whenever I picket or sidewalk counsel at an abortuary. Watching woman after woman go in hurts. I know that the solution to their situations will not be found in there. Problems are not ended by abortion, but only made worse.

Even though I didn't have any say about the abortion, it has had a greater impact on my life than the rape/incest. About nine years ago I accepted Christ as my personal Savior. He has since become not only my Savior, but also Lord of my life. I have repented of the sin of abortion because of my years of silence. I am free. It's because of Christ I am able to tell my story. It's not easy, but I pray that by telling it an abused person will seek help, a baby will be saved, and most importantly, a woman who is considering abortion will save herself.

S E V E N

The Impact of Abortion on Later Children

Once the commitment is made, there is nothing in life which is more important to a parent than his or her children. Everyone who ever hopes to raise children aspires to be the best parent possible. No one wants to be a failure, especially when it comes to raising one's children and providing for their needs.

But the desire to be a "good parent" is not only an internal hope, it is also a social demand. There are only a few condemnations which are worse than being branded a "rotten parent"; it is almost as bad as being called a "child molester." Even a convicted criminal could hope for some respect from his neighbors if at least they remembered him as being a "good father" to his children.

Because of this universal desire to be a good parent, most people are very susceptible to appeals which are made "for the sake of our children." Having long recognized the public's susceptibility to such appeals, and wanting to divert attention from the unborn children killed by abortion, pro-abortion advocates have frequently insisted that abortion is in fact for the *benefit* of children.

Pro-abortionists frequently insist that women who use abortion to ease their burdens today will be in a better position to be good parents in the future. This argument is frequently used during pre-abortion counseling. Women are made to feel that if they don't abort their present "unwanted" pregnancies, for which they are ill-prepared, they will be sacrificing all their future hopes for career, marriage, and family, and so will be unable to provide for the present child, much less for any future children. Or if they already have children, they are told that the "extra mouth" which the unborn child will bring into the family will drain the family of its resources, distract attention from the other children, and otherwise destroy the woman's ability to be a good parent. Thus abortion of an unplanned pregnancy is presented as the best way to be a "good parent" to one's future "planned" children and/or one's present children. Conversely, the option of not aborting the unplanned pregnancy is implied to be an "irresponsible" act which threatens the welfare of "the other" children. In this context the unplanned child is depicted as an external threat to a woman's family rather than as a welcome addition.

This chapter will examine some of the arguments used to promote "abortion for the children's sake." When these arguments are examined in the light of all available evidence, we will see that contrary to pro-abortionists' claims, abortion actually *endangers* the physical and emotional health of a woman's "wanted" children. Rather than preserving resources for a family's other children, abortion instead places the entire family at risk.

How Wanted Children Are Unintentionally Killed by Abortion

Each year 1.5 million unborn children are intentionally killed by legal abortions. But in addition to these intended deaths, an estimated 100,000 infants are the unintended victims of latent abortion morbidity each year.[1] The deaths of these wanted children are especially painful for previously aborted women.

As we discussed in Chapter Three, abortion poses a severe threat to the reproductive integrity of women. Indeed, between 40 and 50 percent of all aborted women will suffer later reproductive problems. Based on current studies, it can be conservatively estimated that previously aborted women will face at least three times more ectopic pregnancies than their unaborted counterparts, three times more first trimester miscarriages, four times more second trimester miscarriages, three times more premature deliveries, and a three times higher incidence of complications during labor.[2] When all of these factors are combined, it can be estimated that for every 100,000 previously aborted women who later attempt a wanted pregnancy, 14,329 will lose their babies. This is over four times the 3,320 losses which would be expected for a group of 100,000 non-aborted women. After subtracting out the "normal" fetal loss rate, it can be concluded that for every 100,000 pregnancies undertaken by previously aborted women, over 11,000 *wanted* babies will die as a direct result of latent abortion morbidity.[3]

These statistical estimates are consistent with recent studies comparing the later reproductive lives of previously aborted women to their non-aborted counterparts. Indeed, based on actual field studies, the above estimates appear to be very conservative. For example, one university study compared the outcome of second pregnancies between 211 women whose first pregnancies were terminated by induced abortion and a parity matched group of 147 women who lost their first pregnancies due to spontaneous miscarriage. The researchers conducting this study found a striking difference in the outcome of pregnancy between the two groups. They discovered a 17.5 percent total fetal loss rate among the induced abortion group compared to only 7.5 percent among the control group, which itself was composed of relatively high-risk patients.[4] These findings suggest that nearly 1 out of every 5 previously aborted women will lose a later wanted pregnancy, and that over half of these losses will be indirectly due to latent abortion morbidity.

Because every type of pregnancy complication also poses a risk to the mother, estimates similar to the ones above can be done to calculate the added maternal death risk which results from latent abortion morbidity. When the proper calculations are made, it can be concluded that for every 100,000 aborted women who later attempt a wanted pregnancy, 12 will die as a result of obstetric complications compared to a "normal" maternal mortality rate of 7.6 per 100,000 pregnancies. Thus, previously aborted women face a 58 percent greater risk of dying during a later pregnancy than their non-aborted sisters.[5]

It can be reasonably expected that at least 900,000 previously aborted women attempt a wanted pregnancy each year. Based on the statistical calculations described above, it is therefore estimated that the latent morbidity of induced abortion results in about 100,000 "wanted baby" deaths and an extra 40 maternal deaths each year.[6]

As is obvious from these figures that the increased risk of death which aborted women face in later pregnancies is significant. But in terms of private decision making, the personal risk which aborted women face is remarkably small compared to the increased risk posed to their wanted children. Margaret and Arthur Wynn, pro-choice researchers for the London-based Foundation for Education and Research in Child Bearing, have clearly pointed out the impact of abortion on later pregnancies.

> "[T]hroughout the crucial stages of human reproduction from conception to the weaning of the child, the risk of death to the child is more than a 100 times the risk of death to the mother. . . . [Therefore,] It is not the mother's life which is primarily at stake but the consequences to subsequent children, if any, of surgical interference with the delicately adjusted reproductive system of women.[7]

Based on the above considerations, it is quite clear that women considering abortion, particularly those who may be likely to seek a wanted pregnancy at a later date, should be warned that the abortion they are contemplating poses a significant, increased risk to their future children and to themselves during later pregnancies.

The loss of a wanted pregnancy is always a personal tragedy for parents who are anxiously anticipating the birth of their child. But for previously aborted women, the miscarriage or birthing loss of wanted children is especially traumatic since their deaths are a painful reminder of the children previously sacrificed through abortion. This loss of a wanted child resurrects buried feelings of guilt and may often be experienced as "punishment" for having undergone the previous abortion. Once this second loss occurs, it is not unusual for a woman to be especially fearful that she has given up her only chance to give birth to a child.

Adamant pro-abortionists might well dismiss the unintended deaths of 100,000 wanted babies each year as an insignificant price to pay for the "freedom of choice." But this hard-core, pro-abortion position does not remove the very real pain which parents feel when they lose a wanted child.

In fact, pro-choicers have long insisted that a human fetus has human value only to the degree it is "wanted" by its parents. According to this relativistic standard, "humanity" is an attribute conferred on a fetus by the opinion of its mother. If pro-choicers are to be consistent in their respect for the subjective standards of pregnant women, they must also admit that *wanted* infants who die as a result of latent abortion morbidity are *human deaths*. Once this fact is recognized, it must then also be admitted that 10 percent of all abortions result in an unintentional death, either of women or of later wanted children.

Thus, at least *one in ten abortions results in an unintentional death*. What reasonable patient, what cautious doctor can accept such a terrible death toll for the sake of short-term convenience?

Finally, women considering abortion should also be aware that for every wanted infant who dies because of prematurity, many more will survive but will suffer mild to severe neurological damage. Dr. Andre Hellegers has conservatively estimated that for every one million aborted women, there will be 20,000 premature births before 32 weeks resulting in 2,000 children permanently handicapped with acquired cerebral palsy.[8] With over 20 million women aborted during the last fourteen years, it can be estimated that the legalization of abortion has resulted in the handicapping of no less than 40,000 children who would otherwise have been normal at birth. It is no wonder, then, that the Wynn report concludes:

> The complications of subsequent pregnancy resulting in children born handicapped in greater or lesser degree could be the most expensive consequence of induced abortion for society and [its] most grievous consequence for the individual and her family.[9]

Thus, given all of the physical risks that abortion poses to a woman's reproductive health, the claim that abortion today is best for one's future children must be dismissed as nothing more than a sales pitch. Women who desire to give birth to healthy babies in the future should exercise extreme caution when considering the abortion option.

Child Battery and Abortion

Pro-abortionists frequently claim that unless unplanned pregnancies are aborted, the resulting "unwanted" children will end up resented and despised by their parents. But, in fact, the evidence overwhelmingly demonstrates that unplanned children almost always end up to be very much wanted and loved by their parents.[10]

Pro-abortionists, however, seem to ignore this fact and instead rely on "common sense" claims that "unwanted" children are not only unwanted but are the most likely victims of child abuse. But once

again, upon investigation, the opposite is found to be true: *It is the children of planned pregnancies who are most at risk of battery.*
This fact first became clear following a University of Southern California study done in 1973 by Dr. E.F. Lenoski, a professor of pediatrics. His investigations into child battery, confirmed by others, found that 91 percent of battered and abused children are the result of planned and desired pregnancies—a rate much higher than the norm of 63 percent found in a matched control group. Furthermore, battered children were much more likely to have been born in wedlock and to mothers who expressed satisfaction with their pregnancies. Not only are battered children wanted, they are central objects of parental aspirations and parental pride. Fully 24 percent of battered children were named after one of their parents, compared to only 4 percent in the control group.[11]

Child abusers cannot be easily categorized. Battery occurs because of maladjusted attitudes, not because of poverty or ignorance. It is clearly not confined to any social or economic class.

Rather than supporting the myth that unwanted children are abused and battered, the evidence strongly suggests that abusing parents carefully plan and desperately want their children. This tendency may in part be related to their "need" to pass on the abuse which they themselves received as youngsters. According to one expert, battering parents typically "grew up in a hostile environment, and were abused themselves. . . . When the children fail to satisfy their emotional needs [unrealistic, neurotic expectations of perfection], the parent reacts with the same violence they experienced as children."[12]

Ray Helfer, an expert on child abuse, describes this cycle of abuse with the acronym W.A.R., meaning the World of Abnormal Rearing.

Although the advent of abortion interrupts a large number of pregnancies, it seems to interrupt less pregnancies of W.A.R. children. Girls who are reared in this unusual atmosphere have a strong desire to become pregnant. They often refuse the use of birth control and dismiss any thought of abortion. . . . Unfortunately, the pregnancy is wanted for very selfish reasons, i.e., to resolve some special problem for the mother. The new baby is supposed to get her away from an unhappy experience in her home, or will keep her company, or even take care of her and comfort her in her loneliness.

As the pregnancy comes to completion, the child may or may

THE IMPACT OF ABORTION ON LATER CHILDREN

not have the capability of meeting the expectation that the parent(s) have developed through the W.A.R. years. Many young mothers who had every desire to get pregnant, with great expectations that the baby would resolve one of their many problems, find themselves even worse off than before. Their baby does not—or is not able to meet these needs.[13]

In fact, instead of reducing the incidence of child abuse, the evidence shows that abortion actually *increases* child abuse. This happens because the abortion mentality reinforces the attitude of treating children like objects, objects that can be wanted or unwanted according to whether or not "it" satisfies parental needs. According to C. Henry Kempe, another child abuse expert, "Basic in the abuser's attitude toward infants is the conviction, largely unconscious, that children exist in order to satisfy parental needs." The same demands for "wanted" children also exist in the abortion mentality. What aborters and abusers have in common, then, is "the assumption that the rights, desires, and ideas of the adult take full precedence over those of the child, and that children are essentially the property of parents who have the right to deal with their offspring as they see fit, without interference."[14]

The evidence linking abortion to child abuse is compelling. Since *Roe v. Wade,* child abuse has increased proportionately with the skyrocketing rate of legal abortions.[15] The same pattern of increased child battery following legalization of abortion has also been observed in many other countries, including Canada, Britain, and Japan. During 1975 alone, the rate of child battery in New York increased 18 to 20 percent, leading to estimates that during the 1980s there would be 1.5 million battered children, resulting in 50,000 deaths and 300,000 permanent injuries.[16] In many cases post-abortion trauma has been directly linked to abuse or neglect of a woman's "wanted" children.[17] This evidence, combined with personal observations, has convinced Dr. Philip Ney, a Canadian psychiatrist who has done extensive work with child abuse cases, that "elective abortion is an important cause of child abuse."[18]

According to Dr. Ney, abortion leads to child abuse in many ways. First, aborted women frequently feel guilt, and "guilt is one of the major factors causing battering and infanticide." This guilt results in "intolerable feelings of self-hatred, which the parent takes out on the child." Second, child abusers almost invariably have a significant lack

225

of self-esteem. Since lowered self-esteem is a well-documented aftermath of abortion, the experience of abortion may help shape an emotional environment which is conducive to the battering of other or later children. Third, maternal bonding instincts are weakened by the deliberate denial of maternal attraction which must take place in an abortion. Once established, this behavior pattern of resisting maternal bonding has a negative impact on bonding in later pregnancies. Finally, Dr. Ney adds, "there is increasing evidence that previously aborted women become depressed during a subsequent pregnancy. Depression interferes with a mother's early bonding with her infant, and children who are not bonded to their mothers are at a higher risk of being battered." He also believes that abortion may "interfere with a mother's ability to restrain her anger toward those depending on her care," because abortion may "weaken a social taboo against harming those who are defenseless."[19]

Because the legal availability of abortion distorts expectations, even women who decide to have their children may suffer from reduced maternal bonding. Instead of facing the old standard where pregnancy meant delivery which meant adjustment, the legal availability of abortion forces the woman to face the temptation of taking "the easy way out." If this temptation is dwelt upon, the period of adjustment is delayed and bonding is inhibited.

Besides the effect of abortion on the abusing mother, Dr. Ney suggests that the marital stress caused by abortion increases family hostilities and thus heightens the possibility of violent outbreaks. If the father felt left out of the abortion decision or only resentfully agreed to the abortion, or if the woman felt pressured into abortion by her mate, deep feelings of resentment and violation of trust might cause frequent eruption of emotions. In the heat of such parental disputes, children are likely to get caught in the crossfire, objects of release for the pent-up rage of adults. "Some men, feeling that size is their only remaining weapon when verbally cornered, beat their wives, who then beat the child. Others, in frustration, leave home, another prominent antecedent to child battering."[20]

Family hostilities might also be aggravated by the non-aborted children who experience symptoms of the "survivor syndrome"—a mixture of guilt and anger. They are confused about why their sibling was aborted and they were not.

Guilt produces depression, which shows as irritability and lethargy, which to the parents smacks of rudeness and disrespect, the very things that trigger many batterings. . . . In some instances, the child triggers the parental aggression because he feels that, as a result of his own aggressive feelings, he should be punished. "You killed my baby brother, go ahead and kill me."[21]

The abortion of a sibling also undermines the survivor's perceptions of his own self-value and the quality of love he is receiving from his parents. According to Ney:

Only two decades ago parents were willing to suffer major deprivation to have and raise children. It seemed like a sacred obligation or a great privilege. Nowadays, people balance having children with wanting a country house, another car, better vacations and early retirement. This might be observed by children in such families. As a result they might feel less confidence in their parents' true concern for their welfare. They might then become so importunate in their demands for care and attention that their parents feel threatened. Not infrequently, the parental response to those attention-demanding children will be physical violence.[22]

In addition to the above factors, Dr. Ney believes that the social acceptance of abortion reduces the esteem with which children are held and undermines the taboo against child abuse:

Abortion diminishes the value of all people, particularly children. When the destruction of the unborn child is socially sanctioned and even applauded, the child can't have much value. More than anyone, children realize they are becoming worth less. Thus, the rate of suicide [among children] has increased correspondingly.
    If society adheres to the ethic that the unborn child only has value when he is wanted, that ethic can easily be applied to small children. Logically, when people stop wanting a child, he has lost value. If the unborn has no value and it is all right to kill him, then it is defensible to kill children who have lost value because they are now unwanted.
    People do not harm what they highly value. As children decline in value, it becomes easier to neglect and dispose of them. Besides, both those who abort children and those who murder them say they do it "out of love."[23]

Because the child is perceived as having no legal rights prior to birth, parents can hardly be expected to respect the child's rights after birth. A battering parent, thinking "I could have aborted you," can quite logically conclude that since pre-natal murder is acceptable, how can anyone object to some post-natal "roughing up."

Finally, Dr. Ney expects that because abortion is expanding the number of families caught up in the W.A.R. cycle, it will have a continuing impact upon future generations:

> Abortion appears to be in the tradition of violent pseudo-solutions, which only compound complex personal and social problems.
>
> Abortion not only increases the rates of child battering at present, it will increase the tendency to batter and abort in succeeding generations. Abortion, producing guilt both in the mother and the children who survive, increases the probability of displaced hostility, which results in so many battered, murdered children. More importantly, by interrupting the formation of the delicate mechanism which promotes mother-infant bonding, it puts at risk millions of babies who are not aborted. . . .
>
> We have disrupted a very delicate balance, turning parents against their own offspring. There may be no turning back.[24]

The Effect of Abortion on Siblings

Abortion of "unwanted" children frequently causes confusion and stress among wanted children. As Dr. Ney observed above, children who survive the "window of vulnerability" only to see, or even suspect, that a sibling was aborted may experience elements of the "survivor syndrome." The result is that wanted children are being made to feel vulnerable to "unwantedness."

The psychological impact of abortion on siblings is significant. In a study of 87 children whose mothers had abortions, researchers found both immediate and delayed reactions. Included under the category of immediate reactions were "anxiety attacks, nightmares, increased aggressiveness, stuttering, running away, death phobias, increased separation anxiety, sudden outbursts of fear or hatred of the mother, and even suicide attempts." Delayed or late reactions included "effects ranging from isolated fantasies to pervading, crucial and disabling [psychosomatic] illness.[25]

Dr. Edward Sheridan, an associate professor of clinical psychiatry at Georgetown University Hospital, has provided therapy for abortion-traumatized siblings for the last twenty-five years. His patients range from one-year-old children to adults who are still coming to terms with the knowledge that they lost a sibling to abortion. According to Sheridan, children sometimes become aware of the abortion through overheard conversations, or even by being directly told by their parents. But frequently, even a very young child will "sense" the mother's pregnancy and then become confused when the anticipated brother or sister does not materialize. If no explanation is given, this confusion may lead the child to somehow feel personally responsible for the loss. On the other hand, if the child becomes aware that the mother actively chose to "get rid" of the sibling, he often begins to fear her.

> When the child hears mother has gotten rid of baby brother or sister, for whatever reason, this makes him dread things in the home. . . . Mother becomes the agent of death instead of the agent of life.[26]

Because the implications of abortion are so clearly hostile to children, a youngster may be disturbed even if the mother has not actually had an abortion. The suspicion that she has, or ever would, may be sufficient to trigger anxiety. Consider, for example, the following conversation between a six-year-old girl and her mother who is vocally pro-choice:

Daughter: Mom? Why didn't you abort me?
Mother: Darling? How can you say such a thing? I wanted you! You're my little girl!
Daughter: But what if you hadn't wanted me?
Mother: But I did!!
Daughter: But what if you stopped wanting me?
Mother: But I won't!!!
Daughter: But how can you be sure? What if you *do* stop wanting me?

This would be an interesting scene to play out, and one must wonder how often it has been played out in real life. No matter how emphatically the mother tries to assure the child that she is wanted, the doubts and questions still persist.

If such conversations do not occur openly between mother and child, they may take place within the minds of children.

Clearly, abortion impacts not only women and their unborn chil-

229

dren, but also the "wanted" children in her family. And despite all the pro-choice rhetoric in the world, these young innocents will simply never understand why the abortion of their brothers and sisters is "for their own good."

Summary

Abortion is sometimes defended as a reasonable way of delaying parenthood until a time when women are better prepared for that role. But women who have had abortions face at least a doubled risk of losing a later wanted pregnancy. Each year nearly 100,000 wanted children die during pregnancy or childbirth because of latent abortion morbidity. Many other children end up permanently handicapped due to abortion-related premature births and complications of delivery. Thus, women considering abortion who plan on future pregnancies should be carefully counseled about the increased risk abortion poses to their later children and to themselves.

Abortion advocates insist that abortion "saves unwanted children" from living miserable lives. But most unplanned pregnancies actually end up very much wanted. In fact, no child is ever truly "unwanted," as is proven by the great surplus of loving people who desperately want to adopt children. "Unwantedness" is simply not a trait of children. Instead, if there is a problem, it lies with "unwanting" adults.

No "unwanted" child has ever been made better off by abortion. Indeed, there is much evidence to indicate that abortion of "unwanted" children has led to increased physical and emotional abuse among the "wanted" children who are allowed the *privilege* of survival.

The rhetorical argument of "aborting for the child's sake" may be effective in making underprivileged women feel obligated to abort, but it does nothing to aid either the woman or the child. It is a spurious argument used only to confuse and gloss over the cruel truth of abortion: a truth which includes violence, death, loss, and pain. Abortion is anti-love because it eliminates those who most need love; it destroys the children who are the "unwanted" opportunities by which parents are compelled to grow and share.

Finally, it should be pointed out once again that most abortions do not kill "unwanted" children. Instead, most women undergoing abortions *do* want the child, or at least feel able to accept it, but they feel unable to raise it, or somehow forced by circumstances to abort. In these cases, then, the aborted child is not an "unwanted" child being spared a miserable life, but a wanted child which is aborted out of fear, frustration, and despair. The distinction is an important one. Given aid and comfort, most aborting women would gladly come to accept their child. Given abortion instead, many will continue to feel obliged to abort "for the child's sake."

E   I   G   H   T

Business Before Medicine

Abortion in America is a commodity, bought and sold for the convenience of the buyer and the profit of the seller. Though abortion
utilizes medical knowledge, it is not *medical*—that is, abortions are not
being prescribed in order to heal the body or cure illnesses. Instead,
over 99 percent of all abortions are provided simply at the request of
desperate women, those who hope that by eliminating their pregnancies they can eliminate their social problems. As we saw in Chapter
Five, even in the rare cases where serious medical problems do exist
because of the pregnancy, abortion is still not good medicine. Given
the physical and psychological risks of this surgical procedure, an
informed and truly "conscientious physician" would almost never pre-
scribe abortion.

For the doctors and clinics engaged in the abortion industry,
decisions about providing abortion services are not based on medical
science, but on consumer demand. Rather than being a medical cure
prescribed by a trained physician, abortion has become just another
service delivered on request, regardless of the patrons' motives or
needs. Abortions are dispensed like haircuts, to whomever can pay the
price—no questions asked—with the hope that it will improve the
client's future social life. Thus today's abortionist/physicians are like
the barber/physicians of the Middle Ages who practiced two trades,
being both merchants and healers.

This dual role is a far cry from the medical standards which existed less than twenty years ago. At that time, the dignity of physicians lay in their devotion to protect human life. This high-minded ideal was summed up in the Hippocratic oath by which they pledged to use their knowledge and skills only to save lives and improve health.

But when some physicians began setting aside their Hippocratic oaths—an oath which specifically forbids participation in abortion, or any other use of medical knowledge for non-healing purposes—they also began to set aside their professionalism. Rather than being medical advisors, they became hired hands. Health care became secondary to consumer demand. Whatever patients asked for, they received, regardless of whether it was necessary for their health or not.

Having turned to the pursuit of business before medicine, abortionists have shed many of medicine's traditional codes of ethics. These professional standards were once seen as necessary to the provision of health care services, but these standards are now viewed as obstacles to providing efficient and profitable abortion services. The five most obvious differences which separate abortion services from strictly medical services are as follows:

First, abortion is the only medical procedure which may be advertised. Normally, the medical community condemns advertising as being undignified and unprofessional. Advertising is forbidden by all codes of medical conduct, and in some states advertising by physicians is illegal. If a physician violates this taboo and advertises his or her services, he will be called before a review board and have his license revoked. Abortionists, however, are the exception. The courts have ruled there can be no restrictions placed on the advertising of abortion services. With this judicial support of their trade, abortion clinics routinely advertise in area newspapers, and even on radio. Sometimes, in order to attract more business, they advertise their clinic under more than one name. These advertisements are seldom coy and are often distasteful. In *The Village Voice*, for example, abortion clinics advertise their services with pictures of smiling women, flowers, or abstract art. To attract customers away from competitors, many clinics advertise loss leaders such as "free pregnancy tests" or "free contraceptive pills." These "medical" services are advertised alongside "adult entertainment" ads for massage parlors and private clubs.[1]

Second, abortion is the only surgery over which there can be no government regulation. According to Supreme Court rulings, federal, state and local governments cannot regulate abortion at all during the first trimester (except to require that it be performed by a physician in a reasonably sterile environment) and may exercise only limited regulations during the second and third trimesters.[2] The exclusion of state or local regulation of abortion is rationalized as being necessary to prevent infringement on the unique "zone of privacy" which patients and doctors share when considering the abortion decision. Ironically, minors may be required by law to have parental permission to have their ears pierced, but no law can require parental permission prior to abortion. States may require waiting periods prior to elective surgeries such as sterilizations, but not so for abortion. Abortion alone is immune from government oversight and consumer protections.

Third, abortion is the only surgery for which the surgeon is not obliged to inform the patient of the possible risks of the procedure, or even of the exact nature of the procedure. Indeed, abortion providers are the only medical personnel who have a "constitutional right" to withhold information, even when directly questioned by the patient.[3] This right is supposedly granted so that "conscientious physicians" might "protect" women from being frightened by the risks they face or upset by what the abortion procedure will do to their unborn children. Unfortunately, this "right" to control and censure the information which is given to women also allows paternalistic control, manipulation, and deceit. *Abortion is the only medical procedure for which legal and medical codes deny the patient the right to informed consent.*

Fourth, abortion is the only surgery for which physicians routinely demand payment in advance; they generally insist on cash or money orders. For every other medical service, cash-at-the-door is considered to be not only unprofessional, but so unethical as to be punishable by the loss of surgical privileges.[4]

Fifth, abortion is the only medical procedure for which clinics pay cash awards, or "finder's fees," to those who bring them customers. For example, in one year alone, the Los Angeles Planned Parenthood-Clergy Consultation Service received $250,000 in kickbacks from clinics to which they referred women for abortions.[5] In addition, some clinics pay their counselors "bonuses" for each phone inquiry they handle in which they convince the client to abort at their facility.[6] If any physician offered kickbacks for referrals in any other branch of medicine, his license would be revoked.

Since abortion is being provided as a commodity, not as a medical necessity, it is understandable that abortionists have rejected those medical standards which would encumber their trade. They are free to promote business before health care. While they present abortion under the guise of medicine (since it lends their commodity an air of respectability which cannot be bought with any amount of advertising), they reject all the obligations, the codes, and the oaths of medicine which through the centuries have given medicine such a high place of honor. While they label their clinics as a "medical" service, they operate them as businesses. And as in any business, profit comes first.

Maximizing Profits

One point on which all abortionists agree is that abortion is a lucrative business. Dr. David Aberman bragged to one reporter that just by moonlighting at an abortion clinic one day a week, he was able to pocket an extra $30,000 per year.[7] Another abortionist, Dr. Kenneth L. Wright, testified at a court hearing that he received $200 per abortion and was able to perform sixty abortions per day, yielding $12,000 worth of business per day.[8] Still another abortionist, Dr. Arnold Bickham, owner and operator of three Midwestern clinics, received $792,266 dollars in 1974 for welfare-paid abortions alone.[9] While no precise profit figures are available, it is not unusual for a physician doing abortions to earn more than eight times the average surgeon's income.[10]

Abortion is big business, as abortion clinic owners are the first to admit. And like other businesses, abortion clinics try to cut costs, increase productivity, and maximize profits.

As in any industry, reducing expensive labor costs is the first avenue towards increasing profit margins. Rather than having high-priced engineers assemble the products they design, low-cost laborers are hired to solder the wires and screw the bolts. Similarly, abortion clinics routinely hire low-cost, unskilled staff members to fulfill the quasi-medical tasks normally performed by physicians or nurses.

Though abortion clinic staff members bear the major responsibility for counseling the patient and caring for her health needs, there are no educational or certification requirements for abortion clinic personnel. Instead, most of these low-cost workers are simply hired "off the street" and receive on-the-job training. The depth of knowledge which abortion staff members have, therefore, is generally far below the usual standards of the medical and nursing professions.

In the typical abortion clinic, these staff members counsel the patients about the procedure, examine the patients, estimate gestation, perform any required tests (e.g., pregnancy tests and blood samples), record vital signs, prepare the patients for surgery, and assist patients through the recovery room. In almost all cases, the physician does not even see the patient until he enters the room to begin the operation. Often the abortionist doesn't even know the patient's name, or vice versa.[11] By delegating responsibility and minimizing patient/doctor interaction, abortionists free themselves to work solely on performing the actual abortions in the least amount of time possible.

This dependency on unskilled workers frequently results in deterioration of services. For example, at more than one clinic investigators have found that records of patients' vital signs were "fudged" or blatantly faked both before and after surgery in order to save time or to make questionable cases look routine.[12] Record keeping is kept to a minimum not only to save time and effort, but also to avoid developing too many records which could be used to incriminate the clinic in the event of a malpractice suit.[13]

Furthermore, in the rush through so many pregnancy and blood tests, abortion clinic lab tests are notoriously unreliable. Non-pregnant women are judged to be pregnant; Rh-negative women are told that they are O-positive; and tests which are paid for are forgotten or mislaid. A lab technician at one abortion clinic shrugged off such mistakes, saying: "We're just too busy to think of everything."[14]

At some clinics mass production techniques are used to increase worker efficiency. Workers pre-fill stockpiles of syringes for later use, and unregistered nursing aides even give the shots.[15]

In the busy, assembly line environment of abortion clinics, sanitation standards often deteriorate. Health inspectors at one abortion clinic found that the lack of sterile conditions extended to:

- Instruments that were "dirty and worn to the point that the stainless-steel finish had deteriorated and the instruments were beginning to rust."
- Recovery room beds made with dirty linens.
- "Supposedly sterile instruments" encrusted with "dried matter."
- Instruments being "sterilized" with Tide detergent, and surgical equipment, including the suction machine, being "cleansed" with plain water.[16]

Besides relying on low-skilled workers to reduce labor costs, many clinics cut back on the medical double-checks normally used to safeguard against accidents. For example, whenever tissue is removed during hospital surgery, it is routinely examined by a licensed pathologist. Tissues extracted during abortion, on the other hand, are often examined only by an on-the-job-trained staff person, *if at all*. A proper pathological examination would determine if there was a failure to extract all the fetal pieces and placental matter. If the common problem is not identified by a pathological exam, the pieces will be left inside the woman's uterus where they may cause lacerations, rotting, and infection. Incomplete abortions such as these are among the most common post-abortion complications.[17]

At many clinics, costs are further cut by avoiding Rh blood tests and expensive Rhogam shots. Most clinics do not provide this service at all, while others offer Rh testing only at an additional cost. A woman who is untested for the Rh factor and is Rh-sensitive is likely to be sensitized during her abortion. If sensitization occurs, the woman's body will become hostile to a later pregnancy with a Rh positive baby and try to reject it. Thus, a woman who is unknowingly Rh-sensitized during her abortion faces a future health risk to herself and to her "wanted" children.[18]

To cut overhead costs even further, many abortion clinics try to minimize such expensive "frills" as "excessive" emergency equipment. As a result of cost-efficient measures, most clinics do not have transfusion supplies and blood type selections available, even though 2 to 12 percent of aborted women bleed enough to warrant a transfusion.[19]

Cost-saving measures like those described above are intended to reduce overhead and maximize profits. To increase profits even further, abortionists try to work as fast as possible in order to handle as many patients per day as possible.[20] Besides the obvious risks in hurrying a blind operation which involves sharp instruments and vacuum pressures capable of tearing out organs, the rush for efficiency often results in "cutting corners" on normal sanitation standards. As one operating attendant told Dr. Denes:

> Our surgeons have a technique, even though I shouldn't really say this, where they don't really scrub between cases. They'll scrub once and they'll do a case and they'll go next door to the next room and put on a new gown and gloves. Without scrubbing between. The surgery is only three to five minutes long. . . . A person who is eight weeks in term only needs two minutes worth of surgery from a good doctor . . .[21]

Similarly, workers at other clinics have reported physicians doing abortions in their street clothes.[22]

Despite the health risks posed by such medical short-cuts, these practices do promote quick and cost-effective abortion services. When everything is flowing smoothly, the assembly line routine at abortion clinics operates at maximum efficiency. One patient recalls her abortion experience, saying:

> I could swear that there was only one doctor and he just went down the line giving abortions. I started crying because I could hear that little [suction] machine going on and off. He just kept getting closer and closer. I heard his gloves pop off in the next room and then he came to me. He didn't say a word. He came in and did it and walked out in three minutes. Then he started down the hall again. . . .[23]

When clinics employ more than one abortionist, the work goes even faster. As a former nurse at one clinic reports: "The doctors race each other. Especially on Saturdays, they compete to see who can get the most patients done."[24]

Because of the huge profits to be made in supplying abortions, the competition between metropolitan abortion clinics is often fierce. Some offer "lunch hour" prices or special "discount days" to attract customers, and at least one abortion referral service uses a sound truck to hype its "Abortion Hot Line."[25] Operators of big city clinics openly admit their desire to drive their competitors out of business. As the owner of one abortion clinic told his staff:

> We have to sell abortions. We have to use all of the tactics we can because just like my other businesses [a trucking firm, a pollution control business, and a real estate sales office] we have competition. Now, we have to go by the rules, but rules have to be broken if we are gonna get things done.[26]

But perhaps the most dangerous cost-cutting activity of abortionists is their failure to provide post-abortion follow-up exams. In most clinics there is little or no post-abortion counseling by the doctor or the staff, and it is extremely unusual for the physician to examine the woman before she is released. Typically, women are told to wait in the recovery room from fifteen minutes to an hour and are then dismissed. By way of comparison, a woman who has a D&C in a hospital is usually hospitalized for observation for two days.[27]

Furthermore, few clinics offer follow-up exams in the days after the abortion. It is rare for any clinic to insist upon the woman's return—except when they have sold her an additional service, such as a fitting for an IUD, or scheduled her for a sterilization. Instead, most abortion clinics tell women to return only if they experience excessive bleeding or fever. But even this lax standard is not observed by all. Some clinics, not wanting to be bothered further, instruct patients to "go to your own doctor" if problems arise. But since most women simply want to put the abortion experience behind them as fast as possible, very few return for follow-up exams even when one is offered. And others, rather than admit what they have done to their family doctor, prefer to endure any post-abortion discomfort in shameful silence.[28]

Like most big businesses, the abortion industry resists all government regulation which might inhibit their profits. For example, it was not women seeking abortion who opposed the Akron city ordinance which established minimum standards of informed consent; it was the abortion providers. In *Akron v. Akron Center for Reproductive Health* abortionists objected to an ordinance which would have required them to inform women of the health risks of abortion, alternatives to abortion, and what the procedure entailed, including facts about the relative development of their fetus. This information, the abortionists complained, would only discourage women from aborting and have a "chilling" effect on their business. Like any salesmen, abortionists wanted to emphasize only the "good" side of their product.

Similarly, when pro-life sidewalk counselors were sued in California, it was not women seeking abortions who sued, complaining that they were being presented with alternatives; it was the owners of the abortion clinic. In this case, the abortionists sued sidewalk counselors for $50,000 worth of "lost customers."[29]

In efforts to prevent any state regulation of abortion, abortion providers have repeatedly gone to court to attack and defeat 24-hour waiting requirements, parental and spousal notification requirements, and state restrictions on welfare-subsidized abortions. They oppose the 24-hour waiting period because it provides too much time for reflection and hinders "impulse sales." In striking down requirements for parental and spousal notification, abortionists have succeeded in separating frightened and vulnerable young women from those who might support them and provide them with alternatives to abortion.[30] But their motive for seeking to force state Medicaid programs to pay for abortions is most obvious of all: it is easier to make large profits from the government than from the poor.

Clinics of Deceit: An Inside Look at the Abortion Industry

In the fall of 1978, the Chicago *Sun-Times* ran a series of articles which shocked the city and the state. Entitled "The Abortion Profiteers," the series detailed the results of a five-month undercover investigation of four abortion clinics. The clinics infiltrated by Better Government Association (BGA) investigators and *Sun-Times* reporters were four of the largest clinics in Illinois, all located on Chicago's high-rent North Michigan Avenue. Together, these four clinics performed over one-third of all the abortions done in Illinois. By all outward appearances, these were big-time, first-class abortion clinics. But undercover investigators found nothing "first-class" about them. Instead, they found callous treatment of patients, lies, greed, injuries, and death.

In order to cushion the impact of these revelations, *Sun-Times* editorials went to great lengths to insist that the abortion right was a sacred one which should not be curtailed. The abuses its investigators had uncovered, the paper insisted, could be corrected by better and more vigilant state regulation of abortion clinics. Furthermore, while decrying the profiteering of the four clinics investigated, the *Sun-Times* boldly insisted that most abortion clinics are probably better and safer than the four which they had investigated.

Unfortunately, there is little basis for this optimism. By looking at the list of "abuses" that the *Sun-Times* and BGA investigators uncovered, we will find that most of the practices condemned were perfectly legal, are common throughout the abortion industry, and years later are *still* outside the scope of government regulation.

Abortions for Non-Pregnant Women

Sun-Times reporters witnessed dozens of cases in which abortions were performed on non-pregnant women. At one clinic an investigator found that 12 percent of all abortions were performed on women with negative or indeterminate pregnancy test results. As the *Sun-Times* reporters pointed out, these non-pregnant women were needlessly exposed to the physical and psychological risks of abortion.[31]

Oddly enough, abortion of non-pregnant women is neither illegal nor even uncommon. Such abortions would be illegal only if clinics attempted to profit by *deliberately and knowingly* deceiving non-pregnant women into believing that they were pregnant. But if there is a "reasonable suspicion" that a woman is pregnant—despite negative or inconclusive test results—then doing an abortion is perfectly legal. Indeed, the accepted practice among many abortionists is always to abort "suspect" pregnancies. They argue that it is medically safer for the woman to perform an early abortion rather than to delay it until tests become conclusive. Furthermore, they insist, performing an early abortion whenever there is a "reasonable suspicion" of pregnancy also saves their patients a great deal of money, time, and worry.

At one national abortion conference, for example, Dr. Ronald Pion, an abortionist from Hawaii, argued that physicians should "protect" women from feeling they killed a fetus by *never* doing a pregnancy test. If a woman could not be sure whether or not an actual abortion had taken place, he argued, she could not feel guilty.[32] At the same conference, New York physician Irwin Kaiser supported Pion's thesis. While admitting that abortion posed inherent risks, Dr. Kaiser questioned the importance of confirming the existence of a pregnancy, saying: "[W]e see no reason at all to be apprehensive about doing a suction evacuation on a patient who isn't pregnant." He added that for the non-pregnant woman, abortion is "probably a very uneventful phenomenon."[33]

Besides "protecting" women from guilt feelings, the most popular defense for doing an abortion even when pregnancy is not confirmed is to "be on the safe side." Early abortions are safer abortions and less costly. If a pregnancy is merely suspected, a physician may honestly perform a "menstrual extraction" (a very early abortion which differs from normal suction abortions only in that the pregnancy is not confirmed.) Many respected medical authorities even believe that doctors should encourage women to have regular "menstrual extractions" instead of waiting to confirm pregnancy. The problem with this policy of being "on the safe side" is that most of these procedures are unnecessary. Studies have shown that 80 percent of these early abortion procedures are done on non-pregnant women.[34]

Finally, it is not a crime to inaccurately diagnose a pregnancy unless it is done with *intent* to defraud—a very difficult allegation to prove. And since most abortion professionals would testify that abortion of non-pregnant women is a "normal risk" of the procedure, it is doubtful that any federal, state, or local regulation of pregnancy testing would be upheld by the courts, since such regulation would encumber "accepted medical practices" and violate the zone of privacy between "the woman and her physician."[35] Furthermore, even if some sort of regulation were upheld, it would be largely unenforceable unless state inspectors reviewed the results of each and every pregnancy test performed.

In sum, abortion of non-pregnant women is not uncommon. It is not a practice limited only to "shady" abortion profiteers; it occurs in clinics around the country. According to one estimate, as many as 10 percent of all women who receive "abortions" are not actually pregnant.[36]

Exceeding Gestational Limits

According to Illinois law at the time of the *Sun-Times* exposé, second and third trimester abortions could only be performed in hospitals. Outpatient clinics were only allowed to do first trimester abortions. But undercover investigators for the *Sun-Times* reported the "shocking" facts that clinics were doing abortions beyond the 12-week cutoff date set by state law. But while these "violations" of state abortion laws were a "shocking" revelation when printed on the front page of a major newspaper, the fact that late-term abortions were being performed in clinics was hardly news to any abortion observer. Instead, late-term clinic abortions were an accepted practice outside the scope of any practical control.

There are two reasons for this. First, honest mistakes in estimating the gestational period of a pregnancy occur all the time. But once again, it is not a crime for a physician to make an honest mistake in estimating how far a pregnancy has progressed. It is a crime only if his *intent* is to defraud the patient.

Second, the Illinois statute limiting outpatient clinics to first-trimester abortions was of questionable validity, as abortionists well knew. Many abortion clinics had successfully challenged similar restrictions in other states. The issue was settled in 1983 when the Supreme Court ruled in favor of the clinics. Today, all outpatient clinics have a "constitutionally protected right" to perform second trimester abortions.[37]

Abortions Performed by "Untrained" Abortionists

The *Sun-Times* series shocked readers with the fact that many abortions were being performed by "moonlighting residents, [and] general practitioners with little or no training in women's medicine." But once again, this "revelation" was not unique to the four Chicago clinics which were investigated. Instead, the use of such "untrained" abortionists is perfectly legal and commonplace.

First, the use of medical residents is an accepted practice in all areas of medicine, abortion is no exception. Residents are routinely allowed to perform minor surgery in teaching hospitals around the country. How else are they to learn? And since abortion proponents all insist that abortion is a "minor surgery," there is no reason to exclude qualified medical students from doing abortions.

Second, in regard to general practitioners who are not specially trained in women's medicine, there are no regulations limiting abortion to gynecologists. Indeed, the Supreme Court ruled that the only qualification necessary to perform an abortion is that a person be a medical doctor. Only non-physicians can be excluded from performing abortions. Attempts to limit abortions to medical specialists (such as obstetricians or gynecologists) have been routinely struck down by the courts as being "unconstitutional."[38]

While it is true that many abortionists have no special training to qualify them to perform abortions, the Constitution as interpreted by the Supreme Court does not allow for any such distinctions in training. Because of this "constitutional law," abortionists are essentially free of oversight by state and local governments or even by state medical boards. Even if an abortionist causes numerous complications or deaths, there is no mechanism to prevent him from continuing to perform abortions short of imprisonment for criminal neglect.[39]

Callousness Toward Patients

Of all the things that they witnessed, the *Sun-Times* investigators seemed most distressed at the discovery that abortionists were "cold, mechanical," and even "sadistic," and often operated with what seemed to be excessive speed.[40] But once more, what these investigators found was not unusual or unique. Instead, as we will see, they are traits common to abortionists at every major abortion clinic.

First, as to the charge of excessive speed, it must be granted that full-time abortionists achieve greater speed with practice. An obstetrician who does only an occasional abortion is unlikely to operate as fast as a full-time professional. In addition, doing abortion after abortion is a monotonous routine, so abortionists tend to develop a pace or rhythm to their surgeries. It is not uncommon for a professional abortionist to do an abortion in less than five minutes, though such speed was seen as shocking by the *Sun-Times* reporters.[41]

Second, the investigators reported many cases where the attending physician was insensitive and rude to patients about to undergo an abortion. For example, in one case the abortionist walked into the operating room and addressed the patient saying: "What do we have here? Ah, too much weight," and proceeded to do the abortion. Another used foul language and shouted at his patient when she began to scream in pain.[42]

But again, it is not a crime for an abortionist to be "cold and mechanical," or even callous and "sadistic." Instead, from all reports, such attitudes seem to be much more the rule than the exception.[43] Indeed, the pressure of doing frequent abortions tends to *make* abortionists callous and "mechanical." Truly compassionate physicians do not have the endurance to stay with the grueling and ugly work of abortion for very long. Only the "tough" (as in "thick-skinned") survive; and it is these abortionists who perform the vast majority of abortions. It is an inevitable result of the abortion business that cannot be corrected by newspaper exposés denouncing "sadism" or by some law requiring "compassion."

Complications and Deaths

Sun-Times reporters shocked their readers with reports of aborted women suffering from complications such as excessive bleeding, incomplete abortions, infections, and internal damage, as well as a number of unreported abortion-related deaths. But once again, this shocking "disclosure" was shocking only because it made the headlines of a major newspaper series.

As we discussed in earlier chapters, complications and unreported deaths resulting from legal abortions are not unusual. Complications are an inherent and "accepted" risk of the abortion procedure. Whether abortions are performed by incompetent interns or experienced surgeons, a significant number of complications will always occur. Unless an abortionist intentionally does harm to his patients or is guilty of criminal neglect, the state can do nothing to regulate his practice simply because he has a high complication rate.[44] In fact, in the state of Illinois, as in most states, not a single physician has ever lost his license because of complications (or even deaths) resulting from his legally-induced abortions.[45]

When these "abuses" were disclosed by *Sun-Times* reporters, there were loud cries for reform. The Illinois governor called for special committees, and there were temporary attempts at change. But in the end, *nothing* changed. In fact, despite all the good intentions of reformers, nothing could be changed. All of the "abuses" cited by the *Sun-Times* are within the "zone of privacy" which the Supreme Court established between abortionists and their clients. No reform was possible because any form of state interference would have been an unconstitutional infringement on the super-rights of abortionists.

In 1984 a spokesperson for the Illinois Department of Public Health was unable to identify any lasting reform which had been implemented following the *Sun-Times* exposé six years earlier. The only attempt at change had been a cosmetic redrafting of health and sanitation standards for "licensed ambulatory center treatment facilities" (abortion clinics). With these new sanitation standards, abortion clinics are now inspected four times a year, but these inspections occur *only* after notifying the clinic in advance of the inspection date.[46] Unfortunately, advance notice inspections are practically useless. With advance notice, clinic operators take special pains to "clean up their acts" before the inspection. Therefore, it is extremely unlikely that these one-day, advance notice inspections will ever uncover the types of abuses which were witnessed by reporters who worked undercover *in clinics* for a period of *five months*.

While the *Sun-Times* series did little in the way of changing state regulation of the clinics, it had even less effect on the careers of the abortion providers who were the targets of the articles. Of all the "sadistic" physicians who were accused of "profiteering" in the series, all but one still practice medicine—and provide abortions—in Illinois.[47] But even that one exception, Dr. Ming Kow Hah, did not lose his license because of the incompetent or dangerous abortions he may have performed. Instead, it was learned that Dr. Hah had previously lost his medical license in Michigan because of allegations that he had sold 384 prescriptions of a rare addictive drug that was later sold illegally on the street. Three years later, after numerous delays and appeals, during which he continued to perform abortions in Illinois, Dr. Hah's Illinois medical license was revoked on the basis of the Michigan drug-related charges. While the *Sun-Times* accused Dr. Hah of giving the "most painful abortions in the city," his Illinois license was revoked not because of his abortion methods, but because of his past record with fraudulent drug prescriptions.[48]

Of the four clinics targeted by the *Sun-Times* investigation, only one was closed when it allowed its license to expire.[49] In this instance, the clinic's owner, Dr. Arnold Bickham, moved his abortion clinic to Indiana. But by 1984 Dr. Bickham had returned to Chicago where he continues to perform abortions today.[50]

A second clinic investigated by the *Sun-Times* closed a little over a year later. The voluntary shut-down of the Chicago Loop Mediclinic was due primarily to financial insolvency. The owners allowed the state license for their clinic to expire; and under pressure from the state, they agreed not to renew their abortion activities in Illinois.[51]

The other two abortion clinics, Biogenetics and Michigan Avenue Medical Center, branded as "abortion mills" by the *Sun-Times*, continue to operate under the same management, with many of the same "cold, mechanical" physicians.

Even if it could have been proved that any of these clinics were operating at standards below those of the abortion industry in general, it is doubtful that any state regulation could have corrected the deficiencies. For example, when the Chicago Board of Health attempted to shut down another clinic where a number of serious complications and deaths had occurred, the owner appealed the decision to the Supreme Court and won. In another case, when it was discovered that an abortion clinic was operating without a state license, the owner was fined only $500 dollars. Three months later, this same operator was granted a license to resume his business.[52]

In the aftermath of the *Sun-Times* exposé, one of the clinic owners, Dr. Arnold Bickham, accused the reporters of malicious "innuendo." He charged that the series was "sensationalism . . . designed to sell newspapers and assist in building esteem for individual reporters who are muckrakers and exponents of yellow journalism at its very worst."[53] The view that the *Sun-Times* stories were exaggerated was shared by many respected members of the medical fraternity. For example, Dr. Clifton Reeder, the president of the Chicago Medical Society, saw "no great urgency" to the problems cited in the abortion series. According to Dr. Reeder, the charges against Chicago's abortion clinics had been "blown all out of proportion to reality."[54]

While we agree with the *Sun-Times* that the abortions provided in the four clinics were indeed dangerous and dehumanizing, we must also agree that Dr. Bickham's accusations are largely correct. The "Abortion Profiteers" articles were sensationalized and biased. These articles were looking for scapegoats and depicting them in the darkest manner possible. The *Sun-Times* investigation discovered little if any-thing that was illegal, except for a few violations of sanitation codes. All that they did was to give a close-up look at a very ugly business: abortion. They highlighted all the lurid warts and human flaws of those who are in the business of providing mass abortion on demand. But these flaws are not unique to the four Chicago clinics. They are common to any abortion clinic, and especially to large abortion clinics, which though highly profitable, are also busy and unwieldly.[55]

The *Sun-Times* abortion series was muckraking. But undercover investigators "raking" for scandal in any abortion facility would find the same unsavory "muck," the same callousness, the same greed, decep-tion, and pain that were the grist which sold the *Sun-Times* series. It is "muck;" but it is also very true and very common. What is unfortunate is that undercover investigators were placed in only four of Chicago's thirteen abortion clinics, only four of Illinois' twenty-four clinics, only four of the nation's 4,000 abortion facilities.

The *Sun-Times* series brought little or no reform to abortion prac-tices in Chicago or Illinois. But at least it momentarily caught the attention of the people of one large city in one large state. But in the other forty-nine states and the other large cities where newspaper reporters have not infiltrated the abortion industry, the unsavory cal-lousness of abortion clinics has yet to become a major public issue.

The Selling of Abortion

Like any other business, the abortion industry has a sales force and a carefully defined marketing strategy. The sales force is composed of abortion counselors who "help" women to make their abortion choice. Their marketing strategy is to tell their clients as little as possible—and never anything negative—about their product. The sales and market-ing divisions of the abortion industry were described in lurid detail in the Chicago *Sun-Times* exposé. Undercover reporters charged that at "Michigan Av. abortion mills, women who are hired to counsel don't—they're paid to sell." And the selling of abortion, they observed, included "sophisticated pitches and deceptive promises."[56]

At one of the clinics investigated, slick brochures assured women that: "From admission to recovery, patient ease and comfort are first considerations. She is encouraged to ask questions, share feelings or misgivings." But in actual practice the same clinic instructed its coun-selors with these three guidelines:

1)   "Don't tell [the] patient the abortion will hurt."
2)   "Don't discuss [the abortion] procedure or the instruments to be used in any detail."
3)   "Don't answer too many questions."[57]

The *Sun-Times* reporters criticized this type of "counseling" as being superficial and deceptive. On both counts the reporters were right. But this type of counseling is not only common throughout the country, it is the accepted and recommended practice of the abortion industry. According to that counseling philosophy, the patient is to be "protected" from information which might discourage her or make her choice more difficult. Instead of "confusing" them with facts, women are to be eased through their abortion choice in a way which will minimize any doubts and regrets.

This philosophy of supportive counseling was developed at a 1971 conference for abortion providers held in Los Angeles. Some of the statements made during a special symposium devoted to the "proper" role of abortion counseling are particularly revealing. For example, one nurse told her colleagues that "whether rich or poor, few women really wanted an abortion."[58] Therefore, she suggested, it was important for counselors to avoid conveying any attitudes which would embarrass, humiliate, or frighten patients out of their reluctantly chosen abortion. Counselors were advised to be particularly careful about their choice of words. They were told never to refer to the procedure as "abortion," but instead to use euphemistic expressions. Another speaker, nurse Henrietta Blackmon, advised that counselors and nurses should be able and willing to describe the procedure, but should never describe the abortion instruments, since this might upset the client. Above all, she warned, counselors should be on guard to keep their own true feelings in check:

If you say "Suck out the baby," you may easily generate or increase trauma; say instead, "Empty the uterus," or "We will scrape the lining of the uterus," but never "We will scrape away the baby."

These may seem very, very insignificant to us, but to the patient it can really imply that you are using a judgment, and quite often we are not aware of what we are saying. We have to be very, very sensitive, and very, very aware of what words we are using to

248

describe the procedures used. Use the word "fetus": This is a fetus; this is not a "baby."[59]

According to these experts, who were establishing the counseling standards to be used across the nation, an abortion counselor's only purpose is to act as "facilitator and participant" in the abortion process—a compassionate friend to help the aborting woman face the unknown and overcome her doubts. Counselors, they warned, were *not* to urge reevaluation of either the client's needs or her decision to abort; they were only to make it as easy as possible for the woman to carry out her decision. Any other form of counseling which challenged her decision, provided new information about risks or fetal development, or dwelled on options, would only increase doubts, anxiety, and guilt. Experience showed, they insisted, that women did not want to be talked out of their abortion decisions. Therefore, the role of the counselor was to provide emotional support, explain the clinic's routine, describe the procedure in a neutral manner, and "—[only] if the doctor approved—warn the patient of the possibility of future sterility." Finally, the counselor should reassure the patient that the decision to abort was good, ethical, and acceptable.[60]

Measured by the standards of respected experts, the counseling offered at the Michigan Avenue clinics was not improper. While their activities might be described as "selling" abortions (and indeed that is what it is), abortion professionals defend such counseling on the grounds that it "protects" women and makes the abortion experience as "easy" as possible.

One factor which allows abortion counselors to get away with telling so little is that many women seeking abortions are vulnerable, frightened, and insecure. In one case, for example, a woman who was counseled in a group situation had several questions she wanted to ask, but she did not, saying: "I was afraid to ask them with all those people around. Maybe it was best I didn't know anyway."[61] Feeling frightened and dependent on others, women seeking abortions generally lack the assertiveness needed to insist on complete answers.

Second, many women do not know what questions they should ask, especially when it comes to complications. In general, the most they are told is that: "There are only slight risks to this procedure, like in any operation. It's nothing to worry about." The vagueness of this reassurance prevents even the slightest possibility for women to ask

questions like: "Will dilation damage my cervix? Will a 'slight infection' reduce my ability to conceive in the future?

But worst of all is the lack of counseling about fetal development:
it *never* occurs. Information about the stage of development of the fetus
to be aborted is available at any local library, but never at the local
abortion clinic. To abortion counselors, discussion of fetal development
is absolutely taboo. It will only upset their patients, they argue, and
increase the guilt which women face. Counselors are so concerned with
"protecting" women from these facts that distortions and lies are an
accepted method of easing the patient's concerns.

An example of such "reassuring" counseling is described by Julie
Engel, who received an abortion when she was three months pregnant.

> Then I asked, "Is abortion a threat to future pregnancies?"
> "Women often have D&C's [dilation and curettage] to help
> them get pregnant," was the perfunctory answer.
> "Are there psychological problems?" I continued.
> "Hardly ever. Don't worry," I was told. . . .
> "What does a three-month-old fetus look like?"
> "Just a clump of cells," she answered matter-of-factly.[62]

In the years that followed, Julie Engel discovered that she was no
longer able to conceive a wanted pregnancy. And then one day she saw
some pictures of fetal development:

> When I saw that a three-month-old "clump of cells" had fingers
> and toes and was a tiny, perfectly formed baby, I became really
> hysterical.
> I'd been lied to and misled, and I'm sure thousands of other
> women are being just as poorly informed and badly served. To
> prove it, John [her husband] and I visited most every clinic in
> Cleveland. I pretended I was pregnant and asked for guidance.
> What we heard was incredible. One counselor told us the
> fetus did not begin to resemble a human being until seven
> months; another said five months and so it went.[63]

Karen Yates, a counselor at Washington, DC's Southeast Crisis
Pregnancy Center, serves a primarily black community. Yates has found
that for most of the young women she serves, facts about fetal development—facts about exactly *what* they would be destroying by having an

abortion—are often the "deciding factor" in a woman's abortion decision. But she also reports that 95 percent of the women she counsels were told by some pro-abortion advocate, their doctors, family planning counselors, or someone else, that the fetus is just a "clump of cells," that it is not really alive. But when Yates and others fully explain the biological facts, the vast majority of women choose not to abort.[64]

Abortion counselors not only avoid the biological facts of fetal development, they also avoid all the moral dimensions of the abortion choice. Instead of helping women to explore their own views on the ethical question, "Do you believe abortion is a moral solution to your problem?" counselors focus attention on utilitarian questions, such as, "Do you want to have a baby? Are you ready to be a parent?" In the long run, however, it is the answer to the ethical question which matters most. It is the question, "Did I do the *right* thing?" which aborted women must live with for the rest of their lives.

Examining this question is especially important since the vast majority of women considering an abortion are uncertain about the morality of what they are doing. Abortion clinics, however, not only avoid such questions, they actively urge clients to suppress and deny their feelings whenever their doubts are raised. At one clinic, for example, when a woman voiced her concern that abortion might be killing, the counselor said, "Don't think of it as killing. Think of it as taking blood out of your uterus to get your periods going again."[65]

Any such counseling which fails to resolve these moral concerns about abortion is leaving a time bomb of guilt and self-condemnation within the woman's psyche. But abortion clinics deny any responsibility for helping their clients explore their moral misgivings. Instead, they emphasize discussion of personal desires rather than personal values. Their avoidance of "moral issues" not only makes the job of abortion counseling easier, it improves clinic profits. According to one study, women who approach abortion as a moral choice are much more likely to keep their pregnancies, while those who approach abortion in terms of furthering their self-interests are more likely to abort.[66]

The desire to "protect" women from the biological facts and moral issues of abortion is all part of the paternalism of abortion providers, which automatically presumes that abortion is the "best" solution for women in trouble, especially if the women they serve are young and destitute. Instead of giving women all the available information and alternatives so that they can decide for themselves, counselors screen the information given so as to "guide" their clients to the "best" solution (and most profitable) which they, the counselors, have already picked out for them. This patronizing concern often becomes the doorway through which the counselor's unconscious biases influence his or her recommendations. Thus a young black girl who would really like to keep her child but doesn't know how is likely to become a victim of a biased abortion equation because of her age, race, and income level. Recognizing that in our society the cards are stacked against this girl, the compassionate counselor sincerely believes that abortion is "best," despite the girl's "naive" desires to keep her baby.

Once counselors decide what is "best" on behalf of their clients, it is an easy matter to influence their final decisions toward the predetermined outcome. Counseling in such cases downplays or even denies the availability of support resources and instead concentrates on the "tremendous burdens" involved in raising a child. Such counseling sessions encourage the women to believe that abortion is not only the "safe and easy" solution, but is in fact "the only practical thing to do." Explaining how she handles such cases, abortion counselor Betty Orr says, "I ask them who is going to take care of the baby while they're in school. Where are they going to get money for clothes?"[67] Faced with such questions of antagonism rather than offers of confirmation and support, frightened and vulnerable young women are easily convinced that abortion is their *only* choice—even when it is contrary to their real desires.

When counseling teenage girls, many family planning abortion counselors are so confident that *they* are the ones with the "best" solutions, that they envision themselves as being "better" parents than the girl's own natural parents. Seeing themselves as being "substitute parents," they jealously guard their "right" to decide what is "best" for their troubled girls. Wanting no interference from the "outside," many clinics will go to great lengths to "protect" a young girl from family members who might encourage birth rather than abortion.[68]

There is one last factor which is common to abortion counseling throughout the country, and that is the high priority placed on providing birth control advice. While abortion counseling is weak in describing the procedure and its risks, totally negligent in describing fetal development, and often paternalistic in the extreme, it is *always* thorough and detailed when it comes to recommending and selling birth control devices.

The emphasis on urging contraceptive protection has long been an established part of abortion counseling. The clear intention of such contraceptive counseling has always been to help clients avoid the need for repeat abortions.[69] But while the contraceptive push seems like a sensible approach to preventing abortions, it is a recommendation which seems strange when coming from those who insist that abortion is "safe and easy." For if abortion is such a "good" solution, why do abortion counselors find it desirable to prevent repeat abortions? Do they think there is something wrong with abortion after all, despite all they say? The answer is yes. Despite what they tell their clients, abortion counselors do not really approve of abortion at all.

Abortion Counselors: the People behind the Rhetoric

In *The Ambivalence of Abortion,* Linda Bird Francke interviewed a Planned Parenthood abortion counselor who was frustrated and angry at repeat aborters, saying:

> I have one kid here, seventeen, who's just had her third abortion. . . . I want to beat the shit out of her. I want to put her through the damn wall. "What's the matter with you" I say to her. Every time she thinks a relationship is going on the rocks, she gets pregnant. Then she has an abortion and starts up a new relationship. She swears every time she has an abortion she won't screw again. I tell her screwing isn't the problem, protection is.[70]

The reason for this anger lies in the ambivalent feelings which abortion counselors and staff, too, have towards abortion. Working side by side with the workers at an abortion hospital in preparation for her book, *In Necessity and Sorrow,* Dr. Magda Denes describes the workers as "dedicated and full of doubt, committed but uneasy."[71]

Like most of the women who come to them seeking abortions, abortion clinic workers are also uncertain about the morality of what they are doing. On a personal level, this uncertainty places a constant stress on the consciences of the workers. Furthermore, on a professional level, this stress is compounded by the requirement to hide their uncertainties in order to "protect" their clients from additional doubts.

The dilemma between what they feel and how they must act is revealed in a number of interviews with abortion counselors. One counselor, for example, recognizes the high level of guilt which aborting women face, saying:

> A lot of people say they're killing their baby. You get a lot of that. Some people afterwards get very upset and say "I killed my baby."

Or even before, they say "My circumstances are such that I can't keep it, but I'm killing my baby."[72]

As a counselor, it is her job to alleviate and deny these guilts. But when asked about her own personal views, she too is ambivalent:

Well, they are killing a baby. I mean, they are killing something that would develop into maturity, but under the circumstances that's necessary, and probably better for the baby. You have to realize that these children would be unwanted and a lot of times uncared for, so it's much better that they are not brought into the world . . ."[73]

Yet another abortion counselor, a college student who was previously aborted herself, hesitantly believes abortion is murder, saying:

I see more of murder the further along they get. Although inside me I know it's murder from the beginning, because there is the fact that when it is conceived it is a potential human being, potential person, potential life, potential organism or whatever you want to call it. There's just so much terminology: is it a human, is it a person, is it a being, is it a life or organism or whatever? I believe that, yes, it is a potential life or being, person, but at the same time it is not independent of the mother and it's not able to live by itself. Until we can reach that point where we can really say that, yes, there is a unit out there that will maintain its life, it's really the mother that has the decision over the life. . . . Does that make sense?[74]

The first of these counselors rationalizes "killing a baby" as necessary to protect the child from a life of potential misery. The second counselor, on the other hand, rationalizes the "murder" of abortion by relying on the pro-abortion double-speak which even she doesn't fully understand or have much faith in. In both cases abortion is recognized as destructive and evil; but it is excused because it is "necessary" either for the freedom of women or for the sake of the "unwanted" children. But as we shall see, these rationalizations are extremely fragile. They are based on the blind hope that abortion has redeeming qualities, rather than on the actual experience of the patients they profess to have "helped."

254

There are two distinct questions to be asked about counselors and other abortion clinic staff. First, what motivates them to work in an abortion clinic? And second, how do they cope with the stress of daily participation in the "evil necessity" of abortion?

The question of what motivates people to work at abortion clinics has many answers. Many see their work simply as a job, an opportunity to make a living.[75] Others see it as an opportunity to help women or as their contribution to the cause of women's liberation. Still others see their abortion-related work simply as a temporary stop on the way to other career goals. As one counselor confided:

> You know, I mean it's gory, and it's really a sad situation to see the abortions, and I have my own opinion about how I feel about abortion. . . . [but to] me it's a job and it's the closest I could get to what I really wanted to do . . . I want to be a nurse-midwife.[76]

While sympathetic to the motives of the abortion counselors she interviews, Dr. Denes is skeptical of their stability and qualifications: "All of them are single, young, exposed and extremely vulnerable themselves to the pitfalls that have brought the majority of patients to this hospital."[77] Often immature and vulnerable themselves, one wonders what these counselors can truly offer the frightened and vulnerable women they are supposed to "counsel." In fact, as many of them admit, they are able to offer the women they serve nothing more than companionship. Rather than counseling patients to reach mature and thoughtful decisions, they are the blind leading the blind, able to offer comfort and encouragement but not guidance or information.

Furthermore, what abortion counselors lack in personal maturity is not compensated for by training. In fact, none of the counselors at Denes' hospital were professional mental health workers. They all received only on-the-job training, a common practice at most abortion facilities. But on-the-job training, at this one facility at least, was carefully limited so as to isolate the counselors from the graphic truth of abortion: "Not a single one among them has ever seen a D&C performed nor watched the explusion of a fetus."[78] Thus, what the counselors did not know could not be revealed to the patients.

Besides those who are motivated to work in abortion clinics because of their desire for a job, their desire to "help people," or their desire to advance the cause of "freedom of choice," there is another class of people who are drawn to this work: aborted women themselves.

It is not uncommon for aborted women to return to clinics to work as counselors or in other capacities. Many clinics, in fact, prefer to hire aborted women since they are more likely to empathize with the situations which compel women to abort. But the willingness of aborted women to work in the clinics does not mean that they were satisfied with their own abortions or have come to terms with their own doubts and ambivalence. Instead, it means exactly the opposite.

Aborted women who work as counselors are almost invariably victims of a disturbing abortion experience themselves. On one level, they choose to work in clinics in the hope of preventing other women from experiencing the traumas which they had faced and may still be facing. But on a deeper level, they return to the abortion clinic in the hope of easing the guilts and traumas which they themselves are still experiencing.[79]

For many women who have been deeply disturbed by their own abortion experiences, working as an abortion counselor is a way of hardening themselves to their own unforgetable experiences. By "returning to the scene of the crime," some women seek to reenact their own abortion decisions through the decisions of others. In this sense, the aborted counselor has a high stake in the final decision of her clients. By watching others choose abortion for the same reasons that she did, she is able to reaffirm the "rightness" of her own decision. In contrast, however, when an aborted counselor witnesses a client suddenly choose against abortion and boldly accept the challenges of an unplanned pregnancy, the counselor may become cynical, ashamed, and envious.[80]

Two WEBA women who had worked in counseling or hospital situations that brought them into contact with women seeking abortions have described how immersion in abortion can be soothing to a troubled conscience. According to one, "I found that in talking to other women about abortion, their decisions to abort satisfied something in me. It made me feel better about what I had done. . . . [It] strengthened my own decisions to abort." Another woman found comfort in being surrounded by people constantly repeating pro-abortion rhetoric as justification for their work: "There's safety in numbers," she says. "I didn't feel really awful about my abortion as long as everyone where I worked was patting me on the back."[81]

This brings us to our second question: How do abortion clinic workers cope with the daily stress of participating in the "evil necessity" of abortion?

The first line of defense lies in the unity of purpose which abortion workers share. Relying on "safety in numbers," they close ranks and reaffirm each other and the "good" that they do. Among them is an unwritten agreement never to openly question what they do, never to admit their doubts, and *never,* under any circumstances, to discuss the destruction of the fetuses over which they preside. Denes calls this collective defense mechanism a "conspiracy of denial."[82]

Denes is adamantly pro-choice, but as a clinical psychologist she is keenly aware of the duplicity which keeps abortion workers from going insane:

> It seems that none who work here can witness the extinction of a segment of the future generation without guilt and fear. The word "murder" surfaces again and again, and it sticks on the tongue like a searing coal of fire that one knows will do further damage whether it is swallowed or spat.
>
> A struggle evolves between reason and conscience, between pragmatic morality and one's own commitment to all human seed. With the struggle there also evolves a shamefaced solution: "I do not decide for these women, I just do my job"; "I give them what they want"; "I only help out." As if disclaiming responsibility could make one free of it."[83]

The importance of denying the reality of abortion sheds additional light on why abortion clinics consistently oppose informed consent requirements, especially requirements for discussing the relevant stage of fetal development. In refusing to provide informed consent, abortion providers are obstensibly "protecting" the woman seeking abortion from disturbing and "confusing" facts. But it may also be true that abortion personnel are seeking to protect *themselves* from the same disturbing facts. The requirement to tell women the facts about fetal development, day after day, would destroy the wall of denial which holds clinics together. By focusing attention on the unborn, informed consent requirements would not only compel women to consider the moral consequences of their acts, they would also force abortion counselors to face their *own* moral doubts about abortion.

After denial, the second line of defense for abortion workers is rationalization. Undoubtedly the most common rationalization lies in the belief that despite all the blood and murder they witness, their work at the clinic somehow improves the lives of the trapped and vulnerable women they serve. By sacrificing one life, they hope, the quality of another's life is improved.[84]

Because their own sanity and "job satisfaction" rests on the belief that abortion is good and worthwhile, it is crucial for counselors to believe that the women they serve really *need* the abortions and really benefit from them. This is the source of the prejudgement by which counselors always believe that abortion is the "best" solution for their clients. But the lurking fear that perhaps their clients' lives are not improved, keeps counselors from looking too closely at their patients' situations or getting too involved in their lives. When the aborted woman walks out the clinic door, the staff wishes her the best; but they are loathe to follow her progress or witness her struggles, her ambivalence, or her guilts. (This is also why post-abortion counseling is so very rarely offered by abortion clinics.)

For counselors who are secretly uncertain and ambivalent about abortion, it is far better to cling to the illusion of "helping others" than to test that belief against reality. To look too deeply at the post-abortion experience, to see the pain and heartache of aborted women is to allow doubt into their own citadels of denial and rationalization. To risk learning that the lives of women are *not* improved by abortion, or are even *worsened,* is to risk destroying the illusion of all the "good" that they do. Their own self-images depend on maintaining the illusion of abortion's "necessity." They *want* to believe in it, they *must* believe in it, and they will ignore any evidence to the contrary. To do otherwise is to invite self-doubt and even self-loathing.

Wanting to believe that their work is "good," abortion counselors believe that abortion is not only an adequate solution for women with unplanned pregnancies, but that it is the "best" solution. Thus, abortion counselors tend to become biased against other alternatives. Abortion is a difficult and sad course for women in "trouble," they believe, but it is *absolutely necessary.* This bias was observed by Cynthia Martin, who studied a large number of abortion clinics for her doctoral dissertation on the psychology of abortion. According to Dr. Martin, abortion counselors are biased against the idea of "a teenager carrying a child to term" and they "refuse to admit that having a child might be a healthier experience for a woman who would go through life blaming herself for the abortion that 'killed her baby.' "[85] Counselors refuse to admit that alternatives to abortion might be better, because to admit that any abortion over which they presided might have been unnecessary is to admit their own guilt in providing it.

Another common rationalization for abortion is the belief that aborting "unwanted" children saves them from miserable lives. But what is most disturbing about this excuse is that it is generally offered by those abortion clinic personnel who are most dissatisfied with their own lives. Many counselors and other abortion workers suffer from low-self esteem and are even self-destructive. It would seem that they find so little comfort in their own lives that they see themselves as doing a favor to others by preventing them from being born. Subconsciously wishing they had not been born themselves, they are quick to believe that abortion is a positive good which prevents other "unwanted" children from being born.[86]

Obviously, denying their own doubts about the morality of abortion and maintaining the rationalization that abortion is a "positive" thing is a constant drain on abortion personnel. Even the strongest of counselors is likely to leave work each day feeling "emotionally beaten up."[87] Thus, in order to survive, abortion workers are forced to harden themselves and take on a depersonalized view of their work.[88] They see themselves and the women they serve as victims of a cold, cruel world, too weak to bring about change. One orderly, for example, admits to feeling that abortion is wrong but feels impotent to interfere, saying:

> I can't tell them [the abortionists], "Hey man, don't do that, that's not right." They want to make money, I need a job. I really don't care. I want to work. The patients come, they have the abortion, I need a job.[89]

This feeling of impotence becomes so great that even when witnessing a woman being forced into an abortion by her boyfriend, counselors will ignore the obvious, and instead join the boyfriend in "guiding" the woman towards the unwanted abortion as their only "sane" choice.[90]

The constant stress faced by abortion workers often manifests itself in hostility. One lab technician, for example, feeling guilty about her own work with abortion, began to take it out on the patients: "I didn't get rude or nasty with the girls, but it was a form of hostility that could be sensed. I would have an attitude."[91]

Sometimes this frustration surfaces as petty fighting between staff members. Reading Denes' inside look at an abortion hospital, one finds frequent outbursts of extreme hostility between abortion personnel. One gets the impression of tense and explosive people, battle-fatigued warriors, driven forward only by the combined motives of duty and greed.[92]

To survive, abortion workers must become detached; and detachment invariably leads to callousness. This callousness may in turn lead to warped behavior and twisted humor. At one New York abortion hospital, a sign is hung for the amusement of the staff: "You rape them. We scrape them. No fetus can beat us."[93]

Charged with "protecting" women from the truth of what they are doing, abortion workers are sometimes forced to bear the guilt themselves. For example, one nurse described the dilemmas she faced when assisting with second trimester saline abortions, saying:

> They always wanted to know the sex, but we lied and said it was too early to tell. It was better for the women to think of the fetus as an "it." Then we'd scoop up fetuses and put them in a bucket of formaldehyde, just like Kentucky Fried Chicken. I couldn't take it any longer, and I quit.[94]

Another nurse, who assisted in over 1,000 saline abortions, eventually resigned from her grisly duty and became a pro-life activist. But even now, the guilt of participating in the "murder" of abortion haunts her:

> The other day I saw an abortion on TV and I had to run to the bathroom. The guilt of having assisted with abortions is so great 10 years later that I sometimes think I need therapy. The trouble is I don't know any therapists I could talk to about this.[95]

At almost every abortion clinic, "staff burnout is a major problem."[96] Studies have found a high incidence of negative psychological reactions among abortion providers, often including ghastly nightmares of giant fetuses seeking revenge.[97]

Like guards at a death camp, abortion workers are uneasy about all that they witness, but they force themselves to continue because it is their duty, their job. If they didn't do it, they rationalize, someone else would, and probably with less compassion than they. But according to

Denes, even this excuse is a frail defense against the weight of the guilt they bear:

> Death is no easy companion. Not even in the veiled and necessary shape abortions lend it. Under pressure, the conspiracy of its denial cracks. In an astonishing turnabout I am sought out by the staff to be told by each what a hell of a business this has been. I am sought out to be told that one has to make a living but otherwise— otherwise, who would such burdens bear?[98]

The Abortionists

Next to the aborted woman, it is the physician who is most directly involved in the actual "killing" of abortion. In fact, whereas the woman's role requires only consent and passive "acceptance" of the abortion procedure, it is the abortionist who is actively employed as the "executioner."[99]

Because most doctors are committed to saving lives, the vast majority of physicians (and obstetricians in particular) are unwilling to play the part of the "executioner" for elective abortions.[100] Rather than 20,000 doctors providing the nation's abortion needs, as was predicted by early abortion promoters, most of today's abortions are provided by only a few hundred "specialists," scattered in metropolitan areas around the country.[101]

According to Edward Eichner, director of medicine at a Cleveland abortion clinic, it is extremely difficult to maintain a staff of doctors willing to perform abortions. He notes that female physicians are especially hard to find and keep on the clinic payroll. Women physicians who have experienced childbirth themselves, he believes, tend to have too much sympathy for the pregnancy and so are not emotionally suited to the rigors of performing repetitive abortions. But besides the moral uneasiness related to performing abortions, Eichner reports, most physicians, male and female, simply find the work unchallenging: "The work is rote and repetitious. Suction abortion is just not stimulating from the point of view of medicine."[102] In other words, abortion is not only a morbid task filled with ethical overtones of murder and death; it is also deathly dull.

Another reason why physicians shy away from doing abortions is that the task of providing abortion on request is not really one of *medicine*. Except for the extremely rare cases when an abortion is necessary to save the life of the mother, abortions are purely "elec-

261

tive." They are a "service" provided for a fee. They do not advance the patient's health in any way; they only satisfy the client's immediate social needs. Thus for a physician trained to save lives and improve health, abortion represents a prostitution of his knowledge and skills. In selling his surgical skills for non-surgical, non-therapeutic reasons, he is simply selling his professional integrity to the highest bidders. It is no wonder, then, that studies of those physicians who do "sell" themselves in the lucrative abortion market report "untoward reactions which include dread, depression, anxiety, guilt and *identity crisis related to the role conflict of healer and abortionist.*"[103] (italics added)

For those physicians who do choose to enter the abortion business, there is no easy solution to this identity crisis. According to one abortionist:

You have to become a bit schizophrenic. In one room you encourage the patient that the slight irregularity of the fetal heart is not important, everything is going well, she is going to have a nice baby, and then you shut the door and go into the next room and assure another patient on whom you just did a saline abortion, that it's fine if the heart is already irregular, she has nothing to worry about, she is *not* going to have a live baby. I mean you definitely have to make a 180 degree turn . . ."[104] (emphasis his own)

The solution which many abortionists attempt is to simply avoid thinking about the ethical question of abortion. Some claim that they are simply doing their jobs and that they are not qualified to "speculate" on morality, not even on their own morality.[105] Others avoid the ethical questions of abortion by focusing on its "practical" values. For example, Dr. Ronald Pion, an abortionist committed to his trade for the purpose of advancing world population control, argues that "we ought not to discuss the ethics of abortion but the ethics of procreation. . . . [W]e have pragmatic and utilitarian involvements to get on with."[106] Similarly, Dr. Edward Allred insists that abortion is necessary for "suppressing poverty, crime, and other problems of society."[107]

The desire to avoid any ethical review of their acts leads some abortionists to insist that the ethical question has already been "decided at law by the Supreme Court."[108] But in fact, the Court specifically avoided making any pronouncement on the morality of abortion. The illusion that it did, however, is a precious salve for uneasy consciences. As we have seen, the simplistic view that "if it is legal, it is moral" also plays a major influence in the decision-making of many of the women who choose abortion. Thus, since the law is a teacher, it is capable of influencing the moral views of both aborters and abortionists.

But while most abortionists try to avoid the moral issue of abortion, few are entirely successful. After interviewing nearly a dozen abortionists in the preparation of her book, *In Necessity and Sorrow,* Dr. Denes reports that "There wasn't a doctor who at one time or another in the questioning did not say, 'This is murder.' "[109]

Some abortionists readily admit their guilt feelings:

I've tried not to make it a moral issue, but a social issue without moral overtones as much as possible. But I think from a straight moral point of view I probably would object to abortion. Because I love kids. From that point of view every fetus is a potential child, and morally I just really don't think that [abortion] should be done. . . .

I suppose that if you want to go below the surface, and thinking about it, I do feel you'd be an abnormal person if you could really honestly say that abortion didn't bother you at all. It goes against all things which are natural. It's a termination of life, however you look at it. It just goes against the grain. It must. . . .[110]

Others are even more schizophrenic, admitting and denying guilt all in the same breath:

In my own case I never had any psychological adverse reaction. Except an occasional feeling that one was destroying life. But in my own mind the issue had already been resolved that this is necessary because otherwise these poor girls are going to risk their own lives . . .[111]

Yet another states:

My feelings about doing abortions were very significant and it was a long period of time for me to work it out. I dare say any thinking sensitive individual can't not realize that he is ending life or potential life, you know. I certainly don't enjoy that. I have no conscious conflict over killing a fetus. There's certainly nothing enjoyable in the act, except providing a necessary something to a person to make their life or burden happier, or easier, or whatever. But there's got to be more to it.[112]

But while this last abortionist claims no "*conscious* conflict over killing a fetus," he later adds: "I think we're certainly living in a time of decreased human respect, of decreased human relationships, and of decreased sensitivity to killing off things."[113]

Sometimes, despite their best attempts to suppress and deny the moral issues which lie at the heart of abortion, the reality of the act refuses to be ignored. One "complication" which is difficult to avoid is always a rude shock for this abortionist who reports:

[O]n a number of occasions with the needle, I have harpooned the fetus. I can feel the fetus move at the end of the needle just like you have a fish hooked on a line. This gives me an unpleasant, unhappy feeling because I know that the fetus is alive and responding to the needle stab. . . . No one has ever mentioned this, but I've noticed it a number of times, you know that there is something alive in there that you're killing. . . ."[114]

For many physicians the weight of guilt is eased by setting an arbitrary limit on how late of a pregnancy they are willing to abort. For example, one physician sets the limit at sixteen weeks of gestation, saying:

I just decided it's not worth it to do, because I have had such terribly strong feelings that it's turned me off. I feel that I am destroying life. I feel that I'm actually killing them. And that kind of feeling I don't like to live with. And I rationalize by saying to myself that from one week to sixteen weeks is to me the upper limits of what I would do. . . . Then after that time I leave it to others, more radical than myself, to do whatever they want to do.[115]

But setting upper limits is one thing, abiding by them is another. Faced with pressure from desperate clients and the prospect of additional revenues, some abortionists find their limits of fifteen and sixteen weeks being stretched later and later into the term.[116] Denial of all responsibility soon leads to an inability to question anything that they do. One doctor who specializes in second trimester saline abortions, for example, insists that doctors should not even ask a woman's reasons for wanting an abortion; he should just "follow orders," so to speak: "We'll just have to face it, that somebody has to do it. And, unfortunately, we are the executioners in this instance."[117]

For doctors as well as women, the moral responsibility for what they do is passed about like a hot potato. Women, in the passive role of "accepting" abortion, perceive it as something done "to" them. Doctors try to excuse it as something "demanded" of them by their patients. And both say that they are only doing what is sanctioned by the law and society. Meanwhile, of course, the law and society disclaim responsibility, saying that abortion is solely a matter for the private consciences of the "woman and her physician."[118]

One abortionist, who recognizes the guilt-passing that occurs, believes that the type of abortion performed has a drastic influence on how the woman perceives the experience:

When we do D&C's it's under general anesthesia, so the patient comes in and the doctor does the dirty work. And when she wakes up, and it's his sin, and she's cured. But with a saline she's participating in this sin, because she's awake, she knows what's going on, she feels it coming out.[119]

The impact on the abortionist is also related to the type of procedure used. Some doctors prefer to do saline abortions during the second and third trimesters because once the instillation procedure is finished, they can leave the hospital and leave the burden of delivering the dead fetus to the patient and nurses.[120] Others, more concerned with easing the emotional shock of the patient, take on the stressful and "grisly" task of dismembering the unborn child and manually removing the fetal parts themselves.[121]

Thus it would seem, rather than avoiding guilt, some abortionists see themselves as *substitute* guilt bearers for the women they serve. In this "martyr's" role, physicians quickly adopt a superior and paternalistic attitude towards their clients. Even the most blatant lies become acceptable in order to "protect" their "girls" from the guilt-laden truths of abortion.[122] But the cost of these lies carries with it the risk that abortion will become overused and that too many patients will suffer from this "safe and easy" procedure. As one abortionist admits:

[W]hat they think are simple solutions are not as simple as they think. They can die, they can become sterile, and they can have many other complications. That unfortunately is the biggest evil of abortions.[123]

Like the other staff members in abortion clinics, abortionists are so busy trying to maintain their own psychic balance that they have little energy left over for worrying about the psychic welfare of their patients. They are so busy trying to remain distant and unimpassioned about what they do that they become distant and unimpassioned towards those whom they "serve."

Dr. Consuelo Sague, a former abortionist who is now vice president of a pro-life group called "Peaceful Solutions," believes that abortion deadens a physician's capacity for compassion.

Once a person becomes accustomed to inflicting pain, he becomes callous in other ways.

One of my teachers, a very clever professor, who performed many abortions, turned very cold in his attitude toward women. He didn't care about them at all. He was unaffected by their physical and emotional pain. He had an academic detachment from women and their feelings. Yes, I think doctors who do abortions become dehumanized. They have to.[124]

Another physician, a practicing abortionist, agrees, though he extends the charge of sexism towards all male gynecologists. According to Dr. Abraham Holtzman (a pseudonym), the Chief of Gynecological and Obstetrical Services at a major New York abortion hospital:

Basically every gynecologist doesn't like women, otherwise he couldn't work with them. He enjoys the position of mastery over them. The fact that he is the god, king, they do what he tells them, which is what he would always want women to do, because every man wants his women to be subservient to him. The patients are subservient to us, and when they rebel it's very simple: "Go to somebody else. Don't come back to me, if you're not going to take my advice." What better relationship can a man have with a woman?[125]

Does abortion make physicians callous, or does abortion attract physicians who are already callous? Dr. Bernard Nathanson, co-founder of the National Association for the Repeal of Abortion Laws, and director of the nation's largest abortion clinic prior to 1973, reports that many of the physicians hired at the clinic experienced drastic personality changes: "I was seeing personality structures dissolve in front of me on a scale I had never seen before in a medical situation. Very few members of the staff seemed to remain fully intact through their experiences."[126] On the other hand, he also reports that the clinic employed several physicians who had already been doing illegal abortions for years. Among this "venal band of scoundrels" were physicians already used to being "vicious, even sadistic with patients."[127] Nathanson himself, after presiding over 60,000 abortions, later became "increasingly troubled by my own increasing certainty that I had in fact presided over 60,000 deaths."[128] This troubling thought eventually led Nathanson to become a leading activist in the national pro-life movement.

While it seems clear that the "burn-out" rate for abortionists is high, it is equally clear that some abortionists are able to ply their trade for decades with few signs of wear, much less repentance. For these sturdy professionals, a hard and detached personality appears essential. Many perform thousands of abortions per year, a task which requires a "robot-like constitution."[129]

Yet some abortionists may not be so unimpassioned about what they do. Some may find a sense of satisfaction in wielding power over life and death. Psychiatrists have observed that some abortionists are motivated by "psychological inadequacy" and "anti-social personalities" and others are motivated by greed.[130] Elements of sadism and even symbolic self-destruction may be the motivating factors for some abortionists.

A trained social worker at one abortion hospital is disquieted by the personalities of the abortionists with whom she works, saying that "there's really pathological things in their involvement with abortion. Like Dr. Rodrigo. He is very sarcastic and he really, you know, like goes after people."[131]

Examples of crude and callous behavior abound in the abortion literature, and not all of it is confined to the abortion "mills" of Chicago. For example, Denes reports witnessing an abortionist who seemed to enjoy inflicting guilt upon his patients. After failing to kill the fetus during the first saline induction, this particular physician attached a heart monitor to his patient's womb and filled the room with the amplified beat of the baby's heart.

"That's it," he cries triumphantly, "that's it—the induction didn't work. Sturdy fellow you have in there, eh?" He gives a loud guffaw, and his broad obscene wink darkens the room.[132]

In reading through interviews with abortionists, few though they are, one is struck by how many of these physicians seem uncertain as to why they even entered medicine in the first place. Frequently they describe themselves as fleeing from family demands that they enter another occupation. Others became doctors only because of family demands. Still others entered medicine simply for the money. All together, many abortionists seem cynical about their medical careers and even their entire lifestyles. Dissatisfied with their own lives, they have little sympathy for the lives of the women they serve or for the unborn they profess to "save" from similar lives of empty "unwantedness." For many, it is clear that they are not devoted to the art of healing or even inspired by it. Instead, medicine, like abortion, is just a job—just a lucrative way to get by one day at a time.

Consider, for example, one New York abortionist who admits to general feelings of guilt yet describes himself as ruthless and cold when it suits his needs:

I would make a good Mafia member, because I honor my friends and destroy my enemies. I never forget a slight, I never forget an encouragement. Those who helped me when I was younger and struggling up, I've lifted them up when they were going down. And those that stepped on me, I stepped on them and crushed them while I was going up.[134]

But despite such cold self-centeredness, it is difficult to believe that any abortionist is ever left unscathed. Having observed several abortionists from close range over a long period of time, psychiatrist Magda Denes sees scars everywhere: "No one is untouched. No one is untorn. Each, propelled by who he is, builds his own mythical world where this is all right, that is wrong, one thing is just, another a crime. Morality is a fluid notion."[135]

Perhaps the comments of Dr. William Rashbaum, chief of family planning services at Beth Israel Medical Center, are prototypical of the "average" abortionist's views. Speaking to reporters, Dr. Rashbaum admitted that there was a time in the midst of every abortion he performed when he was troubled by fantasies of the fetus hanging on to the walls of the uterus with tiny fingernails, resisting the abortion with all its strength.

> How, he was asked, had he managed [to do abortions] while enduring this fantasy? "Learned to live with it. Like people in concentration camps." Did he really mean that analogy? "I think it's apt—destruction of life. Look! I'm a person. I'm entitled to my feelings. And my feelings are: Who gives me or anybody the right to terminate a pregnancy? I'm entitled to that feeling but I also have no right to communicate it to the patient who desperately wants that abortion. I don't get paid for my feelings. I get paid for my skills. . . . I'll be frank. I began to do abortions in large numbers at the time of my divorce when I needed money. But I also believe in the woman's right to control her biological destiny. I spent a lot of years learning to deliver babies. Sure, it sometimes hurts to end life instead of bringing it into the world."[136]

Abortion means money. And for most, if not all abortionists, money is the primary motive for enduring the boredom, the guilt, and the indignity of performing mass abortions.[137] Compared to other "minor surgeries" the cost of abortion is amazingly high, yet to abortionists no price is too high for putting aside his doctors oath. "The high fees may be paying no longer for the criminal risk [involved in doing an illegal abortion], but for the indignity."[138]

Finally, as psychiatrist Conrad Baars, notes: "Abortionists, whether performing their sinister work in hospitals or back alleys, get richer, but not happier or healthier. . . . the emergence of feelings of guilt and depression cannot be suppressed forever."[139] It is an occupation with no joy, and therefore limited to those who are, or are willing, to be callous and mercenary. Truly compassionate doctors have no stomach for the "evil necessity" of abortion, and certainly not the stamina to provide the nation with 1.5 million abortions per year. Such a task takes professionals with that unsavory and "robot-like constitution" which the *Sun-Times* reporters deplored.

While it is clear that the characters who thrive in the abortion industry will never win humanitarian awards, it is also clear that these are the only character types who can survive the pressures of delivering mass scale abortion on demand. There is no way to bring "compassionate" care to what is inherently a compassionless business—clinics held together by illusion, self-deceit, and lucrative profits. It is in the hands of these abortion professionals that the health and "counseling" of desperate, vulnerable women lie. But cold proficiency may not be enough. For as Madga Denes notes after her inside look at the fragile psyche of the abortion industry:

> Renown is no guarantee of skill. Skill is no safeguard against cruelty. Patients are vulnerable to the mental health of their helpers. The helpers should therefore, be watched like potential enemies.[140]

Summary

Abortion in America is not medicine; it is a commodity, delivered with business-like proficiency. In order to facilitate the abortion trade, abortionists (with the blessing of the Supreme Court) have abandoned many of the medical standards which were originally established to protect needy people from unscrupulous health care. These professional codes of ethics were deemed too cumbersome for the business of supplying abortion on demand.

In attempting to make abortion services more efficient and profitable, abortion clinics depend upon low-skill, low-pay workers who are responsible for performing the "routine" tasks normally undertaken by health care professionals. Along with other cost-cutting measures, this dependency on non-medical personnel increases the health risks faced by aborting women in the event of an emergency or an unnoticed complication.

Like all business enterprises, the abortion industry has a special sales force: abortion counselors. Counselors act as "facilitators." Counselors are not supposed to *inform* clients, they are only to help them make the choice for abortion with the least amount of pain and doubt. In fact, "proper" abortion counseling recognizes that women may become "confused" if presented with the facts, and may be "irrationally" dissuaded from choosing an abortion in their own "best" interests. Abortion counselors, therefore, feel obliged to "protect" women from any information which might be "disturbing" or "discouraging." According to the Supreme Court, the right of counselors to withhold any information they feel might have a "chilling effect" on the abortion choice is an absolute right guaranteed by constitutional safeguards. Thus denied the full and complete information they need to make their *own* decisions, it is no wonder that so many aborted women feel betrayed and manipulated by their "counselors."

Though abortion is an extremely lucrative trade for clinics and doctors, it is not a pleasant trade. Staff turnover rates are high; and most workers, counselors and physicians in particular, suffer from guilt and ambivalence about what they do. The dark side of their work is avoided by denial, rationalization, and impersonal attitudes. They avoid thinking about the moral overtones of their work, and they cling to the illusion that the lives of the women they serve are really improved because of their abortions. Any evidence to the contrary is ignored.

Pro-choice advocates who may hope to reform the abortion industry are only deceiving themselves. "Abuses" in the abortion industry are unavoidable, and uncontrollable. The judicial interpretations which elevate abortion to the status of a constitutional right also forbid any regulation to make abortion a *safe* right. Furthermore, the nature of the business naturally attracts "cold, mechanical" profiteers. Compassionate physicians are either repelled by abortion, burn-out after a short time, or develop into "cold, mechanical" profiteers themselves.

Abortion is a grueling, tough business. It is almost as hard on the providers as it is on aborted women.

PROFILES SEVEN

Victims of Prejudice

When women with little or no income become pregnant, they will almost immediately find themselves under the gun of family members, social workers, and family planning counselors who all urge them to have an abortion. Even if a poor woman's pregnancy was planned and the child is wanted, she will find herself accused of "carelessness," "selfishness," and "foolishness." She will hear discouraging descriptions of the increased poverty she will face if she carries the child to term, and she will find herself being described as a negligent mother who will not be able to properly care for the child she loves. She will be told that it is better to "abort for the child's sake," as well as her own. After all, she can always have another child later on when she is more financially secure.

These are the victims of income and age discrimination. Sometimes this discrimination is sincerely paternalistic in nature and the advisors are truly trying to plan the woman's future for her own benefit. At other times there is no real concern for the woman; she is disdainfully viewed as a "welfare bum," and her counselors are simply using every excuse they can to prevent this "unfit" mother from bringing more children onto the welfare rolls. These "socially concerned" counselors believe in the unspoken motto: "It is better to abort than support."

In either case, whether the advisor is sincerely paternalistic or disdainfully manipulative, the woman's own desires, needs, and feelings are ignored. She is not treated as an equal, but as an inferior who has to be pushed into doing the "right thing." These women are among the most exploited persons in our society. They are not only being denied the love and support of society, they are being denied their children.

16) Lorijo Nerad

Lorijo was a victim of pressure and deceit from her social worker, a Michigan state agent appointed to serve and protect the poor. The Nerads' caseworker implied that their welfare benefits would be cut off if Lorijo carried her third child to term. Now sterile due to abortion-related complications, Lorijo and her husband feel they were exploited because of their circumstances.

In January of 1974, my husband Jim lost his job when he injured his elbow. At that time we had one child already, and I was pregnant with our second. Since Jim was unable to find another job, we had to go on welfare.

After having our baby in May, our caseworker at the Department of Social Services made us feel like we had been irresponsible for having a second child. I remember her glaring at us like a disapproving mother who didn't trust her children. She lectured Jim, telling him, "You can't keep your wife barefoot and pregnant the rest of your life. You had better do something about it." She wanted us to stop having children and insisted on making an appointment for us to go to Planned Parenthood for counseling and birth control supplies—conveniently located right next door.

At the clinic I was examined and told that I had a bacterial infection. The doctor said, "I'm not going to touch her with a ten-foot pole." They decided that I couldn't have any kind of birth control, so my husband became the target. The counselor told us that Jim had to have a vasectomy. They really put the pressure on him, making him feel like he was under an obligation to be sterilized. Of course, Medicaid would pay for it. (They were willing to do anything to keep us "welfare folk" from reproducing.) We didn't want to do it, but they told us that there was a 50-50 chance the vasectomy could be reversed later when we wanted more kids *and* had more money. Afraid we would have our finances cut off if we had another child, we went along with it.

273

After this, I went to my doctor to be treated for the bacterial infection, and they ran a pregnancy test on me. We waited in the office for the results. I had missed a period, and I was secretly hoping that I was pregnant. With Jim sterilized, this was our last chance to complete our family. When the phone call from the lab finally came, the nurse talked for a moment, then hung the phone up by slamming it down rather hard. She turned to us and said in a *very* disgusted voice: "Well, it's positive."

I was happy immediately. "All right! I just knew it!" But my enthusiasm was dampened when I saw my husband fall against the wall and look at me with disgust as if it was all my fault. At this point, the nurse started telling us that it was much too soon for me to have another baby. "Either you could die, or the baby could die, or the both of you could die," she told us. The prospect of having me die and leaving him to care for two or three children alone had Jim really nervous. Later that same day my doctor said I could have the baby, but he didn't really offer any encouragement that I should. From all that the nurse had said, we left with the feeling that my life would be in danger if I was to carry the baby full term.

When our caseworker found out that I was pregnant with a third child, she was just disgusted with us. She couldn't believe that we had been "so irresponsible." She urged us to have an abortion, saying "You just can't go around having babies all the rest of your life." After making us feel like dirt, she reassured us that Medicaid would pay for the abortion and that we could always have children later.

From that point on, there was pressure from everyone around me to have the abortion. The only one that didn't want me to do it was my mother-in-law, who was herself a survivor of a failed abortion attempt.

Confusion mounted, tension and pressure took control, and I became another victim of "free choice." I agreed to let them do the abortion, and immediately Medicare came through to prevent another mouth on the welfare roles. (The quick service for aborting my child was a sharp contrast to the six weeks I had to wait before Medicare would treat two rotting teeth.)

On August 18, 1975, I had an abortion. The doctor told me he would slowly dilate my cervix with a series of metal rods and suction out the "blob of jelly called fetal tissue."

I wasn't given anything for pain, the nurse had to hold me down. The nurse kept saying to me, "It will be over in a minute, honey. . . . Oh, come on now, it doesn't hurt that bad. Quit being such a baby!"

The doctor went on with the procedure. Once he stopped and wiped a piece of it on the sheet, showing me and telling me it was a piece of placenta, and saying this is a piece of this or that, using some medical terms.

Afterwards, our caseworker didn't ask about the abortion or how I felt, she just wanted to know that I had had it done.

Looking back, I think that some of the people working with welfare recipients do really want to help them; but when they find out that they can't really "get involved" and help, they buckle under the pressure and quit. Others, like the one who pushed us towards Planned Parenthood and the abortion, have a Margaret Sanger attitude, wanting to weed-out the "depraved," non-working class.

After the abortion, we lied to everyone about it, trying to hide from the guilt. We told my family that I had just had a D&C and that I wasn't pregnant. We never talked about it. Jim felt guilty, too; but he just tried to forget about it, but never really could. He buried it really deep, and he still hurts today when he thinks what he put me and our child through.

As for me, I began to neglect my children, my husband, my home, and myself. I abused my children. I didn't hold them or cuddle with them, because of the looks that they would give me. It was as if they knew what I had done and hated me for killing their brother or sister. The guilt and pain I felt in my heart made me feel so unworthy to even hold a child, let alone have my own. I heard voices saying, "Murderer, murderer, you've slaughtered an innocent baby, your own child."

To cover our guilt we started getting into drugs. We had parties galore. Smoked pot, drank senslessly, and experimented with hard drugs. We wanted to party until we dropped. I was trying anything and everything to get rid of the guilt that stabbed me in the heart every day.

We lived like this for three years after my abortion. Then in 1978 we decided the life we were living was a mess and was burning us out. We turned to our childhood days of churchgoing, and remembered the stories of how God forgave, but I was still in turmoil about my baby. I prayed that I would have another baby to replace it.

Seven years after my abortion, I went back to my doctor to see if all was well enough for me to have the baby I so desperately wanted. After tests, I was told that I had abnormal cells on my cervix, the kind that turn into cancer. Tests led to more tests, and in 1982, at twenty-six years of age, I had to have a hysterectomy. All my hopes of having another baby were ripped away from me.

One month later I got my monthly newsletter from Right to Life. Still a little out of it from my operation, I thumbed through the newsletter only to find a picture of an aborted baby. That did it! I snapped. I cried and screamed at God with my fist in the air, "Why don't you give me another chance?" Then I sat in shock just wondering why I get so hurt and depressed. God had forgiven me, but I didn't forgive myself. So that day, I forgave myself. I decided to take my self-pity and turn it over to God.

But it wasn't until I joined WEBA and saw other women with more problems than I could shake a stick at, that I received complete healing from my abortion. I still mourn the death of my child as anyone who has lost a child will. It is normal; it is what every woman who has had an abortion needs to do. And for the first time in my life, I have felt *normal*, after being told by counselors, friends, and even family that I was crazy for all those years after my abortion.

17) "Vanessa Landry"

Vanessa became pregnant as the result of a rape. But her exploitation did not stop after the rape. She was also victimized by the unrelenting abortion mentality of the social workers and doctors who treated her. Despite the rape, Vanessa was prepared to keep the child until the social worker convinced her that abortion was her only real option. Aftereffects from the abortion have left her sterile. Her anger at being exploited is equalled only by her sadness at being unable to bear children.

One night I went over to the apartment of a girl I knew. Her boyfriend was there. I'd never met him before. He was a stranger to me. After awhile, she went downstairs, and she asked me if I would take care of her baby. I went into the next room to change the baby's diaper. Then the next thing I knew, her boyfriend came in behind me, pulled me down, attacked me, and raped me. After that, I ran into the bedroom and locked the door until he got out. Then I ran downstairs to some other people and told them about it. When I got home, my mom told me not to report it. They didn't quite understand about rape and everything, because my older sister had gotten raped when she was seventeen.

By the time I found out I was pregnant, I was missing a lot of periods, and they told me I was three months pregnant. They also told me that I had gotten gonorrhea and another social disease which at the time there was no cure for. They told me I would have to abort the baby. By that time, I was going through a bad trip, as they say. I was crying and mentally upset, and everything. And because I was diabetic, it was causing my blood sugars to go up, so they placed me in a hospital in isolation.

They didn't counsel me for the rape at all. Now I'm talking to somebody. But six years ago they didn't really have anything in Kansas City to help raped women.

People think that whenever anyone is raped, they have to have an abortion. My social worker was just telling me all kinds of things, encouraging me to have the abortion: "I will come with you to the clinic to help you, since you have to go through your abortion." They didn't offer any option except to abort. They said if I went on and had the baby that I wouldn't have any way of supporting it. And the best option was to abort it since I was low income and I didn't have a job at that time.

I didn't really want to have the abortion. I've always been against abortion all my life. But the doctors told me that if I went on and had the baby, I would have died since I'm diabetic, and I believed them. The social workers and my doctor told me all this stuff, you know, that the baby wouldn't be normal, and it would be retarded and deformed. They were saying it because I was raped, because I was diabetic, and because they thought the gonorrhea would affect the baby. Since then, I've learned that none of this is true. But at the time I was only twenty and didn't know a lot about abortion and everything.

The doctor and social worker that led me to have the abortion, shouldn't have. I would rather have gone on and had the child anyway on my own account. But they pressured me into the abortion saying that welfare wouldn't pay for giving birth but *would* pay for the abortion, since they were saying I would die. They said I was "just another minority bringing a child into the world and there are too many already."

Women who are raped can give their baby up for adoption, you know. But I think that they just didn't want to put the baby up for adoption, they just wanted to see it aborted instead.

By the time this all happened, I was three months along. They said they wanted to go ahead and abort before four months, because conception starts at the time the heartbeat of the baby starts, and that's what I believed. But now I know the heart was already beating by then anyway.

My mother was really trying to get me to keep the baby, but by then I had turned twenty-one and she said, "You're old enough to make your own decision." So like an idiot I signed the papers and went ahead and had it done.

When they did the abortion, I had a real bad reaction from the anesthesia that lasted through the whole abortion. Afterwards, I had a lot of bleeding for two or three weeks. I couldn't get over it. I suffered a lot of mental anguish. Every time I see somebody with a little baby I want to go over and hold it. I very much want to have children.

I'm over the rape now; but because of the abortion, I'm not able to have any kids. I had to have my tubes tied because of complications. They keep telling me I'll die from childbirth; but now I think if I have a positive mind, I can try. Lots of women with diabetes and high blood pressure give birth to normal children, and I'm tired of hearing this from doctors who don't want me to have one. I don't have any children, though I really wanted them. Now the only way I could have them is to have another operation to untie the tubes, and then I can try. . . .

Instead of helping me, all they wanted to do was to prevent the baby. That's why I'm glad I joined WEBA, because I just don't see teenagers and other women going in to have an abortion when they could put the baby up for adoption or just get on birth control so they wouldn't have to have an abortion.

18) Jerri "Porter"

Seven years ago Jerri had an abortion at the insistence of her boyfriend. When she tried to tell the abortion clinic personnel that she did not really want the abortion, they all ignored or belittled her pleas. Instead they paternalistically led her into doing the "best thing for everyone. Jerri and her boyfriend got married one year after the abortion. They both feel grief and guilt over the decision to abort. Though very supportive of each other now, their daily life together is a struggle.

278

When I was eighteen years old, I became pregnant. The father of the baby (now my husband) insisted on an abortion. He was scared because his parents had had to get married with him when his mother was sixteen years old. My boyfriend always felt like his dad resented him for "tying him down." His father drank a lot and would beat him and his mother and sisters. My boyfriend said he wanted to show his father that he could "do it the right way."

But I wanted to have the baby. So I told my boyfriend that he could "get lost" and have no responsibility for the baby. If I felt that I couldn't handle the baby, I could give him up for adoption.

There was one problem: I was so scared! I needed the help of a professional; so like many other girls, I went to Planned Parenthood. After an examination, I talked with a counselor and explained to her that I wanted the baby, but I was scared and that my boyfriend wanted me to have an abortion. She seemed to think that abortion was the wise choice. All she said was, "Well, remember that it's your body, and you have the final say about what happens. However, here's the phone to call and make an appointment for an abortion. The clinic is very busy so you should call as soon as possible." I told her I wasn't ready to jump that fast, and I left feeling lonely and helpless.

I knew I couldn't fight against my boyfriend forever, and I was afraid to tell my parents. So, feeling hopeless, I made an appointment for an abortion at the Harrisburg Reproductive Health Center.

During the pre-abortion group counseling, each girl was asked to tell the others whose choice it was to have the abortion. All the girls had said it was their choice, but I said that I wanted to have my baby but my boyfriend wanted me to have the abortion. I didn't want marriage, though—I wasn't ready for that. The counselor seemed quite upset with me and plainly told me that I was being "romantic," while my boyfriend was being "realistic." How could wanting to give birth to my baby be romantic? I knew it wouldn't be peaches and roses, but the counselor had no right to put me down like that, either. It seems to me that these people are so involved in fighting for abortions that they forget to look at the young girls' and their babies' needs.

Anyway, eight weeks pregnant, I had a suction abortion. About six hours after the abortion, I experienced severe cramps and almost passed out. I've never felt pain like that before—it was as if someone was on the inside of my stomach, slowly cutting it away with a knife. When I finally rocked myself to sleep on my hands and knees then woke up, the pain was gone. The second day afterwards I felt all right.

But on the third day after my abortion, the pain came back, and I had a lot of bleeding and clotting. Nobody told me it would be that bad. I was told to expect some bleeding, which they gave pills for, and some cramps. I was also told that for a couple of weeks I'd feel an emotional loss; but after that, I should be over my experience. If I wasn't, they said, I should seek further counseling, because normally these feelings of guilt, loss, etc. should be gone by then. Well, my symptoms weren't over, but there was no way I was going back to them for counseling.

A year later I married my boyfriend, who also had horrible guilt feelings about what we had done. We have regretted it every day since it happened. We keep wondering what kind of child we murdered: a future President? someone with the answer to our energy problems? Quite on purpose, I got pregnant two weeks before we got married. I knew it was wrong, but the need for another child was so great that it was all I lived for.

About three months after we were married, I started changing emotionally and could not stand having any kind of sexual relationship with my husband. I thought it was a hormone imbalance, due to my pregnancy. When the problem didn't get better after the baby was born, and went on for another year, I went to talk to a Christian friend who was studying to become a marriage counselor. He said I was probably trying to punish myself for what I did, and that I couldn't accept God's forgiveness. It wasn't until two years later that I found out one of the major problems women face after an abortion is not being able to face sexual relationships. The emotional damage done by abortion goes so deep and into so many different areas that it is hard to understand.

I still have problems that need to be worked out. Although I can now enjoy intercourse with my husband, I can't stand any kind of foreplay. I want the lights off and covers on because I don't want God to see what I'm doing. It is going to take a lot to straighten my problems out. Nobody ever told me it would be like this. In fact, I thought I was abnormal until I read information from WEBA and realized that I'm not alone. Sad but comforting.

As a Christian, I can't blame anyone but myself. God allowed me to make my own decision. He was with me all the way, wanting to give me His strength to help me make it through my pregnancy. I was just too scared to reach out for His hand. I still should have gotten better professional help from those agencies. At the age of eighteen, the law says one is an adult. But emotionally, many eighteen-year-olds are not strong enough on the inside to stand up for what they really want.

N I N E

Before and After Legalization

In the preceding chapters we have seen that even those who defend abortion on the grounds of "freedom of choice" admit that abortion is, at best, a "necessary evil," experienced with "ambivalence" and "sorrow." We have shown that abortion is never as "safe and easy" as those who defend it often suggest, and that post-abortion physical and psychological sequelae are common. In light of these facts, we must address the question: Has legalization of abortion improved the lives and welfare of American women, or has it made their lives worse?

The most compelling and repeated argument used by those advocating legalized abortion has been that illegal abortions are dangerous, while medical abortions are safe. Since some women are going to abort no matter what the law says, they argue, it is better that women receive safe, medical abortions rather than being forced to face the risk of dangerous, illegal abortions.

Leaving aside the moral questions associated with abortion, this issue of safety would be a convincing and sufficient argument for legalization—but only if the number of abortions would remain the same. In other words, if legal abortions are N-times safer than illegal abortions, but legalization results in a 5N-times increase in total abortions, then there would in fact be five-times more women suffering physical damage from legal abortions. Under these circumstances, legal abortions would be safer on a percentage basis, but in absolute numbers, more women would suffer damage from legal abortions than had previously suffered from illegal abortions. If this is actually the case, there are compelling health reasons—apart from moral considerations—for restricting abortions.

The fundamental goal of this chapter, then, is to explore whether legalization has increased or decreased the total pain, suffering, and dying experienced by aborted women. In addition, we will examine whether legalization has shifted the pattern of abortion among races, classes, and age groups; since this consideration should also enter into the evaluation of whether or not legalization has freed us of past problems or has merely created new ones.

Abortion-related Deaths: Before and After Legalization

Before legalization, abortion proponents always claimed that "five to ten thousand women die from illegal abortions every year." Repeated frequently enough, this became a "fact of common knowledge" which no one attempted to substantiate. Indeed, informed abortion defenders, as opposed to their less discerning followers, knew that these figures were demonstrably false, but they generally remained silent and allowed the exaggeration to be perpetuated because it was useful to their cause.[1]

Dr. Bernard Nathanson, co-founder of the National Abortion Rights Action League (N.A.R.A.L) and the obstetrician/gynecologist who established and directed the Center for Reproductive and Sexual Health in New York, the largest abortion clinic in the world during the early 1970s, has frankly acknowledged this deception:

> How many deaths were we talking about when abortion was illegal? In N.A.R.A.L. we generally emphasized the drama of the individual case, not the mass statistics; but when we spoke of the latter it was always "5,000 to 10,000 deaths a year." I confess that I knew the figures were totally false, and I suppose the others did too if they stopped to think of it. But in the "morality" of our revolution, it was a *useful* figure, widely accepted, so why go out of our way to correct it with honest statistics? The overriding concern was to get the laws eliminated, and anything within reason that had to be done was permissible.[2]

But where did this "5,000 to 10,000 deaths" figure come from? Investigation reveals that the few people who tried to substantiate the figure all trace their evidence back to a 1936 publication written by Dr.

Frederick J. Taussig, an early advocate of abortion for "socio-econo-mic" indications. But Dr. Taussig's figures were seriously discredited by his contemporaries who noted that his calculations had been widly based on unsupportable assumptions. By 1942, Taussig reversed him-self and insisted that the figure was impossibly high "no matter how we try to cull the various brackets in the mortality statistics."[3] But despite his recantation, the inflated figure was to prove "useful," as Nathanson put it, to abortion proponents of the next generation.

In all fairness, however, not all abortion advocates were silent about this exaggeration. In 1967, for example, Dr. Robert E. Hall, President of the Association for the Study of Abortion, Inc., a re-spected academic group which supported legalization but was less publically active than most other pro-abortion associations, objected to the

. . . . perpetuation of Taussig's thirty-year-old claim that five thou-sand to ten thousand women die every year as the result of criminal abortions. Whether this statistic was valid in 1936 I do not know, but it certainly is not now. There are in fact fewer than fifteen hundred total pregnancy deaths in this country per annum; very few others could go undetected. . . . Although criminal abor-tion is of course to be decried, the demand for its abolition cannot reasonably be based on thirty-year-old mortality statistics."[4]

Once the exaggerations are discounted, the question still remains: How many deaths resulted from abortion prior to its legalization? Again, Dr. Nathanson admits that,

Statistics on abortion deaths [prior to 1973] were fairly reli-able. . . . In 1967, with moderate A.L.I.-type laws [permitting abortion in restricted cases] in three states, the federal govern-ment listed only 160 deaths from illegal abortion. In the last year before the Blackmun era began, 1972, the total was only 39 deaths."[5]

Likewise, Dr. Christopher Tietze, a leading pro-abortion statistician who works with the research arm of Planned Parenthood, has con-cluded that the vast majority of deaths due to illegal abortion were correctly reported as such, and that any understatement of abortion deaths was no more than 10 percent.[6]

There is a high level of confidence in abortion mortality statistics prior to 1973 because these figures were carefully double-checked on several occasions. One long-term study done between 1950 and 1974 in Minnesota (a state representing approximately one-fiftieth of the country's population) used medical teams to investigate case-by-case every death of a female of childbearing age. The investigators made numerous corrections to the official reports and original death certificates, but found that during the 24-year period only 28 deaths could possibly be attributed to criminal abortion. This average of 1.2 abortion deaths per year in Minnesota was *less than one percent* of the 100–200 deaths per year which pro-abortionists claimed for that state.[7] Similar maternal mortality studies in Michigan and California have likewise demonstrated the accuracy of the official statistics on abortion-related deaths.[8]

As the manner of investigation in the above states demonstrates, it was very difficult to conceal an abortion death prior to legalization. A major reason for this was the suspicion of state officials charged with investigating illegal abortions. At one 1970 pro-abortion conference, this fact was candidly admitted by at least one spokesperson:

> I might say we have a fairly high rate of discovery in New York City. The opportunity of obscuring an abortion death is very unlikely. We have a very effective Health Department, which screens all the death certificates, and anything unusual would be referred to us, particularly in a woman of childbearing age.[9]

Some readers might find it curiously inconsistent that previously we argued that *deaths from legal abortions are covered up*, but that now we argue that *deaths from illegal abortions were accurately reported* to within 10 percent of the actual number. Indeed, this is exactly what we maintain. Legalization has worsened reporting procedures for abortion-related deaths. Why were deaths from illegal abortions accurately reported when deaths from abortions today are not? There are many reasons.

First, there was greater concern for identifying abortion deaths prior to 1973 because these deaths resulted from a *criminal* activity— they were illegal deaths, so to speak. Public health officials and physicians alike worked together to track down such "butchers," put them out of business, and place them behind bars.

Second, reporting mechanisms before the legalization of abortion were flexible enough to ensure both accurate reporting and protection of family reputations. In other words, an abortion could still be reported without declaring that it had been illegally induced. This was accomplished by reporting that the death was the result of an "unspecified abortion" resulting from "undetermined" causes. When a physician reported such an "unspecified abortion" death, what the death certificate revealed was that an abortion had actually taken place but that it could not be determined whether it was the result of a spontaneous abortion (miscarriage) or an illegally induced abortion. In some cases the attending physician or coroner truly did not know whether or not the abortion had been spontaneous or induced. But in many other cases, no doubt, physicians chose to list the cause of the abortion-related death as "undetermined" in order to avoid stigmatizing the deceased or embarrassing her family.

The practice of preserving a woman's reputation by listing her death as the result of an "undetermined" abortion was well-known and accepted within the medical establishment. Indeed, nearly 40 percent of all abortion-related deaths were listed under the category of "unspecified abortions." This allowed physicians a way to avoid accusing the deceased of having procured an illegal abortion; while at the same time they were complying with the requirements of the law. But this practice also provided good statistics on abortion-related deaths. In fact, most statisticians automatically included "undetermined" abortion deaths as being the result of illegal abortions. At the academic level, the statistics used on both sides of the abortion debate accept this general rule.[10]

Third, since half-truths are safer than total fabrications, even the physicians who performed illegal abortions were likely to report abortion-related deaths as such. Any physician who would attempt to conceal an abortion-related death as the result of an accident, or cancer, or heart failure, was courting disaster. Such a falsified death certificate would have been quickly exposed during an autopsy, and many states carefully investigated all deaths of females of reproductive age. In such cases, an inaccurate death certificate would not only prove professional incompetence but also suggest that the attending physician had been involved in an illegal abortion. Rather than risk such easy exposure, the physician/abortionist was much more likely to admit that the cause of death was abortion-related, but insist that the cause of the abortion was "undetermined," as described above. Such a listing would be acceptable to the coroner or any other investigator and would not arouse suspicion against the physician/abortionist.

Based on all the available evidence and the three reasons cited above, it is clear that abortion-related deaths were accurately reported prior to 1973. But while the above reasons ensured the accurate reporting of abortion deaths before legalization, they all disappeared after the 1973 ruling. First, legalization means that an abortion death is no longer the result of a criminal act; it is a *legal* way to die. The medical abortionist is no longer criminally responsible for the death, so there is no reason for public health officials to ensure that such deaths are accurately reported and investigated. Indeed, any investigation which proved that a death was abortion-related would serve only to shock, embarrass, or shame the deceased's family.

Second, as we have mentioned before, the courts have established a "zone of privacy" around abortion which protects abortionists from having to report abortion-related complications. This "right" includes the liberty to disguise abortion-related deaths.[11]

Third, abortion is now a "respectable" form of surgery. Therefore, physicians have little interest in correcting erroneous records or in pointing their fingers at the abortionists who are now a legitimate part of their fold. It was one thing to accuse irresponsible "butchers" of killing women; it is another to accuse a fellow doctor.

Fourth, since abortion-related deaths are now "legal" and there is no "butcher" to be apprehended, there is no legal or moral imperative which requires the attending physician to cite the death as abortion-related if doing so would only cause the victim's survivors added stress. Furthermore, the legalizing of abortion deaths has removed all reason for states or cities to investigate such deaths. Since abortionists are operating with the sanction of the Supreme Court, they cannot be arrested, much less convicted.

Because of these changes, the underreporting of deaths from legal abortion is a well-accepted phenomenon among professional statisticians. Even to the layperson, the deterioration of reporting standards is painfully obvious. For example, from 1973 to 1977 only 31 deaths from legal abortions were officially reported for the entire nation.[12] But in a 1978 investigation of only four Chicago-based abortion clinics, 12 deaths from legal abortions were discovered, none of which had been previously reported.[13]

Later on we will compare the number of deaths from induced abortion before and after legalization. For now it is enough to realize that the official reports on abortion deaths prior to legalization were verifiably accurate. The accuracy of these statistics is accepted by experts on both sides of the debate.

The Frequency of Illegal Abortions

Fundamental to the comparison of the health situation before and after legalization is the question: How much has legalization increased the total number of induced abortions? No one doubts that there were more abortions per year after 1973 than before 1973, but the question of degree is in dispute.

A popular figure advanced by abortion advocates is that "of every 10 women now having legal abortions, 7 would resort to illegal abortion rather than be forced to bear an unwanted child."[14] The implication is that 70 percent of legal abortions are merely safe replacements for illegal abortions that would have occurred anyway. The extra 30 percent is considered a population control bonus by some; for others, the increase is accepted as part of the trade-off for eliminating dangerous illegal abortions.

This 70 percent figure was first published by the leading pro-abortion statistician Dr. Christopher Tietze. It was *not* based on interviews with women to determine whether or not they would have sought an illegal abortion if a legal abortion had not been available. Instead, the figure was based solely on his own speculations and elaborate extrapolations. At a 1975 abortion conference, Dr. Tietze was questioned about his assumptions. One person observed that a small adjustment in any of his assumptions would just as easily have yielded a conclusion of 20 percent, rather than the 70 percent figure advanced by Dr. Tietze. Dr. Tietze admitted that a much lower figure was possible and that there was no basis for the assumptions he used in his calculations. Rather, he defended his number-juggling with the comment, "American readers like numbers" and added that he merely wanted to "supply a numerical estimate by way of conclusion."[15]

Despite the failure of Tietze's attempt, accurate estimates have been made. The key problem, however, is to determine an accurate range for the number of illegal abortions prior to legalization.

One way would be to look at the number of reported deaths and calculate the number of abortions that would have been necessary to cause so many deaths. This technique was extensively applied in a study published by Dr. Thomas Hilgers and Dennis O'Hare. Their study begins with the reported statistics on abortion-related deaths. These figures, are considered very accurate prior to 1973. An abbreviated table of the official statistics appears below:[16]

Year	Deaths from legal abortion	Deaths from spontaneous abortion	Deaths from illegal abortion	Deaths from unspecified abortions	Total from all abortions
1940	94	272	501	812	1,679
1950	17	53	91	155	316
1960	10	38	129	112	289
1970	10	9	58	51	128

It is clear from this table that the number of deaths resulting from abortions in all categories had declined dramatically over the decades. A year-by-year graph of these statistics shows a continuous rate of decline. The reason for the decline is simply improved medical treatment. The introduction of antibiotics in the 1940s produced a rapid decline in abortion-related deaths, and continued improvements in health care saved a growing number of people suffering from abortion complications each year.

Adding together the abortion deaths known to be illegal and those suspected of being illegal ("unspecified"), provides the upper limit of deaths resulting from illegally induced abortions. Once the medical improvements over time are considered, these deaths can be assumed to be proportional to the total number of illegal abortions performed. What is necessary, then, is to find a way to account for the improved level of treating complications. This is easier than might be expected, since the treatments for maternal complications and for abortion complications are medically very similar. Therefore, since treatment methods for both maternal and abortion-related complications improve at approximately the same rate over time, the death-to-case ratio for maternal pregnancies must be roughly proportional to the death rate for induced abortions. At this point an assumption must be made as to how many times greater the mortality rate of abortion is compared to the mortality rate of natural pregnancy.

Dr. Christopher Tietze, an abortion proponent, estimated that a "very low estimate" would be 40 abortion deaths per 100,000 abortions.[17] At the time of his estimate, this would correspond to four times the death rate of natural pregnancy. This "very low estimate" was advanced as a knowledgeable guess without any substantiating data. Some limited evidence suggests that the death rate from illegal abortion was probably much higher. Based on data from New York City, it can be shown that illegal abortion was more probably in the range of 5 to 10 times more dangerous than natural pregnancy, and perhaps even as high as 24 times more dangerous.[18]

In order to account for the full range of possibilities, Hilgers and O'Hare used the full range of these assumptions. Assuming that the mortality rate of abortion is 3, 5, 10, or 15 times greater than that for natural pregnancy, they were able to use the known upper limit of abortion deaths to calculate the upper limit of illegal abortions performed. Their data tables are extensive but a simple summation would be to look at the average of their estimates from 1960 to 1969. Assuming illegal abortion is three times more dangerous than natural pregnancy, their data shows an average of 260,000 illegal abortions per year. Assuming illegal abortion is five times more dangerous, their average would be 156,000 abortions per year. At ten times more dangerous, the average number of abortions per year would be 78,000. And finally, at 15 times more dangerous, the average would be 52,000 abortions per year.[19]

What these figures show is that the pro-abortionists' claim of over a million illegal abortions per year was impossibly high. Either the rate of illegal abortions prior to 1973 is much less than pro-abortionists have insisted; or if there were truly a million abortions per year, then illegal abortions are many times safer than legal abortions! The latter is very unlikely.

Based on this statistically derived evidence, it would seem clear that the actual rate of illegal abortions probably ranged somewhere between 100,000 to 200,000 per year. This range is further substantiated by the testimony of women seeking abortion.

In a 1971 survey of 742 women undergoing legal abortions in New York, only 22 percent said that they would have sought an illegal abortion in the absence of legalization. (These women might be classified as "hard core" aborters, demanding abortion regardless of its source or legal status.) On the other hand, 60 percent stated that they definitely would have carried the child to term if abortion had still been illegal, and the remainder were uncertain about what they would have done. (These women would be classified as "soft core" aborters, willing to consider abortion only because it is legal.)[20] Because of the practical barriers in obtaining an illegal abortion, combined with the psychological pressures which work against such a course of action, only a minority of those who were undecided would probably have decided to seek an abortion. Indeed, even of the 22 percent who indicated they were "hard core" aborters, it is probable that many would have changed their minds or would have been unsuccessful in their search to obtain an abortion. Furthermore, the declaration of willingness to seek an illegal abortion in some cases was perhaps more a reflection of personal and political feelings about abortion rather than an accurate reflection of their true determination to abort despite the risks.

This 22 percent figure for "hard core" aborters is brought into perspective by another New York study conducted between 1965 and 1967, a period prior to the state's legalization of abortion. In this pre-legalization survey of 889 women, 8.3 percent of the sample admitted having sought to procure an abortion but only 3.5 percent of the sample reported that an induced abortion had actually been obtained.[21] This would imply that *less than half* of the 22 percent of aborters who express a willingness to seek an illegal abortion in lieu of legalization would have actually persevered and succeeded in their quest.

In 1973, the first year of national legalization, 616,000 legal abortions were performed. Assuming that fully 22 percent of these women would have sought an illegal abortion (though it is likely that less than half would have succeeded), then a maximum of 135,500 illegal abortions would have occurred in 1973 if state laws restricting abortion had remained in effect. Since this was the first year of abortion on demand nationwide, the situation most comparable to that at the time of the 1971 New York survey, this figure is the best representation of the maximum base line for "hard core" aborters in the nation at any given time.

Since 1973, however, the number of legal abortions performed has increased rapidly as more and more "soft core" aborters have been attracted to, or pushed into, abortion as the "safe and easy" solution to their problems. Because today's "hard core" aborters have been numerically diluted by this influx of "soft core" aborters, the 22 percent figure is no longer accurate. Assuming that our base line of 135,000 "hard core" aborters remains constant, only 9 percent of the 1.5 million aborters in 1985 would have sought illegal abortions under 1972 laws. These observations are confirmed by European experience, which shows that only 11 to 16 percent of women denied legal abortions will pursue an illegal abortion.[22] In addition, our own survey (described in Chapter One) found that only 8 percent of the aborters surveyed would have seriously considered seeking an illegal abortion.

Thus, the testimony of women seeking abortions demonstrates three things. First, that only a small percentage of women are willing to seek an illegal abortion. Second, there is a maximum "demand" by "hard core" aborters for somewhere between 100,000 and 200,000 illegal abortions per year. And third, legalization "encourages" more abortions than would otherwise occur.

In sum, rather than merely providing "hard core" aborters with safe, medical abortions, the legalization of abortion has encouraged women who would not otherwise abort to do so. The law is a teacher.

What does all this mean? It means that before legalization there were only 100,000 to 200,000 illegal abortions per year—a range substantiated by both statistical evidence and the testimony of aborted women. But in 1983 there were approximately 1.5 million legal abortions. This means that legalization has caused a *ten to fifteen-fold increase* in the number of abortions performed.

But at least they are safer than the illegal abortions, some might say. Yes, but how much safer? If legalization makes abortion twice as safe, but causes a tenfold increase in total abortions, there is still a five-times increase in women suffering and dying from complications. Only if the improved safety margin is greater than the "encouragement" factor is there any net gain in public health.

Has Legalization Reduced Death and Suffering, Or Increased It?

If abortion was legalized in order to prevent deaths and complications among aborted women, it is important to ask whether or not this goal has been achieved. As we have already shown, deaths and complications occur with legal abortions, too. Though all would agree that legal abortions are safer, the ten to fifteen-fold increase in total abortions indicates that they may not be safe enough.

The number of deaths from illegal abortions had been declining steadily before legalization, due to improved medical treatment. But after legalization the number of abortion-related deaths leveled off. According to the *reported* data, the number of deaths resulting from induced abortions, legal and illegal combined, has not dropped at all since 1973. "While maternal deaths due to criminal abortion appear to be decreasing, *they have been replaced, almost one for one, by maternal deaths due to legal abortion.*" [italics in original][23] Furthermore, although illegal abortions have been reduced, they continue to occur at a rate of approximately 15,000 per year. These remaining illegal abortions result in about ten deaths per year, compared to forty-eight deaths from illegal abortions in 1972, the year before legalization.[24]

This modest reduction in deaths from illegal abortions has occurred at the expense of a massive increase in legal abortions. According to the statistical inferences made by Hilgers and O'Hare, "For each single criminal abortion which has been eliminated, there have been over 18 legal abortions."[25]

But it must also be remembered that the one-for-one replacement of illegal abortion deaths by legal abortion deaths takes into account only the *reported* deaths from legal abortion, which the Center for Disease Control admits to be "selectively underreported."[26] In all probability, then, the number of deaths from legally induced abortion does not simply equal the number of deaths which would have occurred under restrictive abortion laws, but *exceeds* them. Indeed, one isolated study comparing the deaths from legal and illegal abortions in Illinois found that in identical periods of time, before and after 1973, there were three times more abortion-related deaths *after* legalization.[27]

In the simplest of terms, legalization has improved the odds that an individual will survive an abortion, but the astronomical increase in the number of abortions performed means that more women are dying. *The percentage chance of survival is improved, but the absolute number of those who suffer has increased!*

This is true not only in terms of abortion mortality, but also in terms of abortion complications. In 1969 the number of abortion-related complications which were treated in U.S. hospitals stood at 9,000. By 1977 the number of *reported cases* treated in hospitals had risen to 17,000.[28] The total of all reported complications in 1977 was 100,000 and included 16 reported deaths.[29] Again it should be remembered that these are the minimum, *reported* figures. The actual numbers are certainly higher due to "selective underreporting."

On top of the increased physical suffering must be added the deaths which are *indirectly* caused by abortion. Pro-abortionists may dismiss the deaths of tens of millions of "unwanted" children who are the intentional victims of abortion, but each year approximately 100,000 "wanted" pregnancies will end in the sorrow of a spontaneous miscarriage because of latent abortion morbidity.[30] Since abortion advocates insist that only a "wanted" child is a "person," these deaths must be included in the tally of persons inadvertently killed by abortion.

In addition to the increased deaths and physical complications resulting from the increased use of legal abortion, there has also been an increase in the number of women suffering from the psychological complications of abortion. Rather than 100,000 or 200,000 illegal aborters facing the emotional trauma of abortion, now 1.5 million women each year are exposed to the psychological sequelae of abortion.

Beyond even this, the millions of additional women who have legal abortions but would not have sought an illegal abortion face all the other problems associated with abortion, which we previously discussed. They will face a nine-fold tendency towards suicide. They will experience increased marital stress and broken relationships. They will be more and more driven to the escapist and self-punishing abuse of drugs and alcohol. They will be more prone to child battery, and many of their children will face the psychological burden of knowing that mother "killed" their brother or sister.

Is the marginal reduction of illegal abortions worth such a price? Hardly. Instead, it seems clear that the number of women dying and suffering from physical complications alone far exceeds the number who would have suffered similarly if abortion had remained illegal. Rather than reducing the pain and suffering of women, legalization of abortion has increased it by exposing many more women to its inherent risks. The only difference is that now the pain and suffering can be antiseptically ignored because it is "legal." Pro-abortionists go to great lengths to point out the reduced *percentage* chance of complications, but they consistently ignore the increase in the absolute total of complications.

In brief, what has been gained is not fewer deaths among aborted women, but fewer births. This is pleasing to population control advocates—to their minds fewer babies might be worth the cost inflicted upon aborted women. But legalization clearly has not improved the overall health and welfare of American women. Instead, legalization of abortion has only made it easier to pressure women into taking the risk and paying the price.

Legalization Has Not Changed the Abortionists

The common notion of illegal abortions carries with it the imagery of a dirty, "back-alley butcher." The abortionist is seen as dirty, crude, and mercenary. Though such criminal abortionists certainly existed, they did not prevail. In fact, the research of Dr. Alfred Kinsey, much quoted by pro-abortion advocates and considered to be authoritative in many respects, found that 84 to 87 percent of all illegal abortions were induced by physicians, generally using many of the same techniques which are used today. According to Kinsey's surveys, only 5 to 6 percent of illegal abortions were induced by persons not trained in medicine, and the remaining 8 to 10 percent were self-induced. The few other studies available generally support this conclusion.[31]

In a typical case, a woman informed that she was pregnant would ask her physician for help, perhaps fishing with a desperate, "What am I going to do?" In a few cases, if the physician was sympathetic to abortion, he would mention the possibility and perhaps agree to perform it himself. Or if pressed, he might refer her to a professional colleague who would be willing to perform an abortion. Dr. G. Lotrell Timanus of Baltimore was such an abortionist who performed over 5,000 abortions, all on referrals from other physicians who knew of his practice. Finally, if the woman's own physician was uncooperative, she would turn to aquaintances in order to tap the "grapevine" which would lead her to a professional abortionist. In most cases, especially in large metropolitan areas, this would lead her to an "abortion mill" operated by a physician/abortionist.[32] Such physicians, it seems clear, were not in short supply.

Many, if not most, of these same physicians came forward after the legalization of abortion to operate legal abortion clinics where they could openly make $1,000 to $2,000 per day. The former director of one abortion clinic insists that his medical colleagues were "as venal a band of scoundrels as has been collected this side of Ambroise Paré," mercenary and occasionally even sadistic in their treatment of patients.[33]

Putting aside the questionable characters of the physician/abortionists, their technical skills were generally high—at least the equivalent of today's legal abortionists, since obviously they had the same training, and they were often the same people. The skill of these physician/abortionists is attested to by their ability to survive in their criminal practices. The fact that they performed nearly 90 percent of all illegal abortions before 1973 also explains why, with 100,000 to 200,000 illegal abortions performed every year, less than one hundred women died from complications.[34]

The careers of hack abortionists, on the other hand, were generally of short duration. Because abortion was illegal, and the performance of an abortion could so easily lead to complications requiring hospitalization, these less skillful, non-medically-trained abortionists were quickly exposed and convicted. Although they were a minority, these "butchers" provided the colorful lore upon which the over-generalization of back-alley abortions was based. Contrary to this myth, then, the criminal penalties for sloppy abortions effectively served as a "quality control" over illegal abortion. It was a penalty system which successfully weeded out non-professionals, and thus indirectly guided women to the safer domain of physician/abortionists.

In sum, even when abortion was illegal, trained physicians performed 90 percent of the abortions anyway. Today they perform 99 percent of all abortions. This marginal improvement, however, has not resulted in any less pain or suffering among aborted women.

The Women Who Sought Illegal Abortions

There is a common misconception that illegal abortions were generally sought by poor, non-white, lower-class, uneducated, single women who had inadequate access to contraceptives. In fact, the opposite is true on all accounts.

Again we turn to the Kinsey research which provides the most authoritative information about abortion procurers prior to legalization. (Incidently, the authors of the Kinsey study were generally sympathetic to the liberalization of abortion. If there is any bias in their methods and conclusions, it is towards the pro-abortion side.)

According to the Kinsey report, white women were twice as likely to seek an abortion as non-white women. According to Dr. Kinsey:

> The Negro is securing induced abortion less often in comparison to the white female. This is partly a matter of sociology. The birth of a child prior to marriage is not the social disgrace among the socially lower level Negroes that it is among college girls, and this is something that touches upon a reality we must always take into account.[35]

Furthermore, the abortion rate per hundred women was also lower among *married* blacks, despite a considerably higher conception rate.[36]

These data are less race specific than they are reflections of lower economic and lower social status, which blacks disproportionately share. Abortion has always been relatively uncommon among the poor, because the poor are generally more accepting of children and, in fact, are more likely to see a larger family as an ideal.[37]

Indeed, the Kinsey material clearly shows that the rate of abortion increased in direct proportion to increased social status."As a rule," Kinsey researchers conclude, "induced abortion is strongly connected with status-striving."[38] Just as the self-affirmed are more likely to advocate abortion today (see Chapter Four), so these same women were more likely to seek an abortion when it was illegal. Illegal abortion was used primarily to avoid disruption of a higher-than-average lifestyle or to protect the woman's career—the very motives for which there is the least public sympathy.

Finally, the Kinsey study explodes the myth that single women were the primary seekers of illegal abortion. Though it was true that the *rate* of abortion per hundred women was higher among unmarried women, the actual number of abortions done for married women was far greater. This is confirmed by hospital studies of illegal abortion complications which showed that the majority of the patients were married. But by far the highest rate of abortion was among formerly married women. In particular, Kinsey found that college educated, formerly married women used abortion to end over 85 percent of their pregnancies.[39]

Summed up, what all this means is that prior to legalization, the "typical" woman seeking an abortion was an upper-class, well-educated, married white woman. Furthermore, Kinsey and others show that illegal abortion was not used because of the unavailability of birth control. Indeed, it was those who most diligently used contraceptives (again, the better educated, the married, and those from the upper social classes) who turned to abortion as a back-up when it failed. According to one researcher:

[I]n this large sample of respectable white married women . . . those who practice contraception as part of their sex life, by their own admission resort to criminally induced abortion about *three times* as often proportionately as do their comparable non-contraceptor contemporaries. . . . [F]or something like three-quarters of that part of the professional abortionist's business that derives from urban women, he can thank the birth controllers and the current imperfections of their art.[40]

Similarly, Dr. G. R. Venning summarized the British experience in a 1964 article:

This [study] found that the incidence of induced abortion as a percentage of all pregnancies was one percent for women not using birth control and nine percent for women using birth control unsuccessfully. . . . [T]he data illustrate clearly that the likelihood of induced abortion is much greater in women who have contraceptive failures than in women who have not used birth control at all. The data from this survey also showed more induced abortion with rising socio-economic status, the incidence in all pregnancies in the highest social class being more than double that in the lowest group.[41]

Comparing the Past to the Present

As we have already shown, legalization has not reduced the number of women dying and suffering from abortion; in fact, it has clearly increased the number of women suffering from abortion complications. Rather than liberating women, *Roe v. Wade* has only served to make their suffering "legal." Now, instead of 90 percent of abortions being performed by doctors, over 99 percent of abortions are performed by doctors. But this slight improvement has resulted in a more than tenfold increase in abortions. The situation has changed from 100,000 to 200,000 illegal abortions per year to over 1.5 million legal abortions, and the problems have multiplied accordingly.

But this astronomical increase in abortions has also resulted in a major shift of the burden of abortion complications. Previously, the physical and psychological complications of abortion were borne primarily by the "hard-core" aborters, those who were so determined to abort that they would seek out an illegal abortion if a legal one was not readily available. But now the vast majority of aborters (91 percent according to the figures we presented earlier) are "soft-core" aborters, those for whom abortion is only marginally desirable, reluctantly accepted. These "soft-core" aborters might easily be dissuaded from abortion if it were illegal, if they fully understood its risks, or especially if they were offered the emotional and/or financial support which would make the choice not to abort a practical alternative. It is this shift in the abortion burden toward "soft core" aborters which is most disturbing.

The most dramatic change has been towards increased abortion among single women. Before legalization, the majority of abortions were among married women, usually after the family was "finished." Today, over 75 percent of abortions are done on single women.[42] Surprisingly, however, the abortion rate among pregnant teens is relatively low. It is reported that only 27 percent of teenage pregnancies are aborted.[43] Instead, the vast majority of abortions, over 70 percent, are done for women over twenty years of age. Furthermore, of all aborters, 55 percent have no children and 90 percent have fewer than two children. Rather than being used to limit family size, abortion is primarily used to delay childbearing to a more convenient time.

The major area of growth in abortion clientele has been among the "lower classes," particularly the poor and non-whites. Prior to legalization, whites were twice as likely to abort as blacks. Social pressures have now reversed that situation. Today, 40 percent of pregnancies among non-whites are aborted, compared to 25 percent of whites.[44] In 1976 alone, 33 percent of all abortions were performed on non-whites, although non-whites constitute only 13.2 percent of the U.S. population.[45]

But while abortion has increased among non-whites, it has not become more acceptable among them. Polls show that non-whites, particularly blacks and Hispanics, are much more opposed to abortion than the general population.[46] Thus, as we have seen previously, non-white women are aborting in greater numbers against their consciences, because they feel increasingly "forced" to abort because of outside pressures.

The increased frequency of abortion among non-whites and the poor is no accident. Welfare workers, family planning counselors, and government agencies all stress the "wise" choice of abortion to underprivileged clients. In some areas of the country, Hispanics are propagandized to abort with four times more advertising than are their English-speaking neighbors.[47]

This sort of activity has frequently led minority leaders to charge that American abortion policy is intent on genocide. But it should be noted that to the degree such "genocidal" impulses exist, and they do, they are based less on racial bigotry than upon economic prejudice. The latter is attested to by the continued efforts of anti-poor groups which advocate public funding of abortion as a cost-efficient way of reducing welfare rolls: "Better to abort than support." The proponents of this philosophy are not racial bigots; they are simply utilitarians unwilling to support "useless eaters." This anti-natal, anti-poor movement is cautiously silent and introspective in its rhetoric, but it is much larger than most people are aware. In brief, their philosophy is simple: the way to end poverty is to keep the poor from reproducing themselves.[48]

In sum, legalization of abortion has led to an astronomical rise in "soft-core" aborters, especially among the single and the poor. Why this change? And how did it come about?

Before legalization, the only women who were willing to seek an illegal abortion were those who were driven by their own self-concern, their own "status seeking." These were, and remain, the "hard-core" aborters. They were typically well-educated, white, married and regular users of contraceptives. When "mistakes" occurred, these women were determined that their own "rights" or convenience should prevail, and so they were willing to seek abortions outside of the law, regardless of the costs or risks involved.

Legalization, on the other hand, has made abortion *too* easy to obtain. It has now become easier to coax, or even coerce, a woman uncertain about her pregnancy to accept abortion as the "easy out." Such women are made to believe that aborting is something they *should* do, if only for the male, or for their parents, or for their own vague "future" which friends and family hold in such high esteem. Before, these women were protected from being pressured into an abortion because they had ready reasons for refusal: "But abortion is illegal! What if we're caught? Isn't it dangerous?"

But today there are no longer any anchors to which a reluctant aborter can take hold, for all the practical barriers have been taken away. It is legal, and so supposedly safe. Everyone is doing it. Only her own fears and perhaps her own "irrational, moral hang-ups" stand in the way. Isn't it selfish, she's told, to let her own reluctance to abort, her "hang-ups," ruin the lives of others and burden the future her parents have prepared for her?

If legalization had only served to provide "hard-core" aborters with a marginally safer surgery, a surgery which they would have sought anyway, then perhaps legalization would have been a legitimate health goal. After all, having 99 percent of abortions performed by physicians is a marginal safety improvement over the 90 percent rate which prevailed before. But when legalization entices millions of additional women to face the risks of abortion, has not public health been ill-served?

In refusing to judge the morality of "hard-core" aborters, are we not encouraging "soft-core" aborters to compromise their own values for the sake of "practical" considerations? In ensuring the "hard-core" aborter's freedom of choice, are we not undermining the choices of the "soft-core" aborter? Where is the "freedom" when a woman is compelled to believe that abortion is her *only* option, something she is *forced* to choose because of her circumstances?

In the final analysis we must ask: has legalization widened or narrowed the options available to "soft-core" aborters? Is abortion a new social freedom, or a new form of social abandonment?

Summary

Despite all of the promises made by abortion advocates, legalization of abortion has done nothing to lessen the pain and suffering of aborted women. The number of women dying from abortion has not been reduced. Reported deaths from legal abortions replace those which would have occurred from illegal abortions one for one. If unreported deaths from legal abortions are included, the national death toll is higher than when abortion was illegal, though the odds for any single woman are marginally improved.

Similarly, the number of non-fatal abortion complications which occur yearly has skyrocketed since legalization. Over 100,000 complications are *reported* to the Center for Disease Control each year (the actual number must be much higher), as compared to 9,000 reported complications from illegal abortions in 1969.

Legalization has increased the total number of abortions performed ten to fifteen fold. Statistical calculations, supported by the testimony of aborters willing to seek illegal abortions, demonstrate that there was an average of only 100,000 to 200,000 illegal abortions per year prior to 1973. Since legalization, the abortion rate has continually grown. In 1984, an estimated 1.5 million abortions were performed. It is this massive increase in total abortions which has exposed so many women to the physical and psychiatric risks of abortion: that is the primary argument for reinstating abortion restrictions.

The legalization of abortion has brought only moderate improvements in abortion care since almost 90 percent of illegal abortions were performed by physicians prior to 1973, anyway. The growth in the abortion industry has taken place at the expense of "soft-core" aborters, those who would not have chosen abortion if it were still illegal. This shift has been particularly costly among young women, non-whites, and the poor.

PROFILES EIGHT

Illegal Abortions

The pro-choice position has always relied heavily on the graphic horror stories of illegal abortion. Indeed, many of the most radical and angry of pro-choice advocates speak from the experience of having gone through the terrors of an illegal abortion themselves. These women need and deserve to be listened to. They have much to tell. The pressures and fears they faced, the pain and complications they suffered, and the ostracism and isolation they felt were all very real. Everything these pro-choice women report is true; it is only the "solution" of legalized abortion which is false.

Unfortunately, every horror that was true of illegal abortion is also true about legalized abortion. Many veterans of illegal abortion, however, do not realize this. Instead, they cling to the belief that all the pain and problems they suffered could have been avoided if only abortion had been legal. They imagine that if their abortions had been legal, their lives would somehow be better today. Instead of recognizing that it is the very nature of abortion itself which caused their problems, they blame their suffering on the *illegality* of abortion at that time. This is superficial blame shifting, but it is an understandable reaction to what is always a traumatic experience.

Many victims of illegal abortion, however, are no longer caught up in the myth that access to a legal abortion would have lessened its negative impact on their lives. Indeed, nearly 10 percent of WEBA members had illegal abortions before 1973. To these women the greatest tragedy of legalized abortion is that now it is only easier for women to be deceived or pushed into the false solution of abortion.

The next two stories highlight some of the circumstances women faced in obtaining illegal abortions before 1973. These women explain that abortion is just as exploitive and dangerous to women today as it was when it was illegal.

19) "Molly Graham"

Molly was a high school junior when her relatives literally forced her to have an abortion in Mexico. Telling her story is very traumatic for Molly, but she reveals all that she has allowed herself to remember.

Specific details of my story are not clear to me now. I believe I have hidden dates and circumstances deep within me; for whatever reason the Lord has not shown me. I had just turned sixteen in October of 1968 and was a junior at La Sierra High School in Sacramento. I must have found out I was pregnant in December, because I had the abortion sometime in January.

I found out that I was pregnant. For some, this is a terrible event. I had in no way planned for this to happen, but was delighted through and through that I was going to have a baby. My boyfriend Steve and I prepared to tell my mother of the wonderful things that were about to happen: we would get married and in June or July would be having a baby.

We told my mother what had happened. It was not what I had expected. She was furious and ready to kill. She forced Steve out of the house and said that I would not be having this baby. I was in shock and had no grip on what would be happening to me in the next few weeks.

I remember my grandmother coming to town and many, many conversations about this "horrible mess." I believe my mother was trying to prevent me from going through what she went through as a young mother. She wanted so much more for me. I know that it had nothing to do with worry about "family disgrace."

The next day I was forced to take quinine and straight whiskey to get me to abort on my own. I did take the pills, but I couldn't handle the whiskey. After a lot of yelling and crying, I was allowed to quit the booze. Nothing happened.

I believe it was at this point, after Steve had been forcibly removed from my house, that he was told there was a peace warrant issued against him, blocking him from ever coming near me again. He wept bitterly, trying to do all he could to help me. It must have been horrible for him. It was for me. My whole life was confused and turned upside down. I didn't understand anything.

The day after taking the pills, I cut school and went to my doctor who had diagnosed me as pregnant (not my family's doctor). He said it was a miracle that I was not blind with the amount of quinine I had taken, and the baby was surprisingly all right. Steve, his sister and husband and I went out to breakfast afterwards. As we were sitting and talking about the problem, my mother walked in and almost literally dragged me out, threatening all the people I was with. From that point on I was locked in the house.

I really didn't understand even what abortion meant. My mother told me that it was not a baby, but just tissue; and that they would take it all out. This was explained to me at a later date. So at this point in time, I didn't really know they were planning the upcoming abortion.

I think at this point I got to the phone and called my father. I was allowed to go see him. He was of no help. I think he really sided with my mother, but never really said so. He said he didn't have custody of me, and there was nothing he could do. Later, just before the abortion, he came over to see me. I think it was the first time, as a young lady, that I saw my father cry. I did not know and probably will never know (since my father is dead now) what this meant to him.

Next, I was taken to my grandparents' home in Chico. Running away never, ever occurred to me. I am sure it was on their minds, and they guarded against it. Where would I have gone, and to whom? There was no one. My sister (five years older than I) and I were taken up into the foothills. I was basically told to run until I miscarried. My dear sister encouraged me on, saying "If you do this and get it over with, then they will be happy. Then they will leave you alone." Well, I did run. But I was never a runner to begin with. I always was the last in the pack at school. The harder I would run, the slower I think I actually went. I don't think we ran for very long, and I was pooped. I just couldn't go any longer. So grandpa took us back to his home.

At this point I knew they were trying to get a hold of someone in Mexico. My sister apparently had a friend in high school who had had an abortion by this man. Anyway, they were making secret calls and getting secret calls. I only picked up bits and pieces at that time. I really believed that it wouldn't ever work out.

Within a couple of days my grandparents and I were back in

Sacramento, and they were preparing to take me to Mexico. My great grandmother paid the money to my mother for the abortion. You see, she had deliberately aborted her fifth child on quinine and whiskey. And my mother had had a hysterectomy when she knew she was pregnant. What a family history!

Well, we were on our way now. I was in the back seat of a two-door sedan. What would I do with two old people who had been through the mill, first with my mother and then us grandchildren. They were strong in some ways, but weary and broken in others.

It was quiet for awhile, and I had time to think. What should I do? I didn't want to go. If I jumped out of the car, I would hurt the baby and myself. I could run away, but where would I go in some strange city? I heard the preaching I had received earlier: "This is the best thing for you. How can you raise a child? Where will you get the financial support? You will never finish school!"

There was nothing left for me to do but to convince myself that this was the right thing to do. So I did. By the time we got to Mexico, I had surrendered. Now I can say, "I surrendered my baby to death." Although at the time, if I had known what I know now, I would have fought like a tiger. The Lord would have made a way for me.

My grandparents drove straight through to Juarez, Mexico. We found a clean motel room and tried to sleep. All three of us in one room was not an ideal situation. The next morning the secret meetings and endless driving to avoid being followed began. We were transported from one car to another until we reached the house where it was to take place. An ordinary house of death.

Afterwards, my poor grandparents were scared to death when they saw me. They were concerned that I had no color in my face, and kept asking if I was all right. I believe it was ignorance on their part, as well, that encouraged them to take me there. My breasts drained for days, and I was empty, so empty inside. The wonderful dream of being a mother was all over, and I had nothing. Only a miserable memory that I have tucked away in the back of my mind. I don't clearly remember it all. I don't know that I really want to.

I have since forgiven myself and my entire family, as I know that Christ has interceded for me. I shall live forever knowing that I consented to the murder of my baby. Comfort comes as I know that my child is with the Lord, a far better place than where I am at. Someday I will see my child and know from his or her lips that all is well. As Paul must have struggled with his memories of persecuting Christians before he was saved, I too struggle.

20) Ila Ryan

Ila underwent four illegal abortions between 1960 and 1964. She became a pro-choice activist, and after abortion was legalized, she provided anesthesia to women undergoing abortions. Having viewed abortion from both sides of the law, Ila today believes that legalized abortion is a travesty, and she insists abortion is no better today than it was before 1973.

It was 1960. I was in my early 20s. I had just graduated from nursing school and had a new career ahead of me. At this time I found myself pregnant for the first time, and I was scared to death. I was single and living away from home. The young man involved gave me only one suggestion: abortion.

It seemed the easy answer, because (1) I was afraid to tell my mother—I didn't want her to find out about my promiscuous lifestyle, and I knew she would kill me if I went home and told her I was pregnant; (2) I did not want anyone or anything to interfere with my lifestyle, which was party-party-party; (3) I did not want to put forth the time and effort needed to raise a child; and (4) I did not want to face the embarrassment of having people see me pregnant and not married. All my excuses for abortion were self-centered. Abortion is the most self-centered act I know.

I was desperate, and an illegal abortion was the only option available to me—as I saw it. I traveled to Cuba alone and stayed across the street from the gambling casinos of the Havana Hilton. In the morning I was taken to a clinic where I met an abortionist who spoke no English. Following his sign language, I responded in agreement to general anesthesia. I awakened, rid of my "problem." The price was $250.

"Relief" would describe my conscious thoughts and feelings more than "regret." I was free of the "problem," and nobody knew what I had done. I returned to the States to try to live my life in the normal way, for myself.

A year later I was in the same condition, with the same problem, but the procedure for solving it was not as simple. This time I made arrangements in Harlem, New York. I climbed up on a kitchen table in a basement apartment and watched as the instruments were taken out of a dirty linen hamper and boiled on a kitchen stove. Without the

305

benefit of any anesthesia, my cervix was forced open. This caused immediate vomiting. A rubber tube was left in my cervix for a short time and pitocin was administered to stimulate contractions. I was given an antibiotic and sent home.

This treatment was supposed to bring about an abortion in twenty-four hours. It failed and I bled for a full week then returned to the abortionist to have the procedure repeated. The second time it worked, in less than twenty-four hours. After about six hours of good labor, I had the baby in the toilet. I had to fish it out in order to be sure everything had been expelled from the uterus. I had been about four to five months pregnant. My dead baby was a boy and cost $150.

My third abortion was in an abortionist's office in Montreal, Canada. I went in alone. A D&C was performed without anesthesia. I remember being in a great deal of pain, which seemed as though it would never end. Again the "problem" was gone. The father of the "problem" arrived to pick me up, and we returned to the hotel where I found his gift of red roses waiting. The cost of this baby, $350.

My last abortion took place in 1964. It was the most troublesome and difficult to obtain. A friend accompanied me to San Juan, Puerto Rico, with no contact previously arraanged. After a two-day search, I found a man who would do the abortion for $400. I was to receive a spinal anesthetic for this one. The next morning in the abortionist's office I received my spinal, to no avail. I did feel the scraping of my womb; and as with the second abortion, I vomited through the whole thing. I remember that during the entire procedure I stared at a big gold crucifix hanging from the neck of the butcher. What a hypocrite!

On the flight home and for the next month, I suffered various complications: bleeding, abdominal pain, severe headaches. Anemia followed. Reluctantly, I went to a real doctor who pulled out some "tissue" which had not been removed by the abortionist in Puerto Rico.

Each time it seemed abortion was the only answer; but in each case, the final choice was mine alone. After the first one, it was easier to go back for the second, third, and fourth times. My heart was hardened. Not once did I think of my baby as a baby. I couldn't allow myself to think that way.

It was almost twenty years before I began to talk about my abortions. The ultimate truth was hard to face. I had not solved four "problems." I had not simply removed four growths of "tissue" from my womb. The truth was I had murdered four innocent babies who were helplessly dependent upon me for their lives. I had chosen to give them death. I had sought to live my life the normal way, for myself. And I had succeeded. The result was death, but not only for four babies. I was dead, too. And I deserved much more punishment than that which I had inflicted upon the babies. I deserved the life apart from God which I had chosen for so many years. Moreover, I deserved to be shut out of His presence forever.

Before facing these hard truths, I lived in a continuous spiritual and mental state of alienation, guilt, and self-hate. This sent me on a road of almost total self-destruction. I began to drink heavier than ever before. I tried to lose myself in the bottle and in the arms of many, many men and overwork. I could not stand to be alone with my thoughts. I so desperately wanted to be loved and accepted, but I could not allow people to get close to me. I was afraid that if they knew what I had done, they wouldn't like me. My personal relationships were stormy and brief. During the sixties, a pattern formed: drink, fall into sexual relationships, get pregnant, abort, feel guilty, fearful, *lonely,* self-hateful; then start all over again.

I felt God could not possibly love me for all the terrible things I had done. So because I felt He hated me, I hated Him. I denied Him and was very afraid of Him.

My first marriage did not ease the soul-sickness; and because of my drinking and numerous affairs, it ended in divorce after seven years. There were no children born in this marriage. I did not want children. I couldn't look at a baby without crying.

Despite all my inner pain and emptiness, I was still very much in favor of the movement to legalize abortion. I considered myself a feminist, and I supported the idea that abortion was part of a woman's right to control her own body. That is what I believed; that is how I had always acted. There was no room for any thought of what was destroyed in an abortion. I didn't *want* to know. Only my rights mattered, only my convenience.

I, like the whole feminist movement, was too short-sighted to look any deeper than my immediate needs.

Though I was never able to talk about my own abortions, I did not hesitate to recommend abortions for others. In fact, in several cases I helped friends to find illegal abortions. I sincerely thought I was helping them. In 1976 I even took my stepdaughter to the hospital where I worked and arranged for her to have an abortion. Later that year, with my blessings and encouragement, she had a second abortion at a clinic. In both cases I was convinced that it was the "best" thing for her to do.

But the legalization of abortion and its rise to social acceptability did nothing to ease the loss and emptiness I felt. Eventually I became so lonely, guilt-ridden, and desperate, that I saw suicide as the only way out of my torment. I overdosed on Valium and Jack Daniels. When my suicide attempt failed, I was admitted to an alcohol rehabilitation program in October of 1976. It was while in rehab that I began to be aware of a Power greater than myself. I prayed for the first time in many years, and my prayer was answered. I suddenly realized there was a God out there, and He heard me. He must care for me because he answered my prayer. My heart began to be filled with joy and hope, and I was no longer alone. He came to me where I was, in a nut-house with a bunch of drunks.

Shortly after my new relationship with God was established, I accepted Jesus as my personal savior and Lord of my life. After that my life changed rapidly and dramatically. The compulsion to drink left me. I know it had to be God who did this, because no human had ever been able to make me stop drinking before. Three months later I was even able to stop smoking.

By profession I am a nurse anesthetist (the person who puts you to sleep for your operations). I had been giving anesthesia for abortions in the hospital I worked in. I felt I understood the women's dilemmas and sympathized with them. I knew how lonely and scared they were, and I wanted them to know I understood. I don't know how many times I did this. The last time I gave anesthesia for an abortion, it was to be a hysterotomy, because the woman was about 6½ to 7 months pregnant. I put her to sleep as usual, the incision was made in the abdomen, then into the uterus, and a baby was pulled out—I mean a fully developed, moving, breathing baby. It hit me like a ton of bricks—the baby was put into a bucket of water and drowned. I was shaken; I knew at that moment I had stood silently by and condoned murder, not only this time, but many times before. I told my boss I would no longer give anesthesia for abortions and was removed from those duties.

My life really started to improve after this, especially my recovery from alcoholism. I began to like people and learned to not be afraid of them. I prayed on a daily basis. I had an overwhelming desire to go to church, which I did and still do, to thank our marvelous God for all the wonderful blessings He has bestowed on me.

ILLEGAL ABORTIONS

About a year and a half after my suicide attempt, I married again to a most wonderful man. He was so supportive of me, and today gives me all the freedom I need. He can trust me and I trust myself. The compulsion to seek out men has been removed. I am faithful to one man at long last.

Our marriage has been blessed by the birth of a beautiful son in 1980. To me, he is a direct sign of God's forgiveness. I was so happy to be pregnant at the age of forty-one. After four abortions I was able to carry an absolutely normal pregnancy to full-term and give birth to a normal, healthy child. Only through God's grace and protection was this possible.

In my work with the Crisis Pregnancy Center and WEBA, I have learned that legal abortion today is no different than the illegal abortions I received twenty years ago. With my illegal abortions, I was at no time informed of prenatal development, the procedure to be used, possible risks or complications, or what to do if anything did happen. Since it was an illegal procedure, no operative permit was involved and there was no legal protection against malpractice.

I find almost all these things to be the same today. Women are not counseled on alternatives, risks, or complications. They are promised a local anesthetic which does not work most of the time, so they feel the entire procedure. They sign a special operative permit that releases the abortion clinic of responsibility if there is a complication. I know of no other branch of medicine where this is allowed. The result is that millions of women suffer complications from this "safe and easy" procedure and have little or no legal recourse afterwards. At the hospital where I work we treat half a dozen women for abortion complications such as bleeding and infection each month. But perhaps worst of all, women are never informed about prenatal development. The baby is never referred to as a baby, but as the products of conception, uterine contents, blob of tissues, mass of cells—never a baby. Furthermore, then as now, women are being coerced into an abortion during the first twelve weeks of pregnancy, when they are at their lowest ebb, emotionally and physically. What with nausea, vomiting, and the ambiguous feelings about the baby (which is a common symptom of pregnancy), abortion seems like a quick end to the early discomforts of pregnancy. I personally feel that women are being manipulated into making hasty decisions to terminate their pregnancies for the profit of the abortionists. It is a decision she will regret for the rest of her life.

309

ABORTED WOMEN

Today I know I must do all I can to help stop legal abortion in this country. I do this by speaking to groups and by reaching out to aborted women, helping them find the one answer to the emotional hell that follows abortion: forgiveness through Jesus Christ. Only in Him do I have hope for my babies who have died, and for my husband and son who live.

T   E   N

The Future of Abortion

The 1973 Supreme Court decision allowing abortion on demand across the nation has been a constant source of controversy. Even legal scholars sympathetic to abortion have marvelled at the "raw judicial power" which the Court used to force the goals of its own social vision upon the nation. It was a ruling which made it clear that the Constitution could be construed by the Justices into any shape they desired.[1]

The sweeping changes instituted by the Court breeched the principle of separation of powers. The Court not only overruled the abortion laws in every state, but it also defined in precise terms what shape those laws *must* take. Subsequent Court decisions have not only forbidden the states any right to protect the unborn, but have also effectively negated all state power to protect women from coercion and deceit, or to regulate the safety standards of abortion clinics. The issue of abortion aside, these rulings have resulted in tension between the legislative and judicial branches. Only a Constitutional amendment or a Supreme Court ruling reversing the 1973 decision can again give elected representatives the right to regulate abortion. Whether or not an amendment will be passed depends primarily on the force of public opinion.

Most polls agree with this general breakdown: about 20 percent of all people reject abortion under any circumstances, 20 to 25 percent would leave it solely to the woman's choice, and the majority, 55 to 60 percent, would limit abortion to specific circumstances, particularly the "hard" cases.[2] A breakdown of exactly *what* circumstances the middle majority accepts as just cause for abortion shows that they generally lean towards the pro-life position, particularly as the pregnancy advances, and they accept abortion only in the "hard cases." A 1978 Gallup poll found the following results:[3]

PERCENTAGE OF "MIDDLE" GROUP APPROVING OF ABORTION BY CIRCUMSTANCE AND TRIMESTER			
	First trimester	Second trimester	Third trimester
Woman's life is endangered	77%	64%	60%
Woman may suffer severe physical health damage	65%	38%	24%
When the pregnancy is a result of rape or incest	65%	38%	24%
When there is a chance the baby will be deformed	45%	39%	28%
When the woman's mental health is endangered	42%	31%	24%
If the family cannot afford the child	16%	9%	6%

A question they did not ask was: "If the baby would disrupt the woman's career." But considering the low level of sympathy for those who could not financially support a child, it can be assumed that the middle majority would generally be unsympathetic when the life of the unborn was weighed against the woman's career or convenience.

When the 20 percent who are opposed to abortion under all circumstances are added to the generally disapproving middle majority, it would appear that public opinion predominantly favors strong restrictions against abortion. Indeed, polls show strong public support, 71 to 76 percent, in favor of some form of state or local regulation of abortion.[4]

The pressure to regulate abortion is growing. And it is no wonder, because with each passing year the myths of abortion are increasingly exposed, particularly the myth that women want the "right" to abortion. In fact, the opposite is true: "virtually every poll shows that women are significantly more anti-abortion than men are."[5]

In terms of political activists, far more women are working against abortion than for it. In the nation's largest pro-life group, the National

Right To Life Committee, there are 7.5 million women working to stop abortion and provide positive alternatives to women with unplanned pregnancies. In the nation's largest pro-choice organization, the National Abortion Rights Action League, there are only 121,000 female members.[6] Even if one included all of the 250,000 members of the National Organization of Women, the largest feminist group which supports abortion, there are still over twenty women working against abortion for every one woman working for it. And as we saw in Chapter Two, women who have actually had abortions are six times more likely to become anti-abortion advocates than pro-choice activists.

Though it is politically attractive to label abortion as a "women's issue," the history of abortion reform and opinion polls shows that legalization was primarily supported and promoted by upper-class males. Judith Blake, head of the Demography Department at the University of California, Berkeley, and personally favoring the pro-choice position, has noted the general lack of support for legal abortion from women, in contrast to the strong support from upper-class males. Speculating as to why men are more in favor of abortion, Blake suggests that:

[U]pper-class men have much to gain and very little to lose by an easing of legal restrictions against abortion. For some time, these men seem to have been satisfied with relatively small families extending over a limited period of their lives. Thus the increased availability of abortions is not likely to damage whatever interest they have with respect to the family. Furthermore, their sexual freedom has been curtailed, both within marriage and outside it, by restrictions on . . . pregnancy termination, since as a class they are especially vulnerable to being held financially and socially responsible for accidental pregnancies. For this reason, they are likely to favor a lessening of those restrictions. And when one takes into account the fact that birth control reforms—whether advanced contraceptive methods like the pill and the coil, or abortion itself—cost men virtually nothing, their positive attitude toward legalizing abortion becomes even more plausible. After all, it is women who must undergo abortions, not men.[7]

Furthermore, we might add, upper-class males are much more likely to be pro-abortion rather than merely pro-choice. Rather than seeing abortion merely as an individual right, they are more likely to

313

see abortion as a positive social good, useful for reducing the number of welfare children, and valuable as a tool for population control, and as a means of maintaining political power. In other words, upper-class males are more likely to view abortion not as a human rights issue but as a utilitarian one.[8]

In the past, then, the upper-class males who have dominated politics and the judiciary may have found it convenient to hide their self-serving support for abortion under the guise of granting greater freedom to women. But as the voice of women in politics grows stronger, it will become increasingly clear that abortion is a "freedom" which the majority of women do not want inflicted upon them. The only reason that "freedom of abortion" remains a "woman's issue" is that it is still a useful *symbol* for many feminist activists. But pro-choice feminists have never been able to claim that they represent the majority of women. Indeed, the official pro-choice position of mainline feminism is beginning to crack under the pressure of dissenting groups such as Feminists for Life of America.[9]

The "freedom of abortion" ideal, imposed on women by men, will not last as more and more women see through this charade. Change is inevitable. The only question is what form that change will take.

Despair Across the Land

Perhaps the most crucial reason why unrestricted abortion will not be tolerated is that abortion is a defeatist answer, and Americans are seldom satisfied with half-way solutions.

Even to its defenders, abortion is a "necessary evil." It is not a right one exercises with pride. Unlike the proud civil rights gained by blacks—the right to attend all-white universities, the right to eat in any restaurant, the right to live in any suburb, the right to sit at either end of the bus, and so on—the abortion "right" is practiced with shame, not pride.

As we have seen in story after story, women choose abortion because they feel there is "no other option." They abort because it is the "easy way out." They abort because they feel abandoned by their lovers, friends, and families. Without the support to do the right thing, they yield to doing the "easy thing." Or as one WEBA woman put it, "I made the decision to be weak." In today's society, it does not take courage to abort; it takes courage to stand up against all the pressures and inconveniences which push towards abortion. Thus abortion is not a liberating experience; it is a deflating experience which involves a shameful yielding to despair.

In many ways, abortion is like suicide. A person who threatens suicide is actually crying out for help, and so are women who contemplate abortion. Both are in a state of despair; both are lonely; both feel faced by insurmountable odds. Granting the wish for suicide or abortion is not an aid to these desperate people. It is abandonment.

If we were to legalize suicide and create suicide clinics where counselors would ease people into and through their suicide decisions, there would be no shortage of desperate people willing to exercise their "freedom to choose." Suicidal persons would be promised a "quick, easy and painless" solution to their problems. They would be promised compassionate care and a release from their seemingly insurmountable burdens, their feelings of loneliness and pointlessness. And so suicide rates would skyrocket just as abortion rates have soared in the last ten years.

Like the suicide clinics described above (a real proposal recommended by right to die groups), abortion clinics exploit desperate people. They promise to satisfy the dark impulses of our despair. They appeal to our demand for instant solutions to all our problems. They pose as places of compassion, but they are actually reaping huge profits through the harvest of the lonely, frightened, and hopeless people who are "unwanted" by society.

Women who face unplanned pregnancies do not need abortion. They need help and support so they can keep their commitments. They need to be applauded for their bravery against difficult circumstances so their courage might last, their self-esteem might grow, and their integrity might remain firm. As it is, the social acceptability of abortion makes a woman feel that struggling with an unplanned, inconvenient pregnancy is a pointless task. The pride she feels in doing the right thing is taken away from her by those who insist that it is better to do the convenient and "practical" thing.

But as we have seen that abortion is almost always an act of despair by a desperate woman, so too is the abortion system a sign that a society has given in to despair. Abortion signifies an America with crumbling courage, an America which has lost hope in the great dream of justice for all. Abortion is accepted not because it is just but because it gives the appearance of helping a few women at the expense of their as yet unseen children. Too cowardly or too selfish to offer love to *both* the women and their children, "pro-choice" friends, family, and society at large offer women abortion as the "easy way out" which saves everyone from getting too involved with her problems. Abortion is a cover-up; it hides women's problems by eliminating their children and silencing the women themselves with shame. Abortion is a half-hearted solution urged by those who have only a half-hearted concern.

Professor of philosophy Donald DeMarco sees abortion as symptomatic of this surrender. He writes that:

> Without courage, love tends to degenerate into sentimental kindness. . . . The inherent weakness of sentimental kindness is not its lack of benevolence but how it buckles in the face of difficulties. For most people, all that is required to feel kind is that nothing threaten them at that moment. But let a man who is merely kind enter a truly uncomfortable situation and his kindness may quickly give way to cruelty. As C. S. Lewis points out, such "kindness consents very readily to the removal of its object," for it is concerned not with whether its object is good or bad, lives or dies, but only that it escapes suffering.[10]

Abortion has become an excuse for *not* offering real aid to pregnant women. Feminist author Paulette Joyer has complained that the abortion mentality is an "obstacle to true, progressive social reform." In this context, she writes:

> If every unintended pregnancy can be aborted, why should the government and private sector make any special considerations for the single parent? Or even the two-parent family? Logically, only people who can provide for their children without reliance on concessions of others should have children.
>
> Logically, why talk about decent maternity and paternity leaves? Job protection? Flexible career options? Shared jobs? Low cost, high quality child care? . . . If every unintended pregnancy can be aborted, why should local governments feel any obligation to provide additional nutrition and health care to poor women who are pregnant?
>
> If it is known that a child will be born with a physical or mental handicap, but that that fetus can be aborted, why should there be any pressure to provide care and support to handicapped citizens and their families?[11]

The abortion solution is a financially cheap way for society to brush troubled women out of the way while claiming to have done them a service. Abortion is the "cheap love" offered by an uncaring society too busy with "more important" problems than the hardships faced by pregnant women. By promoting abortion, society can avoid addressing the real issues such as those listed by Joyer. By avoiding these issues, by denying women the collective support of the community, society is pressuring more and more women into accepting the abortion "solution."

Abortion is a women's issue, but it is an issue not of women's rights but of women's oppression. The effort to stop abortion is not an attempt to deny women an option; it is a promise to provide them with better options. It is a promise to alleviate their despair, to prevent their exploitation.

Should Laws Reflect Morality?

We have seen that the overwhelming majority of women oppose abortion for convenience. We have seen that abortion is abusive of women and is an excuse by which they are abandoned. But many would argue that we should not "legislate morality." These people insist that anti-abortion laws violate the principle of separation of church and state.

In response to these arguments we might first note that "separation of church and state" is a convenient slogan for those who oppose certain moral or religious convictions, but it is not a principle incorporated in the constitution. What the First Amendment forbids is the "establishment of religion" by Congress. The wisdom of this article was derived from experience with British abuses which attempted to force people to accept the Church of England as the official national denomination. The First Amendment, therefore, was designed to prevent the federal government from instituting such a national denomination or legislating religious doctrines.

But while the first amendment would clearly forbid a national law requiring certain religious observances (such as a requirement to attend church on Sunday or to refrain from meat on Fridays), it was never intended to prevent the government from incorporating religious *values and morals* into its laws. Indeed, all the rights defended by the Constitution are derived from the founding fathers' common belief in God and the sanctity of human life. This view was stated most succinctly in the Declaration of Independence, which recognized the "self-evident truths" that "all men are created equal, that they are endowed by their Creator with certain inalienable Rights, that among these are Life, Liberty, and the pursuit of Happiness."

This was the philosophy upon which this nation was founded, that human rights are inalienably endowed by God, derived from His moral order. First among these is the right to life. It is also worth noting that the founding fathers saw all men as *created* equal," not "born equal." Human dignity, they believed, is God-given at the moment of an individual's creation, at conception, not at birth, not after achieving certain abilities arbitrarily defined as "personhood."

The idea that rights are based on the moral order of God was not new at the time of the American Revolution. Ever since the first civilizations, a belief in a moral order was the basis for all laws which restricted human behavior and guaranteed human rights. Laws against murder, theft, and exhibitionism, for example, were based on the belief that such actions violated the rights and dignity of others.

All laws, since the beginning of time, impose values upon other people. Even traffic laws against speeding impose a value upon those who would like to speed. Every stoplight is an imposition on personal behavior. *Laws always attempt to legislate morality.* To separate morality from the law is to leave the law without purpose.

Pro-abortionists argue that since some people do not believe abortion is immoral, it is not right to prevent them from having abortions. But no law depends on everyone agreeing to it. Not all thieves, rapists, and murderers believe that they are committing immoral acts, and there are many prominent philosophers who would insist that since there is no God nothing is objectively immoral. But even though there is never a perfect consensus on what is moral and what is immoral, it is the purpose of the law to address these issues.

Carried to its logical conclusion, the "freedom of choice" argument is an appeal for anarchy—freedom from any laws, any imposition of values or morality. If "freedom of choice" is made the highest of all laws, then no other laws are possible.

But pro-abortionists are anything but anarchists. While they oppose the anti-abortion "morality" which would legislate against abortion, they are at the same time seeking to impose their own values on society by insisting that there is a moral obligation to provide *free* abortions for the poor. The abortion debate, then, is not one of whether or not the law should be used to impose values upon the people. Instead, it is a debate about *whose* values are going to be imposed upon the rest.

Similarly, politicans who support pro-abortion laws saying, "Personally I don't believe abortion is right, but I refuse to impose my moral views on others," are at best cowards who are unwilling to stand by their own moral convictions, or at worst, nothing more than hypocrites. When these same politicians vote to build defense systems, they are imposing their values on pacifists. When they vote to tax the rich for the sake of the poor, they are imposing their morality on those wealthy persons who don't care about the poor. Writing moral choices into the law is what their jobs are all about.

Above all, laws exist in recognition of the fact that there is a difference between what we *can* do and what we *ought* to do—especially in our relationships with other human beings. It is a means of educating and guiding the members of a society to respect and protect the rights and dignity of others. In large part, these laws are built up by tradition and formulated by trial and error. Thus, it is through the law that the people of one age attempt to teach their values and pass on their wisdom to their descendants.

Laws are also a mechanism by which people are encouraged to do what they know is right, even when it is difficult to do so. Without community support, it is all too easy to give in to despair, to violate one's own principles because it seems like no one cares what you do anyway. Besides condemning evil acts against the dignity of others, the law reminds us that right acts are noble acts. As philosopher and social activist Peter Maurin often reminded his followers, the goal of social justice is to "create a society where it would be easier for people to be good."[12]

In this sense, laws against abortion may seem restrictive to those who want abortions, but they are also an encouragement to those who are tempted by abortion but know that it is wrong. For those women who struggle against the pressures which force them toward abortion, the law is a backstop that reminds them that their sacrifices are worthwhile, that they are doing the right thing if not the convenient thing. Social acceptance of abortion, on the other hand, tells women that they are foolish *not* to abort an inconvenient pregnancy. The choice is one of deciding which of the two different moral viewpoints we want to encourage.

Studies into the psychology of morality reveal that the law is truly a teacher. One of the most significant conclusions of these studies shows that existing laws and customs are *the most* important criteria for deciding what is right or wrong for most adults in a given culture.[13] Whether one wants "morality in the law" or not, most people look to law for moral guidance. Right now the law is teaching that abortion is a moral and presumably effective solution to unplanned pregnancies. As a result, millions of unborn children are being destroyed, an equal number of women are being physically and emotionally violated, and society's compassion for both women and their children is being eroded. Is this really the type of morality we want our laws to teach?

What Changes Are Necessary?

It is our belief that society faces a moral obligation to prevent abortions not only for the sake of the unborn children, but also for the sake of the women who are exploited by the abortion system. This ethical imperative demands that abortion be made not only illegal, but also unthinkable, undesirable. There are two steps towards that end: (1) Society must pass laws which forbid abortions, except when necessary to save the mother's life; and (2) Society must provide love and support to pregnant women both before and after giving birth, because of the added pressures and difficulties they face. Today we are not only failing at both these moral obligations, but we are using the one to excuse the other: we are using the availability of abortion as an excuse to avoid "costly," authentic love for pregnant women.

There are many ways in which the first step, the legal restriction against abortion, can be achieved. The fastest route is for the Supreme Court to reverse the 1973 *Roe v. Wade* decision. A simple reversal would return to the states the right to make their own laws regarding abortion, describing when and under what circumstances abortion would be allowed. A more complete reversal would recognize the unborn as persons entitled to equal protection under the law. In this case, constitutional protection of the individual's right to life would be extended to the unborn, and no state or federal law could allow abortion except when necessary to save the mother's life.

A judicial reversal of *Roe v. Wade* would be quick and effective, but it would not be final. Though it is unlikely, a still later Court could reverse the reversal and again define the unborn as being outside constitutional protection. For this reason, a more permanent solution requires the passage of a human rights amendment to the Constitution which would guarantee basic legal protection to all human beings, born or unborn, regardless of physical or intellectual attributes and talents.

THE FUTURE OF ABORTION

Once there is a renewed restriction on abortion, the rate of illegal abortions would return to approximately pre-1973 levels. "Hard-core" aborters would probably continue to seek out illegal abortions, but the "soft-core" majority of today's aborters would be deterred from abortion. The effectiveness of renewed restrictions against abortion has been demonstrated in Rumania. From 1956 to 1966, Rumania had nearly unrestricted abortions. In 1966 the birth rate was 14.3 per 1000 population, but in 1967, the year after abortion was again restricted, the birth rate jumped to 38.4 per thousand, illustrating a high level of compliance with the new law. But the Rumania experience also shows that once the birth control "back-up" of abortion is withdrawn, people become more careful and responsible in their practice of birth control. Though the birth rate jumped in the year abortion was first restricted in Rumania, it gradually declined to its original level as couples once again learned how to avoid the need for abortion.[14]

There can be no doubt that laws against abortion would be effective in discouraging women from seeking abortions. Studies in foreign countries have shown that 40 to 85 percent of aborting women would not have aborted if it had been illegal.[15] In our own survey of aborted women, over 90 percent said they would not have sought an illegal abortion or attempted self-abortion if the laws had been different. Nearly the same percentage reported that permissive abortion laws strongly influenced their view of the morality of abortion.

If abortion was again totally restricted in the United States, it is likely that the rate of illegal abortions would again decline to around 100,000 to 200,000 per year, representing the demand of "hard-core" aborters. It is also likely that 90 percent or more of these abortions would continue to be done secretly by physician/abortionists, as they were before 1973. A return to illegal abortions, however, does not mean that there would be a return to the death and complication rates of illegal abortion prior to 1973. Instead, the complication and death rates would be much lower. There are two reasons for this. First, medical care for abortion complications has improved during the last two decades (emergency personnel have had lots of opportunities to practice under today's policy of abortion on demand). Second, and more importantly, the abortion techniques used by doctors have also improved; illegal abortionists would continue to use the suction curettage that is used in legal abortion clinics today. In other words, illegal abortions performed by physician/abortionists will be no more dangerous than legal abortions—they will only be far less common, and that alone will

save lives and reduce complications. Even such leading abortion proponents as Garrett Hardin admit that recriminalization would not result in
increased deaths or complications.[16]

But in order to be fully effective, any future restriction of abortion
must also be accompanied by positive programs. Public education
efforts must be launched to expose the myths of the pro-abortion
mentality so as to discourage women from considering illegal abortions.
Towards this end, women must be re-educated about the risks of
abortion and informed about positive alternatives. They must especially be warned about the high risk and foolishness of attempting
self-abortion, that most dangerous form of abortion which provided the
most gruesome stories of the pre-legalization era. Such warnings should
be part of high school health education courses, which should also
include information on positive alternatives and resources which are
available to women with unplanned pregnancies. Women must no
longer be panicked into abortion because of desperation and ignorance
of their options.

This brings us to the second change which must occur: an expansion of support programs for problem pregnancies. Recriminalization of
abortion must not be seen as a restriction of options but as a promise to
provide women with better options. If better options are not provided,
recriminalization will be just another form of abandonment. Therefore,
positive alternatives to abortion must be made a top priority in American social policy.[17]

There is much that can be done to ease the burden on women
with unplanned pregnancies. The needs and approaches are too numerous to be detailed here, but a few major points are worth noting.

First, financial aid must be available to help the pregnant woman
carry her child to term and meet the special medical expenses associated with childbirth. One needed reform is an elimination of insurance
clauses which refuse medical payments to unwed mothers or to married
women who became pregnant prior to marriage.

Second, medical, legal, psychiatric and spiritual counseling should
be immediately available, at no cost, to women and families who find a
pregnancy distressful. In particular, obstetricians and gynecologists
who are among the first to see if a woman is distressed by her pregnancy should be educated about the resources available to aid her
through her pregnancy. Rather than being in the uncomfortable position of being asked to perform an abortion, doctors should accept at
least a minor role in directing women towards crisis counseling centers

where trained professionals can help them through problem pregnancies. Lists of such agencies and brochures of their services should be available in every physician's office, and doctors should take the time to become at least minimally familiar with these alternatives.

Third, counseling and aid centers for women with problem pregnancies should be expanded. Right-to-life groups have done a marvelous job of increasing the availability of such services during the last decade, usually through private donations alone; but there is still much room for expansion. Such services should receive support from public funding because they not only help the women who use these services, but the next generation, as well.

Fourth, institutional barriers against unwed mothers must be abolished. Birth certificates should not stigmatize children or mothers by listing a child as "illegitimate." Employers should not be allowed to discriminate against or fire female employees simply because they become pregnant. School administrators must not be allowed to ban pregnant girls from classrooms and thus add to their stigmatization. Home schooling should be an option, but not a requirement. The more normal the life of the unwed mother, the better are her chances for a healthy adjustment. She needs positive options and support, not demands and rejection.

Fifth, shelters for women with problem pregnancies should be expanded and positively advertised, so that women and girls facing extraordinary pressures from family, friends, or the child's father can have a place of refuge.

Sixth, support programs must continue after the child is born. Women and their children need post-natal care and access to medical and nutritional programs. Furthermore, day-care centers need to be expanded and supported so that young parents can continue their education and single parents can earn a living.

Seventh, adoption options should be expanded so that women and families unable to support a child can have choices about how their child is placed, and those options must be made as painless and reassuring as possible. Since fear of the unknown is the greatest obstacle for women considering adoption, options should exist which would allow a woman to meet, or even choose, the adoptive parents, so that she can be reassured her child will be loved and well cared for. Similarly, many women might prefer the option of finding adoptive parents who would waive rights of confidentiality and provide the natural mother with periodic updates on her child's development, or even visitation rights. An even more radical option would be the development of programs to place the child with a foster family where the mother can come to visit and eventually reclaim her child when she is in a better position to undertake the responsibilities of parenthood herself. There is no need to force women to make an all-or-nothing choice between keeping a child and giving it up for adoption. Compassionate alternatives can and should be found.

Eighth, but least concrete of all, attitudes must change. Men must learn to take greater responsibility for their sexuality and the children they beget. In addition, society as a whole must cease to stigmatize the unwed mother. This can be done without encouraging pre-marital sex, much less unwed pregnancies. The consequences of an unwed mother's behavior are burdensome enough without adding rejection and social stigma, too.

These attitudinal changes can be achieved through education and open discussion of these problems in the media. Of primary importance is teaching parents how to be accepting and supportive of a son's or daughter's unwed pregnancy. At the same time, teenagers need to learn that parental disapproval of sexual activity does not mean that parents will reject them if they get into "trouble." Wisdom counsels against unwed pregnancy, but love accepts and supports those in need, even when the need is of their own making. Just as abortion does not solve the problems of an unplanned pregnancy, neither does rejection. Each is a form of abandonment, and abandonment is cruel no matter what its shape or form.

In short, unplanned children deserve our unconditional acceptance, and women with unplanned pregnancies deserve our unconditional love and support.

If positive alternatives to abortion are made available, and if social support for women faced with distressing pregnancies is increased, there is no reason why illegal abortions could not be reduced far below the pre-1973 level. Women don't *want* abortions; they only feel pressured to have them in order to preserve their relationships, their financial well-being, their careers, or even their public images. Given positive support and unconditional love and acceptance, abortion will cease to be a "necessity" and will be seen as the ugly alternative it is.

Transforming Evil to Good

It has been the theme throughout this book that women are victims of abortion. It is the people who profit by abortion and those who advocate its use as an "easy" solution to real problems who are the perpetrators of this crime.

In many ways, though, this last description includes us all, even those who vocally oppose abortion. Consciously or not, we have created a society where individuals are expected to solve their problems by themselves, or at the very least, to solve their problems in a way which poses the least inconvenience to the rest of us. This attitude of abandoning the unfortunate to deal with their own problems, particularly if the "problems" are of their own making, was the fertile ground from which the abortion mentality sprang. For a society which conceals abandonment under the guise of promoting "individualism," the promotion of abortion as a solution for women "in trouble" was inevitable, because abortion is cheap and "easy"—at least for those who don't have to have them.

Abortion is a symbol of how we have abandoned our ideals of community, love of our neighbors, and care for the weak. To forbid abortion is to promise to strive for our ideals; to accept abortion is to bow down to the non-ethics of the utilitarian counting-house philosophy. Failing to help women cope with the problems of pregnancy is to push them towards the false solution of abortion. There is no neutral ground. If we do not choose life, we choose death.

But just as every scientific experiment yields knowledge, even if it fails, so does every social policy. In seeing failures we learn what to avoid; in seeing evil we learn how to seek good.

Having gone through this period of abortion on demand, and having witnessed its horrors, it is our hope that all of us have learned to look more closely at the needs of women faced with problem pregnancies. Perhaps having recognized the Pandora's box of abortion, we have developed a greater commitment to help women in more constructive, creative, and loving ways. This is the hope of the tens of thousands of aborted women who have now become pro-life activists: that through the deaths of their own children, we might all learn a greater respect for life; that through their own sufferings, we might all build the foundation for increased awareness and the motivation for change. These women and their children paid a horrible price, but if we use this experience as an impetus for change, their sacrifices may ultimately be redeemed.

As we have said time and again, this goal will not be achieved merely by banning abortions. Instead, such a ban must be only one step towards compassionately, and unjudgmentally, supporting pregnant women through inconvenient, unwanted, or otherwise difficult pregnancies. In the wombs of these women live new hopes and dreams, new friends and companions in life. To love these children, we must love their mothers; to care for these mothers, we must love their children. Mother and child are as one, and they cannot be separated without doing violence to both.

Some people complain that such unlimited care is too costly, too inconvenient for society to bear. These critics are half right. Such care is costly, and inconvenient. But such an investment will inevitably pay us back in full; for in learning to love both mother and child, we will learn how to better love ourselves. At the same time, in learning how to rejoice more fully in our own lives, we will learn how to rejoice in the lives of others.

Aborted Women:
How to Find Help

If you or someone you love is suffering from the emotional or physical aftereffects of abortion, you can find compassionate help and support from women who have been through the same experience by contacting any of the WEBA chapters in your state, or any of the other post-abortion counseling groups which are being formed. If WEBA is not listed in your phone directory, call one of your local or state right-to-life organizations and they will be able to give you a phone number for the post-abortion support group nearest you. Most of these groups have a hot-line which you can call to talk to a sympathetic, non-judgmental member at any time, whenever you need them.

If you feel you need the help of a professional counselor, a psychiatrist, psychologist, or a clergy member, look for a counselor who has had experience and training in dealing with Post-Abortion Syndrome (PAS). Most professional counselors are not trained to handle the complicated aftereffects of abortion and therefore may be unable to help you in a meaningful way. Your local pro-life group or crisis pregnancy center may be able to refer you to an experienced PAS counselor.

A P P E N D I X

Survey Results

The survey discussed in Chapter One was distributed through WEBA chapters to 252 women in 42 states. It consisted of two sections: background information and the actual survey questions. The instructions read as follows:

ABORTION EXPERIENCE QUESTIONNAIRE

This survey is being conducted to review the decision-making processes of women who have had abortions, and their subsequent satisfaction or dissatisfaction with their decisions. Please answer the questions as honestly as possible. If you wish to elaborate, please feel free to write further explanations or comments on separate sheets of paper. (If possible, please number your explanations according to the number of the question which prompted your comment.) Your written comments may be used in published results of this study. Names and addresses will not be used and will remain confidential unless written permission for use is requested and granted. If you know of anyone else who has had an abortion and may be willing to answer this survey, please make a photocopy of this form for them, or write to the survey address for an additional copy.

The first section of the survey requested the following background information:

Name:_____   Age:_____
Address:_____ Race or
City:_____   ethnic origin:_____
State:_____

Highest grade
completed:_____

Was your abortion ☐ legal, or ☐ illegal?

Name of clinic or hospital where abortion was performed:_____
_____

City:_____ State:_____
Abortion referral or counseling agency (if any):_____
_____

City:_____ State:_____

How many weeks pregnant were you at the time? _____ wks.
How old were you at the time? _____ yrs.
Marital Status: ☐ single   ☐ married
               ☐ engaged   ☐ divorced

How many children did you have at that time? _____
Income level at the time: ☐ less than $5,000 per year
(of your parent(s) or   ☐ $5,000 to $10,000
yourself and/or spouse)   ☐ $10,999 to $15,000
                              ☐ $15,000 to $20,000
                              ☐ over $20,000

Was the cost of your abortion subsidized by an outside source?   ☐ Yes   ☐ No

Source, if known: _____
_____

Tabulation of the background information yielded the following results:

AGE DISTRIBUTIONS

Age at time of abortion:	≤15 yrs	15–19	20–24	25–29	>30
	3%	42%	33%	14%	8%

Average age at time of abortion: 21.2 yrs
Low age at time of abortion: 12   yrs
High age at time of abortion: 40   yrs

Age at time of survey:	<20	20–24	25–29	30–34	>34
	1%	11%	33%	35%	20%

Average age at time of survey: 31.2 yrs
Low age at time of survey: 16   yrs
High age at time of survey: 64   yrs

Average time since abortion: 10.0 yrs
(Survey age—abortion age)
Greatest time since abortion: 36   yrs
Least time since abortion: 7   months

RACE OR ETHNIC ORIGIN

White—87%
Other—13%

LEGAL AND ILLEGAL ABORTIONS

Legal —92%
Illegal— 8%

EDUCATION LEVEL

No Answer	Under 12 yrs	High School (12 yrs)	Degree Equivalent			
			Associate or Trade (13–14)	Bachelors (15–16)	Masters (17–18)	Ph.D. (>18)
5%	6%	39%	26%	19%	4%	1%

WEEKS PREGNANT AT TIME OF ABORTION

<5 wks	5–6	7–8	9–10	11–12	13–24	>24
2%	13%	23%	18%	24%	19%	0%

Average gestation at time of abortion: 10.2 wks
Low gestation at time of abortion: 4 wks
High gestation at time of abortion: 23 wks

MARITAL STATUS

Single:	65%		Married:	17%
Engaged:	8%		Separated:	11%

NUMBER OF CHILDREN

Number of children:	0	1	2	3	>3
	73%	14%	9%	4%	1%

INCOME LEVEL

Under $5,000 per year:	33%
$5,000 to $10,000:	25%
$10,000 to $15,000:	14%
$15,000 to $20,000:	7%
Over $20,000:	21%

Though the above figures tend to show that the women surveyed generally had low incomes at the time of their abortions, these numbers should be interpreted with caution. These figures are not necessarily indicative of the general incomes or social classes of these aborters. At the time of their abortions, most of these women were in their early twenties or late teens; many were college students. While some respondents elsewhere indicated that they were from middle- or upper-class families, they considered themselves independent at the time of their abortions (whether working or attending college) and so reported only their personal incomes. Thus, the income *potential* of many of these aborters may have been significantly higher than the above figures indicate. Moreover, these income levels are not adjusted for inflation.

SUBSIDY OF ABORTION

This question was meant to identify government subsidized abortions (i.e. through federal or state Medicare programs). Another frequent response, however, was that insurance (usually the insurance policy of the woman's parents or college insurance) covered the costs of the abortion. Responses such as "paid for by boyfriend," or "parents" were tallied as being abortions that were *not* subsidized.

Subsidized:	23%	Government subsidy:	64%
		Insurance subsidy:	36%
Unsubsidized:	77%		

Following the background questions was a list of 58 questions which were to be answered on a scale of 0 to 5. According to the directions for this final section:

Instructions: Unless otherwise indicated, most questions require answers on a scale where 1 = Not At All, ranging up to 5 = Very Much. Unsure is always indicated by circling 0.

In practice, most of the women did not answer any question which they felt was not applicable to their circumstances. If, for example, they had not consulted with their parents before their abortions, they simply did not circle a response to the question as to whether or not their parents influenced their decisions. Since computer tabulation of the results would have been overly complicated by unanswered questions, all unanswered questions were recorded as a "0" response. Therefore, all "0" responses include those respondents who were unsure of their response to a particular question, as well as those who were sure that the question was "Not Applicable" (N/A) to their particular circumstances.

In general, most answers clustered at the extremes of the 1 to 5 scale. Therefore, in the description of these survey results found in Chapter One, 1-2 responses were generally combined into a single percentage, as were 4-5 responses, and the middle response, 3, stood alone. The few exceptions to this rule were noted in the text.

The following is a complete listing of the questions asked, with answers recorded according to the *percentage* of respondents falling in each category.

	N/A or Unsure	Not at All				Very Much
	0	1	2	3	4	5
1. Were you satisfied with the abortion services you received?	10%	44%	8%	18%	10%	8%
2. Were you satisfied with your choice at the time?	8%	42%	14%	13%	10%	14%
3. Are you satisfied with your choice today?	3%	95%	0%	1%	0%	1%
4. Was the decision made for reasons of:						
mental health?	40%	34%	4%	6%	6%	11%
physical health?	41%	48%	2%	3%	1%	6%
financial limits?	32%	27%	5%	9%	5%	23%
social acceptance?	20%	12%	3%	7%	10%	47%
family size?	42%	48%	1%	2%	1%	6%
career goals?	41%	30%	4%	7%	5%	13%
long-term needs?	43%	22%	4%	7%	6%	18%
short-term needs?	41%	14%	2%	5%	9%	28%
other:——(see Chapter One)	54%	2%	0%	3%	2%	39%
5. Do you feel you were "forced" by outside circumstances to have an abortion?	4%	12%	10%	10%	10%	54%
6. Were you encouraged to have an abortion by:						
parents?	34%	35%	2%	6%	2%	21%
other family members?	41%	39%	3%	3%	2%	12%
husband?	54%	33%	1%	1%	2%	9%
boyfriend?	27%	27%	2%	4%	7%	33%
social worker?	52%	32%	2%	0%	4%	10%
abortion counselor?	39%	20%	2%	4%	8%	27%
doctor?	41%	27%	3%	6%	5%	18%
friends?	38%	28%	2%	7%	6%	18%
other:——(see Chapter One)	77%	5%	0%	2%	3%	13%
7. Would your choice have been different if any or all of the above had encouraged you differently?	8%	4%	2%	3%	7%	76%
8. Do you feel you were "forced" by others to have an abortion?	4%	23%	10%	10%	14%	39%
9. If abortion had not been legally available, would you have sought an illegal abortion?	16%	72%	3%	4%	2%	4%
10. Would you have attempted a self-induced abortion?	4%	87%	2%	2%	2%	3%
11. Did you feel rushed to have an abortion?	3%	8%	3%	5%	12%	69%

	N/A or Unsure	Not at All				Very Much

12. How long did you take to decide?
☐ 1–4 days, ☐ 1wk., ☐ 2–3 wks., ☐ 4–6 wks., ☐ longer
    51%   24%   12%   6%   6%

13. Do you feel your decision was well thought out?
| | 1% | 74% | 8% | 9% | 2% | 6% |

14. Do you feel you had all of the necessary information to make the decision?
| | 2% | 88% | 5% | 3% | 1% | 2% |

15. Have you had more than one abortion?
24% Yes   76% NoNo

How many?
    1   2   3   >3
    76%   20%   3%   2%

16. Would you ever have another abortion?
| | 4% | 95% | 1% | 0% | 0% | 0% |

17. Were there any physical complications following the procedure?
47% Yes   44% No   9% Unsure

18. If so, were they severe or minor? (minor-1; severe-5)
| | 47% | 15% | 6% | 14% | 4% | 15% |

Please list, if any: ——(see Chapter One)

19. Was there any permanent damage?
18% Yes   47% No   35% Unsure

Please list, if any: ——(see Chapter One)

20. Have any subsequent pregnancies resulted in miscarriage or premature birth?
23% Yes   67% No   10% Unsure

If so, does your doctor attribute it to your previous abortion?
5 % Yes   5% No   88% Unsure

21. Were there any negative psychological effects you attribute to your abortion?
94% Yes   2% No   4% Unsure

22. If so, were they minor or severe? (minor-1; severe-5)
| | 6% | 4% | 3% | 14% | 19% | 54% |

23. Did they persist: ☐ 1–6 mos. ☐ 1–2 yrs ☐ over 3 years
              8%   10%   82%

24. Do they still persist?
| | 7% | 25% | 23% | 19% | 8% | 18% |

25. Was post-abortion counseling available through the clinic or referral agency?
| | 16% | 76% | 4% | 1% | 1% | 2% |

26. Did you require professional counseling and/or treatment?
| | 8% | 45% | 4% | 6% | 6% | 31% |
What other forms of counseling did you receive?
——(see Chapter One)

APPENDIX: SURVEY RESULTS

	N/A or Unsure	Not at All				Very Much
27. Were you using a form of birth control when you conceived? If so, what type?——(see Chapter One)	23% Yes	74% No			3% Unsure	
28. Were you familiar with the available forms of birth control?	1%	7%	8%	15%	7%	63%
29. Knowing where your life is today, would you still have chosen abortion?	4%	94%	1%	0%	0%	1%
30. Did you discuss your decision with others?	1%	25%	28%	19%	10%	18%
31. When you went to the clinic or counselor, was your decision already firm?	5%	30%	9%	16%	10%	31%
32. Were you still looking for options?	9%	29%	9%	7%	8%	36%
33. Did the clinic, doctor, or counselor help you to explore your decision?	2%	84%	7%	3%	1%	3%
34. Do you feel their opinions were biased?	23%	6%	3%	3%	7%	59%

If so: ☐ for abortion, or ☐ against abortion
        79%   1%   20% n/a

	N/A or Unsure	Not at All				Very Much
35. Were you adequately informed about the procedure?	4%	49%	17%	15%	10%	6%
36. Were you given information about the biological nature of the fetus?	4%	90%	3%	2%	0%	2%
37. Were you well informed about the procedure and fetus through other sources *before* seeking an abortion?	1%	83%	7%	5%	0%	4%
38. Was your decision made in consultation with your doctor?	2%	70%	4%	5%	6%	14%
39. Were you encouraged to ask questions?	6%	64%	16%	8%	3%	2%
40. Were your questions thoroughly answered to your satisfaction?	19%	52%	12%	8%	4%	4%
41. Do you believe there was information you were not given, or were misinformed about?	8%	10%	1%	4%	4%	73%

If so, what? ——(see Chapter One)

	N/A or Unsure	Not at All				Very Much
42. Were risks and dangers discussed?	7%	65%	16%	5%	4%	4%

43. What *was* your opinion about the nature of the fetus?

    4% no answer   26% human   30% non-human   40% other

What *is* your opinion about the nature of the fetus?   3% no answer   97% human   0% non-human   0% other

ABORTED WOMEN

	N/A or Unsure	Not at All				Very Much
44. If counseling a friend who was in a situation such as yours, would you encourage her to choose an abortion?	1%	98%	0%	0%	0%	1%
45. Was your self-image improved or worsened by your decision? (worsened-1; improved-5)	2%	89%	4%	3%	1%	1%
46. Is your life today better or worse because of your decision? (worse-1; improved-5)	21%	60%	6%	8%	1%	4%
47. Was the period of your pregnancy before the abortion emotionally traumatic?	4%	11%	6%	10%	11%	60%
48. Did you feel in control of your life when making your decision?	3%	65%	8%	9%	6%	10%
49. Did you feel your life was controlled by others?	4%	16%	8%	12%	14%	47%
50. Did the knowledge that abortion was legal influence your opinion about the morality of choosing abortion?	11%	12%	1%	6%	12%	58%
51. Did you consider carrying the pregnancy to term?	5%	19%	12%	15%	12%	38%
52. Did you consider keeping the baby?	6%	23%	10%	13%	10%	49%
53. Did you consider adoption?	4%	62%	13%	7%	6%	8%
54. Under better circumstances, would you have kept the baby?	10%	1%	2%	3%	3%	81%
55. After your abortion, did you hope to have children at a later time?	6%	6%	1%	2%	1%	84%
56. Were there periods when you felt good or excited about your pregnancy?	9%	23%	8%	6%	10%	43%
57. What were your feelings about abortion prior to becoming pregnant? (negative-1; positive-5)	21%	33%	8%	20%	6%	12%
57. What are your feelings about abortion today? (negative-1; positive-5)	1%	98%	1%	0%	0%	0%

336

Planned Parenthood Group

After the overall analysis, survey respondents who received counseling and/or their abortions at Planned Parenthood clinics were sorted out and tabulated separately, as discussed in Chapter One. A total of 53 respondents (21% of all respondents) fell into this subgroup. Their answers to the following questions were selected to provide a comparison of Planned Parenthood services to those of abortion providers as a whole.

1. Were you satisfied with the abortion services you received?	11%	45%	11%	13%	8%	11%
6f. Were you encouraged to have an abortion by (your) abortion counselor?	26%	10%	2%	2%	12%	48%
28. Would your choice have been different if any or all of the above had encouraged you differently?	8%	0%	0%	0%	13%	80%
31. When you went to the clinic or counselor, was your decision to abort already firm?	2%	36%	11%	23%	4%	25%
32. Were you still looking for options?	11%	19%	6%	9%	9%	45%
33. Did the clinic, doctor, or counselor help you to explore your decision?	2%	85%	13%	0%	0%	0%
34. Do you feel their opinions were biased?	19%	4%	2%	4%	6%	66%

If so, ☐ for or ☐ against abortion?
      89% for   0% against   12% no answer

35. Were you adequately informed about the procedure?	2%	43%	15%	23%	11%	6%
36. Were you given information about the biological nature of the fetus?	2%	85%	8%	4%	0%	2%
37. Were you well informed about the procedure and fetus through other sources *before* seeking an abortion?	2%	81%	4%	6%	0%	8%
38. Was your decision made in consultation with your doctor?	2%	89%	2%	2%	0%	6%
39. Were you encouraged to ask questions?	4%	60%	19%	11%	4%	2%
40. Were your questions thoroughly answered to your satisfaction?	17%	53%	11%	13%	2%	4%
41. Do you believe there was information you were not given or were misinformed about?	4%	13%	0%	4%	6%	74%
42. Were risks and dangers discussed?	6%	62%	19%	8%	4%	2%

ONE: *A Survey of Women Who Aborted*

1. Howard and Joy Osofsky, eds., *The Abortion Experience* (New York: Harper and Row Publishers, Inc., 1973), 500–01.
2. Linda Bird Francke, *The Ambivalence of Abortion* (New York: Random House, 1978), 29.
3. U. S. Department of Commerce, *Statistical Abstract of the United States 1984*, 104th Edition, 1983; and Illinois Department of Public Health, "Abortion Data Report to the General Assembly," July 19, 1982.
4. *Statistical Abstract*, 71.
5. Ibid.
6. Ibid.; and Elasah Drogin, *Margaret Sanger: Father of Modern Society* (Coarsegold, CA: CUL Publications, 1980), 31.
7. Germain Grisez, *Abortion: the Myths, the Realities, and the Arguments* (New York: Corpus Books, 1972), 52–54.
8. Francke, *Ambivalence of Abortion*, 46.
9. Ibid.; and IDPH, "Abortion Data Report."
10. Mary K. Zimmerman, *Passage Through Abortion* (New York: Praeger Publishers, 1977), 62–70; and James Tunstead Burtchaell, *Rachel Weeping* (Kansas City: Andrews and McMeel, Inc., 1982), 104.
11. The responses to this question were slightly distorted by the fact that 8 percent of the women surveyed actually did have illegal abortions prior to 1973. Some of these illegal aborters answered this question by saying they would have strongly considered an illegal abortion; others felt this hypothetical question was not applicable to them because abortion was illegal at that time and answered "Unsure."
12. Zimmerman, *Passage Through Abortion*, 62–63.
13. Since 60 percent of those who sought counseling at Planned Parenthood were uncertain about their decision, as compared to about 50 percent of the total sample, it can be concluded that Planned Parenthood clinics are more likely to attract and counsel women who are ambivalent about their decision. This is especially likely since Planned Parenthood specializes in birth control programs targeted at teenagers and low income

women. Women from these groups are especially likely to want the baby, but feel unable to do so and are thus more likely to seek help in finding options through personal counseling. Self-affirmed women, on the other hand, are unlikely to seek any counseling from a family planning clinic, and instead they come to a firm decision on their own and go straight to the abortion clinic.

14. A causal link between abortion and cervical cancer has not yet been verified and is only now being investigated by medical researchers. This 4 percent rate, however, is many times higher than the national average, especially for young and middle-aged women.

15. Ann Saltenberger, *Every Woman Has a Right to Know the Dangers of Legal Abortion* (Glassboro, NJ: Air-Plus Enterprises, 1982), 154–55.

TWO: *Evidence from the Pro-Choice Side*

1. Zimmerman, *Passage Through Abortion*, 42.
2. Ibid.; and Francke, *The Ambivalence of Abortion*, 82. Also see the testimonies of WEBA members Nancyjo Mann (Preface) and Jackie Bakker, pp. 206–10.
3. Zimmerman, *Passage Through Abortion*, 43. For an example of parental pressure on WEBA members, see the story of "Molly Graham", pp. 302–04.
4. Ibid. 78–79.
5. Ibid., 122.
6. Ibid., 110.
7. Ibid., 110–12.
8. Ibid., 122.
9. Ibid., 143.
10. Ibid., 146–47.
11. Ibid., 193.
12. Ibid., 139.
13. Ibid., 129.
14. Ibid., 139.
15. Ibid., 140–41.
16. Ibid., 189–90.
17. Ibid., 69.
18. Ibid., 193.
19. Ibid., 194–95.
20. Ibid., 55 and 150.
21. Ibid., 186.
22. Ibid., 182.
23. Jane Doe, "There Just Wasn't Room in Our Lives Now for Another Baby," *The New York Times*, 14 May 1976, Op-Ed section.

24. Francke, *The Ambivalence of Abortion*, 253–55.
25. Ibid., 11.
26. Ibid., 18.
27. Francke's low grades for factual accuracy are discussed in Burtchaell's *Rachel Weeping*, 53–55.
28. Francke, *Ambivalence of Abortion*, 43.
29. Francke, *Ambivalence of Abortion*, 50, 64, 71, 84, 100, 111, 168, 169, 175, 200, 203, 229.
30. Ibid., 49. 56, 61, 78, 85, 86, 89, 91, 95, 96, 99, 107, 110, 151, 153, 155, 166, 191, 192, 199, 205, 226, 235.
31. Ibid., 49, 65.
32. Ibid., 85.
33. Ibid., 84, 95.
34. Ibid., 167.
35. Ibid., 55–56.
36. Ibid., 49–51, 53, 56–68, 61, 64, 66, 67, 71, 75, 77, 79, 84, 88–91, 94–100, 107–08, 110–12, 152, 155, 167–69, 171, 174, 188, 192–94, 198, 200, 203, 205, 227–28, 231, 235, 238.
37. Ibid., 61.
38. Ibid., 167.
39. Ibid., 74–75.
40. Ibid., 78–81.
41. Ibid., 91.
42. Ibid., 201.
43. Ibid., 63.
44. Ibid., 77.
45. Ibid., 99.
46. Ibid., 101–03.
47. Ibid., 96.
48. Ibid., 93.
49. Ibid., 64.
50. Ibid., 65.
51. Ibid., 63–66.
52. Ibid., 105–06.
53. Ibid., 98 and 103.
54. Ibid., 55–56.
55. Magda Denes, *In Necessity and Sorrow: Life and Death in an Abortion Hospital* (New York: Basic Books, Inc., 1976), xiv.
56. Ibid., 94.
57. Ibid., 97–98.
58. Ibid., 101.
59. Ibid., 122.
60. Ibid., xvii.
61. Ibid., 6.

62. Ibid., 14.
63. Ibid., 50.
64. Ibid., 58–61.
65. Ibid., 126.
66. Ibid., 222–23.
67. Ibid., 240.
68. Ibid., 246.
69. Ibid., 134–35.
70. Ibid., 199.
71. Ibid., 203.
72. Ibid., 191.
73. Ibid., xv.
74. Ibid., 57.
75. Ibid., xv–xvi.
76. The Boston Women's Health Collective, Inc., *Our Bodies, Ourselves* (New York: Simon and Schuster, 1973), 234.
77. Ibid.
78. Ibid., 236.
79. Ibid.
80. Ibid., 236–37.
81. Ibid.
82. Reprinted in "Mother Is The Other Victim Of Abortion," *The National Right to Life News*, 22 December 1983, 10.
83. *Catholics United for Life Bulletin*, March 1982.
84. Reprinted quotes from Dr. Herbert Ratner, "A Baby On Her Mind," *Life and Family News* brochure.
85. See the moving testimony by Audra Stevens, "But Nobody Said Think," *Abortion and Social Justice*, eds. Thomas W. Hilgers and Dennis J. Horan (New York: Sheed and Ward, 1972), 267. See also page 187.
86. Donald Granberg, "The Abortion Activists," *Family Planning Perspectives*, July–August 1981, 157–63.
87. Ibid., 163.
88. Ibid., 161.
89. *Encyclopedia of Associations*, 18th Edition, 1984, 906 and 1105.
90. Granberg, "The Abortion Activists," 161; and *Encyclopedia of Associations*.
91. Francke, *Ambivalence of Abortion*, 48–51. Also see, for example, WEBA member Karen Sullivan's story, pp. 73–77.

THREE: *The Physical Risks of Abortion*

1. See for example the declaration of Esther Pratt that "The brutal consequences of illegal abortion—mutilation, blood poisoning and even

death—have been almost nonexistent in the United States since January 22, 1973, when the Supreme Court ruled. . . ." in "Is An Acorn An Oak Tree?," *The Weekly*, Champaign-Urbana, Illinois, Volume 4, No. 3, 1.

2. Lynn D. Wardle and Mary Anne Wood, *A Lawyer Looks at Abortion* (Provo: Brigham Young University Press, 1982), 122.

3. Robert A. Destro, "Abortion and the Constitution: The Need for a Life-Protective Amendment," *California Law Review*, 1975, Volume 63, 1303 (footnote 274).

4. John and Barbara Willke, *Handbook on Abortion* (Cincinnati: Hayes Publishing Company, Inc., 1979), 78–80, 89. See also Pamela Zekman and Pamela Warrick, "The Abortion Profiteers," *Chicago Sun Times*, special reprint 3 December 1978 (original publication 12 November, 1978). Zekman and Warrick reveal how undercover investigators in abortion clinics found that clinic employees routinely checked off "no complications" before the abortion was even performed.

5. Ann Saltenberger, *Every Woman Has a Right to Know the Dangers of Legal Abortion* (Glassboro, N.J.: Air-Plus Enterprises, 1982), 19.

6. Ibid.; Willke, *Handbook on Abortion*, 78–79; and Thomas Hilgers, Dennis Horan, and David Mall, *New Perspectives on Human Abortion* (Frederick, Md.: University Publications of America, 1981), 145–50.

7. Magaret Wynn and Arthur Wynn, "Some Consequences of Induced Abortion to Children Born Subsequently," Foundation for Education and Research in Child Bearing, London 1972, reprinted in *Marriage and Family Newsletter*, vol. 4, nos. 2–4, February, March, April 1973, Collegeville, Mn., 8–9.

8. Willke, *Handbook on Abortion*, 78, 80, 86.

9. Hilgers, et al., *New Perspectives on Human Abortion*, 147.

10. Wynn, "Some Consequences," 17.

11. D. A. Grimes and W. Cates, Jr., "Abortion: Methods and Complications," *Human Reproduction*, 2nd ed., 796–813.

12. Willke, *Handbook on Abortion*, 29.

13. A 1971 German study of 1,234 abortions reported an "early complication" rate of 12.2 percent, cited in Wynn, "Some Consequences," 17. Another study of 2,498 vacuum abortions found 285 incidents of obvious post-abortion complications either immediately after the procedure or at an eight-week follow-up exam, yielding a "early complication" rate of 11.4 percent. (Edelman, Brenner, and Berger, "Abortion by Aspiration versus Curettage," *American Journal of Obstetrics and Gynecology*, 15 June 1974, vol. 119, no. 4, p. 476.)

14. See Wardle and Wood, *A Lawyer Looks At Abortion*, 112–13, for statistics and a comparison of the morbidity and natural childbirth definitions.

15. Wynn, "Some Consequences," 20.

16. Saltenberger, *Every Woman*, general.

17. Ibid. For accounts of incomplete abortions, see the stories of WEBA members Cathe Birtwell (32–36); Debbie "Nelson" (210–12); and Monica Harshbarger (157–60). For an account of an incomplete abortion which necessitated a lifesaving hysterectomy, see the story of WEBA member Debbie "Nelson" (210–12). For an account of an incomplete abortion which resulted in later fertility and childbirth problems, see the story of WEBA member Monica Harshbarger (157–60).
18. Ibid., 30–32.
19. See Saltenberger, *Every Woman*, and Grimes and Cates, "Abortion: Methods and Complications." Also see the story of WEBA member "Vanessa Landry" (276–78).
20. Wardle and Wood, *A Lawyer Looks At Abortion*, 114.
21. See Saltenberger, *Every Woman*, in general; WEBA brochure "Before You Make the Decision"; and the Profile sections of this book.
22. Saltenberger, *Every Woman*, 84, 180–81.
23. Wynn, "Some Consequences," 20.
24. Grimes and Cates, "Abortion: Methods and Complications," 810.
25. Willke, *Handbook on Abortion*, 31.
26. Hilgers and Horan, *Abortion and Social Justice*, 292.
27. Ibid.
28. Saltenberger, *Every Woman*, 33.
29. Wardle and Wood, *A Lawyer Looks At Abortion*, 123.
30. See Saltenberger, *Every Woman*, 81. Also see the story of WEBA member Jackie Bakker (206–10).
31. Saltenberger, *Every Woman*, 36.
32. Ibid. in general; and Wardle and Wood, *A Lawyer Looks At Abortion*, 115.
33. Bernard Nathanson, M.D., with Richard Ostling, *Aborting America* (Garden City, New York: Doubleday and Company, Inc., 1979), 276.
34. Liz Jeffries and Rick Edmonds, "Abortion: The Dreaded Complication," *The Philadelphia Inquirer*, 2 August 1981.
35. Thomas J. Marzen, "The Supreme Court on Abortion: Doctor Knows Best," *The National Right to Life News*, 30 June 1983, 15.
36. "The Doctor's Dilemma—When Abortion Gives Birth to Life," *Chicago Tribune*, 15 August 1982, Section 12.
37. Jeffries and Edmonds, "Abortion: The Dreaded Complication."
38. See Franke, *Ambivalence of Abortion*, 34, for an example of a physician's refusal to treat a live-born aborted fetus. He commented, "That's not a baby. That's an abortion."
39. Mike Masterson, "Baby Survives Abortion in Arkansas," *The National Right to Life News*, 4 August 1983, 6.
40. Jeffries and Edmonds, "Abortion: The Dreaded Complication."
41. Ibid.
42. Gretchen Kaiser, "Abortion Technique Injects Digitoxin into Baby's

Heart," *The National Right to Life News*, 13 September 1984, 1. See also Saltenberger, *Every Woman*, 192.

43. See Dr. Thomas Hilgers' "The Medical Hazards of Legally Induced Abortion," in Hilgers and Horan, *Abortion and Social Justice*, 69. See also Saltenberger, *Every Woman*, 75.

44. Willke, *Handbook on Abortion*, 53-54. For accounts of abortion-caused infections which resulted in fertility and childbirth problems, see the stories of WEBA members Gayle "Hayes" (36–40); Deborah Hulebak (81–88); and Monica Harshbarger (157–60). For accounts of abortion-caused infections which necessitated lifesaving hysterectomies, see the stories of WEBA members Carolyn Walton (144–47); Debbie "Nelson" (210–12); and Jackie Bakker (206–10).

45. See Saltenberger, *Every Woman*. See also "Ectopic Pregnancies Increasing," *The National Right to Life News*, 16 August 1984, 4 (from a health report printed in the *New York Times*).

46. Dr. and Mrs. J. C. Willke, *Abortion: Questions and Answers* (Cincinnati, Ohio: Hayes Publishing Company, Inc., 1985), 104, citing U.S. Dept. H.H.S. *Morbidity and Mortality Weekly Report*, April 20, 1984.

47. Hilgers and Horan, *Abortion and Social Justice*, 73.

48. Willke, *Questions and Answers*, 103, citing the *British Journal of OB/GYN*, August 1976.

49. Wynn, "Some Consequences," 7.

50. Willke, *Questions and Answers*, 91.

51. Willke, *Handbook on Abortion*, 92.

52. Saltenberger, *Every Woman*, 177; see also the profile story of Deborah Hulebak (81–88).

53. Willke, *Handbook on Abortion*, 94.

54. Hilgers and Horan, *Abortion and Social Justice*, 70.

55. Wynn, "Some Consequences," 5; Willke, *Questions and Answers*, 105–06.

56. Hilgers, et al., *New Perspectives on Human Abortion*, 128–33.

57. Saltenberger, *Every Woman*, 182; Willke, *Questions and Answers*, 109.

58. Willke, *Questions and Answers*, 107.

59. Wynn, "Some Consequences," 18.

60. Willke, *Questions and Answers*, 118.

61. Ibid., 107; Wynn, "Some Consequences," 15.

62. *Science*, vol. 215, 1589.

63. For personal testimonies revealing the high incidence of cervical cancer among aborted women, see the stories of WEBA members Carol St. Amour (77–81) and Lorijo Nerad (273–76).

64. Willke, *Questions and Answers*, 97–98.

65. Ibid., 193.

66. Hilgers, et al., *New Perspectives on Human Abortion*, 92–123.

67. Willke, *Handbook on Abortion*, 96.
68. Ibid., 97; and Hilgers and Horan, *Abortion and Social Justice*, 69.
69. Wynn, "Some Consequences," 17.
70. Ibid., 7.
71. Hilgers, et al., *New Perspectives on Human Abortion*, 94 and 112; and Saltenberger, *Every Woman*, 175.
72. Willke, *Handbook on Abortion*, 89–90.
73. Ibid., 93.
74. Wardle and Wood, *A Lawyer Looks At Abortion*, 112.
75. The 70 percent complication rate was found in an Australian study cited in testimony by Pat Goltz, International President, Feminists for Life, Inc., before the Senate Subcommittee on Constitutional Amendments, 21 August 1974.
76. See U.S. Supreme Court Decisions *Akron v. Akron Center for Reproductive Health*, 1983 and *Thornburg v. ACOG*, 1986.
77. Willke, *Handbook on Abortion*, 96; and Hilgers and Horan, *Abortion and Social Justice*, 69–70.
78. Saltenberger, *Every Woman*, 189.
79. Ibid., 27.
80. Zekman and Warrick, "The Abortion Profiteers."
81. See Willke, *Handbook on Abortion*, 81–82. See also Hilgers, "Medical Hazards of Abortion," *Abortion and Social Justice*, 61.
82. Destro, "Abortion and the Constitution," 1303 (footnote 274).
83. Willke, *Handbook on Abortion*, 78.
84. Saltenberger, *Every Woman*, 51.
85. Willke, *Handbook on Abortion*, 80.
86. Ibid. This ten percent rate fits with the discrepancy in the reported mortality rates from the New York experience. See Hilgers, "Medical Hazards of Abortion," *Abortion and Social Justice*, and Willke, *Questions and Answers*, 98–99.
87. Saltenberger, *Every Woman*, 52.
88. Hilgers, et al., *New Perspectives on Human Abortion*, 82.
89. Andrew M. Kaunitz, M.D., et al., "Causes of Maternal Mortality in the United States," *Obstetrics and Gynecology*, May 1985, vol. 65, no. 5, 607. It is noteworthy that this listing of abortion deaths excludes indirect deaths resulting from embolism, obstetric hemorrhage, obstetric infection, anesthesia complications, and deaths from ectopic or other pregnancies complicated as a result of a previous abortion. Deaths from these cases were listed under other maternal mortality categories even though they might more appropriately be apportioned under abortion-related deaths.
90. Saltenberger, *Every Woman*, 32.
91. Ibid., 40.

92. Saltenberger, *Every Woman*, pamphlet edition.
93. Frances Frech, "Comparing the Figures," *The Human Life Review*, Fall 1982, vol. VIII, no. 4, 72.
94. Hilgers, "Medical Hazards of Abortion," *Abortion and Social Justice*, 63.
95. Ibid., 61.
96. Ibid.
97. Ibid.
98. Hilgers, et al., *New Perspectives on Human Abortion*, 82-83.
99. Frech, "Comparing the figures," 62.
100. Willke, *Handbook on Abortion*, 87.
101. Ibid.
102. Frech, "Comparing the Figures," 69–72, and Hilgers, et al., *New Perspectives on Human Abortion*, 69–91. Also, it should be noted that spontaneous miscarriage is the only natural phenomenon which is truly comparable to induced abortion. When this comparison is made, the maternal mortality rate for induced abortion is found to be two to five times greater than the maternal death rate for miscarriage during all stages of gestation. See Robert G. Marshall, "Spontaneous Abortion Deaths," *A.L.L. About Issues*, Sept. 1985, vol. 7, no. 9, 49.
103. "Is Abortion Safer Than Childbirth?", *The National Right to Life News*, 3 February 1983.
104. It is reported that there is only a 2 percent morbidity rate for childbirth, (Wardle and Wood, *A Lawyer Looks at Abortion*, 112) as compared to abortion morbidity rates which are commonly reported to be in the 20 to 40 percent range.
105. Wynn, "Some Consequences," in general.

FOUR: *The Psychological Impact of Abortion*

1. Howard Fisher, "Abortion—Pain or Pleasure?", *The Psychological Aspects of Abortion*, 51.
2. Hilgers, "Medical Hazards of Abortion," *Abortion and Social Justice*, 77, referring to studies by Fleck and Kummer.
3. Saltenberger, *Every Woman*, 136.
4. Hilgers, et al., *New Perspectives on Human Abortion*, 153.
5. Willke, *Handbook on Abortion*, 54.
6. Saltenberger, *Every Woman*, 138.
7. Ibid., 145.
8. Francke, *Ambivalence of Abortion*, 253.
9. Ibid., 254.
10. Saltenberger, *Every Woman*, 165–66.
11. Osofsky, *The Abortion Experience*, 199–200.
12. Saltenberger, *Every Woman*, 154–55.

13. For example, when testifying before a Senate Subcommittee, abortionist and pro-choice advocate Dr. Richard Berkowitz admitted that of the hundreds of patients he has seen who have had abortions the "overwhelming majority" had "tremendous deep-seated psychological reactions. . . . They have a very real awareness of the fact that there was a little, recognizable human being inside of them." Debra Braun, "Unborn Children Can Feel Pain, Senate Subcommittee Told," *NRL News*, 30 May 1985, 8. See also Francke, *Ambivalence of Abortion*, 11 and 47.

14. Dr. Monte Harris Liebman and Jolie Siebold Zimmer, "The Psychological Sequelae of Abortion: Fact and Fallacy," in David Mall and Dr. Walter Watts, eds., *The Psychological Aspects of Abortion* (Washington, D.C.: University Publications of America, 1979), 127.

15. Willke, *Handbook on Abortion*, 51.

16. Saltenberger, *Every Woman*, 141.

17. Ibid., 145.

18. Ibid., citing Kent et al., 136, 138, and 140.

19. Dr. Philip G. Ney, "Infant Abortion and Child Abuse: Cause and Effect," *The Psychological Aspects of Abortion*, 29. For an example of abortion as an aggravation of psychological problems, see the testimony of WEBA member "Tammy Conrad" (179–82).

20. Saltenberger, *Every Woman*, 140.

21. Ibid., 138–39.

22. Ibid., 136.

23. Ibid., 146.

24. Lawrence Lader, *Abortion* (New York: Bobbs-Merrill Company Inc., 1966), 21.

25. Francke, *Ambivalence of Abortion*, 32.

26. Zimmerman, *Passage Through Abortion*, 69.

27. Burtchaell, *Rachel Weeping*, 104.

28. Francke, *Ambivalence of Abortion*, 63.

29. Liebman and Zimmer, "Psychological Sequelae of Abortion," 133.

30. Francke, *Ambivalence of Abortion*, 99.

31. Liebman and Zimmer, "Psychological Sequelae of Abortion," 131.

32. Willke, *Handbook on Abortion*, 51.

33. Burtchaell, *Rachel Weeping*, 104–05.

34. Saltenberger, *Every Woman*, 140.

35. Francke, *Ambivalence of Abortion*, 47–48.

36. Liebman and Zimmer, "Psychological Sequelae of Abortion," 132. Also, for accounts of such resentment by aborted women toward their spouses or boyfriends, see the stories of Cathe Birtwell (32–36); Carol St. Amour (77–81); Deborah Hulebak (81–88); and Alice Gilmore (147–50).

37. Francke, *Ambivalence of Abortion*, 53, 130–32, 165–70
38. Ibid., 116. For accounts of such resentment of boyfriends or husbands toward the aborting woman, see the profile stories for "Sarah Logsdon" (185–87); "Molly Graham" (302–04); and Donna Merrick (151–57).
39. For example, see Nathanson, *Aborting America*, 14–15.
40. See Francke, *Ambivalence of Abortion*, 53–54, 61–62, 65, and 116–47. See also Arthur B. Shostak and Gary McLouth, *Men and Abortion: Lessons, Losses, and Love* (New York: Praeger Publishers, 1984), in general. This book is definitely pro-choice in perspective yet confirms most of the conclusions drawn in this book, and specifically focuses on ambivalence and doubts of men. Like Francke's and Zimmerman's books, *Men and Abortion* has a very limited, short-term perspective on abortion reactions, but is nonetheless very instructive.
41. Ibid., 107.
42. See Ibid., 105 and 110 for examples.
43. Ibid., 108. For examples among WEBA members, see the testimonies of Carol St. Amour (77–81); "Sarah Logsdon" (185–87); and Alice Gilmore (147–50).
44. Saltenberger, *Every Woman*, 131. For an example among WEBA women, see Jerri "Porter" (278–80).
45. Ibid., 131 and 138. See also Francke, *Ambivalence of Abortion*, 116.
46. Fisher, "Abortion—Pain or Pleasure?," 48. For accounts of promiscuity see Ila Ryan (305–10), and Donna Merrick (151–57). For examples of intentional "replacement" pregnancies, see the stories of Jerri "Porter" (278–80); Jackie Bakker (206–10); and Karen Sullivan (73–77). For a cycle of repeat pregnancies and abortions, see the story of Deborah Hulebak (81–88).
47. Grisez, *Abortion: Myths, Realities, and Arguments*, 79.
48. Liebman and Zimmer, "Psychological Sequelae of Abortion," 133.
49. Ibid., 132.
50. Ibid., 133.
51. Ibid., 132.
52. Quoted by Dr. Monte Harris Liebman of the Pregnancy Aftermath Helpline, *Medical Tribune*, 26 August 1981.
53. Saltenberger, *Every Woman*, 137–38.
54. Dr. Conrad Baars, "Psychic Causes and Consequences of the Abortion Mentality," *The Psychological Aspects of Abortion*, 122.
55. Ibid., 125.
56. Ibid., 122–23.
57. Saltenberger, *Every Woman*, 139 and 155.
58. Ibid., 153. For examples of self-destructive behavior, see the testimonies of Cathe Birtwell (32–36), Carol St. Amour (77–81), Carolyn Walton (144–47), Gayle "Hayes" (36–40), Deborah Hulebak (81–88),

Lorijo Nerad (273–76), "Tammy Conrad" (179–82), Martha Wenger (182–84), and Donna Merrick (151–57).

59. Fisher, "Abortion—Pain or Pleasure?", 48–50.

60. Saltenberger, *Every Woman*, 132. Also, Greenglass, "Therapeutic Abortion and Psychiatric Disturbance in Canadian Women," 21 *Can. Psychiatric A. J.* 45 (1976) found a 3 percent suicide rate. For examples of suicide attempts among WEBA members see the stories of Carolyn Walton (144–47), Gayle "Hayes" (36–40), "Tammy Conrad" (179–82), and Ila Ryan (305–10).

61. Overduin and Fleming, *Life in a Test-Tube*, 1982, 144.

62. Debra Braun, "Woman Kills 3-Year-Old Son One Day After Obtaining Abortion," *The National Right to Life News*, 13 October 1983, 12.

63. Liebman and Zimmer, "Psychological Sequelae of Abortion," 132–34.

64. Ibid, 134.

65. Ibid, 135.

66. Ibid.

67. Ibid.

68. Ibid., 132.

69. Saltenberger, *Every Woman*, 153.

70. Dr. Myre Sim and Dr. Robert Neisser, "Post-Abortive Psychoses: A Report from Two Centers," *The Psychological Aspects of Abortion*, 1–13.

71. Saltenberger, *Every Woman*, 146.

72. Ibid., 160.

73. Wardle and Wood, *A Lawyer Looks At Abortion*, 117.

74. Ibid.

75. Saltenberger, *Every Woman*, 152.

76. Baars, "Psychic Causes and Consequences of Abortion Mentality," 122.

77. Hilgers, et al., *New Perspectives on Human Abortion*, 478–80.

78. Regis Walling, "When Pregnancy Is A Problem," *The National Right to Life News*, 12 January 1984, 1.

79. Hilgers, et al., *New Perspectives on Human Abortion*, 479.

80. Ibid.

81. *Newsweek*, 31 October 1983, 86.

82. See "*In A Different Voice* by Carol Gilligan," book review by Dr. Wanda Franz, *NRL News*, 24 November 1983, 11; and *NRL News* special supplement, "Carol Gilligan and 'The Victims of Caring' ", 23 February 1984.

83. Fisher, "Abortion—Pain or Pleasure?" 48.

84. Mall and Watts, *The Psychological Aspects of Abortion*, xi.

85. Ibid., xi–xii.

86. Dr. Thomas Hilgers, Marjory Mecklenburg, and Gayle Riordan, "Is Abortion The Best We Have To Offer? A Challenge to the Aborting Society," *Abortion and Social Justice*, 179.

87. Saltenberger, *Every Woman*, 146. Also, Pare and Ravin, "Follow-up of Patients Referred for Termination of Pregnancy," *Lancet*, 28 March 1970, 635.

88. Baars, "Psychic Causes and Consequences of Abortion Mentality," 119–20.

89. Ibid, 118–20.

90. Zimmerman, *Passage Through Abortion*, 186.

91. Editorial by Dana Tueth Motley of the Abortion Rights Coalition, *Daily Illini*, University of Illinois at Champaign-Urbana, 9 February 1982, 17.

92. Franz, *NRL News*, 24 November 1983, 11; and "Carol Gilligan" supplement, *NRL News*, 23 February 1984.

93. Saltenberger, *Every Woman*, 154; and Hilgers, "Medical Hazards of Abortion," *Abortion and Social Justice*, 76. See also testimony of Dr. Richard Berkowitz, reported by Braun, *NRL News*, 30 May 1985, 8.

FIVE: *The "Hard" Cases*

1. United States Supreme Court, *Roe v. Wade*, *U.S. Reports*, October 1972, 164–66.

2. What the Court upheld was not the woman's choice per se, but the physician's freedom to treat his patient in whatever way he saw fit. Only the woman's own doctor, the Court insisted, is qualified to determine her "health needs." Therefore, state governments may not forbid any surgery (including abortion) which the doctor deems necessary to preserve her "health." In fact the Court placed little or no emphasis on the woman's choice, but instead insisted that the final decision "is inherently, and primarily, a medical decision, and basic responsibility for it must rest with the physician." (*Roe*, at 166.)

  Thus, it was not woman's rights which the Court upheld, it was doctor's rights. States are simply not allowed to second-guess a physician's "professional judgment" on such a sensitive matter as abortion.

3. See *Akron* and *Thornburg*.

4. Saltenberger, *Every Woman*, 44–45. See also Hilgers, et al., *New Perspectives on Human Abortion*, 140–41.

4a. Saltenberger, *Every Woman*, 44.

5. Burtchaell, *Rachel Weeping*, 67.

6. See Willke, *Handbook on Abortion*, 34.

7. Grisez, *Abortion: Myths, Realities, and Arguments*, 73–77; Nathanson, *Aborting America*, 240–49; and Hilgers and Horan, *Abortion and Social Justice*, 38.

8. For example, see Nathanson, *Aborting America*.

9. Grisez, *Abortion: Myths, Realities, and Arguments*, 75.

10. Hilgers, et al., *New Perspectives on Human Abortion*, 121.

11. See Nathanson, *Aborting America*, 37–45. Also see the testimony of Linda Viewegh in Milton Rockmore's "Are You Sorry You Had An Abortion?," *Good Housekeeping*, July 1977, vol. 185, 120.
12. Burtchaell, *Rachel Weeping*, 68.
13. IDPH, "Abortion Data Report."
14. Grisez, *Abortion: Myths, Realities, and Arguments*, 81–82.
15. Burtchaell, *Rachel Weeping*, 69.
16. Ibid.
17. Ibid.
18. Mall and Watts, *The Psychological Aspects of Abortiion*, ix.
19. Lawrence Lader, *Abortion* (New York: Bobbs-Merrill Company, 1966), 22; Sim and Neisser, "Post-Abortive Psychoses," 8; and Burtchaell, *Rachel Weeping*, 69–70.
20. Grisez, *Abortion: Myths, Realities, and Arguments*, 79.
21. Hilgers and Horan, *Abortion and Social Justice*, 40.
22. Grisez, *Abortion: Myths, Realities, and Arguments*, 79; and Hilgers, et al., *New Perspectives on Human Abortion*, 156.
23. Hilgers and Horan, *Abortion and Social Justice*, 40.
24. Grisez, *Abortion: Myths, Realities, and Arguments*, 79.
25. Sim and Neisser, "Post-Abortive Psychoses," 12.
26. Saltenberger, *Every Woman*, 132.
27. Ibid., 48; and Destro, "Abortion and the Constitution," 1301 (footnote 264).
28. Willke, *Handbook on Abortion*, 52.
29. Hilgers and Horan, *Abortion, and Social Justice*, 40.
30. Willke, *Handbook on Abortion*, 52.
31. Saltenberger, *Every Woman*, 134. See also Baars, "Psychic Causes and Consequences of Abortion Mentality," 123; Burtchaell, *Rachel Weeping*, 70; and Grisez, *Abortion: Myths, Realities and Arguments*, 80.
32. Grisez, *Abortion: Myths, Realities, and Arguments*, 81.
33. Saltenberger, *Every Woman*, 134–35.
34. Hilgers, et al., *New Perspectives on Human Abortion*, 54.
35. Ibid., 51–52.
36. Ibid., 443.
37. Ibid., 50
38. See the letter by Dr. Hymie Gordon on amniocentesis in *Primum Non Nocere*, the newsletter published by The World Federation of Doctors Who Respect Human Life, September 1980, 4–6.
39. Hilgers, et al., *New Perspectives on Human Abortion*, 54.
40. The use of ultrasound reduces the risk of accidentally puncturing the child with the amniotic needle, but it also reduces the chance of a successful test. According to one study of 65 amniotic fluid specimens taken from patients who had been exposed to ultrasound, 35 failed to

grow in culture media. See Robert S. Mendelsohn, *MalePractice: How Doctors Manipulate Women*, (Chicago: Contemporary Books, 1981), 164.
41. Hilgers, et al., *New Perspectives on Human Abortion*, 49.
42. Gordon, "Amniocentesis." 5–6.
43. Hilgers, et al., *New Perspectives on Human Abortion*, 55.
44. Gordon, "Amniocentesis," 4–6.
45. Rayna Rapp, "The Ethics of Choice," *MS. Magazine*, April 1984, 97.
46. Hilgers and Horan, *Abortion and Social Justice*, 14–19.
47. Since the legalization of abortion in 1973, court rulings have placed physicians under even greater pressure to urge the testing for and abortion of handicapped babies. Today, a physician who fails to recommend amniocentesis and abortion may face the risk of a "wrongful life" malpractice suit in which parents hold him or her responsible for the costs of raising a handicapped child which they could have aborted. This legal and financial pressure is forcing many physicians who are not biased against the handicapped for eugenic reasons to join in the movement toward aborting handicapped infants. See Leonard Nelson, ed., *The Death Decision* (Ann Arbor, Mich.: Servant Books, 1984), 57–68.
48. Saltenberger, *Every Woman*, 137.
49. Ibid., 142–43.
50. Gordon, "Amniocentesis," 4–6.
51. Ibid.
52. Wilke, *Handbook on Abortion*, 117.
53. Susan Austin, "The Aborting Community," *The Human Life Review*, Fall 1982, vol. III, no. 4, 61.

CHAPTER SIX: *Hostages of Rape, Victims of Abortion*

1. Mary Meehan, "Accepting the Unjust," *National Catholic Register*, 18 April 1982, citing questions and testimony with respect to *Doe v. Bolton*.
2. Hilgers, et al., *New Perspectives on Human Abortion*, 182.
3. Sandra Kathleen Mahkorn, "Pregnancy and Sexual Assault," *The Psychological Aspects of Abortion*, 55.
4. Hilgers, et al., *New Perspectives on Human Abortion*, 188.
5. Ibid., 189.
6. Mahkorn, "Pregnancy and Sexual Assault," 56.
7. Hilgers and Horan, *Abortion and Social Justice*, 49. Also see "Rape, Incest, and Abortion," pamphlet published by Decatur, Illinois Right to Life, 2.
8. Ibid.
9. Mahkorn, "Pregnancy and Sexual Assault," 56.
10. See "Life or Death," a publication of the Hayes Publishing Company, citing *The Educator*, September 1970.

11. Hilgers, et al., *New Perspectives on Human Abortion*, 190.
12. Ibid., 191.
13. Ibid., 182.
14. Ibid., 183.
15. Ibid., 185.
16. Mahkorn, "Pregnancy and Sexual Assault," 66.
17. It is likely that many "rape" pregnancies are in fact the result of sexual intercourse between women and their husbands or boyfriends which occurred shortly before the attack. Though the child in such cases is not actually the "rapist's," the victim's genuine belief that it is, or may be, causes the same psychological distress as would be faced in any true rape pregnancy. Because such cases are psychologically and emotionally indistinguishable, the need for compassionate treatment is still imperative. See Mahkorn, 65.
18. Mary Meehan, "Accepting the Unjust," a brochure reprinted from *The National Catholic Register,* 18 April 1982.
19. Mahkorn, "Pregnancy and Sexual Assault," 53.
20. Ibid., 53–72. See also Hilgers, et al., *New Perspectives on Human Abortion,* 182–98.
21. Mahkorn, "Pregnancy and Sexual Assault," 58–59.
22. Hilgers, et al., *New Perspectives on Human Abortion,* 194.
23. Mahkorn, "Pregnancy and Sexual Assault," 65–69.
24. Hilgers, et al., *New Perspectives on Human Abortion,* 193.
25. Meehan, "Accepting the Unjust."
26. For examples of the triumphant attitudes of women who delivered children conceived by rape, see John Powell, *Abortion: The Silent Holocaust* (Allen, Tex.: Argus Communications, 1981), 122.
27. See Meehan's "Accepting the Unjust"; and Meehan's "Facing the Hard Cases," *The Human Life Review,* Summer 1983, 24.
28. Dr. George Maloof, "The Consequences of Incest: Giving and Taking Life," *The Psychological Aspects of Abortion,* 84–85. Dr. Maloof's article, pages 73–110, is the primary source for all information used in this section on incest.
29. Meehan, "Facing the Hard Cases," 25.
30. Ibid.
31. Maloof, "The Consequences of Incest," 76.
32. Ibid., 73–83. Also, it is worth noting that the desire for parental attention is also a factor which accounts for many non-incestuous teenage pregnancies. First, many teenagers use sexual activity as a warning flag to attract parental concern. But many parents fail to see that the teenagers' promiscuity is actually an appeal for greater parental involvement and even discipline. So instead the parents tolerate or even condone the sexual activity by simply telling the teen to "be careful." This response simply drives the daughter (or son) to even more outrageous conduct.

Frequently, pregnancy is seen as the last taboo—it is one thing the parents can't ignore. So the daughter subconciously seeks to become pregnant in order to finally arouse her parents and force them to see her life and be a part of it. (Maloof, 73) The victim of incest, also seeking a true parental care and concern, thinks and acts similarly.

33. Ibid., 81.
34. Ibid., 84.
35. Ibid., 75.
36. Ibid., 89.
37. Ibid., 81.
38. Hilgers and Horan, *Abortion and Social Justice*, 50.
39. Maloof, "The Consequences of Incest," 82 and 99.
40. Ibid., 99–101.
41. Grisez, *Abortion: Myths, Realities, and Arguments*, 86.

SEVEN: *The Impact of Abortion on Later Children*

1. D. C. Reardon, "An Estimate of the Number of Maternal and Infant Deaths Resulting From Latent Abortion Morbidity," unpublished. The methodology and some of the sources used to reach this estimate are briefly described in the following footnotes.

2. See Chapter Four, and also: Richardson and Dixon, "Effects of legal termination on subsequent pregnancy," *British Medical Journal*, 29 May 1976, 1303–4; Wynn, "Some Consequences of Induced Abortion," op. cit.; Lembrych, "Fertility Problems Following an Aborted First Pregnancy," *New Perspectives on Human Abortion;* Iffy, "Perinatal Statistics," *New Perspectives;* V. Logrillo, "Effect of Induced Abortion on Subsequent Reproductive Function," N.Y. State Dept. of Health, Contract #1-HD-6-2802, 1975-78.

3. From the studies mentioned above it can be conservatively estimated that for every 100,000 confirmed pregnancies among previously aborted women, there will be 1,200 ectopic pregnancies, 4,300 first trimester miscarriages, 8,500 second trimester miscarriages, 13,700 premature births resulting in 221 infant deaths, and 13,000 complications of labor resulting in 108 infant deaths, for a total loss of 14,329 wanted infants per 100,000 pregnancy attempts. In contrast, for a control group of 100,000 non-aborted women with confirmed pregnancies, one would expect only 400 ectopic pregnancies, 1,400 first trimester miscarriages, 1,400 second trimester miscarriages, 5,200 premature births resulting in 84 infant deaths, and 4,300 complications of labor resulting in 36 infant deaths, or a total overall loss of 3,320 wanted babies.

4. Richardson and Dixon, "Effects of legal termination," op. cit.
5. Reardon, "An Estimate of Maternal and Infant Deaths", op. cit.
6. Ibid.

7. Wynn, "Some Consequences," 7.
8. Andrea E. Hellegers, "Abortion: A Help or Hindrance to Public Health?", Testimony to the Senate Judiciary Subcommittee on Constitutional Amendments, 25 April 1974. Also see Saltenberger, *Every Woman*, 179.
9. Wynn, "Some Consequences," 6.
10. Burtchaell, *Rachel Weeping*, 75–77; Saltenberger, *Every Woman*, 135; Hilgers et al., "Is Abortion the Best We Have to Offer?", *Abortion and Social Justice*, 181; and Willke, *Handbook on Abortion*, 58–59.
11. Willke, *Handbook on Abortion*, 61.
12. Ibid.
13. Burtchaell, *Rachel Weeping*, 80–81.
14. Ibid., 81.
15. Willke, *Handbook on Abortion*, 60.
16. Ney, "Abortion and Child Abuse," 25.
17. Ibid., 33. Also see Braun, "Woman Kills 3-Year-Old Son One Day After Obtaining Abortion," (see Chap. 5, n. 64), 12.
18. Burtchaell, *Rachel Weeping*, 79.
19. Ibid., see quotes on 77–78. See also Ney, "Abortion and Child Abuse," 29–32.
20. Ney, "Abortion and Child Abuse," 30.
21. Ibid., 29–30.
22. Burtchaell, *Rachel Weeping*, 77–78.
23. Ney, "Abortion and Child Abuse," 28–29.
24. Ibid., 34.
25. Hilgers, "Medical Hazards of Abortion," *Abortion and Social Justice*, 76.
26. Leslie Bond, "The Surviving Sibling: Another Victim of Abortion," *NRL News*, 25 September 1986, 11.

EIGHT: *Business Before Medicine*

1. Wardle and Wood, *A Lawyer Looks At Abortion*, 159; Willke, *Handbook on Abortion*, 99; and *The Village Voice*, 1 March 1983.
2. Wardle and Wood, *A Lawyer Looks At Abortion*, 120–25.
3. See the U.S. Supreme Court decisions, *Akron v. Akron Center for Reproductive Health*, 1983, and *Thornburg v. ACOG* 1986; also Willke, *Handbook on Abortion*, 99.
4. Willke, *Handbook on Abortion*, 99.
5. Ibid., 98.
6. Zekman and Warrick, "Abortion Profiteers."
7. Ibid., 12.
8. *Catholics United for Life Newsletter*, October 1981.
9. Zekman and Warrick, "Abortion Profiteers," 8.

10. Willke, *Handbook on Abortion*, 100.
11. Zekman and Warrick, "Abortion Profiteers"; and Denes, *In Necessity and Sorrow*.
12. Zekman and Warrick, "Abortion Profiteers"; and Saltenberger, *Every Woman*, 170–71.
13. Willke, *Handbook on Abortion*, 100; Zekman and Warrick, "Abortion Profiteers," 16–18.
14. Zekman and Warrick, "Abortion Profiteers," 19.
15. Saltenberger, *Every Woman*, 161.
16. Zekman and Warrick, "Abortion Profiteers," 15.
17. Willke, *Handbook on Abortion*, 99.
18. Ibid., 100; Saltenberger, *Every Woman*, 180–81; and Zekman and Warrick, "Abortion Profiteers."
19. Willke, *Handbook on Abortion*, 100.
20. Zekman and Warrick, "Abortion Profiteers," 14–16.
21. Ibid.; and Denes, *In Necessity and Sorrow*, 236.
22. Saltenberger, *Every Woman*, 170.
23. Zekman and Warrick, "Abortion Profiteers," 12.
24. Ibid., 6; and Nathanson, *Aborting America*, 112–13.
25. Zekman and Warrick, "Abortion Profiteers," 3.
26. Ibid., 9; and Denes, *In Necessity and Sorrow*, 226.
27. Willke, *Handbook on Abortion*, 102.
28. Ibid., 101; Zekman and Warrick, "Abortion Profiteers."
29. *Catholics United for Life Newsletter*, October 1981.
30. Donald DeMarco, "The Family at Bay," *The Human Life Review*, vol. VIII, no. 4, Fall 1982, 44–54.
31. Zekman and Warrick, "Abortion Profiteers," 32.
32. Paul Marx, *The Death Peddlers: War on the Unborn* (Collegeville, Minn.: St. John's University Press, 1971), 124.
33. Ibid., 142.
34. Ibid.
35. Wardle and Wood, *A Lawyer Looks At Abortion*, 120–24; and Thomas J. Marzen, "The Supreme Court on Abortion: Doctor Knows Best," *The National Right to Life News*, 30 June 1983, 15.
36. Willke, *Handbook on Abortion*, 101.
37. John Noonan, Jr., "The Akron Case," *The Human Life Review*, vol. IX, no. 3, Summer 1983, 8.
38. Wardle and Wood, *A Lawyer Looks At Abortion*, 110.
39. Willke, *Handbook on Abortion*, 102–03.
40. Zekman and Warrick, "Abortion Profiteers," 11–15.
41. Denes, *In Necessity and Sorrow*, 211–24 and 236.
42. Zekman and Warrick, "Abortion Profiteers," 12–13.
43. Mary Arnold, "Abortion Burnout," *Catholic Twin Circle*, 5 August 1984, 3–4; Denes, *In Necessity and Sorrow*; and the stories of WEBA members

Carol St. Amour (77–81); Alice Gilmore (147–50); Donna Merrick (151–57).

44. Hilgers and Horan, *Abortion and Social Justice*, 69–70; and Willke, *Handbook on Abortion*, 103.
45. Personal communication with the Illinois Department of Public Health (IDPH).
46. Personal communication with IDPH.
47. Personal communication with the Illinois Department of Registration and Education (IDRE), 1984.
48. Zekman and Warrick, "Abortion Profiteers," 14–15 and 31.
49. Ibid., 8 and 41.
50. Ibid., 43; and personal communicaton with IDRE.
51. Personal communication with IDPH.
52. Zekman and Warrick, "Abortion Profiteers," 8.
53. Ibid., 45.
54. Ibid., 10.
55. See, for example, the discussion regarding the abortion hospital studied in Denes, *In Necessity and Sorrow.*
56. Zekman and Warrick, "Abortion Profiteers," 2–3 and 33.
57. Ibid., 33.
58. Marx, *The Death Peddlers*, 19.
59. Ibid., 21.
60. Ibid., 18–19.
61. Zekman and Warrick, "Abortion Profiteers," 33.
62. Rockmore, "Are You Sorry You Had An Abortion?"
63. Ibid.
64. Debra Braun, "Nation's First Black Crisis Pregnancy Center Stresses Family Involvement," *National Right to Life News*, 12 January 1984, 4.
65. Liebman and Zimmer, "Psychological Sequelae of Abortion," 133.
66. Burtchaell, *Rachel Weeping*, 80.
67. Francke, *Ambivalence of Abortion*, 179.
68. DeMarco, "The Family At Bay," 44–54; Thomas and Catherine Yassu, "The Abortionists Betray a Family," brochure printed by Sun Life, Thaxton, Virginia; and "Court OKs Abortion for Suicidal Minor," *Illinois Right to Life Committee News*, Sept./Dec. 1986, 1.
69. See Marx, *The Death Peddlers*, 19, 29–30.
70. Francke, *Ambivalence of Abortion*, 182.
71. Denes, *In Necessity and Sorrow*, 17.
72. Ibid., 76–77.
73. Ibid.
74. Burtchaell, *Rachel Weeping*, 135–36.
75. See Denes, *In Necessity and Sorrow*, 18, 156, and throughout several other interviews.

76. Burtchaell, *Rachel Weeping*, 136.
77. Denes, *In Necessity and Sorrow*, 32.
78. Ibid., 8.
79. See the intervieews with counselors who have been aborted in Francke, *Ambivalence of Abortion*, 71–75, 86–89, and 228-30. Also see the testimony of WEBA member Karen Sullivan (73–77).
80. See Denes, *In Necessity and Sorrow*, 134; and the testimony of WEBA member Deborah Hulebak (81–88).
81. See the testimonies of WEBA members Karen Sullivan (73–77) and Deborah Hulebak (81–88).
82. Denes, *In Necessity and Sorrow*, 243.
83. Ibid., 89–90.
84. Ibid., 245.
85. Maloof, "The Consequences of Incest," 92.
86. Denes, *In Necessity and Sorrow*, 21 and 39.
87. Ibid., 80.
88. Ibid., 18.
89. Ibid., 156.
90. Ibid., 177–78.
91. Ibid., 19.
92. Ibid., 131.
93. Francke, *Ambivalence of Abortion*, 40; and Denes, *In Necessity and Sorrow*, 246.
94. Francke, *Ambivalence of Abortion*, 34.
95. Mary Arnold, "Abortion Burnout," *Catholic Twin Circle*, 5 August 1984, 3–4.
96. Ibid; and Denes, *In Necessity and Sorrow*, in general.
97. See Hilgers and Horan, *Abortion and Social Justice*, 77; and Francke, *Ambivalence of Abortion*, 33.
98. Denes, *In Necessity and Sorrow*, 243.
99. Ibid., 69.
100. Burtchaell, *Rachel Weeping*, 220.
101. Ibid., and Nancy Koster, "Abortionists Incriminated By Their Own Statistics," *National Right to Life News*, 27 September 1984, 7.
102. Francke, *Ambivalence of Abortion*, 40; and Burtchaell, *Rachel Weeping*, 218.
103. Liebman and Zimmer, "Psychological Sequelae of Abortion," 128.
104. Denes, *In Necessity and Sorrow*, 67.
105. Burtchaell, *Rachel Weeping*, 210. See also the interview with abortionist Edward Allred in the film, "A Matter of Choice" (New Liberty Pictures). When asked if there were any moral or ethical principles by which he justified abortion, Dr. Allred answered: "It's philosophical, as much as anything. I don't choose to get into that aspect of it. I'm not much of a philosopher. I try not to delve into things like that too much."

106. Marx, *The Death Peddlers*, 125; and "The New Ethic for Medicine and Society," *California Medicine*, (official journal of the California Medical Association), vol. 113, no. 3, September 1970, 67–68 (editorial).
107. See the interview with Dr. Allred in the film, "A Matter of Choice."
108. Burtchaell, *Rachel Weeping*, 210.
109. Powell, *Abortion: The Silent Holocaust*, 67.
110. Denes, *In Necessity and Sorrow*, 146–47.
111. Ibid., 141.
112. Ibid., 64.
113. Ibid., 64–65.
114. Ibid., 141.
115. Ibid., 144.
116. Ibid., 68.
117. Ibid., 69.
118. Burtchaell, *Rachel Weeping*, 213; and see Mendelsohn, *MalePractice*, 77–78 for additional examples of how physicians blame their own irresponsibility on the "demands" of their patients.
119. Denes, *In Necessity and Sorrow*, 140.
120. Ibid., 64 and 147.
121. See the comments of Dr. Kerenyi in "The Doctor's Dilemma—When Abortion Gives Birth to Life," *Chicago Tribune*, 15 August 1982, Section 12.
122. Denes, *In Necessity and Sorrow*, 68.
123. Ibid., 232.
124. Arnold, "Abortion Burnout," 4.
125. Denes, *In Necessity and Sorrow*, 227.
126. John T. Noonan, Jr., *A Private Choice: Abortion in America in the Seventies* (Toronto: Life Cycle Books, 1979), 170.
127. Nathanson, *Aborting America*, 110.
128. Ibid., 146.
129. Grisez, *Abortion: Myths, Realities, and Arguments*, 51.
130. Ibid.; and Fisher, "Abortion—Pain or Pleasure?", 50.
131. Denes, *In Necessity and Sorrow*, 79.
132. Ibid., 134.
133. Ibid., especially 62, 225, and 230. For an explanation of how the competition created by medical schools encourages the development and selection of compassionless doctors, see Mendelsohn, *MalePractice*, 89.
134. Denes, *In Necessity and Sorrow*, 145.
135. Ibid., 239.
136. Burtchaell, *Rachel Weeping*, 216–17.
137. Denes, *In Necessity and Sorrow*, 144.
138. Burtchaell, *Rachel Weeping*, 50.

139. Baars, "Psychic Causes and Consequences of the Abortion Mentality," 121.
140. Denes, *In Necessity and Sorrow*, 240.

NINE: *Before and After Legalization*

1. Grisez, *Abortion: Myths, Realities, and Arguments*, 67.
2. Nathanson, *Aborting America*, 193.
3. Grisez, *Abortion: Myths, Realities, and Arguments*, 68 and 226.
4. Ibid., 71.
5. Nathanson, *Aborting America*, 193.
6. Grisez, *Abortion: Myths, Realities, and Arguments*, 70.
7. Burtchaell, *Rachel Weeping*, 65.
8. Grisez, *Abortion: Myths, Realities, and Arguments*, 69–70.
9. Hilgers, "Medical Hazards of Abortion," *Abortion and Social Justice*, 80 (footnote 56).
10. See Destro, "Abortion and the Constitution;" and Hilgers, et al., *New Perspectives on Human Abortion*, 82.
11. Destro, "Abortion and the Constitution," 1303; and Willke, *Handbook on Abortion*, 78. Also see Chapter Three.
12. Hilgers, et al., *New Perspectives on Human Abortion*, 82.
13. See Chapter Five of this book; and Zekman and Warrick, "Abortion Profiteers."
14. Burtchaell, *Rachel Weeping*, 94.
15. Ibid., 95.
16. See Hilgers, et al., *New Perspectives on Human Abortion*, 82; and Destro, "Abortion and the Constitution."
17. Hilgers, et al., *New Perspectives on Human Abortion*, 170. Since Tietze admits elsewhere that deaths from illegal abortion were accurately predicted to within 10 percent, his assessment of a minimum of 40 deaths per 100,000 must also lead him to conclude that there were under 100,000 illegal abortions per year prior to legalization, since only 38 such deaths were reported in 1972.
18. Ibid., 166.
19. Ibid., 169. Willard Cates and Roger W. Rochat, pro-choice statisticians with Abortion Surveillance at the Atlanta Center for Disease Control, using the same technique but assuming a rate of 30 deaths per 100,000 illegal abortions, have estimated that the total number of illegal abortions performed in 1972 was only 130,000. See Cates and Rochat, "Illegal Abortions in the United States: 1972–1974," *Family Planning Perspectives*, 8:125
20. Osofsky, *The Abortion Experience*, 196–98.
21. Hilgers, et al., *New Perspectives on Human Abortion*, 166.

22. See "Abortion and the Supreme Court," published by the National Committee for a Human Life Amendment (NCHLA), Washington, D.C., 1979. Also, our own survey found that only 8 percent of the aborted women surveyed would have considered seeking illegal abortions.

23. Ibid. Also see Hilgers, et al., *New Perspectives on Human Abortion*, 84.

24. Hilgers, et al., *New Perspectives on Human Abortion*, 169. These are conservative estimates. See Nathanson, *Aborting America*, 193, for an account of only 39 deaths in 1972.

25. Hilgers, et al., *New Perspectives on Human Abortion*, 180.

26. Saltenberger, *Every Woman*, 51.

27. "Voice of the People," *Chicago Tribune*, 26 January 1983.

28. NCHLA, "Abortion and the Supreme Court."

29. Grimes and Cates, "Abortion: Methods and Complications," 796.

30. See Chapter Seven.

31. Grisez, *Abortion: Myths, Realities, and Arguments*, 48; and Nancy Howell Lee, *The Search for an Abortionist* (Chicago: University of Chicago Press, 1969), 84–93.

32. Grisez, *Abortion: Myths, Realities, and Arguments*, 49. Studies of illegal abortionists found that they almost invariably "claimed to be performing socially valuable work," yet were also clearly motivated by "a combination of greed and psychological inadequacy." These physician abortionists were typically only average achievers in medical school and had failed to establish profitable careers in legitimate medicine. According to one of these studies, "Unfortunately, almost without exception, the physician/abortionist is a deviate in some manner." Abortion, then, was a lucrative and "justifiable" market in which these otherwise non-successful physicians could excel. Ibid., 51.

33. See Nathanson, *Aborting America*, 93–116 (especially page 110), for a description of how illegal abortionists were attracted to lucrative legal abortion clinics.

34. Grisez, *Abortion: Myths, Realities, and Arguments*, 70; and Lee, *Search for an Abortionist*, 104.

35. Grisez, *Abortion: Myths, Realities, and Arguments*, 52.

36. Ibid.

37. Ibid., 52–54.

38. Ibid., 53.

39. Ibid.

40. Ibid., 56.

41. Ibid.

42. "Abortion Data Report to the General Assembly," Illinois Department of Public Health, 19 July 1982.

43. Francke, *Ambivalence of Abortion*, 178–79.

44. See "Legal Abortions by Selected Characteristics," *Vital Statistics*, 1978.
45. Drogin, *Margaret Sanger,* 31.
46. Rita Radich, "Disaffection Within Democratic Party Offers Opportunity For Pro-Life Voice To Be Heard," *The National Right to Life News,* 22 March 1984, 6.
47. Drogin, *Margaret Sanger,* 31.
48. A thorough examination of this anti-poor, "eugenic" philosophy will presented in this author's next book.

TEN: *The Future of Abortion*

1. Wardle and Wood, *A Lawyer Looks At Abortion,* 163–68.
2. Burtchaell, *Rachel Weeping,* 96–105; Raymond J. Adamek, "Abortion and Public Opinion in the United States," National Right to Life Education Trust Fund, 1982; and Judith Blake, "The Supreme Court's Abortion Decisions and Public Opinion in the United States," *Population & Development Review,* March/June 1977.
3. Nathanson, *Aborting America,* 266.
4. Burtchaell, *Rachel Weeping,* 100.
5. Nathanson, *Aborting America,* 189 and 265.
6. See Granberg, "The Abortion Activists"; and Chapter Three of this book.
7. John Noonan, Jr., *A Private Choice: Abortion in America in the Seventies* (Toronto: Life Cycle Books, 1979), 49.
8. Abortion is in fact a tool of social engineering which a portion of the upper class believes it must use in order to preserve its privileged position against the demands of a growing population of poor people in America and Third World nations. Driven by an "us against them" mentality, these elitists believe they must suppress the population of these "lower classes" in order to preserve social order and advance their interests. Abortion is seen as a primary tool in this social engineering attempt. Thus, the pro-abortion movement can be clearly traced to these elitist eugenic and population control movements of earlier decades. While these elitists were the power brokers behind the pro-abortion movement, they manipulated the feminist movement into promotion of abortion as a key "woman's rights issue." But the true goal of these elitists was not women's rights but social engineering and suppression of "unfit" populations.
9. Ibid.
10. Hilgers, et al., *New Perspectives on Human Abortion,* 447.
11. Paulette Joyer, "Abortion Hasn't Helped Solve Women's Problems," *Sisterlife,* a publication of Feminists for Life of America, September 1984, 3.

12. Peter Maurin, *The Catholic Worker,* May 1976, 5.
13. Arthur Dyck, "Is Abortion Necessary to Solve Population Problems?", *Abortion and Social Justice,* 169.
14. NCHLA, "Abortion and the Supreme Court."
15. Ibid.
16. Garrett Hardin, *Mandatory Motherhood: The True Meaning of "Right to Life"* (Boston: Beacon Press, 1974), 13; and Nathanson, *Aborting America,* 194.
17. Hilgers and Horan, *Abortion and Social Justice,* 177–197.

A SELECTED BIBLIOGRAPHY

Burtchaell, James Tunstead, C.S.C. *Rachel Weeping*. Kansas City: Andrews and McMeel, Inc., 1982.

Denes, Magda. *In Necessity and Sorrow*. New York: Basic Books, Inc., 1976.

Francke, Linda Bird. *The Ambivalence of Abortion*. New York: Random House, Inc., 1978.

Hilgers, Thomas W. and Dennis J. Horan and David Mall, eds. *New Perspectives On Human Abortion*. Frederick, Maryland: University Publications of America, 1981.

Mall, David and Walter F. Watts. *The Psychological Aspects of Abortion*. Frederick, Maryland: University Publications of America, 1979.

Saltenberger, Ann. *Every Woman Has The Right To Know The Dangers Of Legal Abortion*. Glassboro, New Jersey: Air-Plus Enterprises, 1982.

I N D E X

therapeutic abortions, 166–70
Psychosomatic illnesses, following abortion, 130
Pulmonary embolism, as post-abortion complication, 92, 94–95

R

Race, of aborted women, 5–6, 330
Rape pregnancies, 188–90
abortions for, 206–212
in perspective, 190–91
psychology of women with, 191–99
Rashbaum, Dr. William, 268
Reeder, Dr. Clifton, 246
Reik, Theodore, 126
Relationships, disruption of, and abortion, 45–46
Remorse, as post-abortion complication, 52, 120, 121–22
Repeat abortions, of aborted women, 6–7
Replacement babies, 23, 126, 133
Reproductive health, abortion as threat to future, 93, 95
Residents, as abortionists, 242–43
Rh blood tests, lack of, in many abortion clinics, 237
Rhogam shots, provision of, in abortion clinics, 237
Rh sensitization, as post-abortion complication, 95
Rodrigo, Dr. 267
Roe v. *Wade* (1973), 111–12, 161, 225, 297, 320
Rovinsky, Dr. Joseph J., 112
Russell, Dr. J. K., 101
Ryan, Ila, 305–10

S

Sague, Dr. Consuelo, 266
St. Amour, Carol, 77–81
Saline abortions, 96
Salting out. *See* Saline abortions
Self-affirmed, advocation of abortion by, 138–39, 296
Self-destructive behavior, as psychological reaction to abortion, 23
Self-image, deterioration of, following abortion, 127–29
Sex selection, use of amniocentesis for, 172
Sexual coldness, following abortion, 50–51
Sexual dysfunction, post-abortion, 123–126
Sheridan, Dr. Edward, 228–29
Siblings, effect of abortion on, 228–30
Single women, myth of, as seekers of abortion, 296
Situation factors, in the abortion decision, 9–10
Smith, Kathleen Trueland, 143
Social status, correlation of, with abortion rate, 295–96
"Soft-core" aborters, 297–300, 321
Spina bifida, use of amniocentesis to diagnose, 173
Spina Bifida Association, 177
Sterility, post-abortion, 21
Stress infertility, 190
Subjective approach, to the abortion experience, 1–2
Suction curettage, 93–95
Suicidal tendencies, post-abortion, 22, 129, 168–69
Suiciders Anonymous, 129
Sullivan, Karen, 73–77
Surrogate mothers, aborted women as, 126–27
Survey of women aborted, 1–2
comparing statistics, 4–8
limitations of, 2–4
questions asked on, 333–37
results of, 328–32
Survivor syndrome, 226
Swanson, Gloria, 69
Swanson on Swanson (Swanson), 69
Sweden
abortion death rate in, 112
evidence on abortion from, 104